D1617317

The Rise of
Modern Society

For Ray Pahl
with whom much of this was discussed

The Rise of Modern Society

Aspects of the Social and Political
Development of the West

KRISHAN KUMAR

Basil Blackwell

Copyright © Krishan Kumar 1988, except for chapter 1 copyright © 1988 by Encyclopaedia
Britannica, Inc. and chapters 8 and 11 copyright © 1978 and 1980 by Martinus Nijhoff
Publishers.

First published 1988

Basil Blackwell Ltd
108 Cowley Road, Oxford, OX4 1JF, UK

Basil Blackwell Inc.
432 Park Avenue South, Suite 1503
New York, NY 10016, USA

British Library Cataloguing in Publication Data

Kumar, Krishan, 1942–
    The rise of modern society: aspects of the
social and political development of the West.
1. Western world. Industrialised countries.
Development
I. Title
303.4′4′091772

ISBN 0-631-16007-8

Library of Congress Cataloging in Publication Data

Kumar, Krishan.
    The rise of modern society: aspects of the social and political
development of the West / Krishan Kumar.
    p.   cm.
Includes index.
ISBN 0-631-16007-8
    1. Social history—Modern, 1500– 2. Mass society.
3. Industrialization. 4. Capitalism. 5. Marxian school of
sociology.   I. Title.
HN13.K85 1988
301—dc19   88-10376 CIP

Typeset in 10 on 11 pt Ehrhardt
by Photo·graphics, Honiton, Devon
Printed in Great Britain by T.J. Press Ltd, Padstow, Cornwall

Contents

Preface

The writings collected in this volume are essays in the theory and history of industrial society. In one form or another they revolve around a central question: what is the sociological theory of industrialism, and how far do the actual histories and practices of industrial societies match up to this theory? The first chapter maps out in the most general way the sociological account of modern industrial society, and its contrast with other forms of society. The other chapters in Part I deal with selected aspects of this model. They consider the debates surrounding the origins and development of capitalist industrialism, and they discuss also the future of industrialism. Are industrial societies becoming 'post-industrial'? Have they reached the limits of their development in current forms? Is there a crisis of industrial society? The chapters in Part I operate at a fairly high level of generality: the title 'Continuities and Discontinuities' sums up their main theme.

Part II, 'Politics, Work and Society', interrogates the general model of industrialism at more specialized levels. The Marxist theory of class and class action is set against the actual picture of nineteenth-century English society, with suggestions as to the general theoretical shortcomings of the Marxist model. The theory of revolution, based on the 'classic' examples of France and Russia, is examined for its relevance to the conditions of advanced industrial societies. The concepts and forms of work, employment and unemployment are traced over the course of the development of Western societies, with the emphasis on changing meanings and changing practices. In many of these chapters England, as the oldest industrial society, comes in for special consideration. The final chapter therefore looks at current views of Britain's future, and raises the question of how far both Britain's problems and the suggested remedies point the way to the future of other industrial societies.

I expect this collection to be of use mainly to students and teachers of sociology, politics and history, but I hope it may also have a wider appeal. There is nothing in either the language or the approach that should cause any difficulty to the general reader. The topics are of the kind that I hope would interest anyone reflecting on the long-term problems and prospects of industrial society.

All the chapters have appeared before. I have made only minor revisions to the original texts although in most cases I have added a bibliographical note indicating some of the more recent literature on the subject.

I should like to thank Sean Magee, of Basil Blackwell, for his encouragement and support. It was he who made me see that these essays might make up a reasonably coherent whole. Other staff at Basil Blackwell have also been unfailingly helpful. I also owe a great debt to the secretarial staff of Keynes College in the University of Kent. All of them, but especially Kate Ralph, have had to struggle with almost indecipherable handwriting and mounds of photocopies. They have discharged the arduous task with good humour and enormous efficiency. I am most grateful to them.

Krishan Kumar
Canterbury, Kent

Acknowledgements

The author and publishers acknowledge with thanks permission granted to reproduce material published elsewhere:

'The Rise of Modern Society' as 'Modernization and Industrialization' in the *Encyclopaedia Britannica* (*Macropaedia section*), 1989 edition. Copyright © 1988 by Encyclopaedia Britannica, Inc. Reprinted by permission.

'Pre-capitalist and Non-capitalist Factors in the Development of Capitalism: Fred Hirsch and Joseph Schumpeter' in A. Ellis and K. Kumar (eds), *Dilemmas of Liberal Democracies: Studies in Fred Hirsch's Social Limits to Growth* (London, Tavistock Publications, 1983).

'Continuities and Discontinuities in the Development of Industrial Societies' in R. Scase (ed.), *Industrial Society: Class, Cleavage and Control* (London, Allen and Unwin 1977; in association with the British Sociological Association).

'The Industrializing and the 'Post-industrial' Worlds: on Development and Futurology' in E. de Kadt and G. Williams (eds) *Sociology and Development* (London, Tavistock Publications 1974; in association with the British Sociological Association).

'The Limits and Capacities of Industrial Society' in a shortened form in R. Scase (ed.), *Divisions in Western Capitalism and State Socialism*, (London, Unwin Hyman, 1988).

'Class and Political Action in Nineteenth-century England: Theoretical and Comparative Perspectives', *Archives Européennes de Sociologie*, 24 (1983), 3–43. Reprinted by permission of Cambridge University Press.

'Twentieth-century Revolutions in Historical Perspective' as 'Le Rivoluzioni del Ventesimo Secolo in Prospettiva Storica', in L. Pellicani (ed.), *Sociologia delle Rivoluzioni* (Naples, Guida Editori, 1976). A shorter version was published as 'Revolution and Industrial Society', *Sociology*, 10 (1976), 245–69. Reprinted by permission of Guida Editori and the British Sociological Association.

'Can the Workers be Revolutionary?' *European Journal of Political Research*, 6 (1978), 357–79. Copyright © 1978 by Martinus Nijhoff Publishers. Reprinted by permission of Kluwer Academic Publishers.

'The Social Culture of Work: Work, Employment and Unemployment as Ways of Life', *New Universities Quarterly*, 34 (1979/80), 5–28.

'Unemployment as a Problem in the Development of Industrial Societies: the English Experience', *Sociological Review*, 32 (1984), 185–233. Reprinted by permission of Associated Book Publishers (UK) Ltd.

'Thoughts on the Present Discontents in Britain', *Theory and Society*, 9 (1980), 539–74. Copyright © 1980 by Martinus Nijhoff Publishers. Reprinted by permission of Kluwer Academic Publishers.

PART I

Continuities and Discontinuities

1

The Rise of Modern Society

INTRODUCTION

Modern society is industrial society. To modernize is to industrialize. It might be possible to give some other meaning to modernity, but to do so would be perverse and misleading. Historically, the rise of modern society is intrinsically connected to the rise of industrial society. All the features that we associate with modernity can be shown to be related to the set of changes that, no more than two centuries ago, brought into being the industrial type of society. What this immediately suggests is that the terms 'industrialism' and 'industrial society' cover far more than the economic and technological components that make up their core. Industrialism is a whole way of life. It encompasses economic, social, political and cultural changes. It is by undergoing such a comprehensive transformation through industrialization that societies become modern.

Modernization is a continuous, long-term and open-ended process. Historically and originally, the scale of time over which it occurred has to be measured in centuries, although later there can be examples of 'speeded-up' modernization. In either case, the work of modernization is never done. It is not a once-and-for-all-time achievement. There is a dynamic principle built into the very system of modern societies. Modern societies never settle, never reach equilibrium. Their development is always irregular and uneven. Whatever the level of development, there are always 'backward' regions and 'peripheral' groups. This is a persistent source of strain and conflict in modern societies. Such a condition is not confined to the internal development of individual states. It is replicated on a world scale, as modernization extends out from its original Western base to take in the whole world. The existence of unevenly and unequally developed nations introduces a fundamental element of instability in the world system of states.

Modernization seems to have two main phases. Up to a certain point in its course, it carries all the institutions and values of society along with it, in what is generally regarded by the bulk of the population as a progressive, upward movement. Resistance to modernization can be sharp and prolonged, but is generally doomed to failure. Beyond that certain point, however, modernization breeds discontents on an increasing scale. Partly this is due to the phenomenon of 'rising expectations' caused by the very success and dynamism of modern society. All groups come to make escalating demands on society, which are increasingly difficult to meet. More seriously, modernization on an intensified level and on a world scale brings new social and material scarcities which threaten the very principle of growth and expansion on which modern society turns. In this second phase, modern societies find themselves faced with an array of new problems whose solution often seems to lie beyond the confines of the traditional nation state. At the same time, the world remains dominated by a system of nation states of unequal strength and conflicting interests. The resulting impasse makes the resolution of common problems very difficult.

But challenge and response is the very stuff of modern society. In considering its nature and development, what stands out initially at least is not so much the difficulties and dangers as the extraordinary success with which modern society has mastered the most profound and far-reaching revolution in human history.

BECOMING MODERN

The Revolution of modernity

If, in its temporal dimension, human social evolution is charted on a twelve-hour clock, then the modern industrial epoch represents the last five minutes, no more. For more than half a million years, small bands of men and women roamed the earth as hunters and gatherers. With simple stone tools, and a social order based on kinship ties, they successfully preserved the human species against predators and natural calamities. In observing contemporary Australian aborigines, the Bushmen of South Africa, the Eskimos and Pygmy groups in Africa, Malaysia and the Philippines, we can get some glimpse of the social life of Old Stone Age society – the oldest and most enduring type of human society.

Around 10,000 BC – fifteen minutes ago on our evolutionary clock – some of these hunters and gatherers invented agriculture and the domestication of animals. It is this that is somewhat misleadingly called 'the Neolithic Revolution'. But if new stone tools were not the central element in the change, revolutionary it certainly was. Mobile bands became settled village communities. The development of the plough raised the productivity of the land a thousandfold. The population of the earth increased dramatically. More significantly, herding and agriculture for the first time created a surplus of food. This allowed some members of the population to cease from subsistence activities and to become craftsmen, merchants, priests and bureaucrats. The vast increase in the division of labour took place in a new, concentrated, physical environment. Around 4000 BC cities arose, and with them trade, markets, government, laws and armies.

The technology and social organization of the Neolithic Revolution were the basis of all civilization until the coming of industrialism. With remarkably few additions – the invention of the stirrup was an important one – what served ancient Mesopotamia and ancient Egypt of the third and second millennia BC remained the essential foundation of all states and empires of the ancient world, from China and India to Greece and Rome. The same is true of the European Middle Ages, which in some respects, notably the technical sphere, actually fell below the level of the ancient world. Not until the seventeenth and eighteenth centuries in Europe did mankind make another leap comparable to that of the Neolithic Revolution.

It is against this evolutionary background that the revolution of modernity must be seen. It is one of the only two 'quantum' jumps that human social evolution has made since the primal hunting and gathering stage of early *Homo sapiens*. The Neolithic or Agricultural Revolution produced – paradoxically – urban civilization; the Industrial Revolution lifted mankind to a new plane of technological development that set no limits to the transformation of the material environment. Comparisons are treacherous, as well as odious, but it is perhaps fair to say that in its speed and scale the change brought about by the Industrial Revolution has had a greater impact on human life than the Neolithic Revolution. Neolithic civilization remained throughout confined by its limited technical and economic base; industrial civilization is the 'unbound Prometheus', for whom change and growth are normal and indeed necessary. Nevertheless, an understanding of agrarian society is essential for the analysis of industrial society. For it is largely through the contrast with its agrarian past that modern society stands out. The meaning of the modern is to be sought as much in what it renounced as in what it aspired to, in its revolutionary mutation.

The West and the world

What produced this leap into modernity? Why, just as some hunters and gatherers gave rise to agrarian society, did some agrarian societies give rise to industrial society? We will always be more or less in the dark about the first of these momentous changes. About the second, too, the precise causes are still the subject of fierce and probably endless debate. But at least we know reasonably well when it occurred, and where. It took place between the sixteenth and eighteenth centuries; and it began in the countries of north-western Europe – especially England, The Netherlands, northern France and northern Germany.

There was an unexpected aspect to this. Compared to the Mediterranean, not to mention Arabic and Chinese civilization, north-western Europe at the time was backward, technically and culturally. In the sixteenth and seventeenth centuries it was still absorbing the commercial and artistic innovations of the

Italian city-states of the Renaissance, and making piratical raids where it could on the wealthy Spanish Empire. It seemed an unlikely candidate for economic leadership. Yet it was here that the changes took place that propelled north-western Europe into the forefront of world development.

One possible reason for this has always seemed persuasive. North-western Europe was the origin and heartland of the Protestant Reformation of the sixteenth century. In his great work, *The Protestant Ethic and the Spirit of Capitalism* (1904), the German sociologist Max Weber suggested this as the principal explanation of the economic success of the region. Catholicism, said Weber, and even more non-Western religions such as Hinduism and Buddhism, were 'other-worldly' religions. They placed all their doctrinal emphasis on religious contemplation and the life hereafter. Protestantism, on the other hand, was a 'this-worldly' religion. It broke down the distinction between the Church and 'the world', between the monastery and the marketplace. Every man was a priest; every thing he did, at work or at play, he did in the sight of God. Weber sought to show that Protestantism, and especially its Puritan variety, developed a particular type of character which led to an ascetic life of thrift, frugality and hard work. Especially it promoted a particular work ethic. For the Protestant, to work was to pray. All work, all occupations, were a religious vocation. Work was therefore endowed with a sacred character. It had to be pursued with a fitting seriousness and methodicalness, in a spirit of rational enterprise which eschewed waste and frivolous adventurism. Such an attitude was admirably suited – though not intendedly – to the development of industrial capitalism. The Protestant nations therefore invented modern capitalism, and so launched the world on a course which it still follows.

In a similarly persuasive way, the rationality of the Protestant work ethic seems linked to the development of modern science. This too took place largely in north-western Europe, in the course of the seventeenth century. In no other place, at no other time, was there anything like the 'scientific revolution' of these years in England, France and The Netherlands. It is true that the Industrial Revolution, in its early phases at least, did not depend on the theoretical science of Newton, Lavoisier and others of this period. But what was more important was the scientific culture and the scientific habits of mind that they nurtured. It was this that became the bedrock of industrialism. Moreover, the scientific method of observation, experimentation and verification could be applied not just to nature but to society. Eventually, towards the end of the eighteenth century, 'social science' – economics and sociology especially – began to find a place alongside natural science. The scientific outlook became the hallmark of modern society, so much so that the term 'scientific-industrial' became almost synonymous with it.

Already, by the seventeenth century, Western Europe had embarked on the path of transoceanic expansion that was to become one of its most notable features in the succeeding centuries. America had been discovered and colonized, thereby adding at a stroke a vast new domain to the West. The West took a commanding lead over the rest of the world. Linked to the enormous potentialities of science and industry, it acquired a momentum and a dynamism that suggested a future immeasurably grander than anything previously achieved. For the first time, moralists and philosophers began to conceive the possibility that the modern world could be the equal and even the superior of the ancient world of Greece and Rome. The idea of progress, and with it the idea of modernism, was born: latest was best. The present must be seen in the perspective of the future, as prologue to the swelling act. The world was growing in power and enlightenment and, barring 'unnatural' accidents, would continue indefinitely to do so. Western society was not merely leading the way, it was showing to the rest of the world, as in a mirror, its future condition. 'The country that is more developed industrially,' said Karl Marx, 'only shows, to the less developed, the image of its own future.'

The dual revolution

Modern society owes its direct origin to two great revolutions of the eighteenth century, one political, the other economic. But both are part of a broader pattern of change that, since the Reformation, had set the West on a different path of development from the rest of the world. This included the individualism and, in the end, the secularism, that was the legacy of Protestantism. It also included the rise of science, as a method and as a practice. Both of these culminated explosively in eighteenth-century society. The first produced political revolutions in America and France. The second, more diffusely, gave rise to the Industrial Revolution in England.

The American and French Revolutions established the political character of modern society. They announced that modern society would be constitutional and democratic. What sort of constitution, and how democratic in practice, were matters left unresolved, as they still are. But from the time of those revolutions it was clear to practically all thinkers that no political system could now claim legitimacy that was not in some sense based on 'the will of the people', constitutionally expressed. It was this message that was so brilliantly and influentially spelled out by the clear-sighted French aristocrat Alexis de Tocqueville in his two works *The Ancien Régime and the French Revolution* (1856), and *Democracy in America* (1835–40).

That the new democratic legitimation could be accorded to popular or constitutional dictatorships such as those of Napoleon III in France or Adolf Hitler in Germany only showed how flexible the formula could be. But it was not infinitely expandable. The idea of 'tacit' or 'implicit' popular consent resorted to by several old-fashioned monarchies and empires fell before the onslaught of modern democratic theory as developed from the American and French Revolutions. In England this was done through a gradual extension of the franchise in the nineteenth century. In Russia, and elsewhere in eastern and central Europe, violent revolution seemed the only means in the face of autocratic intransigence.

But however accomplished – whether grudgingly conceded, seized in popular revolution, or imposed from on top by modernizing elites – the democratic constitutional state has come to be accepted as in principle the only fully legitimate polity of modern society. All apparent deviations from the norm, as for instance with the Communist states of Eastern Europe or the military dictatorships of Africa and Latin America, have to offer elaborate justifications. These, where they are not simply specious denials, generally take the form of pleading special or emergency conditions. Full democracy, at some time in the future, remains the confessed and committed goal. The tortuousness of most of these pleas and denials is the clearest testimony to the normative strength of the democratic ideal in modern society.

The American Revolution added a further ingredient to the political form of modern society. It asserted the principle of self-determination. Only those states were legitimate which were ruled by the people 'naturally', by virtue of a common culture and a common territory, subject to them. Foreign rule, or rule by alien elites as in the Turkish and Habsburg Empires, was illegitimate. Only nation states were natural political entities; only they were permissible. 'National self-determination' became one of the most powerful watchwords of the liberal and radical ideologies that were largely instrumental in shaping the modern states of the nineteenth and twentieth centuries.

That, as with democracy, this was a highly contentious and ambiguous demand, was shown especially in the experience of central and eastern Europe, where the question of *whose* presumed nationality should be the basis of the state divided ethnic groups bitterly and murderously. Who, in Hungary, was 'the' national group – Magyars, Slovaks, Croats, Serbs, Rumans? Only superior force could resolve the issue. But, once again, it was not the practical difficulties that mattered. As with democracy, it was the pure theory of nationalism, nationalism as an ideal, that became the irresistible force. And, once invented by the West, it could not be contained there. Along with democracy, it was one of the ideals absorbed by the colonies of the Western powers, eventually becoming the dynamite that exploded Europe's overseas empires.

We might say, lastly, that the American and French Revolutions were important not just in establishing the substance of the modern polity but in the example they provided of how to bring it into being. They invented, that is, the modern concept of revolution. In so doing they charged an old word with new meaning. Before the eighteenth century the term 'revolution' in politics echoed its older uses in astronomy, as in Copernicus's *On the Revolutions of the Celestial Spheres*. That is to say, it referred, as its etymology clearly implies, to cyclical motions – to the cycles of growth and decay that were as inevitable in the affairs of men as in the natural world. Applied to the political realm, this suggested that all 'revolutionary' change was part of a recurring cyclical pattern, not the creation of something fundamentally new. It was in such a sense that the English revolutionaries in 1640 and 1688 used the term, and there was still an echo of this even in the American Revolution of 1776.

With the French Revolution, however, the word decisively acquired its modern meaning. It now meant the conscious attempt to bring into being a new order of things (of which, it was assumed to be self-evident, 'freedom' and 'democracy' would be an essential part). Societies could transform themselves, could establish themselves on new principles, as the French had attempted to do, by the act of revolution. From that time 'revolution' entered the political vocabulary and the political practice of the modern world as the willed re-ordering of all social and political relations. It was a message that was, once more, not lost on the new subjects, internal and external, of states that had themselves come into being through revolutions, anxious though their rulers might be to forget their origins.

If the American and French Revolutions laid down the political pattern of the modern world, the English Industrial Revolution laid down the economic pattern. The changes that took place in England during the nineteenth century became an almost copy-book example of the process of industrialization. To choose to industrialize – and not so to choose meant risking backwardness and dependence – was to imitate the English Industrial Revolution. Since England was the pioneer industrial nation of the world, there simply was no other available model to fix on. Even later, when it was clear that the English method of industrialization might not be universally applicable, the general form of society that emerged in England in the course of the Industrial Revolution was widely regarded as the typical industrial form.

With some pardonable elision, certain episodes and tendencies in the English case were selected out as characterizing industrial development as such. These included the movement from the land to the cities, the massing of workers in the new industrial towns and factories, and the rise of new distinctions between family life and work life, and between 'work' and 'leisure'. Such features, along with others which I shall consider shortly, were compounded into a powerful image of industrialism, as a whole social system and way of life. To industrialize was to commit oneself, more or less irrevocably, to this whole way of life – to become something like English industrial society.

The English themselves, with the usual Anglo-Saxon disinclination to theorize, did not contribute much to this image of industrialism, at least in so far as it was turned into a systematic account of society. Certain powerful symbols and images of urban and industrial life were indeed picked up from English novelists such as Charles Dickens and Elizabeth Gaskell, but it was left to others, from societies only just beginning to industrialize, to blend these artistic impressions into a systematic analysis of the new society. Foreigners such as Alexis de Tocqueville, Friedrich Engels and Karl Marx came to England to observe and to reflect on the changes that they saw there. They were convinced that what was happening in England would be repeated, more or less exactly, in other societies as they underwent industrialization. Industrial England could therefore be seen as a social laboratory of inestimable value to those other societies. In works such as Engels's *The Condition of the English Working Class in England in 1844* (1845), and Marx's *Capital* (1867), English experience was examined for the light it shed on the general process of industrialism, and for what it suggested of future developments, there and elsewhere. Through such works, the English Industrial Revolution became the property not just of the English nation but of the whole world. All societies, it was felt, would have their 'Coketowns', the generic industrial town of Dickens's *Hard Times*; all would have industrializing ideologies and institutions of the kind – referred to by Germans as '*Manchesterthum*' – that nineteenth-century observers came to associate with the world's leading industrial city, Manchester. Manchester was indeed the symbol of the new industrial society, and hence the image of the world's future. 'The age of ruins is past,' declared Benjamin Disraeli in his novel *Coningsby* (1844); 'have you seen Manchester?'

One consequence of this tendency to generalize the English experience was that industrialism itself grew in scope and significance. It came to symbolize and to embody not just the economic and techological changes that lay at its heart, but other political, social and cultural changes that appeared to be intrinsically connected with it, whether as causes, concomitants or consequences. Thus the 'democratic revolution' triggered by the American and French Revolutions was seen as the necessary political transformation that, sooner or later, must accompany all movement to an industrial society. Similarly, changes in urban life, in family form, in individual and social values and in intellectual outlook, were all seen as correlated changes that were part and parcel of industrialism as a way of life. Industrial society came to stand as the type of modern society. It redefined all relevant earlier developments, such as Protestant individualism and the scientific revolution, as 'preconditions' or 'presentiments' of industrialism; and it reinforced them by incorporating them in a systematic and wider movement of change which had its own compelling logic of development. Industrialism, it was widely agreed, was a 'package', and had to be purchased as such. To embark on industrialization was, willy-nilly, to take on board all the multifarious features of modernity.

THE NATURE OF MODERN SOCIETY

General features

Modernity has to be understood, in part at least, against the background of pre-modernity. Industrial society emerged out of agrarian society, the type of society that had been dominant in the world for more than 5,000 years, ever since the Neolithic and Urban Revolution. Not only did this mean that, against so enduring a system, industrialism had to struggle to establish itself, and often did so only patchily and unevenly, in a long-drawn-out process of change; it also meant that industrial structures took much of their characteristic form and colour from a rejection, conscious or unconscious, of pre-industrial ways. Industrialism certainly added novel features of its own, in the course of development. But it always remained at least partly a 'contrast concept', one that both in its theory and practice had to be understood as much by what it denied as what it affirmed. The force of the modern has always been partly a reactive force, a force that gained meaning and momentum by a comparison or contrast with what went before and what was negated.

Considered at the most general level, this leads us to see modernization as a process of individualization, differentiation or specialization, and abstraction.

Put more concretely: first the structures of modern society take as their unit the individual rather than, as with agrarian or peasant society, the group or community. Secondly, modern institutions are allotted to the performance of specific, specialized tasks in a social system with a highly developed and complex division of labour, they do not carry out many and diverse tasks, as for instance the family does in peasant society, where it is at once the unit of production, consumption, socialization and authoritative decision-making. Thirdly, as opposed to attaching rights and prerogatives to particular groups and persons, or being guided by custom or tradition, modern institutions are governed and guided by general rules and regulations that derive their legitimacy from the methods and findings of modern science. In principle at least, they are not the agents of particular individuals, such as a king or priest, endowed with divine or prescriptive authority, but act solely according to the rational and impersonal precepts formulated by scientific experts.

These contrasts by no means exhaust the content of modern society, nor are they the only ones that can be drawn. Moreover, they treat modern society as an ideal entity, in terms of its self-professed principles, rather than as it actually operates. The two do not always match. Nevertheless they do illustrate, as do most other lists of such principles, the dependence of the concept of modernity on past structures that form the basis of comparison and exclusion. It is indeed such a set of contrasts, not necessarily carefully distinguished, that most people have in mind when they think or speak of 'modern' as opposed to 'traditional' society.

So far as the more positive features of industrialism go, industrial society can best be thought of as constituted by an economic core around which other, non-economic, structures crystallize. In Marxist terminology, this is rendered in the more deterministic form of an economic 'base' conditioning a non-economic 'superstructure'. This seems an unnecessarily rigid and misleading formula. The relation of the economic to the non-economic realm is mutual and interactive, as can best be seen by considering the impact of scientific ideas on economic and technological development. Still, it is true to say that, in its origins, it is the economic changes that most dramatically affect industrial society. Economic institutions and practices moreover continue to define if not determine industrialism. So it is only common sense to pick them out first.

Economic change

Economic historians and theorists have been inclined to stress *economic growth* as the central defining feature of an industrial as opposed to a non-industrial economy. Thus the English historian E. A. Wrigley declares that 'industrialization is said to occur in a given country when real incomes per head begin to rise steadily and without apparent limit'. The American economic historian W. W. Rostow popularized a similar conception in suggesting that with industrialization, the economy 'takes-off' into 'self-sustained growth'. It becomes airborne: all the relevant statistical indices of the economy −

investment, output, growth rate etc. – take a sudden, sharp, almost vertical upward turn.

Linked to this phenomenon of growth are certain core components of the industrial system. These include: technological change, such that work is increasingly done by machines rather than by hand; the supplementing or replacement of human labour power by inanimate sources of energy, such as coal and oil; the freeing of the labourer from all feudal and customary ties and obligations, and the creation of a free market in labour; the concentration of workers in single, comprehensive, enterprises (the factory system); a pivotal role for a specific social type, the entrepreneur.

It would be easy to vary and extend this list. Not all components are of equal importance, nor all equally indispensable to the industrial economy. They are drawn largely from the experience of the first industrializing nations, in Western Europe and North America. Later industrializers were able to dispense with some of them, or at least to try to do so. The Soviet Union for instance industrialized on the basis largely of forced rather than free labour, while in Japan the entrepreneur was throughout stimulated and sustained by strong state involvement in industrialization. Moreover it needs to be remembered that societies – as for instance Denmark and New Zealand – can industrialize largely through the commercialization and mechanization of agriculture. Agriculture simply becomes another industry; farms are simply rural factories.

Even in this latter case, there is no place for a distinctively rural way of life in industrial society. Mechanization brings an increase in productivity which decimates the rural population. Even where agriculture remains an important part of the industrial economy, the proportion of the labour force employed in agriculture drops steadily with industrialization. This is the 'sectoral transformation' that is one of the clearest and most obvious effects. A majority of the work force comes to be employed in the production of manufactured goods and in services, rather than in the 'primary' sector of agriculture. In both the United Kingdom and the United States, for instance, by the mid-1970s more than 95 per cent of the employed population were in manufacturing and services, and only 4 per cent in agriculture. Japan, as an example of a 'late-developer', shows the same pattern: in 1970, 80 per cent of the employed population were in manufacturing and services, only 20 per cent in agriculture. These figures should be compared with the normal condition of pre-industrial agrarian societies, where typically 90 per cent of the adult population are peasant farmers or farm workers.

The vast increase in agricultural productivity which this sectoral change in employment indicates is symptomatic of the economic achievement of industrialism as a whole. Industrial society breaks through the historic limits of scarcity. In the past, economic growth was always cut off by Malthusian checks, by limitations of food supply or the shortage of easily available raw materials such as wood. Industrialization allows for the creation of large food surpluses which can feed a largely urban population. It ceaselessly scours the world, its lands and its seas, for fresh materials and new energy sources to feed the industrial machines. Science finds substitutes for those sources which dry up and those materials which become dangerously scarce. There may be limits to such a process but if so they have not yet become visible. The problems it throws up are political and social, not technical. As an economic mechanism the industrial system, linked to science, is unprecedented in its promise of indefinite growth. It can in principle bring abundance for all. In the words of John Maynard Keynes, it announces, for the first time in human history, that 'the economic problem may be solved', that 'the economic problem is not the permanent problem of the human race'.

Population change

There have been two major population explosions in the course of human social evolution. By the end of the Old Stone Age, the world's population is estimated to have been between 5 and 6 million (an average of 0.04 persons per square kilometre of the earth's land area). Following the Neolithic or Agricultural Revolution, the population made its first major leap, over the short span of 8,000 years reaching around 150 million by the year 1000 BC (1 person per square kilometre). For the next 2,500 years there was relatively little change. World population had reached about 500 million by the end of the seventeenth century. During this time, 'Nature audited her accounts with a red pencil'. Any tendency for population to grow was punished by the Malthusian checks of starvation and pestilence. Only with the Industrial Revolution of the eighteenth century did population break out again from its Malthusian prison.

From about 1700, there was a second and far more rapid population explosion. In the past 300 years the world's population has increased more than eightfold, reaching 4.6 billion by the mid-1980s. It is expected to reach just over 6 billion in the year 2000 (which will mean an average of 46 persons per square kilometre of the earth's land area). This gives some measure of the difference between the two population revolutions of human history: it is the speeding up of the rate of increase that has occurred so dramatically since industrialization. Between 1650 and 1850, the average annual rate of increase of the world's population doubled; it had doubled again by the 1920s, and more than doubled, once more, by the 1970s. The rate of increase is now 2 per cent per year, and is expected to accelerate to 3 per cent by the end of the century.

If we take as our measure the time taken to double the world's population over the past 350 years, we find a 'doubling time' that has been shrinking fast. It took 200 years, from 1650 to 1850, to double the world's population from 500 million to 1 billion. It took only another seventy-five years to make the next doubling, bringing the total to 2 billion by 1925; and only fifty-five years to make yet another doubling, to 4 billion by 1980. There are signs of a slowing down in the last part of this century, and clearly doubling on this scale and at this pace cannot be endured for much longer. Even so experts predict 8 billion by the early part of the next century. This would mean a doubling time that has been cut down to about forty years.

It was in Western Europe, birthplace of the Industrial Revolution, that the second population revolution began, thereby making clear the connection between the two phenomena. Europe's population doubled during the eighteenth century, from 100 million to 200 million, and doubled again during the nineteenth century, to 400 million. It was in Europe, too, that the pattern first emerged which has come to be known as the 'demographic transition'. The population of non-industrial countries is normally stable (and low) because high birth rates are matched by high death rates. With industrialization, improvements in medical knowledge and public health bring, together with a more regular food supply, a drastic reduction in the death rate. There is not, however, for the time being, a corresponding decline in the birth rate. The result is a population explosion, as experienced in nineteenth-century Europe. In time, however, as European societies showed in the early twentieth century, the urbanized populations of industrial societies voluntarily lower their birth rates, and population growth flattens out. A new population plateau is reached. Japan, industrializing some fifty years later than the West, provided an almost textbook demonstration of the pattern of the demographic transition. Its population grew rapidly after 1870, during its industrializing phase, and fell equally rapidly after the Second World War. Japan's population history, a compressed version of the West's, as befitted a late-developer, seemed a most satisfying corroboration of the association between industrialization and the demographic transition. So too, in an even more speeded-up form, was Russia's population development in its century of industrialization that began in the 1880s.

Would the demographic transition hold good for the developing societies of the Third World? These nearly all experienced rapid population growth after the Second World War, at rates greater than ever occurred anywhere in the West. Western aid and medical science spectacularly reduced the high death rates, often by more than 50 per cent. But, unlike the West, the high birth rates have shown little tendency to fall. Determined efforts in a few countries, such as Singapore, Sri Lanka and China, are beginning to produce some results. But on the whole the attempts by national governments and international agencies to persuade people to have smaller families have failed. One result is the persistence of predominantly youthful populations in societies which can least afford the charge of feeding and educating its non-productive young. Young people under fifteen make up about 40 per cent of the populations of the Third World, as compared with about 25 per cent in the industrialized world. It has been shown that only low fertility rates, and not low mortality rates alone, can produce an older population.

Why has the birth rate remained stubbornly high in these societies? Partly this is because industrialization has been so slow and fragmentary in the Third World. Hence the reasons that weighed with the populations of the West, once industrialization has passed a certain point, do not yet signify. In addition, where a certain real degree of development has taken place, as in Brazil or Malaysia, it has largely affected a small elite and left the great mass of the people untouched. In both cases it remains rational for the bulk of the population to continue, as of old, to have large families, for the traditional reasons that many hands make light work, and also so that parents will have the security of many children to provide for them in their old age. Lower fertility will come, not only when these societies are more highly developed, but when the wealth is more evenly spread and social security systems well established.

Urbanism as a way of life

Industrialism does not just increase numbers; it distributes them in a particular way, spatially. It concentrates them in cities. Modern life is urban life, unquestionably. But so obviously and overwhelmingly is this a fact of everyday experience that we are apt to forget that cities have been part of society for more than 5,000 years. It may even be said that it was in the ancient world, in the cities of Egypt, Greece and Rome, that the distinctively urban type of life was brought to perfection. It was here that the city came to be identified with civilization. Certainly it is hard to imagine a more refined urban existence than could be found in the Athens of Plato or the Rome of Horace. The Italian cities of the Renaissance, too, are there to remind us of the heights urbanity could reach before the coming of industrialism.

Industrial urbanism differs from pre-industrial urbanism in two ways. The first is in its quantitative reach and intensity; the second is in the new qualitative relationship it sets up between the city and society.

For all the culture and sophistication of the pre-industrial city, it remained a distinctly minority experience. Full urban participation ranged narrowly from the 3 or 4 per cent of the population who were city dwellers in third millennium BC Egypt and Mesopotamia, to the 10–15 per cent of Italians who lived in cities at the zenith of imperial Rome (but who were heavily dependent on food supplies from North Africa). This represents a highpoint of pre-industrial urbanism. Until the advent of industrialization in the eighteenth century, the rural population of most countries rarely dropped below 90 per cent – the figure that applies, for instance, to both France and Russia on the eve of their revolutions.

Industrialization brings a growth in trade and manufactures. It sets up a requirement for centralized sites of production, distribution, exchange and credit. It demands a regular system of communications and transport. It calls into being duly constituted political authorities with the power to establish a dependable coinage, a standard system of weights and measures, a reasonable degree of protection and safety on the roads and regular enforcement of the laws. All these developments conduce to a vast increase in urbanization. Whereas in agrarian societies 90 per cent or more of the population are rural, in industrial societies the tendency is for 90 per cent or more to be urban.

The growth of cities with industrialization can be illustrated by the example of Britain, the first industrial nation. In 1801 about one-fifth of its population lived in towns and cities with 10,000 or more inhabitants. By 1851, two-fifths were so urbanized; and if we include, as did the Census of that year, smaller towns of 5,000 or more, more than half the population could be counted as urbanized. The world's first industrial society had become the world's first urban society, suggesting thereby a clear connection. By the year of Queen

Victoria's death, in 1901, the Census recorded three-quarters of the population as urban (two-thirds in cities of 10,000 or more and half in cities of 20,000 or more); in 1911, it was four-fifths. In the space of just over a century a largely rural society had become a largely urban one.

The pattern was repeated, with appropriate time-lags, on a European and world scale as industrialization proceeded. At the beginning of the nineteenth century, continental Europe (less Russia) was less than 10 per cent urbanized, with respect to cities of 10,000 or more; by the end of the century it was about 30 per cent urbanized (10 per cent in cities with 100,000 or more), and by the mid-1980s, the urban population was more than 70 per cent. In the United States, in 1800 only 6 per cent of the population lived in towns of 2,500 or more; in 1920, the Census reported that for the first time more than half of the American people lived in cities. By the mid-1980s this had risen to nearly 80 per cent – about the same as Japan's urban population – and more than two-fifths of the population lived in cities of 1 million or more. Taking the world as a whole, in 1800 no more than 2.5 per cent of the population lived in cities of 20,000 or more; by 1965 this had increased to 25 per cent, and by 1980, 40 per cent. It is estimated that by the year 2000 about half the world's population will be urban, by this measure. At the same time there has been a great growth of very large cities, of a type virtually unknown in the pre-industrial world. Cities of more than 1 million inhabitants numbered 10 in 1900, 49 in 1950 and 250 in 1985.

As with population growth, it is in the Third World that the fastest rates of urban growth are to be found. The rapidly expanding population in the countryside sought the city as the only escape route, though in many cases it turned out to be perilous. Between 1900 and 1950, while world population grew by 50 per cent, the urban population as a whole grew by 254 per cent; but in Asia urban growth was 444 per cent and in Africa, 629 per cent. By the mid-1980s, Africa and Asia were about 35 per cent urbanized, and Latin America nearly 70 per cent so. Cities such as São Paulo (10 million), Mexico City (12 million) and Calcutta (8 million), had mushroomed to rival and even overtake in size the large cities of the developed West and Japan.

But while Third World urbanization repeats some of the more distressing features of Western urbanization – overcrowding, insanitary conditions, unemployment – the compensation and eventual remedy of economic growth has been largely lacking. With some partial exceptions, such as Brazil, Mexico, Singapore and Hong Kong, the Third World has known urbanization without industrialization. The result has been the rapid growth of shanty-towns – *bidonvilles, callampas* – on the edges of the big cities. It has been estimated that about 4 or 5 million families in Latin America live in shanty-towns. While these settlements are not as disorganized and intolerable as they may seem from the outside, they add considerably to the problem of already overstretched urban facilities and urban administration.

Urbanism cannot be grasped simply by statistics of urban growth. It is a matter too of a distinctive culture and consciousness. Urbanism is a way of life, as classically analysed by the German sociologist Georg Simmel and the American sociologist Louis Wirth. In the massing of people in large modern cities, as opposed to the small towns of pre-industrial society, they saw great opportunities but also great dangers. City life, with its tendency to nervous overstimulation, led to a bored and blasé attitude to life. It encouraged frivolous and fleeting cults and fashions. It detached people from their traditional communal moorings, leaving them morally stranded and so inclined to harbour unreal expectations and feverish dreams. In the very number of social contacts it necessarily generated, it compelled individuals to erect barriers, to protect their privacy. Individuals are forced into an attitude of reserve and isolation. Hence, as Simmel noted, the superficial paradox that 'one nowhere feels as lonely and lost as in the metropolitan crowd'.

At the same time, cities promoted diversity and creativity. They attracted the best and the brightest to them. If anything was to be accomplished in modern society, it must be in the city. Karl Marx spoke of 'the idiocy of rural life'. Only in cities, many sociologists felt, would human beings be able to realize to the full all their potentialities. Cities were the forcing house of change and growth. 'Great cities,' declared the French sociologist Émile Durkheim, 'are the uncontested home of progress; it is in them that ideas, fashions, customs, new needs are elaborated and then spread over the rest of the country . . . Minds naturally are there oriented to the future.'

But whether they deplored or praised urban life, most commentators have agreed that, with industrialism, the city moved into a new pivotal position in relation to the society as a whole. Pre-industrial cities were isolated fragments, urban islands in an agrarian sea. They hailed each other across vast alien tracts of non-urban life, which remained largely indifferent to and unaffected by their practices. Essentially they were parasitic on the countryside and the peasant masses whose labour and food production sustained them. Their disappearance not only would not have mattered to the peasants but would in most cases have been welcomed.

With industrial urbanism, this relationship was reversed. The countryside now became dependent on the city. It became an integral part of a single economic system, centred on the cities. Largely emptied of people, the countryside was now in effect simply another theatre of industrial operations for city merchants and bankers. All political and economic power resided in the city; industrial and financial corporations became the dominant landowners, replacing individual proprietors. Except as quaint retreats for tourists, no areas of rustic life remained, none at any rate that significantly affected the values and practices of society. Now that it no longer existed, 'country life' could become a persuasive motif in the fertile minds of advertising copywriters, preying on the fantasies of urban man.

The city became both the symbol and the reality of industrial society as a whole. No longer, as in the past, standing in a mechanical relation to other parts of society, it was now placed at the centre of an organic whole. Industrialism created a centralized web of social relationships, and the city was the nodal point from which and to which all influences flowed. It dictated the style and set the standard for the whole society, providing it with its economic, political and cultural framework. When in their novels Dickens and Balzac treated London and Paris metaphorically as the representation of the whole system of industrialism, they came nearer to the truth than most of those investigators patiently accumulating statistics of rural–urban migration.

Work and the family

In pre-industrial or non-industrial society, the family is the basic unit of production. All its members engage in a cooperative set of subsistence activities. In a typical English example from the early eighteenth century, the man might be a weaver, his wife a spinner, with the younger children acting as assistants in the joint domestic enterprise. Mixed in with this would probably be the cultivation of a small plot of land, together with access to common land to forage for fuel and to hunt small game. The family need not necessarily be very large – in north-western Europe and North America it seems to have been relatively small – but on the whole extra hands are an economic asset as well as carrying an extra mouth to feed. The family is a collective enterprise; all its members regard themselves as part of that collectivity, and their contributions as swelling a common store; any servants or other non-family members such as apprentices are 'adopted' or treated as family members, for no other relationships but family ones are recognized. For its members, the family is, to all intents and purposes, the whole society, or at least society in miniature.

Industrialization radically disrupts this more or less autonomous family economy. It takes away the economic function of the family, and reduces it to a unit of consumption and socialization. Production moves away from the household to the factory. The commons are enclosed, and the land commercially exploited for national and international markets. Some individuals become the owners and the managers of the new system. But the bulk of family members must become either landless agricultural labourers or, as increasingly happens, workers in the factories of the new industrial towns. In either case, the family becomes dependent for its livelihood on structures and processes external to itself. It lives by the jobs and wages of its members, and these are affected by forces which it barely comprehends, still less controls. From being, as in the past, more or less coterminous with society, the family becomes one dependent part of a system whose dynamism determines its fate.

In the early stages of industrialization, the family tends to struggle to maintain its traditional collective unity. Its members, whether employed as farm workers in the country, industrial workers in the towns, or domestic servants in well-to-do urban homes, continue to pool their resources. They make regular visits home and continue to think of themselves as a collectivity. Their wages still contribute to a common family fund. This is used to support the non-working young as well as temporarily unemployed members, and to provide for members in sickness and old age. In the absence of a comprehensive system of social security, the family itself is forced to become a 'welfare state in miniature'. In these circumstances, as in the past, a large family can be as much an asset as a burden. For a considerable time, therefore, large families, especially among the working classes, continue to be the norm in industrial society.

Eventually the forces of individualization, which are so powerful in the industrial economy and the society at large, affect also the family. Family members, male and female, increasingly come to think of their wages as their own, to be disposed of as they individually see fit. The state is forced to step in to provide for those members unable to earn their own living, either because they are chronically unemployed, or because they are too young, too sick or too old. The family increasingly becomes restricted to child-rearing, and even here it has to compete with the school, peer groups and child-care agencies. For its older members, it becomes merely the site of recreation and a certain amount of sociability. Physically they may spend a good deal of time at home, but their minds are formed more by influences operating outside it. Their lives are led largely outside the family, in their work and in association with non-family friends and colleagues. They do not think of their identity in terms of a collective family identity. Hence the tendency for young adults to marry young, to break away from their families of origin and to set up their own independent families.

Shorn of so many traditional functions, the family becomes almost exclusively the sphere of private life. It attends to the needs of children and the emotional and sexual satisfaction of the spouses. A small unit is best suited to these tasks. The larger families of the pre-industrial and early industrial periods, which sometimes included grandparents and married offspring, give way to the small, two-generation nuclear family of parents and dependent children only. Whether or not the nuclear family precedes industrialization – as for instance it seems to have done in England – in industrial society it certainly becomes the norm.

With the shrinking and privatization of the family, the sphere of work grows correspondingly. It becomes the principal source of individual identity. In pre-industrial society, the question 'Who am I?' is likely to be answered in terms of place of origin or family membership. I am John of Winchester, or John, Robert's son. In industrial society the question is typically answered in terms of one's occupation in the formal economy. The occupational role, as miner or machinist, clerk or cleaner, becomes the determining role. It is the source generally of one's identity, status and income. Work, throwing off its religious sanctification in the Protestant ethic, itself becomes a religion. Not to work, to be unemployed, is to be stigmatized as much in one's own eyes as in the eyes of society.

Work is redefined as applying more or less exclusively to formal employment in the industrial economy. All other kinds of work – unpaid domestic work, voluntary work, work done for friends or family – are devalued and treated as marginal or 'unproductive'. The paradox is that the elevation of the sphere of employed work is accompanied by a decisive fragmentation of work as an activity. Industrialization brings about a massive increase in the division of labour. But this involves not just, as in pre-industrial urban life, a specialization of crafts and the rise of new occupations. This certainly takes place. But more important is the new kind of division of labour, what Adam Smith and Karl Marx called the 'detailed' division of labour, in the work task itself. The set of tasks involved in the making of a whole product, which was previously performed by a single craftsman or worker, is now separated out and allocated to a number of different individuals. In his famous example of a pin manufactory in *The Wealth of Nations* (1776), Adam Smith showed how by dividing up the task of pin-making into eighteen distinct operations, each performed by 'distinct hands', productivity could be increased more than a thousandfold. It was this form of the division of labour that became the source of the fantastic productivity of the industrial system, especially once Henry Ford had organized it around the continuously moving assembly line, and Frederick Winslow Taylor had supplied the method for the splitting of the task into an infinity of the simplest operations.

The English social critic John Ruskin pointed to one consequence of this new division of labour when he said that 'it is not, truly speaking, the labour that is divided, but the men'. The problem of motivating the work force, of providing sufficient inducement to work discipline and performance when the tasks themselves were so intrinsically uninteresting, haunted all industrial societies. But the new division of labour itself pointed, rather ominously, to the likely resolution of this problem. Once tasks had been so minutely sub-divided that the least skilled workman could do them, it was an inevitable next step to mechanize the tasks and dispense with the human worker altogether. Full automation was implicit in the industrial principle of the division of labour from the very start. It was ironic that the form of society which had so unprecedentedly put work at its very centre should also, in its further evolution, threaten to take it away altogether from its citizens.

Social structure

Given the importance of economic institutions in general, and occupational position in particular, it is not surprising to find that industrial society tends to produce a new principle in the ordering and ranking of individuals. Economic position and relationships become the key to social position and class membership. This is new, in its extent at least. While wealth or the lack of it have always been important in determining social position, they have not usually been the sole or even the central determinant. In all non-industrial societies, attributes of race, religion, age and gender are of equal and often greater importance in assigning individuals to a position in the social hierarchy. In the traditional Indian caste system, for instance, the religious eminence of even the poorest Brahmin marked him out as a member of the highest and most esteemed caste.

Industrial society tends to subordinate all these pre-industrial principles of ranking to the economic one. One's position in the system of production, or, more generally, in the marketplace, allocates one to a particular class or group. Ownership of property, level of education and training, all affect one's market position. Karl Marx was convinced that in the course of its development capitalism – the only form of industrialism he considered – would eventually throw up only two main economic classes, the propertyless workers or proletariat and the capitalist owners or bourgeoisie. These he expected to engage in a revolutionary struggle which would eventually lead to socialism.

One reason why this has not happened in any developed society is that, though perhaps dominant in the long run, economic relationships have not so sweepingly eliminated other non-economic considerations. Older sources of identification have continued to exercise considerable power. Groups based on ethnic, religious and regional ties have overlapped with and occasionally submerged those based solely on the tie of economic interest. Thus the working class of Northern Ireland has preferred to stress its Protestant identification over its proletarian one. Workers and capitalists in the Basque and Catalan regions of Spain have united in a long-drawn-out opposition to Madrid. In the United States, black identity has continued to override any other based on income or occupation. Indeed throughout the industrial world in this century, conflicts of a racial, religious, or regional kind have equalled if not surpassed conflicts arising out of economic interests.

This is one way in which it is brought home that even radical changes involve continuities as well as discontinuities. There are gainers and losers in the process of change, and the losers are apt to hark back to past ways and values. Industrialization, though making a fundamental break with past forms of society, does not abolish all the elements of traditional society. It carries many of them over and may even intensify them, with that peculiar power that industrialism confers on all activities – even those, such as war, which threaten to annihilate it.

Secularization and rationalization

At the most abstract level of development, modernization leads to what Max Weber called 'the disenchantment of the world'. It eliminates all the superhuman and supernatural forces, the gods and spirits, with which non-industrial cultures people the universe, and to which they attribute responsibility for the phenomena of the natural and social worlds. In their place it substitutes as the sole cosmology the understanding of modern science. Only the laws and regularities discovered by the scientific method are allowed as providing a valid explanation of any earthly or non-earthly happening. If it rains – or doesn't rain – it is not because the gods are angry but because of atmospheric conditions, as measured by the barometer.

Specifically, modernization involves a process of secularization. It systematically, that is, devalues religious institutions, beliefs and practices, substituting for them those of reason and science. This process was first observable in Christian Europe, towards the end of the seventeenth century. It is possible that there is something inherently secularizing about Christianity, for no other religion has ever spontaneously given rise to secular beliefs. At any rate, once invented in Europe, especially Protestant Europe, it was carried as part of the 'package' of industrialism that was exported to the non-European world. Wherever modern European cultures impinged, they diffused secularizing currents which undermined all traditional religions and non-rational ideologies.

Secularization does not imply that religion is driven out altogether from society. It is a general tendency or principle of development in modern societies. Against a background of societies dominated for millennia by religion, it inevitably leaves many religious practices still in being, and may even stimulate new ones. Religious rituals such as baptisms and church weddings persist in all industrial societies; the Church may, as in England and Italy, continue to play an important moral and social role. The generality of the population may hold, however insecurely, traditional religious beliefs alongside more scientific ones. There may even be, as in the United States, waves of religious revivalism, involving large sections of the population.

The important thing is that all such religious phenomena, real as they might be in the lives of the people who participate in them, lose their centrality in the life of society as a whole. As compared with their place in traditional society, they increasingly take on the character of marginal, even leisure-time, activities. They no longer carry that crucial legitimating power that religious activities have in all non-industrial societies. The Church is aware that to confront the modern state too openly is to risk disestablishment, as in France, or even, as in communist societies, dissolution. Baptisms and church weddings persist more for social reasons than because of a belief in their religious significance. Even the fervour of American revivalism often seems stamped more with the character of American commercialism than with any specifically anti-secular religiosity. Certainly the world's largest and most powerful industrial society, for all it declares itself to be 'one nation under God', seems perfectly capable of absorbing a considerable degree of religious activity without abandoning its avowedly secular constitution and its undeniably secular economy.

Secularization is a sub-development of a larger cultural process that affects all modern societies: the process of rationalization. While this refers centrally to the rise of the scientific world-view, it encompasses many more areas than we usually associate with science. It refers, for instance, to the capitalist economy, with its rational organization of labour and its rational calculation of profit and loss. It refers also to artistic developments, such as the achievement of the rational utilization of lines and spatial perspective in painting, and of a rational system of notation and rational harmonic principles in music. For Max Weber, however, the most careful student of the process, it referred above all to the establishment of a rational system of laws and administration in modern society. It was in the system of bureaucracy, seen as the impersonal and impartial rule of rationally constituted laws and formal procedures, that Weber saw the highest development of the rational principle in modern life. Bureaucracy meant a principled hostility to all traditional and 'irrational' considerations of person or place, kinship or culture. It expressed the triumph of the scientific method and scientific expertise in social life. The trained official, said Weber, is 'the pillar of both the modern state and of the economic life of the West'.

Weber was aware that bureaucracy had two faces. It could also be despotic and irrational, in actual operation. The triumph of a principle did not guarantee its strict performance in practice. Rationalization was a process that operated at the highest, most general, level of social development. It would have been surprising if its presence were to be found in every nook and cranny of modern society. Everywhere one should expect to find the persistence of non-rational and even anti-rational attitudes and behaviour. Religion was one example; the occasional rise of personal, 'charismatic', leadership, breaking through the rationalized routines of bureaucracy, was another. These should not be thought of simply as vestiges or 'hangovers' from traditional society. They were also the expressions of essential needs, emotional and cultural, that were in danger of being stifled in a scientific and 'disenchanted' environment. The rise of modern Fascist leaders such as Mussolini and Hitler, and of modern cults of mysticism and magic, would not have surprised Weber – these were, to him, the more or less predictable consequence of a rationalized and bureaucratized world.

Weber stressed another significant point. Rationalization did not entail that the populations of modern societies were, as individuals, any more reasonable or knowledgeable than the populations of non-industrial societies. What it meant was that there was, in principle, scientifically validated knowledge available to modern populations, by which they could enlighten themselves about their world and seek to govern their behaviour. In practice, as Weber knew, such knowledge tended to be restricted to scientifically trained elites. The mass of the population of a modern society might in their daily lives be more ignorant than the most primitive savage. The savage usually has a comprehensive working knowledge of the tools he uses and the food he consumes. Modern man can use an elevator without the slightest idea of its working principle; he can eat food manufactured in ways and with materials of which he is blissfully and totally unaware. The crises and disasters this ignorance can occasion are only one example of the fundamental ambivalence of modernity as a principle of development.

Social problems

As with bureaucracy, so with practically all the other features: they show the two faces of modernity. One face is smiling, expressing the dynamic, forward-looking, progressive aspects. It promises unprecedented abundance, freedom and fulfilment. The other face shows the dark side of modernity. It expresses the new problems that modernity brings in its wake by virtue of the very scale and novelty of its achievements. Social progress is matched by social pathology. Every forward step seems to evoke a corresponding penalty.

Thus, the historic achievement of supporting a large population also brings crowding, pollution and environmental destruction. Quietness, privacy and space become scarce commodities. Massed together in cities, seeking rest and recreation, the large populations of industrial societies open up the whole world to mass tourism. Soon every rural haven, every sunswept coast, is turned into an administered holiday camp, each a uniform replica of the other. The industrial principle of mass production and mass distribution can readily be turned from the production of goods to the production of services, including those of leisure and entertainment. Quantity increases; quality declines.

Urban-industrial life offers unparalleled opportunities for individual mobility and personal freedom. It also promises the attainment of dazzling prizes, in wealth and honours, for those with the enterprise and talent to reach for them. The other side of all this is the loneliness of the city dweller, and the desolation of failure for those many who cannot win any of the prizes. As Durkheim analysed it, the individual is placed in the pathological condition of 'anomie'. He experiences 'the malady of infinite aspirations'. The decline of religion and community removes the traditional restraints on need and appetite, causing these to rise morbidly and without limit . At the same time the competitive modern order which feeds these unreal expectations provides insufficient and unequal means for their realization. The result is an increase in suicide, crime and mental disorder.

Industrial work, too, demands a high price for the enormous increase in productivity brought by the intensification of the division of labour. It was Karl Marx who offered the most systematic analysis of this under the heading of 'alienation'. The industrial worker feels estranged from the activity of work because the work is so meaningless, fragmented and undemanding. He does not realize himself, his human potential, in his work. It makes no call on his constructive and creative faculties, unlike for instance traditional craft work. The industrial worker also feels alienated from the product of his work, as he has no control over its manufacture nor over the terms and conditions of its disposal. As the sum of its parts, the industrial system of production is phenomenally powerful; but at the cost of reducing those parts, the human workers, into mere 'hands', helpless semblances of humanity. Eventually, Marx hoped, the surplus wealth produced by the industrial system would free workers altogether from the necessity of work; but until that time the degraded condition of the worker would be the most eloquent testimony to the dehumanization wrought by the system.

Marx's optimism about the future was perhaps as excessive as his pessimism about the present. But he was by no means the only one who felt that industrial society demanded too high a price of many of its members. Repeatedly it was disclosed that industrialism had created new and apparently ineradicable pockets of poverty. Despite steady economic growth, there was the persistent finding throughout the industrial world that between 15 and 20 per cent of the population remained permanently below the officially defined levels of poverty. It appeared that industrialism by its very mechanism of growth created a 'new poor', whose who, for whatever reason – deprived backgrounds, low enterprise, low intelligence – were unable to compete according to the rules of the industrial order. Lacking the communal and kinship supports of the past, there was no alternative for the failed and the rejected but to become claimants and pensioners of the state.

There were other victims too. The small nuclear family offered, to a greater extent than ever before, the opportunity for intense privacy and emotional fulfilment. But the very intensity of the relationships it demanded seemed to put an intolerable burden on it. Added to that, it became the only remaining primary group in society, the only social unit where personal face-to-face relationships continued to any great extent. Elsewhere bureaucratic or commercial relationships prevailed. The nuclear family was called upon to do all the work of restoration and repair of its members on their return from the impersonal, large-scale, bureaucratic world of work and, increasingly, play. Under this unprecedented pressure it showed all the symptoms of distress. Adolescent alienation and teenage rebellion became the accepted features of modern family life. Divorce rates soared; and when people sought to re-marry – 'the triumph of hope over experience' their second marriages proved even more unstable than their first. There was a steady increase in one-parent families, headed usually by a woman. Marriage and re-marriage nevertheless remained popular; the nuclear family remained the norm, despite occasional communal experiments. No one, it appeared, had much confidence in these institutions but nor could anyone think of anything better to put in their place.

Modernization, finally, put a number of political and cultural problems on the agenda. The decline of local communities, and the great growth in scale of political centralization, put a strain on civic loyalties and the willingness to participate in political life. As the mass political parties monopolized public life, individual citizens retreated increasingly into private life. Political apathy and low turn-outs at elections became matters seriously affecting the democratic pretensions of modern liberal societies. A similar danger stemmed from the spread of mass communications, which in the twentieth century came to monopolize the cultural life of modern societies. The cultural uniformity and conformity bred by the press, radio and television threatened the pluralism and diversity on which liberal society prided itself, and which it regarded as its chief security against totalitarian challenge.

Together, political and cultural centralization pointed to the creation of a 'mass society'. As Tocqueville had warned, individuals lacking strong intermediate institutions with which to identify would become atomized, and might look to the protection of strong men and strong governments. Once more, this had to be seen as a general tendency and possibility, not an inevitability. Plural institutions remained strong in many societies. But the rise and success of totalitarian movements in some industrial societies showed that the tendencies were real, and present in some degree in all modern societies.

MODERN SOCIETY AND WORLD SOCIETY

Western and non-Western routes to modernity

The Western experience of industrialization became the model for world industrialization. To become modern was to become something like Western industrial society. Non-Western societies were not always given much choice in the matter. As formal or informal colonies of Western powers they often found themselves being 'developed' in a Western direction before they took political control of their own destinies. Once on the way, there was no going back. But even where some choice was involved, it was clear to everyone that the only viable form of society in the modern world was industrial society. Only industrial societies could be active agents in the world system: all others must become clients or dependants. It was above all Japan which demonstrated this. From a poor nation humiliated at the hands of the West, Japan rose through industrialization to become one of the most powerful societies in the world. More pointedly, it showed that, by meeting the challenge of industrialization, a non-Western society could become not merely the equal but the superior of some of the strongest Western powers.

Japan confirmed what Western experience had already made clear: that there were several routes to modernity. In the nineteenth century, England, Belgium, France and the United States industrialized largely on the basis of the individual entrepreneur and the free market economy. Germany, and even more Japan, industrialized from 'on top': the state and political elites played a major role, organizing credit, coordinating and planning the nature and pace of development and restricting markets in the interests of home industry. Later still came the even more authoritarian model of modernization under the aegis of the one-party state. Taking their lead from the Soviet Union, following the Russian Revolution of 1917, many developing countries in Asia, Africa and Latin America sought to industrialize according to economic plans drawn up by highly centralized political elites, and stringently imposed on their populations.

Not all such attempts were formally socialist or communist, on the Soviet pattern. But even where, as in India, formal liberal democracy was instituted, industrialization was largely guided by a single national party – identified with the struggle for independence from colonial rule. In any case there were plenty of socialisms to choose from, many departing substantially from the Soviet model as well as from each other. There was the 'African socialism' of Nkrumah's Ghana and – differently – Nyere's Tanzania; the 'Chinese socialism' of Mao's China; the 'Cuban socialism' of Fidel Castro; the 'Yugoslav socialism' of Tito. All could aspire to be 'models of development' to Third World societies, and many were prepared to lace the model with suitable offers of economic aid and technical expertise.

Japan and the Soviet Union suggested, in their different ways, that there was a general pattern of 'late development', appropriate to all those who attempted to industrialize in the shadow of already existing industrial powers. This variously involved strong protectionism, directed labour, control of unions and central supervision of banking and credit. It also meant circumventing the sharp management–worker divide which marked most early Western industrializers, and which continued to hamper them in their later industrial history. If unions were allowed at all, they tended to be 'company unions', as in Japan, involving all plant workers and many levels of management as well. Above all, late-developers put the power of the state at the centre of the modernizing effort. The state was the prime mover and guardian of the whole enterprise. Unlike Britain or the United States, where the state played merely a 'nightwatchman' role, keeping the peace and enforcing the laws, in countries such as Japan, the Soviet Union and China, the state directed the industrializing process from the start and supervised it throughout. It took major decisions about investment, transport and communications, and education. It developed the media of mass communications as agencies of mass cultural socialization into modern values and attitudes. Whether or not, therefore, the economy was formally nationalized, in practice economic develpment was placed firmly under national auspices and directed to nationalist ends.

Late development tended to produce a different social structure from that of the pioneering West. In the West, industrialization was largely a private affair, carried out by middle-class entrepreneurs. The social structure it produced was typically one of private proprietors and managers at the top, with professionals and technicians in the middle as the service class and industrial workers at the bottom. Japan and Germany added public officials as key members of the top class. In later cases, in the Soviet Union and most Third World societies, industrialization was carried out by a middle-class intelligentsia which seized control of the state and the army. The senior party officials and military personnel became the new ruling class. Seeking to mobilize the whole nation in the effort at modernization, they prevented the emergence of a new entrepreneurial middle class, and strictly controlled developments among the peasants and industrial workers (for instance by collectivizing agriculture). The typical structure of these societies is one of elite and mass, linked by party agencies at every level of society. Classes, in the usual Western sense, do not exist. But, though most of these societies espouse some form of socialist ideology, such 'classlessness', even in the Soviet Union, is worlds away from Marx's vision of the future socialist society. Certainly it seems compatible with a high degree of inequality and exploitation.

One world or many?

Japan has been, so far, the only non-Western country in the world to become fully industrial. It may be important that it began its industrialization in the nineteenth century, while the West was still itself industrializing, and before it had built up a truly commanding lead. The same is true of the Soviet Union, the only other major case of industrialization outside Western Europe and North America (taking South Africa and Australia as 'European'). In the twentieth century it has become increasingly clear that industrialization is not something that nations can decide about entirely by themselves. They operate within a context of world industrialization, in a world system of states of decidedly unequal wealth and power.

The world system can be divided up according to political or economic criteria. If we take the former, we get the familiar 'West–East' divide. This is primarily an ideological division between the developed capitalist nations, such as the United States, Germany and Japan (counted as ideologically 'West'), and the developed Communist or 'state socialist' nations, such as the Soviet Union and Hungary. Attached to these are respectively underdeveloped capitalist nations – such as Bolivia and Bangladesh – and underdeveloped Communist nations – such as China and Cuba.

A more significant and in many ways more realistic division arises from taking the level of economic development as primary, and the political or ideological differences as subsidiary. This gives us the 'North–South' divide. With some anomalies – South Africa, Australia – the world is seen as divided essentially between the wealthy and powerful countries of the northern hemisphere, and the poor, less developed countries of the southern hemisphere.

But the 'North–South' terminology, though handy in debate, is inaccurate and misleading. The economic model of the world system more precisely distinguishes between the Superpowers, the United States and the Soviet Union; other developed countries, such as Japan and Hungary; and the underdeveloped countries, such as China and Bolivia. We then have First, Second and Third Worlds.

The attraction of this model is that it points to the interconnections and flow of power in the world system. It shows especially the global domination of the two Superpowers, who despite being divided by divergent ideological and strategic interests, also share a common interest in maintaining their joint world hegemony. The Superpowers compete with each other, drawing into their respective spheres of influence the less powerful countries of the Second and Third Worlds; but, in order to maintain the balance of power, they also collude, choosing on occasion to ignore profitable opportunities for making trouble in each other's sphere, and undermining political movements which seek too independent a 'third way' (as shown for instance by Soviet policy during the Spanish Civil War).

A further refinement of the economic model is to see not three worlds of development but only one developing world system. Taking a historical perspective, this view, advanced especially by the American theorist Immanuel Wallerstein, argues that there is but a single world economy, the capitalist world economy which has been expanding since the seventeenth century. This economy has, over the centuries, been moving outward from its north-west European base to incorporate increasing sections of the globe. East European societies are seen as full participants in this system, and are accordingly regarded not as socialist but as 'collective capitalist firms'. Countries can be classified according to their nearness to the centre of the system. There are 'core countries', such as the United States and Japan; 'semi-peripheral countries', such as Brazil, most East European states and China; and 'peripheral countries', such as Cuba, and most of the poor countries of Africa and Asia. Depending on economic fortunes and fluctuations, as well as the logic of the developing system itself, countries can move in and out of these categories – for instance, the Soviet Union moved from semi-periphery to core, and India from periphery to semi-periphery; Britain may well be moving from core to semi-periphery.

The plausibility and appeal of this model lie in its recognition of the growing internationalization of the industrial economy. Nation states, whether capitalist or Communist, are becoming increasingly subordinate to world economic developments. The politics of energy – oil, gas, nuclear power – are world politics (just as, for some considerable time, military strategy has been world strategy). Decisions about capital investment and growth are taken in a world context, on a world scale. The giant multinational corporations are the most significant new actors on the world stage. They have been establishing a new international division of labour. From their point of view, it makes more sense to manufacture their goods in South Korea or Taiwan, where labour is still cheap and governments compliant, than in the United States or Britain, where labour is expensive and unions powerful. Central planning, research and development can be retained in their Western homelands, where there are the necessary reserves of highly qualified professional and scientific personnel. Profits can be declared in those countries where taxes are lowest. In such a way do the multinationals show the interdependence of core and periphery nations. At the same time they are powerfully transforming the economic and social life of their base areas, the Western industrial societies.

'POST-MODERN' AND 'POST-INDUSTRIAL' SOCIETY

New developments in economy and social structure

Industrialism never reaches a point of equilibrium or a level plateau. It ceaselessly, by its very principle of operation, innovates and changes. Having eliminated the agricultural workforce, it moves on to decimate manufacturing employment. New technology increases manufacturing productivity and displaces workers. Manufacturing, from accounting for a half or more of the employed population of industrial societies, shrinks to between one-quarter and one-third. Its place is filled by the service sector, which in all industrial societies comes to employ between a half and two-thirds of the workforce, and to account for more than a half of the Gross National Product. Most service occupations – in government, health and education, banks, leisure and entertainment – are white-collar. The typical industrial worker comes to be not, as in the past, the blue-collar worker but the white-collar worker. 'White-bloused' might be more accurate, since the majority of service workers are women. In the late stages of industrial development, women tend to make up nearly a half of the total workforce.

The move to a 'service society' is marked by a great expansion in education, health and other private and public welfare services. The population typically becomes not just healthier, better housed and better fed, but also better educated. Most young people complete secondary or high school education; between a quarter and a half of them go on to full-time higher education. Professional and scientific knowledge becomes the most marketable commodity. The 'knowledge class' of professional, scientific and technical workers becomes the fastest growing occupational group. The link between pure science and technology, loose and imprecise in the early stages of industrialization, is pivotal in the later stages. New industries, starting with chemicals and pharmaceuticals, and later including the aeronautical, space and nuclear industries, are spawned by developments in pure science and come to depend largely on further theoretical research. Theoretical knowledge in the social sciences also comes to be widely applied, as in Keynesian management of the national economy, and in complex models of technological and economic forecasting.

Struck by these changes, as compared with the 'classic' industrial society of the nineteenth and early twentieth centuries, some theorists, notably the American sociologist Daniel Bell, speak of the movement to a new 'post-modern' or 'post-industrial' society. Such assertions seem premature. Most of the changes can be seen as the product of long-term developments intrinsic to the process of industrialism from the start. The rise of service work comes out of the continuing process of mechanization and technical innovation, which constantly replaces men with machines. The growth of services is premised on the consequent growth in productivity of the manufacturing sector. It can also be seen as the consequence of the growth of multinational corporations, and their strategy of removing their manufacturing operations to Third World countries, while centring their service operations in the developed world. This too is the result of the increase in scale and complexity of industrial organization which has been a tendency from the very start. The growth of knowledge-based industries, finally, represents no break with the past. Science has always been at the basis of industrialism, and its closer union with industry and society in this century is simply the fulfilment of the rationalizing drive which, as we have seen, is the major impulse of modernization.

But while there may be no new society, these changes do add a new dimension to modern societies. Beyond a certain point of economic development, new values and problems emerge. The activities of the multinationals are causing a decisive 'de-industrialization' of many modern societies, a collapse of manufacturing output and employment as these shift out to the Third World. While services have for the time filled the breach, this cannot be expected to continue, at least as far as employment goes. The new microelectronic technology, itself simply the latest wave of industrial tools, is making inroads into service employment faster than ever machines displaced manufacturing workers. The application of computers to information-processing in a wide range of service work – government offices, banks, insurance companies, department stores – is threatening to displace the vast mass of routine white-collar workers. Nor are the more skilled workers necessarily much safer: computer-aided design takes over much of the draughtsman's and architect's work, electronic audiovisual equipment much of that of the teacher, self-service diagnostic machinery much of that of the nurse and doctor.

At the same time, a more highly educated population is less compliant with such threats to its livelihood. It demands protection or compensation on a scale which puts heavy pressure on the fiscal resources of the state. Moreover it is no longer satisfied with merely material remuneration or compensation. Industrial societies have crossed a historic threshold in consumption levels which complicates the needs and satisfactions of their populations. Non-material values – the desire for satisfying work, for unpolluted towns and countryside, for a more human scale of organization, and a more harmonious relationship with the natural environment – figure strongly in the inventory of things thought requisite for 'the good life'. The rise of environmentalist and ecological movements, such as the British 'Friends of the Earth' and the 'Green Parties' of Europe, testify to this new concern.

If the new technology can be so productive that large numbers of the population need not work at all, or only for short periods, then a new 'post-industrial' way of life may be possible. The organization of time and leisure will become the main social concern. If, however, the new technology simply produces mass unemployment without adequate compensation or support, the conflicts of late twentieth-century industrial society will bear a striking resemblance to the strife of the early Industrial Revolution. 'Post-industrial', for those societies which cannot compete successfully in the world, will look uncomfortably like early industrial, without the hope of that heroic period.

New patterns of urban life

Many features of modernity, intensified beyond a certain level, produce a reactive response. Urbanization, having reached practical saturation point, leads to sub-urbanization, the desire to live in neighbourhoods with green spaces and at least a breath of country air. As the suburbs fill up, the more prosperous citizens become 'ex-urban': they colonize the villages and small towns of the countryside which are within commuting distance of their work in the city. Aiding this trend is the industrial decentralization and depopulation of many cities, as old manufacturing industries decline and new service industries move out to the suburbs and small towns. For the first time since the onset of industrialization, the countryside begins to gain population and the cities to lose it. According to the 1980 US Census, cities such as St Louis, Buffalo and Detroit lost beween 21 and 27 per cent of their population over a thirty-year period. In England, London lost 20 per cent of the population of its inner boroughs between 1961 and 1971, and Liverpool almost 25 per cent of its population in the twenty-year period to 1971.

But there is a deceptive aspect to this movement. The main forces of industrialism, here as elsewhere, continue to dominate the process. Suburbanization and ex-urbanization do not mean de-urbanization. On the contrary they lead to a spreading of urban life over greater and greater areas. They involve the filling up, at lesser densities, of large urban areas and regions. There is the 'metropolitan area', comprising a large city of around 10 million people together with a surrounding community socially and economically dependent on it. The metropolitan areas themselves have a tendency to merge into even larger urban agglomerations, known as 'megalopolises', which serve populations of 40 million or more. The biggest of these is the conglomeration of cities and surrounding regions that stretches from Boston to Washington, DC along the north-eastern seaboard of the United States. Others in the United States include the Chicago–Pittsburgh area around the Great Lakes, and the San Francisco–San Diego region along the Pacific coast. In Britain there is an emerging megalopolis in the region between London and the Midland cities, in Germany in the industrial basin of the Ruhr, and in Japan in the Tokyo–Osaka–Kyoto complex.

The Greek urbanist Constantine Doxiadis has argued that this process is part of a long-term evolution that must eventually culminate in the world-city, or 'ecumenopolis'. This will incorporate many areas of reserved spaces for recreation and agriculture, as well as desert and wilderness conservation areas. But essentially it will be a web of interconnected cities throughout the world, all parts being closely linked by rapid transport and the electronic media of communication, and all contributing to a single functional unity. In ecumenopolis, the entire surface of the globe will have become recognizably the dwelling place of urbanized humanity.

What is seen here is the contradictory pattern typical of late industrial life. Subjectively, individuals wish to escape from the city. They leave the older urban centres only to find themselves cocooned by larger urban structures in the region at large. The objective structural forces of industrialism have in no way abated. But increasingly they give rise to reactions and protests which have a 'de-modernizing' character.

Thus there has been the reaction to the large-scale bureaucratic organization that Max Weber saw as the hallmark of industrial society. 'Small is beautiful', declare the protesters, and seek to re-establish communal and craft environments characteristic of the pre-industrial period. Parallel with this is the movement of 'alternative' and 'intermediate' technology which aims to design tools that put skill and creativity back into the human worker, rather than into the machine.

At the political level too there is the reaction to large scale and centralization. In many industrial societies, such as Britain, France, Spain and Canada, there have been strong regional movements demanding autonomy or outright independence. Often these are areas, such as Scotland in Britain or the Basque provinces in Spain, which wish to restore historic nations that have been incorporated in larger, more centralized, units. These movements are assisted by the internationalization of the world economy and polity which, over the world as a whole, gives rise to new nationalisms. Lacking economic and often genuine political autonomy, small societies assert their cultural identity and autonomy – an autonomy which the great powers and multinationals are often happy to grant since it often facilitates their local operations. New nations emerge, their main symbols of independence being often no more than a national anthem and an international airport.

The assertion of cultural values opposed to modernity is a general characteristic of late industrialism. There is the revival of ethnicity, a claim for a culture and way of life that often harks back to older communal traditions, and which denies the legitimacy of any uniform culture propagated by the large nation state. Thus in the United States, blacks, Hispanics, Italians and many others have made strong claims on behalf of a distinctive ethnic way of life which they variously seek to defend against the encroachments of the dominant national Anglo-Saxon culture. Such ethnic assertions are generally made in terms of the collectivity or community, rather than the individual. They also refer to concrete and particularistic values which run against the formal rationality and bureaucratic uniformity of modern societies.

Protests against such rationality and uniformity are seen, as well, in the successive waves of youth cultures and religious revivals which mark late industrial society. At the objective level, the large-scale bureaucratic institutions continue to give the main direction to national life. All revolts against them, such as the 'May events' in France in 1968, fail against their indispensability to modern society. But subjectively they are incapable of satisfying the emotional and social needs of individuals. The consequence is the repeated rise of sub-cultures, often of a bizarre mystical or hedonistic kind, which aim in their practice to reverse the main features of modernity, and which give their members a sense of participation and belonging of an almost tribal nature. The Hippie youth movement of the 1960s was one such kind, as were religious cults such as the Hare Krishna based on Eastern mysticism and religion. Central to most of these 'antinomian' movements and ideologies is a wholesale rejection of the scientific world-view, seen as alienating and de-humanizing.

To embark on modernization is to be caught up in a whirligig. Once started, there is a ceaselessly spinning motion which cannot be stopped or slowed down for long. A nation that modernizes is set on a path of development that has its own logic and an inseparable mixture of good and bad. Modern society brings progress in the form of material abundance. Less certainly, it brings increasing control of the natural and social environment. But its scientific and technological achievements are bought at high cost to spiritual and emotional life. Moreover, in unifying the world, it establishes uniform standards, higher in many cases than previously prevailed. But at the same time it ensures that failures and disasters will also be magnified on a world scale. There are no retreats and escape routes, except those which modern society itself invents as pastimes. No Stone Age aborigine or Neolithic peasant farmer can escape the impact of modernity. With full modernization, the world becomes one and its fate that of all its inhabitants.

To measure the balance of gains and losses in modernity, and to increase the former against the latter, require forms of social accounting and social engineering which have so far defied the efforts of social science and government. But in practice this does not matter. No one can wait for that problem to be solved, if it ever can be. To modernize is to take everything, the bad with the good. Not to modernize is to play no part in the life of contemporary humanity. One of the unusual, and historically unprecedented, aspects of modernization is that it leaves no choice in the matter.

BIBLIOGRAPHY

Classic accounts

Durkheim E., *The Division of Labour in Society* (1893). Eng. trans. Glencoe, Ill., The Free Press, 1964.
McLellan D. (ed.), *Karl Marx: Selected Writings*. Oxford, Oxford University Press, 1977.
de Tocqueville A., *Democracy in America* (1835–40). Eng. trans. London, Fontana, 1968.
Weber M., *The Protestant Ethic and the Spirit of Capitalism* (1904). Eng. trans. London, Allen and Unwin, 1976.

General accounts

Berger P., Berger B. and Kellner H., *The Homeless Mind: Modernization and Consciousness*. Harmondsworth, Penguin Books, 1974.

Chodak S., *Societal Development*. New York, Oxford University Press, 1973.

Kemp T., *Industrialization in the Non-Western World*. London, Longman, 1983.

——, *Historical Patterns of Industrialization*. London, Longman, 1978.

Kerr C., Dunlop T., Harbison P. and Myers C., *Industrialism and Industrial Man*, 2nd edn. Harmondsworth, Penguin Books, 1973.

Kumar K., *Prophecy and Progress: The Sociology of Industrial and Post-Industrial Society*. Harmondsworth, Penguin Books, 1978.

Landes D. S., *The Unbound Prometheus: Technological Change and Industrial Development in Western Europe from 1750 to the Present*. Cambridge, Cambridge University Press, 1969.

Polanyi K., *The Great Transformation: The Political and Economic Origins of Our Time*. Boston, Mass., Beacon Press, 1957.

Pollard S., *Peaceful Conquest: The Industrialization of Europe 1760–1970*. Oxford, Oxford University Press, 1981.

Wallerstein I., *The Capitalist World Economy*. Cambridge, Cambridge University Press, 1980.

Worsley P., *The Three Worlds: Culture and World Development*. London, Weidenfeld and Nicolson, 1984.

Useful collections of specialist articles

Alavi H. and Shanin T. (eds), *Introduction to the Sociology of Developing Societies*. London, Macmillan, 1982.

Bendix R., *Embattled Reason: Essays on Social Knowledge*. New York, Oxford University Press, 1970.

Bernstein H. (ed.), *Underdevelopment and Development*. Harmondsworth, Penguin Books, 1976.

Eisenstadt S. N. (ed.), *Readings in Social Evolution and Development*. Oxford, Pergamon Press, 1970.

Germani G. (ed.), *Modernization, Urbanization, and the Urban Crisis*. Boston, Mass., Little, Brown, 1973.

Hoselitz B. F. and Moore W. E. (eds), *Industrialization and Society*. UNESCO/The Hague, Mouton, 1966.

de Kadt E. and Williams G. (eds), *Sociology and Development*. London, Tavistock, 1974.

Particular topics

Pre-industrial economy and society: C. M. Cipolla, *Before the Industrial Revolution* (London, Methuen, 1976); W. W. Rostow, *How It All Began: Origins of the Modern Economy* (London, Methuen, 1975). Population: R. K. Kelsall, *Population* (London, Longman, 1979); H. J. Habakkuk, *Population Growth and Economic Development since 1750* (Leicester, Leicester University Press, 1972). Cities: R. Sennett (ed.), *Classic Essays on the Culture of Cities* (Englewood Cliffs, NJ, Prentice–Hall, 1979); F. Baali and J. S. Vandiver (eds), *Urban Sociology* (New York, Appleton–Century–Crofts, 1970); R. E. Pahl, *Patterns of Urban Life* (London, Longman, 1970); P. Abrams and E. A.

Wrigley (eds), *Towns in Societies* (Cambridge, Cambridge University Press, 1980); B. J. L. Berry, *The Human Consequence of Urbanisation* (London, Macmillan, 1973). Work: H. Braverman, *Labour and Monopoly Capital* (New York, Monthly Review Press, 1974); H. G. Gutman, *Work, Culture and Society in Industrializing America* (New York, Vintage Books, 1977), R. Bendix, *Work and Authority in Industry* (New York, John Wiley, 1956); K. Thompson (ed.), *Work, Employment, and Unemployment* (Milton Keynes, Open University Press, 1984). Family: P. Laslett, *The World We Have Lost*, 2nd edn (London, Methuen, 1975); E. Shorter, *The Making of the Modern Family* (London, Fontana, 1977); M. Young and P. Willmott, *The Symmetrical Family* (London, Routledge and Kegan Paul, 1973). Social structure: A. Giddens, *The Class Structure of the Advanced Societies*, 2nd edn (London, Hutchinson, 1981); S. Giner and M. S. Archer (eds), *Contemporary Europe: Social Structures and Cultural Patterns* (London, Routledge and Kegan Paul, 1978). Social Problems: J. Ellul, *The Technological Society* (New York, Vintage Books, 1974); F. Hirsch, *Social Limits to Growth* (London, Routledge and Kegan Paul, 1977); A. Ellis and K. Kumar (eds), *Dilemmas of Liberal Democracies* (London, Tavistock, 1983); W. Leiss, *The Limits to Satisfaction* (London, Marion Boyars, 1978). Social change: D. Bell, *The Coming of Post-Industrial Society* (New York, Basic Books, 1973); A. Toffler, *The Third Wave* (New York, Bantam Books, 1980); J. Naisbitt, *Megatrends* (New York, Warner Books, 1982).

2

Pre-capitalist and Non-capitalist Factors in the Development of Capitalism: Fred Hirsch and Joseph Schumpeter

The habit of looking at the last ten thousand years as well as at the array of early societies as a mere prelude to the true history of our civilization which started approximately with the publication of the *Wealth of Nations* in 1776 is, to say the least, out of date. It is this episode which has come to a close in our days, and in trying to gauge the alternatives of the future, we should subdue our natural proneness to follow the proclivities of our fathers.

Karl Polanyi, *The Great Transformation*

I

The question as to the long-term future of capitalist industrial society – whether or not so-called – has been raised since its very beginning. Much of the speculation has turned on that society's capacity or otherwise for indefinite expansion and growth. Capitalism, all admitted, was a unique social formation. It had a dynamism and a self-propelling energy unprecedented in mankind's history. All other civilized societies – Egypt, China, Rome, Byzantium – had gone into stagnation or decline through the self-limiting principles of their economic systems. In these societies, Nature had indeed 'audited her accounts with a red pencil'. Only Western capitalism seemed to have discovered the secret that would enable it to escape from the cosmic trap of hunger and poverty, inertia and decay.

Or had it? Fred Hirsch stands in a long line of critics and commentators who have cast doubt on this optimistic belief. In eighteenth-century England, in the very springtime of modern capitalism, an intense debate raged over the inherent 'progressiveness' of the new economic order.[1] On one side were ranged the passionate opponents of mercantilist regulation and advocates of free trade, such as Adam Smith and Josiah Tucker. These argued that the capitalist nations could look forward to a future of more or less unlimited growth and prosperity. Freed of mercantilist rivalries and restrictions, they would maintain and increase their superiority over the rest of the world, turning the non-capitalist societies into peripheral and dependent provinces supplying raw materials for the capitalist core.

Against these were those who held that the very principle of the free market in goods and people would ultimately impoverish the capitalist nations. David Hume propounded a general law of economic decay:

There seems to be a happy concurrence of causes in human affairs, which checks the growth of trade and riches and hinders them from being confined entirely to one people . . . Where one nation has gotten the start of another in trade, it is very difficult for the latter to gain the ground it lost . . . But these advantages are compensated . . . by the low price of labour in every nation which has not an extensive commerce, and does not much abound in gold and silver. Manufactures, therefore, gradually shift their places, leaving those countries which they have already enriched and flying to others, whither they are allured by the cheapness of provisions and labour, till they have enriched these also and are again banished by the same causes.[2]

Thus any nation embarked on the capitalist course will, in the long run, descend from the heights of prosperity to the depths of misery and unemployment for the mass of its population. It was this melancholy cycle that prompted Hume's friend, Lord Kames, to see 'chrematistic' society as 'Janus double-faced', and as providing a clear illustration of the general law that 'nations go round in a circle from weakness to strength and from strength to weakness'.[3]

The thinkers of the Scottish Enlightenment – notably Adam Ferguson – were indeed among the most sceptical about the glowing promise of the new commercial society.[4] Smith's own admiration was, as we know, itself highly qualified. Vanity, the striving for the admiration of others, rather than the desire for utility or convenience, he saw as the irrational passion behind the ceaseless activity of the modern world. 'And thus place, that great object which divides the wives of aldermen, is the end of half the labours of human life.'[5] All the 'toil and anxiety' bestowed upon the pursuit of wealth issued from the chimerical delusion that it would bring security and fulfilment. But 'it is well that nature imposes upon us in this manner. It is this deception which arouses and keeps in continual motion the industry of mankind. It is this which first prompted them to cultivate the ground, to build houses, to found cities and commonwealths, and to invent and improve all the sciences and arts'.[6] Smith was moreover, as is well known, fully alert to the spiritual and moral deficiencies of capitalism; and in his later writings he came even to see an inevitable material decline, in which to the 'cheerful and hearty' progressive state there would succeed a 'dull' stationary state and a 'melancholy' declining one.[7] Thus, even in Adam Smith's case, we are faced with 'the deeply pessimistic prognosis of an evolutionary trend in which both decline and decay attend – material decline awaiting at the terminus of the economic journey, moral decay suffered by society in the course of its journeying'.[8]

At the very outset of the capitalist era, therefore, we find a fundamental ambivalence and anxiety about the capacity of the capitalist system to fulfil the goals variously set for it. The welcome generally given to the new commercial order was cautious and qualified. There was an inherent element of irrationality and arbitrariness about it that boded ill. Even those most fervent in their advocacy feared for its future. Hence it is not really surprising to find that the arguments in its favour that appeared most convincing were directed as much to the *past* as to the future of society. Hirschman has suggested that capitalism appealed to many thinkers and statesmen of the seventeenth and eighteenth centuries not because of any alleged positive virtues, since people of this kind were generally united in an aristocratic and intellectual disdain for commerce; but because, to an age frightened and exhausted by the continuous civil and international wars of the seventeenth century, the 'interest' of money-making appeared an altogether safer channel for the people's unruly energies than more exciting pursuits such as power and glory.[9] The appeal, in other words, was political rather than economic, and certainly never moral. 'In an age in which men were searching for ways of limiting the damage and horrors they are wont to inflict on each other, commercial and economic activities were ... looked upon more kindly not because of any rise in the esteem in which they were held; on the contrary, any preference for them expressed a desire for a vacation from (disastrous) greatness, and thus reflected continuing contempt'.[10] Dr Johnson's remark, that 'there are few ways in which a man can be more innocently employed than in getting money', captures both the basis of the appeal and the condescending manner in which it was often couched. Other writers, more deeply impressed by the point that commerce would restrain the passions not just of subjects but also of their rulers, were inclined to be less snobbish: Savary wrote of 'this commerce [that] makes for all the gentleness of life'. *Le doux commerce*, declared Montesquieu, 'polishes and softens barbarian ways, as we can see every day'. Capitalism triumphed, according to Hirschman, in part at least because it was dull and passionless. The features that were later to be denounced by romantic critics – those that made it 'alienating' and 'one-dimensional' – were precisely those that made it so attractive in the earlier stages.

Hirschman's account, however debatable,[11] has the particular merit of insisting on a point often overlooked: that the emergence of capitalism can only be understood by relating it directly to the (pre-capitalist) society out of which it came. What might seem an obvious banality becomes more interesting when we consider the usual method of dealing with this. In the standard Marxist accounts, for instance, capitalist society emerges out of feudalism on the basis of a principle – the market – and a class – the bourgeoisie – wholly antithetical to their feudal counterparts. Some of the liveliest passages of the *Communist Manifesto* dwell on the deep-seated differences between the heroic–chivalric feudal aristocracy and the prosaic bourgeoisie (the bourgeoisie 'has drowned the most heavenly ecstasies of religious fervour, of chivalrous enthusiasm, of philistine sentimentalism, in the icy water of egotistical calculation', etc.). Although the new society is said to mature in the womb of the old, the newborn infant is born with remarkably few parental characters. This is an oddity indeed, and it should be seen as such in society as much as in nature.

Max Weber, like Marx, also stresses discontinuity. His problem is to account for the emergence of 'the spirit of capitalism' in the modern West, a spirit totally at variance with the prevailing attitude to money-making in medieval Christendom, and to be found nowhere else in the world. Unlike Marx, however, Weber is driven by his comparative method and his *verstehen* principles to search more deeply in late medieval society for the roots of the capitalist outlook. He accepts that in a civilization permeated by religious belief, only religion can be the source of a new ethic that will be sufficiently strong and resilient to maintain itself against the hostility of the traditional culture. In *The Protestant Ethic and the Spirit of Capitalism* he sought to show how, through the beliefs and activities of certain Protestant sects, money-making was made respectable for its members and, to the extent that they became influential, for the particular society as a whole.

This is moving halfway to Hirschman. But it still leaves a problem. Weber has shown how certain social groups, of relatively humble origin, by reforming and re-working traditional religious ideology were able both to motivate themselves in an economic direction, and to offer a justification of their practices to the wider society. Economic activity was thereby sanctified and promoted, even though of course with ultimate consequences – the capitalist system – that were quite unintended by sixteenth and seventeenth century Protestants. Hirschman himself puts the pertinent question: Weber accounts plausibly for the motivation of the 'aspiring new elites', but what of the 'gatekeepers' of medieval society? His own discussion is intended to show how the traditional elites and their advisers, acting essentially on prudential motives of statecraft and self-interest, were led to advocate commercialism as the possible antidote to internecine war:

the expansion of commerce and industry in the 17th and 18th centuries has been viewed here as being welcomed and promoted not by some marginal social groups, nor by an insurgent ideology, but by a current of opinion that arose right in the center of the 'power structure' and the 'establishment' of the time, out of the problems with which the prince and particularly his advisors and other concerned notables were grappling. Ever since the end of the Middle Ages, and particularly as a result of the increasing frequency of war and civil war in the 17th and 18th centuries, the search was on for a behavioral equivalent for religious precept, for new rules of conduct and devices that would impose much needed discipline and constraints on both rulers and ruled, and the expansion of commerce and industry was thought to hold much promise in this regard.[12]

Hirschman therefore, even more than Weber, emphasizes the intimate connection between the new order of capitalism and the prevailing structure of power in early modern Europe. In this he shows the greater sociological realism. Capitalism could not have arisen in total opposition to medieval feudal society, nor could it have been the accomplishment of marginal social groups acting on their own. There is no example of social change of this kind and magnitude that exhibits such a pattern.[13] Revolutionary change – whether or not overtly political – always involves a Frondist element, the collusion or connivance of at least some representatives of the old ruling class. The dominant groups of feudal society were necessarily implicated in the emergence of the system that ultimately undermined their own order. It should be stressed that this relates to a quite different matter from the case of those members of the upper classes, as in England, who went in for capitalist ventures themselves, in trade and agriculture. The upper classes who promoted capitalism in the early modern period did so primarily for reasons of state, and not in order to join in a capitalist free-for-all.

This suggests a further dimension to the question of the origins and development of capitalism. If pre-capitalist groups and preoccupations were so important in the crucial nascent stages, might it not be possible that they remained so in the later stages as well? Might it not be that, in general, 'non-capitalist' elements formed a significant component in the social order of capitalism, not simply as residues or hang-overs but as essential props to its regular functioning? The conventional answer, even among those who give considerable weight to pre-capitalist factors in the origins of capitalism, is to deny them much of a role in its later development. Capitalism, once set going, seems to acquire a logic of it own, which governs its further course. For both Weber and Hirschman, the principle of 'unintended consequences' removes to a large extent the significance of the original factors in subsequent evolution. For Weber, Protestants see religion gradually undermined by the secularizing force of the economic system they have helped to create. The pious Richard Baxter is succeeded by the free-thinking Benjamin Franklin. For Hirschman, the principle operates somewhat differently – people intend things that *don't* happen – but the effect is the same. The hopes that capitalism would spell peace were blasted first by the French Revolution and the Napoleonic Wars, and later by the world wars and revolutions of the twentieth century. The social interests associated with those hopes shared the same fate.

It is here that we encounter directly the contributions of Hirsch and Schumpeter. As against these orthodox views, they insist on a degree of relationship between capitalism and its pre-capitalist past that, going well beyond mere overlap and co-existence, amounts to something like an integral symbiosis.

II

'Market capitalism has never been the exclusive basis of the political economy in any country at any time.'[14] Hirsch's contention is that liberal market capitalism, taken at its own estimation and in its own terms, is unviable. The attempt to make it work according to its principle of 'possessive individualism' – an attempt it is ultimately forced into by the very logic of its own development – drives it into crisis. Hirsch here accepts the view put forward earlier by Karl Polanyi, who postulated that 'the idea of a self-adjusting market implied a stark utopia. Such an institution could not exist for any length of time without annihilating the human and natural substance of society; it would have physically destroyed man and transformed his surroundings into a wilderness'.[15]

Market society therefore never actually functioned according to its own expressed principle of self-regulation through the 'invisible hand'. It couldn't have done so without destroying itself. How then was the impression created that it had, that the natural order of liberal society was market society? Hirsch argues that there were special historical conditions which made the equation of 'self-love and social' plausible. Part of the predicament of present-day liberal democracies has been to mistake these special conditions for the natural framework of liberal capitalist society. Market capitalism came into being under 'transient inaugural conditions'.

Adam Smith's invisible hand has linked individual self-interest with social need. But the conditions in which this link has been achieved over a wide area can now be seen not as stable conditions that can be relied on to persist or to be readily maintainable by deliberate action. Rather, they can be seen in important respects to have been special conditions associated with a transition phase from an earlier socioeconomic system. The generally benign invisible hand was a favourable inaugural condition of liberal capitalism.[16]

What were these favourable but transient 'inaugural conditions'? The first is that 'full participation was confined to a minority – the minority that had reached material affluence before liberal capitalism had set the masses on the path of material growth'.[17] This condition was undermined by the very success of liberal capitalism. Its economic performance made possible the idea of plenty; its liberal principle made it impossible to deny anyone a share – increasingly, an equal share – in that plenty. The frustrations consequent upon the removal of this original condition – the 'crowding' effect – are analysed by Hirsch under the themes of 'the paradox of affluence' and 'the distributional compulsion'.

The second inaugural condition is that 'the system operated on social foundations laid under a different order of society'. It is these foundations that 'underlie a benign and efficient implementation of the self-interest principle operating through market transactions'. Those who, such as Keynes, have sought to correct the admitted imperfections of the free market by selective acts of public intervention and public provision – e.g. through tax laws and subsidies – have been guilty of a superficial analysis. They have ignored the critical role played by 'the supporting ethos of social obligation both in the formulation of the relevant public policies and in their efficient transmission to market opportunities. Why expect the controllers, alone, to abstain from maximizing their individual advantage?' The fact is that 'the principle of self-interest is incomplete as a social organising device. It operates effectively only in tandem with some supporting social principle.' Adam Smith and John Stuart Mill, in their different ways, could more or less take this supporting ethos for granted in the earlier period of capitalism, and so do not comment much on it. Their successors have neglected it at the very time that it is being eroded by the triumph of the individualistic ethic of the market. Hence it is ignored at the time of its greatest need. Keynesian-style interventions to modify the principle of *laissez-faire* have only intensified the problem. 'Correctives to *laissez-faire* increase rather than decrease reliance on some degree of social orientation and social responsibility in individual behaviour. The attempt has been made to erect an increasingly explicit social organization without a supporting social morality.'[18]

Hirsch in this account, under the general theme of 'the depleting moral legacy'[19], thus directly links the successful operation of capitalism to its pre-capitalist past. The buoyancy of the market system in its initial phase is seen as resting squarely 'on the shoulders of a premarket social ethos'.[20] 'The social morality that has served as an understructure for economic individualism has been a legacy of the precapitalist and preindustrial past. This legacy has diminished with time and with the corrosive contact of the active capitalist values.'[21] The content of this morality, as well as its direct relevance to market society, is best suggested by Durkheim's crisp rejoinder to the pure market philosophies of nineteenth-century liberals such as Herbert Spencer: 'All in the contract is not contractual.' That is, market relationships depend on non-market norms. 'Wherever a contract exists, it is dependent on regulation which is the work of society and not that of individuals.'[22] Like Durkheim, Hirsch attaches great importance to the restraints on individual appetites and behaviour imposed by traditional morality. For him, these restraints derive largely from the virtues inherent in traditional religious belief which, predating capitalism, were carried over into the capitalist era to act as the necessary checks on unfettered individualism. 'Truth, trust, acceptance, restraint, obligation – these are among the social virtues grounded in religious belief which are ... now seen to play a central role in the functioning of an individualistic, contractual economy.'[23] The depletion of the moral legacy of capitalism is coupled therefore to the decline of traditional religion. For 'religiously based norms' were a 'fortunate legacy from a set of principles that was being replaced'. The very force and success of market values gradually undermined religious belief and practice. Once more, the result is seen as having a special historical pathos: 'The market system was, at bottom, more dependent on religious binding than the feudal system, having abandoned direct social ties maintained by the obligations of custom and status. Yet the individualistic, rationalistic base of the market undermined the unseen religious support.'[24]

It is striking how many current commentators on 'the crisis of liberal society' also discern the core of the problem in the deteriorating moral foundations of the capitalist economy: a problem made well-nigh insoluble by the fact that these foundations are themselves the ruins of older pre-capitalist structures.[25] The keynote was struck as early as 1921 by Tawney when he wrote of 'the nemesis of industrialism'. Industrialism – 'the perversion of individualism' – was destroying itself not through any 'flaw or vice in human nature', but by the very 'force of the idea, which ... reveals its defects in its power'. Stripped of any concept of a common social or moral purpose, as supplied for instance by medieval Christianity, industrialism (sc. capitalism) committed men and nations 'to a career of indefinite expansion, in which they devour continents and oceans, law, morality and religion, and last of all their own souls, in an attempt to attain infinity by the addition to themselves of all that is finite'.[26] The general form of the argument is clear enough. Capitalism, by itself, is essentially amoral and anomic. Individual outcomes are the result simply of the 'free play' of the market. But no social system can work without a morality. Capitalism lives on borrowed time off a borrowed morality. For long, capitalism has lived off 'the accumulated capital of traditional religion and traditional moral philosophy',[27] elements which are extraneous to the market. Even the secular philosophies of liberalism and utilitarianism were able to offer a sustaining set of values to capitalism only because, as Dunn shows, they were buttressed by 'the shadowy frame of a Christian ideological inheritance'.[28] Their own logic and that of the capitalist system they served, gradually undermined that inheritance, finally yielding a reductive and mechanical egoism which was as potentially threatening to liberal values of tolerance and democracy as it had once seemed benevolent to them. In a sense therefore we might say that the Protestant ethic was not simply the origin but the persisting condition of capitalism. It restrained the wants and appetites which, in the pure utilitarian felicific calculus, are unlimited and insatiable. 'When the Protestant ethic, which had served to limit sumptuary (though not capital) accumulation, was sundered from modern bourgeois society, only the hedonism remained.'[29] Generally, then, as Michael Waltzer puts it, 'what made liberalism endurable for all these years was the fact that the individualism it generated was always imperfect, tempered by older restraints and loyalties, by stable patterns of local, ethnic, religious, or class relationships. An untempered liberalism would be unendurable. That is the crisis . . . : the triumph of liberalism over its historical restraints.'[30]

These observations, together with those of Hirsch, all seem to me undeniably true. They are of crucial importance in understanding the development of capitalism: both its expansive growth, and the counter-movement of the 'self-protection of society' which, stemming from other value systems, was necessary to preserve the social conditions for that growth.[31] But there is a worrying aspect to them. They are couched in vague, general, terms. We are offered abstractions such as 'a pre-market social ethos', 'a traditional moral philosophy', 'older restraints and loyalties'. The role they are expected to play is central to the drama of capitalism as expounded by these authors. Yet they exist as rather mysterious, free-floating entities, lacking any real material embodiment. What was the social substance of these influences? In what groups were they embodied? Whose interest and outlook did they express? Merely to point to the existence of these non-capitalist factors is a necessary first step towards understanding; but the account remains historically and sociologically in a highly unsatisfactory state if it rests there.

Schumpeter to a good extent supplies the want. In the space of remarkably few writings, Schumpeter sketched a sociology of modern capitalism that in its breadth and brilliance is scarcely inferior to that of Marx and Weber. Reworking 'the ancient truth, that the dead always rule the living',[32] he gave an account of capitalism whose distinctive aspect was the stress on capitalism as a *compound* social formation. It was a compound in two linked senses. Historically, it exhibited the features of two epochs, the 'feudal' and the 'capitalist'; sociologically, it carried the impress of two leading classes, the aristocracy and the bourgeoisie, which were the products of those two very different historical epochs. Capitalism in this respect was simply an instance of a more general feature of social systems:

Every social situation is the heritage of preceding situations and takes over from them not only their cultures, their dispositions, and their 'spirit', but also elements of their social structure and concentrations of power . . . The social pyramid is never made of a single substance, is never seamless. There is no single *Zeitgeist*, except in the sense of a construct. This means that in explaining any historical course or situation, account must be taken of the fact that much in it can be explained only by the survival of elements that are actually alien to its own trends . . . The co-existence of essentially different mentalities and objective sets of facts must form part of any general theory.[33]

Applied to the case of capitalism, such a view explains the persistence of a 'pre-market social ethos' not as some generalized carry-over from the feudal era but as the class expression of a still powerful aristocracy. As Schumpeter describes the process, the absolutist monarchies of the sixteenth to eighteenth centuries in Europe increasingly shaped their policies according to the needs of capitalist development, the more so as they depended to an increasing extent on revenues created by the capitalist process. But the monarchy, and the aristocracy which – however capriciously – was allied to it, never allowed themselves to become the captives of bourgeois interests, still less politically subordinate to the bourgeoisie. The 'feudal presence' in the structure of the absolutist state was no mere ghost.

The steel frame of that structure still consisted of the human material of feudal society and this material still behaved according to precapitalist patterns. It filled the offices of state, officered the army, devised policies – it functioned as a *classe dirigente* and, though taking account of bourgeois interests, it took care to distance itself from the bourgeoisie . . . All this was more than atavism. It was an active symbiosis of two social strata, one of which no doubt supported the other economically but was in turn supported by the other politically.[34]

This was, says Schumpeter, 'the essence of that society'; and the structure thus established extended well beyond the early phase of capitalist development. 'The aristocratic element continued to rule the roost right to the end of the period of intact and vital capitalism.'[35] Controversial as such a statement is, and subject to many qualifications, it seems to me broadly true. As a perspective on the long-term development of European societies it helps to explain many things which do not fit at all satisfactorily into alternative sociological theories (such as the Marxist). It can explain phenomena as diverse as the French Revolution,[36] the British pattern of industrial development,[37] the success or otherwise of English working-class movements in the first half of the nineteenth century,[38] and the nature of German politics and society up to the rise of Hitler.[39] In all cases what is at issue is a cluster of class actions and alliances that do not make sense within the concept of a single unified bourgeois society. Inconvenient 'deviations' and 'archaisms' have to be explained away, as for instance the active role of the French nobility in bringing about the French Revolution of 1789. Schumpeter enables us to see that these are not 'atavisms' or 'cultural lags', but the expressions of the normal patterns of bourgeois politics and bourgeois social development. 'A purely capitalist society – consisting of nothing but entrepreneurs, capitalists and proletarian workmen – would work in ways completely different from those we observe historically if indeed it could exist at all.'[40]

It is the *normal* order of bourgeois society to be variegated. Its social structure is marked by a fundamental heterogeneity. It is formed not simply by synchronous elements in relationships of conflict and cohesion – e.g. bourgeoisie and proletariat – but also by relationships between strata – aristocracy and bourgeoisie – which look towards different historical periods for their characteristic outlook and principles of action. Bourgeois society is Janus-faced, one face turned towards the past, the other towards the future. 'The social pyramid of the present age has been formed, not by the substance and laws of capitalism alone, but by two different social substances, and by the laws of two different epochs.'[41.]

The fact of this structural dichotomy can complicate how classes perceive their 'normal' or 'natural' class interest. Schumpeter gives the example of imperialism. How is it that the bourgeoisie came to be linked, as it was in the late nineteenth century, with an imperialist policy and outlook? The natural tendency of bourgeois society is pacific. The bourgeoisie is 'inclined to insist on the application of the moral precepts of private life to international relations'.[42] In an ideal bourgeois world, war is irrational and anti-utilitarian, a distraction and a diversion of energy from the central activity of trade and industry.[43] The bourgeois interest should be the peace interest, and so it often is: as for instance with the Cobdenite English middle class for most of the nineteenth century.

Imperialism in capitalist states is therefore partly explained as the expression of the tendency and outlook of a politically dominant aristocratic class, who owe their very title to rule to their fitness for war, and for whom war once constituted the main business of life. To this extent it represents a persistence of forms of behaviour characteristic of the era of absolutism. But it was not simply the aristocracy that was formed by the absolutist state. The bourgeoisie too carried its stamp. Especially on the Continent, the bourgeoisie was as much brought into being by the absolutist monarchy in the latter's struggles with the aristocracy, as it made itself by its own independent efforts. Systems of tariffs and trading rights were created and regulated by mercantilist states in pursuit of their own autocratic and dynastic interests. The bourgeoisie in its early stages was critically dependent on the patronage and protection of the monarchy against the feudal aristocracy. It became habituated to protectionist and paternalist strategies, and adept at exploiting these to further its own interests against those of other classes and other national bourgeoisies.

Thus the bourgeoisie willingly allowed itself to be moulded into one of the power instruments of the monarchy . . . Trade and industry of the early capitalist period remained strongly pervaded with precapitalist methods, bore the stamp of autocracy, and served its interests, either willingly or by force. With its traditional habits of feeling, thinking, and acting moulded along such lines, the bourgeoisie entered the Industrial Revolution. It was shaped, in other words, by the needs and interests of an environment that was essentially non-capitalist, or at least precapitalist – needs stemming not from the nature of the capitalist economy as such but from the fact of the co-existence of early capitalism with another and at first overwhelmingly powerful mode of life and business. Established habits of thought and action tend to persist, and hence the spirit of guild and monopoly maintained itself . . . Actually capitalism did not fully prevail *anywhere* on the Continent. Existing economic interests, 'artificially' shaped by the autocratic state, remained dependent on the 'protection' of the state. The industrial organism, such as it was, would not have been able to withstand free competition.[44]

Since the bourgeoisie never fully wrested political power from the aristocratic state, 'the state remained a special social power, confronting the bourgeoisie'. But schooled by its past experience the bourgeoisie came to look to the state for 'refuge and protection against external and even domestic enemies. The bourgeoisie seeks to win over the state for itself, and in return serves the state and state interests that are different from its own.'[45] Its existence as a child of autocracy makes it highly vulnerable to ideologies which are essentially antithetical to capitalism. It espouses, often with no need of prompting from outside, militarism, nationalism, imperialism and so proves itself to be a truly national bourgeoisie. Such readiness 'bears witness to the extent to which essentially imperialist absolutism has patterned not only the economy of the bourgeoisie but also its mind – in the interests of autocracy and against those of the bourgeoisie itself.'[46] In the final analysis, then, imperialism is 'not only historically, but also sociologically, a heritage of the autocratic state, of its structural elements, organizational forms, interest alignments, and human attitudes, the outcome of precapitalist forces which the autocratic state has reorganised, in part by the methods of early capitalism. It would never have been evolved by the "inner logic" of capitalism itself.'[47]

It is immaterial, for present purposes, how plausible one may find this account of imperialism; although the imperialist wars of the twentieth-century Leviathan may well seem confirmation rather than refutation of Schumpeter's analysis, and, with the recrudescence of the 'warfare' state, make him appear unduly optimistic as to the waning influence of 'precapitalist elements'. What matters more, however, is the method of the analysis. Social theorists have become only too expert at conjuring abstract 'social systems' out of thin air, or out of some undifferentiated substance – 'values', 'power', 'productive mode' – in their conceptual bubble-blowers. Schumpeter is no less theoretical in intent than any of these. But the materials of his 'social system' are the materials of actual history: history as both event and process. He avoids the temptation, succumbed to by most social theorists of the past 200 years, to impose an evolutionary scheme on social development, such that more or less whole stages or states of society appear, with their leads and lags, vestiges and residues. By giving due weight and respect to the social elements as actually found and constituted in society at any time, undismayed by 'atavisms' and 'archaisms' which on the contrary he acknowledges as the normal phenomena of any social order, he is able to give an account of modern capitalist society which at the very least passes the test of credibility: a rare achievement in recent social theory. More than that for the moment it is unnecessary to claim.[48] The important thing is that by emphasizing the normality of the non-capitalist elements in the development of capitalism, Schumpeter is able to deal with not simply the familiar features of capitalism but also the irregular and 'aberrant'. He can, that is – in a way that Hirsch for instance cannot – explain how capitalism can be both unboundedly expansive and market-oriented, and at the same time for long sufficiently restrained to prevent this pure capitalist ethos from tearing the system apart.

For Schumpeter's non-capitalist aristocracy is, of course, not simply warlike and imperialist. It embodies other traditional values as well. It has an almost religious attachment to the land, it is suspicious or contemptuous of commerce and it is the upholder of a social philosophy of paternalism which, if its obligations were often carelessly discharged, remained an ideology potentially exploitable by all parties. It preserves, in other words, a rich store of pre-capitalist values and images which can be drawn upon as occasion demands in the social conflicts engendered by capitalism. In alliance with other non-capitalist interests – at various times the Church, the army, the bureaucracy, the peasants and the workers – it intervened, often decisively, in the capitalist process to slow down or otherwise regulate the pure operations of the market system. As the landed interest and the guardian of territorial integrity, it resisted, in common with the peasants, the full effects of the commercialization of the soil and international free trade which threatened a complete mobilization of land and the destruction of all small proprietors.[49] It succeeded in retaining protection until the middle of the nineteenth century in England, and throughout the century on most of the Continent. Together with the workers it fought the factory owners on factory legislation and the utilitarians on Poor Law reform. The Tory–Radical alliance in England in the first half of the nineteenth century was indeed the source of one of the most successful and sustained counter-movements to capitalism to be found anywhere in Europe (so successful as to deceive Marx and Engels into thinking that they had uncovered the revolutionary proletariat). Elsewhere, as in Germany, a strongly paternalist state run by the traditional landowning class brought in impressive measures of social welfare. In all this, it hardly needs to be said, considerations of class interest were no doubt uppermost in the minds of the protagonists, and social duty often only the public facade. But the effect nevertheless was to save capitalism from itself, at least for the time being. The checks to the market system served to blunt and divert the social forces unleashed by capitalism, which might otherwise have led to social war.

III

America did not occasion class war; but in other respects it offers a fascinating glimpse of what happens in a largely Europeanized society lacking a feudal tradition. America was a European invention but without a European past. It was forged in the crucible of European thought but not of European social experience. Its development was conditioned by the fact that, as Tocqueville said, Americans were 'born equal, instead of becoming so'. Unlike Europe, it did not gain its democracy through a revolutionary struggle with feudal aristocratic forces. There were few feudal relics in colonial America. Its society of small farmers and small traders, having shrugged off the English crown, was able to develop in relative freedom from a constraining feudal presence. It is one of the few cases we have of a pure bourgeois society, bourgeois in origins and bourgeois in development.[50]

This was in many ways, as Tocqueville declared, a 'great advantage', a beneficent inheritance. It gave to all aspects of American life a uniquely liberal and democratic character. But it had a damaging consequence too. As Louis Hartz brilliantly showed, it led to the enthronement in America of an 'absolutist liberalism', a 'dogmatic Lockeanism', which dominated American politics and which effectively precluded the emergence of a tradition of political thought at all.[51] Political thought feeds on political conflict and political diversity. These were the very things denied, in principle and to a good extent in practice, by the force of the prevailing liberal ideology. The result was a deadweight liberal consensus which killed off for more than a century all significant political speculation and political growth.

In Europe, feudal, bourgeois and proletarian forces met in 1789. All three continued to interact throughout the nineteenth century and beyond. Their mutual interaction gave rise not just to a rejuvenated conservatism and a militant liberalism, but also to socialism. All three were absent in America. America's 1776 was a purely bourgeois affair. Thereafter the liberal ethos enclosed the American community like a vice. All subsequent developments were the play of variations – Horatio Algerism, Progressivism, New Dealism, – on the liberal theme. There were no conflicts between bourgeoisie and aristocracy to generate the conservatism of a Bonald or Burke: 'Southern Toryism' collapsed under the weight of its own contradictions. In this most bourgeois of societies, lacking the social conflicts of Europe, there was not even the growth of a self-conscious and complex liberalism, playing off the people against the aristocracy, and aristocracy against people, being pushed in one direction – as by James Mill and Macaulay – by fear of the mob, and in a more radical direction – as by John Stuart Mill and Lloyd George – by a sharp reminder of its birth in a popular struggle against the feudal state. The fate of Hamilton's 'high' Whiggery, and the Republican Party's subsequent embrace of the democratic capitalist ideology of Algerism, showed how difficult it was for liberalism of a European kind to gain a foothold in the United States.

Socialism, as is well known, failed even more dismally to establish itself in

American life and thought. This was not simply due to the absence of a truly proletarian class, a dubious enough assertion in any case, still less to the moving frontier. It was at least as much the result of the lack of a feudal tradition and a feudal class, whose presence in Europe provided the explosive matrix for the development of socialism. The socialist movement in Europe was nourished as much by the aristocracy as by the bourgeoisie in their mutual struggles. The landowning aristocracy could pose – and even act – as the historic protector of the people against a selfish and rapacious bourgeoisie. Out of the 'feudal socialism' of a Carlyle and a Disraeli ('half echo of the past, half menace of the future', as Marx put it), there could develop that Tory Radicalism that played so important a part in nineteenth-century Europe. As an ideological component of socialism, indeed, the feudal element remained highly significant. The reception of Proudhon, Ruskin and Morris showed that a good part of the appeal of socialism was its promise to restore something like the communal and craft-based order of the Middle Ages. Moreover, the aristocracy continued to be serviceable to socialism when its role shifted from ally to antagonist. Socialism critically depended for its growth on the presence not simply of the bourgeois enemy but of the feudal remnant as well. As Marx saw, and as the Dreyfus affair so well demonstrated, in the conditions especially of continental Europe socialism would draw its strength as much from the struggle against the forces of the feudal order as from that against capitalism. This was the 'dual revolution', against both feudalism and capitalism, which Marx foresaw would have to be the task of European socialism, and which Lenin and Trotsky later generalized into a 'law' for all 'backward' countries (which in practice seems to have been every country except England and, ironically, the United States).

The fateful fact of being 'born equal' therefore deprived the United States of the fertilizing currents of all the main varieties of European social thought: conservatism, liberalism and socialism. This cultural impoverishment would have mattered less if the rough equality that prevailed among the early colonial farmers and traders had persisted. It was a crippling deficiency when, quite apart from the problem of the 'peculiar institution' of slavery, social inequality grew to European proportions in the second half of the nineteenth century. It meant that the United States lacked both the social resources and the ideas with which to confront the problems of the world's fastest-growing capitalist economy. It is startling to think that the United States got through the age of the robber-barons with nothing more impressive to hand than refurbished Herbert Spencer. But there was a costly price to pay. For all the harshness of the European patterns of industrialization, there is really little to compare with the brutality and bitterness of the labour conflicts in the United States from the 1870s to the 1930s. Tocqueville had already observed of America in the 1830s that 'the manufacturing aristocracy which is growing under our eyes is one of the harshest which ever existed in the world.'[52] In the mass strike of 1877 more than 100 strikers were killed by a combination of employers' private armies, special police and federal troops. The federal government continued to bless this combination of private and public violence throughout the period. A similar strike-breaking force of 14,000 men was involved in the bloody Pullman strike of 1894 in which thirty-four strikers were killed and hundreds badly wounded. No policy of legal and non-violent strike action was proof against the ability and ready willingness of employers, judiciary and government to resort to armed force against the strikers. As a result, right up to the Second World War nearly every major strike turned into a bloody confrontation, with many dead and wounded.[53] Every big strike was treated as incipient rebellion or civil war, every attack on the employers' prerogatives seen as a challenge to the state.

Marx wrote in the preface to *Capital* that England was the country that showed other industrializing countries the 'image of their future'. It was a poor prediction in more than one respect. Tocqueville judged better in casting America in that role. The United States is the Hirschian nightmare realized. It is capitalism unleashed, capitalism without the historical restraints that contained its destructive tendencies for so long in European societies. Some have argued that, despite the absence of a pre-capitalist class, religion in the form of Protestantism provided a real degree of restraint on the American capitalist system.[54] The evidence is hard to find; and, in any case the claim seems to be based on a misunderstanding and misapplication of the Weberian argument. Weber showed that the Protestant ethic restrained the *individual* in his own consumption and style of life, the more freely and efficiently to exploit to the full the resources of nature and society. On the social plane, in other words, the ethic encouraged the most limitless expansion and growth. It provided no compensating social principle to restrict that growth. Hence while Protestantism might have had some regulatory influence on individual psychology, it was quite incapable of containing the capitalist beast at large in society: quite the contrary. It was only, as Schumpeter showed, the existence of social forces with interests and outlooks outside or beyond the market that endowed societies with the capacity to exercise any real degree of restraint on the pace and logic of capitalist development. It was these social forces that the United States conspicuously lacked. There were no social groups of whom it could truly be said – as it could be said, for instance, of the landed aristocracy in Europe – that they were in the capitalist system but not of it. All groups were drawn more or less willingly into the struggles of the marketplace, and imbibed its ethic to the full. State and society, the public and the private realms, were collapsed into each other. Hence neither within the state nor within the social ethos of a class could there be found a non-market tradition of social responsibility or enlightened paternalism.

What was left to Americans was the freedom of the void: the 'malady of infinite aspirations', as Durkheim defined anomie. 'The limits are unknown between the possible and the impossible, what is just and what is unjust, legitimate claims and hopes and those which are immoderate.'[55] The possibilities were or seemed dizzying; the only unpardonable sin was not to seize them, the only acceptable form of worship that of the 'bitch-goddess', success. The United States became classically the land where all that mattered was success or failure. Never mind that 'within the American world there was no escape from the race even for those who won it';[56] or that, as taught by countless examinations of 'the American Dream' from the novels of Scott

Fitzgerald to the *film noir* of the 1940s, success remained forever elusive and fleeting. Failure was after all much worse, especially as American society supplied no other values to support an alternative way of life outside the competitive commercial system. And since success was the supreme criterion, how it was achieved could only be a relatively minor concern. Thus not only were the ends of American society 'de-regulated' by the capitalist ethic, so were the means, making it a perhaps unique case of a social system whose defining principle was anomie.[57] What distinguished a Carnegie from a Capone was not the ends pursued, nor even the means adopted, which were in both cases remarkably similar; it was the success which blessed the enterprise of the former as compared with the *fortuna* that damned that of the latter. It is in this reduction of society to a game in which luck plays a cosmic role that we most clearly see the 'pure logic' of an untrammelled capitalism.

IV

The general message of both Hirsch's and Schumpeter's accounts is that capitalism is killed not by its failure, as Marx expected, but by its success. Its own logic undermines it, by sweeping away all the pre-capitalist and non-capitalist baggage that has accompanied it on its journey. Capitalism itself is unconscious of the necessary labour of sustenance performed by this pre-capitalist inheritance. It sees it at best as an unnecessary burden, at worst as an obstacle to its progress. It regards it therefore variously with indifference or calculated hostility. It saps the force of religion, dissolves all corporate organization such as workers' guilds and village communities, and gradually either eliminates the power and influence of non-capitalist groups or draws them fully into its system. It thereby exposes itself fatally to tendencies within its own system which are preparing its downfall.

In breaking down the pre-capitalist framework of society, capitalism broke not only barriers that impeded its progress but also flying buttresses that prevented its collapse. That process, impressive in its relentless necessity, was not merely a matter of removing institutional deadwood, but of removing partners of the capitalist stratum, symbiosis with whom was an essential element of the capitalist schema.[58]

The argument, therefore, by a different route, arrives at a general conclusion not so far from Marx's. As Schumpeter urbanely says, 'in the end there is not so much difference as one might think between saying that the decay of capitalism is due to its success and saying that it is due to its failure.'[59] Hirsch and Schumpeter disagree of course not only with Marx but with each other on what it is about capitalism itself that drives it into crisis. Hirsch picks out particularly the consequences of successful growth in the material economy, forcing upon society a self-defeating struggle for equal shares within the 'positional economy'. For Schumpeter, capitalism's economic success brings about the atrophy of the entrepreneurial function, the bureaucratization of the enterprise and the disintegration of the bourgeois family. Assailed by a class of alienated intellectuals which is its own creation, capitalism loses both its basic legitimacy and its motivating force.

This is not the place to adjudicate between Hirsch and Schumpeter,[60] nor to assess the host of other theories variously contending over the causes of capitalism's current ills. What is interesting is that despite the differences in their analyses, both Hirsch and Schumpeter see emerging out of the strains of developed capitalism what Hirsch calls a 'reluctant collectivism'. For Schumpeter this is 'socialism', but since he defines socialism narrowly as 'control over the means of production by a central authority,'[61] this is not so far removed from Hirsch's perception of collectivism as a 'trend towards collective provision and state regulation in economic areas.'[62]

Hirsch is concerned to make that collectivism less reluctant: more full-blooded and so more effective in achieving its ends. This is not the place to discuss the precise measures he suggests. Here I simply want to observe, by way of concluding, that Hirsch's prescriptions are generally flawed by the same feature that marks his analysis of the pre-capitalist moral framework of capitalism. That is, they hang in the air; they are irredeemably idealist. On the last page of *Social Limits to Growth* Hirsch states the general goal:

the prime economic problem now facing the economically advanced societies is a structural need to pull back the bounds of economic self-advancement. That in turn requires a deliberate validation of the basis of income and wealth distribution that these economies have managed to do without in a transition period that is ending . . . We may be near the limit to explicit social organization possible without a supporting social morality. Additional correctives in its absence simply do not take . . . the first necessity is not technical devices but the public acceptance necessary to make them work.[63]

It is not too much to say that this either presumes or calls for revolution, or something very similar. This inference is qualified only slightly by the consideration of one of the key mechanisms suggested by Hirsch for achieving this goal: the adoption of an 'as if altruism', whereby self-interested motives are put at the service of collectively oriented behaviour to overcome the felt deficiencies of privately directed behaviour:

the best result may be attained by steering or guiding certain motives of individual behaviour into social rather than individual orientation, though still on the basis of privately directed preferences. This requires not a change in human nature, 'merely' a change in human convention or instinct or attitude of the same order as the shifts in social conventions or moral standards that have gone along with major changes in economic conditions in the past.[64]

The fact that Hirsch puts the 'merely' in quotation marks confesses an understandable uneasiness, but it cannot disguise the immensity of the change contemplated, as his parallel with past changes only too clearly underlines.

What social agency is to accomplish so momentous a change? Whose interests are furthered by promoting such a social morality? Everyone's in the end, of course, but that is simply to state the problem in a different form. Is the change to come about by a blinding flash of collective self-enlightenment? For Hirsch himself is only too well aware of the difficulty of getting people to act in a collectively enlightened way while private ends and motivations still predominate.[65] 'Individuals can perceive a need for themselves and their fellows and yet have no rational basis to act on it in isolation. The socially concerned individual then faces a dilemma between social and individual needs.'[66] This brings us back to the need for 'collective means', which remains a highly abstract entity, especially as Hirsch rules out on the grounds of 'primary liberal values' the 'subjugation of individual judgement on moral issues and behavioural choices to the thought of some Chairman Mao.'[67] Now that would be a solution, of a kind, but renouncing it Hirsch is left in the familiar position of having to hoist himself up by his own boot-straps. It is a particularly despairing admission of failure to fall back on the belief that 'the functional need for a change in the social ethic can be expected, over time, to promote it.'[68] His own analysis suggests quite otherwise.

Truly, one cannot blame Hirsch for not providing a convincing account of how the change is to come about. Many others have seen the need for comparable changes without being any more successful.[69] For his part, Schumpeter's account of 'the march into socialism' has its own problems, and it is certainly not my intention here to offer it as an alternative to Hirsch. Moreover, Schumpeter's task is easier inasmuch as he is describing as well as prescribing. But, although his attitude to socialism retains a characteristically detached irony, he clearly sees it not only as more or less inevitable but also as capable of delivering at least as efficiently all that capitalism delivered.

The whole of our argument might be put in a nutshell by saying that socialization means a stride beyond big business on the way that has been chalked out by it or, what amounts to the same thing, that socialist management may conceivably prove as superior to big business capitalism as big business capitalism has proved to be to the kind of competitive capitalism of which the English industry of a hundred years ago was the prototype ... As a matter of blueprint logic it is undeniable that the socialist blueprint is drawn at a higher level of rationality.[70]

What is in any case more important, here as in the earlier discussion, is not so much the correctness or otherwise of Schumpeter's view of socialism as the form of analysis he adopts. Schumpeter points to concrete tendencies within late capitalist society which, he argues, whether or not we choose to call the outcome 'socialism', are transforming capitalism to such an extent that it becomes simply erroneous to use the same term for the emerging social order. These include the growth of an interventionist state, a technical and managerial bureaucracy in both public and private enterprises and a salaried professional middle class with interests and attitudes very different from those of the classic private capitalist and entrepreneur. The exigencies of war and depression further encourage these developments. Socialism is merely the recognition and rationalization of these tendencies. The main work has already been done. 'The capitalist process shapes things and souls for socialism.'[71]

Simply to mention Burnham's *The Managerial Revolution* (1941) and

Galbraith's *The New Industrial State* (1969) is to indicate the kinship of this argument with that vast concurrence of contemporary social thought to which Schumpeter himself is of course a major contributor. But the very familiarity of Schumpeter's analysis is its strength in the present context. It suggests at the very least that the transforming forces he points to are real observable entities in the recent history of Western societies. Whether or not they can fulfil quite the task that he sets them is disputable, but he certainly presents us with some very plausible means to his designated ends. This is precisely what Hirsch does not do, and on the available evidence the future seems to lie much more with Schumpeter's commissars than Hirsch's 'jaded social democrats'.

Comparisons can be artificial as well as invidious. Actually Hirsch and Schumpeter go together very well. Both break through the conventional categories of discipline and ideology to cast a refreshing and revealing perspective on the development of Western capitalist societies. Both emphasize important features of that development too often ignored or treated as peripheral. In contemplating the future, Schumpeter is the greater realist, consistent with the greater sociological realism of his treatment throughout. But he is a realist at the cost of the sacrifice of values he obviously cherishes. Hirsch is certainly no wild-eyed visionary. The impressiveness of his achievement lies in the sense of a man grappling with some of the most intractable problems of modern society without abandoning the commitment to liberal and humane values. Who has yet done more?

NOTES

1 J. M. Low, 'An eighteenth century controversy in the theory of economic progress', *The Manchester School*, 20 (1952), 311–20.
2 D. Hume, 'Of money', in *Essays: Moral, Political and Literary* (London, Grant Richards, 1903), pp. 290–1.
3 Low, 'Eighteenth century controversy', p. 322.
4 D. Forbes, '"Scientific" Whiggism: Adam Smith and John Millar', *Cambridge Journal*, 7 (1954), 643–70; and Introduction to his edition of Adam Ferguson, *An Essay on the History of Civil Society* (Edinburgh, Edinburgh University Press, 1966).
5 Adam Smith, *The Theory of Moral Sentiments* (Indianapolis, Liberty Classics, 1969), p. 122.
6 Ibid., p. 303. See also N. Rosenberg, 'Adam Smith, consumer tastes and economic growth', *Journal of Political Economy*, 76 (1968), 361–74.
7 Adam Smith, *The Wealth of Nations* (2 vols, London, Dent, 1910), vol. 1, p. 72.
8 R. Heilbroner, 'The paradox of progress: decline and decay in *The Wealth of Nations*', *Journal of the History of Ideas*, 34 (1973), 243.
9 A. O. Hirschman, *The Passions and the Interests* (Princeton, NJ, Princeton University Press, 1977).
10 Ibid., pp. 58–9.
11 E. Gellner, 'The withering away of the dentistry state', in *Spectacles and Predicaments: Essays in Social Theory* (Cambridge, Cambridge University Press, 1979).

12 Hirschman, *The Passions*, p. 129.
13 The view that there was no radical break of any kind – in England at least – in the sixteenth and seventeenth centuries has been provocatively put by A. Macfarlane in *The Origins of English Individualism* (Oxford, Basil Blackwell, 1978). Space, as well as general competence, forbids any discussion of that theme here. But one might at least say that Macfarlane takes a very restrictive and narrow view of what is implied by 'the rise of capitalism', and the question cannot be resolved by a concentration on legal or customary definitions of land ownership and tenurial rights. A good deal more is involved by way of changes in social values, attitudes to work and religion and the sense of communal ties. Macfarlane does not discuss any of these.
14 F. Hirsch, *Social Limits to Growth* (London, Routledge and Kegan Paul, 1977), p. 118.
15 K. Polyani, *The Great Transformation* (Boston, Mass., Beacon Press, 1957), p. 3.
16 Hirsch, *Social Limits to Growth*, p. 11.
17 Ibid.
18 Ibid., pp. 11–12, 120.
19 Ibid., pp. 117ff, 161ff.
20 Ibid, p. 12.
21 Ibid., p. 117.
22 E. Durkheim, *The Division of Labor in Society*, trans. G. Simpson (New York, The Free Press, 1964), p. 211.
23 Hirsch, *Social Limits to Growth*, p. 141.
24 Ibid., p. 143.
25 S. Brittan, 'The economic contradictions of democracy', *British Journal of Political Science*, 5 (1975), 48; D. Bell, *The Cultural Contradictions of Capitalism* (London, Heinemann, 1976); J. Habermas, *Legitimation Crisis*, trans. T. McCarthy (London, Heinemann, 1976), pp. 48–9; J. H. Goldthorpe, 'The current inflation: towards a sociological account', in F. Hirsch and J. H. Goldthorpe (eds), *The Political Economy of Inflation* (London, Martin Robertson, 1978); M. Gilbert, 'A sociological model of inflation', *Sociology*, 15 (1981), 185–209. John Goldthorpe has seen in this a key difference in the treatment of capitalism by economists and sociologists: 'There are, and have been historically, clear differences between economists and sociologists in their evaluations of the capitalist market economy. Economists tend to see this as having an inherent propensity towards stability or, at least, as capable of being stabilized through skilled management on the basis of the expertise that they can themselves provide. Sociologists, on the other hand, tend to view the market economy as being inherently unstable or, rather, to be more precise, as exerting a constant destabilizing effect on the society within which it operates, so that it can itself continue to function satisfactorily only to the extent that this effect is offset by exogenous factors: most importantly, by the integrative influence of some basic value consensus in the society, deriving from sources unrelated to the economy; or by some measure of "imperative coordination" imposed by government (or other agencies) with the ultimate backing of force' ('The current inflation', p. 194).
26 R. H. Tawney, *The Acquisitive Society* (London, Fontana, 1961), p. 47.
27 K. Kristol, *Two Cheers for Capitalism* (New York, Mentor Books, 1979), p. 61.

28 Ibid., p. 43.
29 Bell, *Cultural Contradictions*, p. 224.
30 M. Waltzer, 'Nervous liberals', *New York Review of Books*, 11 October 1979, p. 6.
31 Polyani, *The Great Transformation*, pp. 130ff.
32 J. A. Schumpeter, *Imperialism and Social Classes: Two Essays* (New York, Meridian Books, 1955), p. 98.
33 Ibid., p. 111.
34 J. A. Schumpeter, *Capitalism, Socialism and Democracy*, 5th edn (London, Allen and Unwin, 1976), p. 136.
35 Ibid., p. 111.
36 K. Kumar (ed.), *Revolution: The Theory and Practice of a European Idea* (London, Weidenfeld and Nicolson, 1971), pp. 52ff.
37 M. J. Wiener, *English Culture and the Decline of the Industrial Spirit 1850–1980* (Cambridge, Cambridge University Press, 1981).
38 D. C. Moore, *The Politics of Deference* (London, The Harvester Press, 1976); and see my 'Class and political action in nineteenth-century England', ch. 6 below.
39 R. Dahrendorf, *Society and Democracy in Germany* (London, Weidenfeld and Nicolson, 1968).
40 J. A. Schumpeter, 'Capitalism in the post-war world', in R. V. Clemence (ed.), *Essays of J. A. Schumpeter* (Cambridge, Mass., Addison Wesley, 1951), p. 172.
41 Schumpeter, *Imperialism*, p. 92.
42 Schumpeter, *Capitalism*, p. 128.
43 Schumpeter, *Imperialism*, p. 69.
44 Ibid., pp. 90–1.
45 Ibid., p. 93.
46 Ibid., p. 94.
47 Ibid., p. 97.
48 Perhaps one might add, as a particularly telling example of the undogmatic quality of Schumpeter's thinking, that even in his most 'purely' economic analysis, *The Theory of Economic Development* (New York, Oxford University Press, 1961), he concedes so important a role to 'accidents' – i.e. history – in the aetiology of the crises of the business cycle as calmly to suggest the possibility that no general theory might be needed at all (p. 222).
49 Polanyi, *The Great Transformation*, pp. 178ff.
50 The United States of America is only the best studied example of a fascinating exercise in comparative analysis that can be undertaken by looking at societies such as those of Latin America and Australia, which have been formed out of 'fragments of Europe'. See, for example, the studies in L. Hartz, *The Founding of New Societies* (New York, Harcourt, Brace and World, 1964).
51 L. Hartz, *The Liberal Tradition in America* (New York, Harcourt, Brace and World, 1955).
52 A. de Tocqueville, *Democracy in America* (2 vols, New York, Schocken Books, 1961), vol. 2, p. 194.
53 J. Brecher, *Strike!* (Boston, Mass., South End Press, 1972).
54 Bell, *Cultural Contradictions*, pp. 55ff; Kristol, *Two Cheers for Capitalism*, p. 245.
55 E. Durkheim, *Suicide: a Study in Sociology*, trans. J. A. Spaulding and G. Simpson (London, Routledge and Kegan Paul, 1952), p. 253.

56 Hartz, *The Liberal Tradition*, p. 221.
57 R. K. Merton, 'Social structure and anomie', in *Social Theory and Social Structure*, rev. edn (Glencoe, Ill., The Free Press, 1957).
58 Schumpeter, *Capitalism*, p. 139.
59 Ibid., p. 162.
60 For Schumpeter see A. Heertje (ed.), *Schumpeter's Vision: Capitalism, Socialism and Democracy after Forty Years* (New York, Praeger, 1981).
61 Schumpeter, *Capitalism*, p. 167.
62 Hirsch, *Social Limits to Growth*, p. 1.
63 Ibid., p. 190.
64 Ibid., p. 146.
65 Ibid., especially pp. 137ff.
66 Ibid., p. 179.
67 Ibid., p. 180.
68 Ibid., p. 179.
69 See, for example, Hirsch and Goldthorpe, *The Political Economy of Inflation*, pp. 214–16.
70 Schumpeter, *Capitalism*, pp. 195–6.
71 Ibid., p. 220.

BIBLIOGRAPHICAL NOTE

As with most original thinkers, Hirsch has not fitted very well into the compartments in which academics teach their subjects and conduct their research. Hence the paucity of systematic treatments of the main themes of his *Social Limits to Growth*. Among the few critical commentaries, see the volume in which this chapter first appeared: Adrian Ellis and Krishan Kumar (eds), *Dilemmas of Liberal Democracies: Studies in Fred Hirsch's Social Limits to Growth* (London, Tavistock Publications, 1983). Two noted economists have used Hirsch as the point of departure for some stimulating reflections: Frank Hahn, 'Reflections on the invisible hand', *Lloyds Bank Review*, no. 144 (1982), pp. 1–21; A. K. Sen, 'The profit motive', *Lloyds Bank Review*, no. 147 (1983), pp. 1–20. A specific test of Hirsch's concept of 'positionality' is Elim Papadakis and Peter Taylor-Gooby, 'Positional satisfaction and state welfare', *Sociological Review*, 34 (1986), 812–27. Some broadly similar issues to Hirsch's are considered in Lester Thurow, *The Zero-Sum Society* (Harmondsworth, Penguin Books, 1981). On the disappointments and dissatisfactions of economic growth, see also Albert O. Hirschman, *Shifting Involvements: Private Interest and Public Action* (Princeton, NJ, Princeton University Press, 1982); Tibor Scitovsky, *The Joyless Economy: An Inquiry Into Human Satisfaction and Consumer Dissatisfaction* (Oxford, Oxford University Press, 1977); William Leiss, *The Limits to Satisfaction* (London, Marion Boyars, 1978). Broader, but touching on a number of topics central to Hirsch, is the stimulating essay by Michael Ignatieff, *The Needs of Strangers* (London, Chatto and Windus, 1984). Hirsch-type themes also crop up at various points in the essays by Claus Offe, *Disorganized Capitalism: Contemporary Transformations of Work and Politics* (Oxford, Polity Press, 1985). And see also two collections which raise many of the questions discussed by Hirsch: Herman E. Daly (ed.), *Economics, Ecology, Ethics: Essays Toward a Steady-State Economy* (San Francisco,

W.H. Freeman, 1980); M. Gaskin (ed.), *The Political Economy of Tolerable Survival* (London, Croom Helm, 1981).

On the Hirsch–Schumpeter view of Western capitalist development, there is a good chapter on Schumpeter, and other relevant matters, in Tom Bottomore, *Theories of Modern Capitalism* (London, Allen and Unwin, 1985). Two recent works by R. J. Holton on the rise of capitalism are also pertinent: *The Transition from Feudalism to Capitalism* (London, Macmillan, 1985); and *Cities, Capitalism and Civilization* (London, Allen and Unwin, 1986). For the supposed link between capitalism and 'possessive individualism', see N. Abercrombie, S. Hill and B. S. Turner, *Sovereign Individuals of Capitalism* (London, Allen and Unwin, 1986). Also interesting, for its break with conventional theories of industrial development, is Suzanne Berger and Michael J. Piore, *Dualism and Discontinuity in Industrial Societies* (Cambridge, Cambridge University Press, 1980).

See also the notes to 'The limits and capacities of industrial capitalism', chapter 5 in this volume.

3
Continuities and Discontinuities in the Development of Industrial Societies

One cannot assume, and ought not to expect, that any theoretical or conceptual apparatus that fits the analysis of industrialisation will be equally appropriate for the study of the further development of societies already industrialised.

T. H. Marshall, summing up at the end of the 1964 British Sociological Association Conference on the Development of Industrial Societies

It is one of the most interesting of Joseph Schumpeter's many provocative suggestions that we consider the era of capitalist industrial society as a residual phase of transition between feudalism and socialism. He does not, of course, mean this in Marx's sense, as a social order which succeeds feudalism and precedes socialism. He literally wants to suggest that capitalist industrialism is a hybrid, a temporary period during which the forces and structures of European feudalism were gradually being overcome. But 'in breaking down the pre-capitalist framework of society, capitalism broke not only barriers that impeded its progress but also flying buttresses that prevented its collapse'.[1] When the process was more or less completed, some time in the earlier part of this century, not only had feudalism gone, but capitalism also. Seen in this light, capitalism appears as 'the last stage of the decomposition' of feudalism.[2]

What this perspective suggests is that there was something exceptional, aberrant almost, about the hundred years or so which followed the English Industrial Revolution, and which is generally regarded as the era of classic industrialism. And indeed this is a view which, looking back from the vantage point of the late 1970s, seems increasingly plausible; and is correspondingly being increasingly aired. So, for instance, George Steiner, noting a widespread current alertness to and anxiety about violence and disorder, observes that 'when we lament safeties, courtesies, legalities now eroded, what we are in fact referring to is the *belle époque* of middle-class hegemony, notably in Western Europe, from about the 1830s to the Second World War.'[3] He cautions us against drawing topical comparisons on the basis of this 'nagging sense of "paradise lost"'. For 'far from being the historical rule, the stabilities, the general absence of violence, the law-abidingness, the sanctity of property and contract, the spaciousness of work and play which we associate, erroneously or not, with the epoch from Waterloo to the economic and social crises of the 1930s, were an exception, a rare and fragile *entente* between ruler and ruled . . . So far as Western history goes, the long peace of the nineteenth century . . . begins to look like a very special providence.'

In a similar vein Ernest Gellner also observes, apropos contemporary debates about the 'free market' versus the planned (i.e. politicized) economy, that such an opposition is based on an illusion fostered by a too schematic view of nineteenth-century European history.[4] The proponents believe that they are dealing in sociological and historical 'universals' – or, at any rate, categories which they can take to be roughly equivalent. But in fact the sociological norm, across time and place, is overwhelmingly 'politics in command'. What has led people to think otherwise is the fact that in the era of 'classical' capitalism there took place a separation of the economic and political realms that was 'highly eccentric, historically and sociologically speaking'[5] and which gave rise to the unprecedented and erroneous belief in a 'natural' economy based on the operations of the untrammelled market. Such a separation could only take place in historical circumstances that were 'rather peculiar and highly specific',[6] depending mainly on the existence of a state which for various reasons had neither the inclination nor the need to interfere with the economy. 'So the miracle occurred – a society in which, for once, wealth was mightier than the sword.'[7] These historical circumstances have now changed; the customary norm has re-asserted itself; politics once more dominates economics. Clearly it is unwise to conduct debates about present political dilemmas on the basis of principles derived from a unique historical phenomenon.

These observations have more than the customary virtues in serving as a point of departure. They reveal an unfamiliar and illuminating perspective on a period of history hallowed by frequent sociological invocation (which is a poor substitute for actual investigation). Two features implied in these accounts are particularly relevant in any exercise in contemporary stock-taking. One is that the epoch of classic industrialism is, in broad terms, over. However we assess the present situation of the industrial societies, we would be ill-advised to cast our reflections in the categories appropriate to the developing industrial society of the nineteenth century. The second point emphasizes the *openness* of the options available to the industrial societies at the present time. It warns us against relying on the schematization of history that so often serves sociology as a shorthand for historical knowledge, and which leads us to expect social orders or epochs to succeed each other in orderly progression – as 'feudalism', 'capitalism', 'socialism' and so forth. If there were indeed something peculiar and exceptional, or at the least historically highly specific, about nineteenth-century industrial society, then we should not expect to discern any future state of that society either by a simple extrapolation of trends, or by conjecturing some sort of 'natural' or determined evolutionary supersession. The relationship between the past and the future of industrial society is likely to be far more disjunctive than is implied in either of these modes of procedure. If anything, as Gellner's argument suggests, it is the *pre*-industrial past of European societies that may well turn out to be the better guide to the future. That this might appear surprising is only an indication of how firmly we have become the prisoners of a progressivist, evolutionary tradition of thought.

The general lines of this Schumpeterian perspective seem to me correct; and in this chapter I want mainly to look at the prospect for the occurrence of fundamental *discontinuities* with the past development of industrial societies, and to contemplate the possibility of a future very different from what might be expected by an extrapolation of that development. But first it seems important to reflect a little on the alternative and more commonly held view, that the future of industrial society will be merely the past 'writ large', the result in the main of persistencies, continuities, intensifications and accelerations of past trends. The purpose here is not so much to question the evidence adduced for this view; for the main point of disagreement has less to do with the existence of particular trends than in the interpretation of them as still existing growths or as fossilized and decaying persistencies. Rather there is the need to re-assess the frequently asserted conclusion that seems to follow from this view: that the traditional concepts and theoretical framework created for the analysis of nineteenth-century industrial society will still do for the analysis of present and future industrial society.[8]

I

It is not difficult to see how a contemporary observer might build up a picture of current social realities that is both highly plausible and squares remarkably well with the expectations of nineteenth-century sociology. Thus he would show the continuing process of urbanization, so that, for instance, in this century the United States and France could be added to the list of 'urban–industrial' societies, and the percentage of the world urban population increased from 9.2 in 1900 to 28.1 in 1970. He would show the continuing trends towards the greater centralization, 'rationalization' and bureaucratization of politics, commerce, communications and culture; in the transformation of national economies into one global economy, under the oligopolistic management of a small number of transnational regional economic groupings; in the concentration of wealth both within nations and between them, so that the gap between the industrial societies and the 'Third World' continues to grow. In the more local, immediate concerns of an individual's life, too, developments could be indicated which broadly conform to nineteenth-century expectations. Kinship ties, particularly in a residential and community context, have narrowed. The nuclear family becomes the effective norm. Stable residential communities are broken up, particularly among the working classes; 'substitute communities', of the occupational community or voluntary organization kind, are thin and uninvolving, leaving the individual increasingly 'privatized', centring his existence on his home, family and leisure pursuits. This tendency is intensified by the increasing meaninglessness of work, as the fragmentation and bureaucratization of the work process continues. As Marx expected, 'the worker feels himself at home only during leisure time, whereas at work he feels homeless'. Nor are the consolations of the other world available to any effective degree. True to expectations, the process of secularization of beliefs has continued, so that even if the motions of church-going are attended to, the meanings these have for the actor have been substantially altered in the direction of secularism.

There is not much here that would have perplexed a Saint-Simon, Marx, Durkheim or Weber. It was in these terms, more or less, that they marked out the destinies of the industrial societies. And who would seriously quarrel with Nisbet's forthright assertion that 'we *are* urban, democratic, industrial, bureaucratic, rationalized, large-scale, formal, secular, and technological'.[9]

What is curious and somewhat paradoxical is that theories that essentially insist on this version of contemporary realities are currently finding their strongest expression under the banner of 'post-industrialism'. The term suggests, as indeed its authors intend it to, that the industrial societies have now moved so far from their original base that they have undergone a qualitative transformation, giving birth to a new social order which is *beyond* industrialism. And yet when we examine the most influential accounts of the post-industrial idea, as in Bell[10] and Touraine,[11] it becomes quite plain that what they are referring to are long-term continuities within the social order of industrialism.[12] Bell and Touraine point to the explosive expansion of the service sector in this century, the accelerating growth of the white-collar occupational groups, the increasing number and significance of scientific and technical personnel, above all the new pivotal role of knowledge itself as the crucial resource of present-day industrial society. All these, they claim, add up to structural forces so different in kind from those propelling the old industrial society that we must acknowledge the rise of a new order, post-industrial society.

But was not Marx in his *Theories of Surplus Value* already in the 1860s commenting on the growing white-collar army of 'the labour of superintendence' and reproaching Ricardo for ignoring 'the constantly growing number of the middle classes, those who stand between the workmen on the one hand and the capitalist and landlord on the other'?[13] And had not Saint-Simon, even earlier, singled out the scientist and the engineer as the most representative figures of the new order which he called industrialism; and called upon them to impose their expert rule on a society whose fundamental basis was scientific knowledge? Most obvious of the links with the classic order of industrialism are seen in Weber's account of the relentless process of 'rationalization' in Western civilization, marked by the constant bureaucratization of all sectors of social life, and the spread of scientific or 'technical' reason to problems of politics as well as those of production. If the post-industrial society is 'the knowledge society', then in the late nineteenth century Weber was already sketching its structure and pointing up its strains.

The impression of novelty created by the post-industrial idea comes from the selection of tendencies often overlooked in the historical and sociological analyses of industrialism: a neglect partly accounted for by a popular and powerful image of industrialism which overstresses the significance of factories and the industrial worker in the development of industrial society. One of the uses of the post-industrial idea is indeed to direct us back to the history of European industrialization, on examining which it is not difficult to discover the growth and spread of most of the tendencies later characterized as 'post-industrial'. At this level of analysis, therefore, it seems fair to regard the 'post-industrial' label as a misnomer, and to suggest that it is simply a newer and glossier version of the general analyses of industrialism as a generic type which were common in the 1950s, and which we associate with the theses of 'convergence' and 'the end of ideology', and the names of Lipset, Kerr, Aron, Galbraith and, of course, Bell himself.[14]

To put the matter thus is not necessarily to dismiss wholly the post-industrial analysis or its heuristic usefulness. It is incapable of sustaining its major claim that a new era, comparable in scope to that of industrialism, has been entered. But may its proponents not argue, more modestly, that although the features picked out are not novel to this century, they have reached such a prominence in the past twenty-five years (say) that we need to regard our current condition as in significant ways very different from that obtaining at the beginning of this century – not to mention nineteenth-century industrial society? Even at this level I do not think that the post-industrial theorists have selected the most interesting or significant tendencies to speculate upon. But the point does nicely raise the more general issues: the difficulty of analysing the present with the intellectual tools of nineteenth-century sociology. The problem is that the organising concepts which the sociological tradition offers us – such as 'capitalism', 'rationalization', 'secularization' – operate at too high a level of abstraction to be suitable for the kinds of distinctions which we need to make in the recent history of the industrial societies. As a consequence every sociological theory that stresses continuity with past development is forced to suppress the recognition of some very important changes.

Consider, for instance, that in discussing the process of 'rationalization' or 'secularization' we need to go back at least to the Reformation of the sixteenth century and the scientific revolution of the seventeenth century; perhaps even, as Saint-Simon would have us do, to the outburst of scientific activities in the twelfth and thirteenth centuries. Similarly with 'capitalism'. Its development can quite conventionally be traced from the sixteenth century or even earlier: E. P. Thompson speaks, without apparently any need of qualification, of 'the bourgeois revolution of the fifteenth to the eighteenth centuries'.[15] By the same token, with the capitalist system established, we are asked to consider a host of diverse twentieth-century phenomena – Fascism, Keynesianism, de-colonization – as 'essentially' capitalist. In this perspective, it is quite clear that we are still in the classical age both of sociology and of the industrial society.

The approach along these lines can be fertile, as Marx and Weber amply showed. But it is the long view, which for many important aspects of social change can become excessively so. Let us get nearer to the history of the societies in question. We are then struck forcibly by some very powerful contrasts. There is the whole decline and dissolution of the characteristic nineteenth-century system of the liberal polity and economy: the free market, the independent entrepreneur, the parliamentary assembly and the judiciary with some degree of real independence of and control over the executive. As against this we have since had the rise of large oligopolies and monopolies in the market, usually with some form of state backing, and which virtually puts an end to competition; the unification of the executive and the legislature through the rise of the mass political party with its extra-parliamentary organization; the spread of 'administrative law' as a general phenomenon of increasing bureaucratic rule; the massive stimulus given to governmental power by the exigencies of organizing for two world wars, a power further strengthened in peacetime by some startling developments in weapons technology, the spread of a centralized system of mass communications and the extension of systems of public education and welfare to the point where they become potentially all-embracing agencies of social control of the population. No wonder a Lord Chief Justice in the 1920s, seeking for historical parallels for the new legal developments that so concerned his profession, was forced to jump over the age of liberal constitutionalism and come down finally in the age of the Star Chamber and 'Tudor despotism.'[16] A nineteenth-century time-traveller, stepping into this brave new world, might surely be driven to speculate on what grand events, what spectacular revolution, had produced such a transformation in the life of society.

He would not have been entirely unprepared, of course, had he happened to read the gloomy prognostications of Mill, Tocqueville and Burckhardt. And, from the lofty heights of the sociological tradition, we could indicate to him the continuities with long-established processes in Western societies; the extent to which most of these changes can be seen as the maturing of some of the most basic principles of industrialism. But he would surely be right to think that it was a strange view of social change which buried these momentous changes so smoothly under general, all-purpose concepts, and which refused to treat this mass, corporatist, late twentieth-century society in terms very different from those we might use for nineteenth-century liberal industrial society. For at this level of analysis, Schumpeter and Gellner are right to insist that, at the very least, we should consider the original phase of industrialism as over, and try to take stock of the current phase with a vocabulary and a set of concepts that acknowledge the distance that industrial society has moved from its original base.

It is, of course, in the end all a matter of the level of analysis. In the perspective of classical sociological theory all these twentieth-century developments can readily be comprehended by a few general concepts – 'rationalization' would indeed probably serve to cover them all. What I am arguing is that the embrace might be too close, and is potentially deadly; and that we need to develop a more limited, historically grounded, approach to contemporary social changes, in addition to the grand theorizing that no doubt will continue to serve us for other purposes (especially perhaps comparisons with other cultures). This is especially necessary when we are considering the future as basically an extension and a continuation of long-established and deep-lying structural tendencies; for it is only thus that we will be able to see both the original theme and any significant variations that have been and will be played on it. The categories of 'advanced industrial', 'late capitalism', 'neo-capitalism' and so forth, with their themes of a fundamental persistence are thin and insufficient ways of conceptualizing changes of the dimension that the twentieth century has seen: as would be felt perhaps particularly keenly by the subject of a Fascist state (or even of its numerous, less brutal, 'managerial' successors), when asked to believe that he is in the same 'essential' position as his counterpart of nineteenth-century capitalist Europe.

II

What, however, of the alternative possibility, that the future will mark a truly radical break with even the most basic structural tendencies of industrialism – the drive towards ever greater degrees of scale, centralization, bureaucratization and rationalization? One's views here have to become very tentative, because the evidence, even where it exists, has not been gathered in the systematic manner that makes firm generalizations possible. But some indication can be given of certain trends that would suggest a genuine movement beyond industrialism: to a post-industrial society in the proper sense of the term, rather than to the 'hyper-industrial' society that is envisaged in most contemporary theories of industrialism, including the 'post-industrial' theory itself.

Illich has advanced the interesting idea that the history of industrialism be considered as marked by two watersheds.[17] In the first phase, leading to the first watershed, science is applied to a range of traditional problems – scarcity, disease etc. – which it resolves with unprecedented efficiency, bringing about the widespread provision of goods and services previously available only to the very few, the rich or powerful. In the second phase, leading to the second watershed, the first phase becomes the basis for a further expansion and increased legitimation which actually reverses the progressive tendencies of that earlier phase, and which largely continues for the benefit of 'self-certifying professional elites'. A number of the major institutions of industrial society are now seen as having moved over their second watershed. 'Schools are losing their claim to be effective tools to provide education; cars have ceased to be effective tools for mass transportation; the assembly line has ceased to be an acceptable mode of production.'[18] The answer is seen in the development of a contrary mode which Illich designates 'convivial' production, and which is based on the design and use of simple tools, renewable resources, personal skills, small-scale operations and the 'de-professionalized' provision of services such as health, education and transportation.

This may seem familiar utopian stuff. What gives it a concreteness and a foothold in contemporary reality are various indications that industrialism is in a state of genuine crisis, and that certain varieties of utopian thought, new or traditional, might now have a relevance previously denied them by the powerful currents of a developing and triumphant industrialism. Something of this is in any case indicated by an impressive convergence of thought during the 1970s which agrees with Illich in stressing, as a matter of necessity as much as desire, alternatives to the present industrial mode.[19]

In urging us to consider these alternatives, the first point to which these thinkers draw our attention is the illusion of progress generated by the industrial societies' fixation on Gross National Product as the primary index of prosperity. This is a misleading index not simply in terms of more rounded notions of progress but even within its own terms of economic productivity. GNP measures the *total* volume of goods and services bought and sold on the market. But this total can be swollen in curious ways. If, for instance, an activity which causes pollution, spoliation or ill-health – e.g. chemical plants, motor cars, noisy aeroplanes – leads to further economic activity to remedy the damage – e.g. purifying processes, medical services – the resulting chain of activities appears as a contribution to an overall increase in national wealth, since both kinds of activities count as additions to the total volume of goods and services in the national economy.

This is clearly insane; and while insanity of this kind does not necessarily drive a society to self-destruction, pointing it up does put a different complexion on that 'superindustrialism' so euphorically anticipated by contemporary futurologists.[20] For, given the pronounced growth in services in this century, it could mean that much of the increase in national wealth amounted to no more than vast increases in pollution, environmental destruction and personal suffering, with the consequent expenditure of fresh capital and labour to repair, maintain and renovate the physical, social and psychological fabric of the society. We might think this an apt symbol of an exploitative and predatory industrialism, which ends up creating its wealth by a process of self-laceration. At any rate it should warn us against the common argument that, although industrialism is unpleasant in many ways, it justifies itself in the end by producing the goods, and ever more of them. This now seems an elaborate sleight of hand, and makes a poor case for the extension of industrialism into the future. If increases in productivity mean mainly the more and more intensive laundering of each other's dirty washing, we might reasonably begin to fear for the very survival of the clothes.

The illusion of greater welfare is fostered by a further quirk of social accounting. The growth of services in this century is rightly seen as one of the most distinctive features of recent economic history. But does it represent a real increase in services? Pigou, in *The Economics of Welfare*, long ago pointed to the problem by observing that if a widowed vicar paid his housekeeper a weekly wage, this was an addition to the national income; if he married her, it became a subtraction. The visibility of the 'service revolution' of this century has tended to conceal the fact that what has mainly happened has been a vast transfer of services from the home, where they were not counted as 'productive', to the market, where they have generated much employment and many monetary transactions. Thus work done at home, such as cooking, cleaning, educating, tending and caring, have moved into the marketplace as the restaurant industry, the laundry industry, public and private systems of education, health and social welfare. Undoubtedly this movement has had enormous consequences, especially in the rise of female employment and the extension of state activity. But, again, we must be careful to recognize the spurious aspects of this growth in employment and welfare, and to see that our societies are not necessarily the richer, or more comfortable, or more civilized for it.

So much might be admitted, and even regretted, by the proponents of industrialism. But as hard-headed realists, looking for the sociological fact or tendency as against the mere nostalgic or utopian wish, they may ask what grounds there are for supposing that these predominant trends, undesirable as many of them may be, will be seriously interrupted. It is here that desire and necessity seem, as at other rare moments in the past, to be moving towards a detente. Industrialism is being increasingly seen as not simply wasteful and unpleasant, but unworkable.

There has been a fundamental contradiction in the manner of development of most of the major industrial societies over the past two centuries. As the heritage of sociology insistently points out, these development have all been in the direction of greater scale, centralization, mechanization, specialization and bureaucratization. They have involved, correspondingly, a progressive decline in the skills, competence, autonomy and responsibility of the bulk of the population. Knowledge and skills have gone into machines and bureaucratized service institutions; authority and autonomy into the hierarchical and bureaucratic structures of large-scale organizations. Once again, this is a phenomenon largely disguised by the ideological features of industrial societies. So, for instance, the real loss of skills and competence is hidden by a system of occupational classification which, by postulating a certain hierarchy of occupations, can record an actual rise in the general level of skills in this century. A massive increase in the number of 'semi-skilled' over 'unskilled' workers is shown by the simple device of classifying as 'semi-skilled' all workers associated, in whatever capacity and with whatever actual skill, merely with machines: as watchers, tenders, feeders etc. Given the mechanization of factory and office, an 'upgrading' of the workforce follows automatically. But as Braverman says, 'it is only in the world of census statistics, and not in terms of direct assessment, that an assembly line worker is presumed to have greater skill than a fisherman or oysterman, the fork lift operator greater skill than the gardener or groundskeeper, the machine feeder greater skill than the longshoreman, the parking lot attendant greater skill than the lumberman or raftsman.'[21] Much the same, *mutandis mutatis*, can be said of theories of the increasing 'professionalization' of the workforce, or of a more educated and 'knowledgeable' population in general. All such views confuse the acquisition and use of real knowledge and skills with such tokens as a certain number of years spent in formal educational institutions, or the gaining of professional or academic certificates which often bear very little relation to the needs of the jobs for which they supposedly qualify their holders.[22]

This wholesale 'de-skilling' of the population would probably have found its retribution in any case at some point in the future. What has brought that somewhat sooner is the wider context in which the process of de-skilling took place. The mode of industrialization of the West, basically a form of capitalistic or economistic rationalization of the world, led to the parcelling up of the world into specialized and differentiated 'resource areas' for the benefit of the industrial societies. So long as these areas remained politically weak, the industrial societies could pursue the logic of the rationalizing mode with scant regard to the long-term consequences. Hence in particular the progressive shifts towards increasingly 'high', capital-intensive large-scale technology, with accelerating consumption of non-renewable fossil fuels. The high point of this long-term tendency can in retrospect be seen as the boom period of the post-1945 economies when, as Geoffrey Barraclough convincingly shows,[23] the availability of abundant supplies of cheap oil prompted most industrial societies into a near-suicidal dependence on it, and caused a shift away from other energy sources, especially coal. At the same time technological innovation was either slowed down or skewed as the industrial societies basked in the great oil lake.

That high point can also be seen as a turning point (it may yet turn out to be a terminal point). The sharp increases in the price of oil in the early 1970s were not of course themselves the source of the industrial societies' problems; but the effects were symptomatic of those problems, and were remarkably effective in highlighting the profound historic significance of the crisis. Ultimately the crisis was created by a mode of development that came to depend on energy sources which have long been known to be limited and of a relatively fixed term, and whose cheapness was premised on the continuing political weakness of the non-industrial world. As Barraclough says, 'What we are experiencing is not a short-term emergency but a last desperate attempt by industrial society . . . to climb out of a crisis of its own making.'[24] The writing is on the wall, and the industrial societies are being forced into a readjustment for which they are psychologically and structurally extremely unprepared. In particular they have now to contemplate a future – at least within the medium term – of increasingly costly resources of the kind their technologies have come to depend upon; a future in which consequently, not only must they expect to be less wealthy, but one in which also they will need to be far more imaginative and resourceful in the husbanding of what they have and can afford, and in the search for other, renewable sources of energy and technologies appropriate to them.

It is in this historical context that the loss of general skills and competence is seen at its most damaging. The industrial system of plentiful consumer goods and expensive professionalized services is under severe strain. It can no longer support itself, in its traditional form, at reasonable cost. It requires a population that, once more, should be able to rely upon itself for the repairing and maintenance of much of the physical structure of the society, and for the invention of tools that are modest and flexible in the use of resources, and relatively easy to service. Above all it requires that people should come to depend much more upon themselves, their families and their community for the provision of many services to do with general health and welfare, at present supplied by professionalized private and public bodies. But the industrial bureaucracies have expropriated the individual craftsman of his skill; the service bureaucracies have dispossessed the population both of the knowledge and of the confidence to attend to many of their medical and general welfare problems, such as having their babies at home, rather than in hospitals, in the rearing of their children, in the cure of minor illnesses and injuries and in the care of the old and mentally ill. The ability to transform the classic pattern of industrialism into the 'convivial' mode is lacking at precisely the time that it is most urgently needed; and that lack is a direct consequence of the classic mode.

The difficulty is compounded by a further consequence of the rationalizing tendency of industrialism. The traditionally claimed economies of scale, centralization and bureaucratization are increasingly revealing their other face, of dis-economies and dys-functions. Beyond a certain size and a certain degree of centralization of institutions, the advantages gained up to that point seem to be outweighed by the losses incurred as a result of the endemic problems of large-scale organization. The 'economies of scale' all too often turn out to be a Panglossian version of the misguided philosophy of putting all your eggs in one basket. Comprehension and control of the workings of the organization become difficult at any point, even the highest, leading to waste and inefficiency due to duplication, delayed or distorted communication and the pursuit of contradictory aims by different departments. Errors of a relatively minor kind can be magnified on such a scale as to become major disasters. And so on. In recent years there have been serious grounds for questioning the very survival of national centralized systems of health and education, so patently inefficient, uncontrollable and costly have they become.

In the end the most important problem may well be that of keeping the commitment of the workforce of these large-scale organizations. The high degree of dissatisfaction and alienation caused by the rationalized technology and work organization of these institutions has been evident from a number of diverse expressions in recent years: absenteeism (causing in Britain a loss in working days more than thirty times that due to strikes), industrial sabotage, a preference for leisure and early retirement over higher income and promotion (significantly observed at managerial level), and, at the more extreme edges, a movement of 'deprofessionalization' and withdrawal (or radical re-commitment) on the part of a considerable number of professionals – doctors, architects, lawyers and social workers. The evidence from the top, as it were, underlines this impression. Schemes of job-enrichment and work-reorganization have become a common theme of discussion in managerial circles, reflecting the growing concern at the difficulties of keeping the loyalty and commitment of the workforce. It was not the workers but the management at Saab, Volvo and Philips who set on foot schemes involving a radical breaking-up of the assembly-line organization, and the creation of autonomous work units responsible for a diversity of tasks and the construction of more complete components; while the French government creates a post of Minister of Job Enrichment.

III

Only a fool would attempt to predict the outcome of the clash of tendencies currently observable in contemporary industrial societies. Industralism may – as I believe – be driving itself, and the societies subject to it, into an impasse.

But the fossils of numerous civilizations bear eloquent testimony against any view that holds this to be an improbable direction for society to take. Indeed if we were to take our guidance from history we would have every reason to expect the massive and settled routines of classic industrialism to negate the more recent, more fragmentary, opposing currents. In the short run, at least, they clearly have the predominant economic, political and cultural power; and in history as in politics it is usually the short run that counts.

As against this, one could argue that at least the alternatives have been posed; and they have been posed in a contemporary situation which daily and in a hundred manifest ways points up the relevance both of the critique of industrialism and of the alternatives posed. Critics of industrialism there have been since its very origins at the beginning of the nineteenth century. But however passionate the criticism, it has always had the problem that, to the majority of the population, the benefits of industrialism seemed to outweigh the costs. Set against the material scarcity of the past, above all, the industrial mode promised to lift societies above a material level virtually unchanged since the norm was established by the Neolithic Revolution more than 6,000 years ago.

It is this situation which has now changed and, I think, changed decisively. At the objective level, industrialism has run into the ground. For two centuries it has developed its institutions and technology on the basis of more or less unchanging expectations as to both the material resources and the political configuration of the world. Both these premises now are clearly revealed as shaky, and a most precarious basis on which to confront the future. The need now, as a matter of sheer survival, is to restructure those institutions and technologies to meet the new situation – and that simple way of putting it has to suppress the recognition of the truly formidable problems involved in this readjustment.

Some hope that this can be achieved in time comes from the subjective expression of dissatisfaction and dissent. For the first time in the history of industrialism large numbers of people of all classes are beginning to show signs that, on balance, they do not feel that the benefits of industrialism now outweigh the costs. Both as workers in the industrial and clerical bureaucracies, and as the consumers, clients, claimants and victims of those same bureaucracies, they are in their daily lives experiencing a sense of deep frustration with the routines to which they are subjected. In a variety of direct and local action movements over the past fifteen years they have given vent to some of that frustration, and have attempted to reconstruct and to take control of small, localized, aspects of their lives. This is hardly revolutionary, either in intention or in effect. But as the large-scale institutions continue to become more frustrating, costly, inefficient and brutal; as services deteriorate and taxation and public spending grows to meet the ever increasing need of 'patching up' the material and moral environment; so we might hope and expect these small seeds to grow.

NOTES

1 J. Schumpeter, *Capitalism, Socialism and Democracy* (London, Allen and Unwin, 1917), p. 139.
2 Ibid.
3 G. Steiner, 'The many faces of violence', *The Listener*, 9 October 1975, pp. 460–1.
4 E. Gellner, 'A social contract in search of an idiom', *The Political Quarterly*, 46 (1975), 127–52.
5 Ibid., p. 135.
6 Ibid., p. 134.
7 Ibid., p. 140.
8 For example, R. A. Nisbet: 'We live, and we should not forget it, in a late phase of the classical age of sociology. Strip from present-day sociology the perspectives and frameworks provided by men like Weber, and Durkheim, and little would be left but life-less heaps of data and stray hypotheses'. *The Sociological Tradition* (London, Heinemann, 1967), p. 5.
9 Ibid., p. 317.
10 D. Bell, *The Coming of Post-industrial Society* (New York, Basic Books, 1973).
11 A. Touraine, *The Post-industrial Society* (New York, Random House, 1971).
12 I have attempted a detailed examination of this version of the post-industrial idea in my 'Industrialism and post-industrialism: reflections on a putative transition', *Sociological Review*, 24 (1978), 430–78.
13 A. L. Harris, 'Pure capitalism and the disappearance of the middle class', *Journal of Political Economy*, June 1939, pp. 328–56.
14 S. M. Lipset, *Political Man* (London, Heinemann, 1960); C. Kerr, J. T. Dunlop, F. Harbison and C. A. Myers, *Industrialism and Industrial Man* (Cambridge, Mass., Harvard University Press, 1960); R. Aron, *The Industrial Society* (London, Weidenfeld and Nicolson, 1967); J. K. Galbraith, *The New Industrial State* (Harmondsworth, Penguin Books, 1967); D. Bell, *The End of Ideology* (New York, Collier Books, 1961).
15 E. P. Thompson, 'The peculiarities of the English', in R. Miliband and J. Saville (eds), *The Socialist Register* (London, The Merlin Press, 1965), pp. 311–62.
16 The Lord Chief Justice was Lord Hewart. His book, published in 1929, was called *The New Despotism* (London, Ernest Benn).
17 I. Illich, *Tools for Conviviality* (London, Calder and Boyars, 1973).
18 Ibid., p. 8.
19 See, for example, M. Bookchin, *Post-scarcity Anarchism* (Berkeley, Ca, The Ramparts Press, 1971); E. F. Schumacher, *Small is Beautiful* (London, Blond and Briggs, 1973); T. Roszak, *Where the Wasteland Ends: Politics and Transcendence in Post-industrial Society* (London, Faber and Faber, 1973); D. Dickson, *Alternative Technology and the Politics of Technical Change* (London, Fontana, 1974); E. Goodman, *A Study of Liberty and Revolution* (London, Duckworth, 1975).
20 For example, A. Toffler, *Future Shock* (New York, Random House, 1970).
21 H. Braverman, *Labor and Monopoly Capital: The Degradation of Work in the Twentieth Century* (New York, Monthly Review Press, 1974).

22 See, for example, I. Berg, *Education and Jobs: The Great Training Robbery* (Harmondsworth, Penguin Books, 1973).
23 G. Barraclough, 'The Great World Crisis', *New York Review of Books*, 23 January 1975, pp. 20–9.
24 Ibid., p. 21.

BIBLIOGRAPHICAL NOTE

Some of the ideas of this chapter are developed further in my *Prophecy and Progress: The Sociology of Industrial and Post-industrial Society* (Harmondsworth, Penguin Books, 1978; 3rd reprint, with a new Preface, 1986). For the rest, the most useful literature is that dealing with the broad sweep of modern industrial development and the social theory that has accompanied it. Two helpful surveys of that literature are Timothy Leggatt, *The Evolution of Industrial Systems: The Forking Paths* (London, Croom Helm, 1985); and Richard J. Badham, *Theories of Industrial Society* (New York, St Martin's Press, 1986). On actual structures and patterns of development, a solid and reliable introduction is Howard Davis and Richard Scase, *Western Capitalism and State Socialism* (Oxford, Basil Blackwell, 1985).

Daniel Bell, the most influential proponent of the post-industrial idea, has developed his thinking in *The Cultural Contradictions of Capitalism* (London, Heinemann, 1976) and *Sociological Journeys: Essays 1960–1980* (London, Heinemann, 1980). A powerful complement to this, especially strong on the historical side, is James R. Beniger, *The Control Revolution: Technological and Economic Origins of the Information Society* (Cambridge, Mass., Harvard University Press, 1986).

For the 'radical' post-industrialists, not just Illich and Schumacher but their 'Green' successors such as Rudolf Bahro and André Gorz, see Boris Frankel, *The Post-industrial Utopians* (Oxford, Polity Press, 1987).

See also the references and bibliographical notes to the other chapters in Part I of this volume, especially chapter 2 'Pre-capitalist and non-capitalist factors in the development of capitalism'.

4

The Industrializing and the 'Post-industrial' Worlds: on Development and Futurology

INTRODUCTION

The purpose of this chapter is not to predict the future relations between the 'developed' and the 'underdeveloped' societies. Less grandly, it is to consider some of the attempts that have been made in that direction, with a view to assessing their value for the sociology of development. For some years now, and especially during the past decade, a number of social scientists in all the major industrial countries of the world have been engaged in what many of them have been pleased to call 'the futurological enterprise'.[1] They have been attempting to discern the main structural outlines of future industrial society. They have conjectured, many of them, that industrial society is entering a new phase of its evolution, marking a transition as momentous as that which a hundred years ago took some European societies from an agrarian to an industrial social order. They have called this new society variously: the 'post-industrial society' (Daniel Bell), the 'post-modern era' (Amitai Etzioni), 'post-civilization' (Kenneth Boulding), 'post-economic society' (Herman Kahn), and – to vary the phrase a little – 'the knowledge society' (Peter Drucker), 'the technetronic era' (Zbigniew Brzezinski), and, more modestly, 'the service class society' (Ralf Dahrendorf).[2]

Very few of these theorists deal extensively or in detail with the likely framework of relationships between the 'post-industrial' and the industrializing worlds. Their focus, as with so much social theory in the past, is on the intrinsic mechanisms of societal change. Consequently their interest is in the new society in the making, as it expresses itself in the various stages of formation in the different industrial societies of the developed world. We are largely left to make our own inferences as to the probable impact of the new type of society on its environment, especially as that is constituted by other societies outside the 'post-industrial' pale. Perhaps this lack of curiosity reflects no more than the indifference commonly displayed by the strong to the weak. But it is obvious that the developing societies cannot respond with a similar indifference. The industrial societies only too promptly, massively and forcibly manifest themelves as an active presence in the environment of these other societies, who are constantly required to adjust to changes induced by the continuing evolution of their host societies.

Thus the sociology of development cannot ignore the work of the futurologists. If, as they declare, the industrial societies are moving into a radically new era, with different demands and requirements from the present, then the developing societies will equally radically be affected. The forces shaping their internal evolution will have taken on a new character. To be able to say anything about the direction of that evolution we shall need to know something about those new forces.

I

That development theorists and futurologists are strangers to one another appears all the more unjustified when we consider that development theory and futurology taken together constitute one of the best examples of convergence and complementarity in the history of social theory. They both, in their different spheres, re-establish the study of social change as the central preoccupation of their studies, following a period of over half a century of neglect of that topic.

One hardly need elaborate these days on the extent to which the heroic period of sociology was dominated by the awareness of social change. Saint-Simon, Comte and Spencer, Tocqueville and Marx, Weber and Durkheim all wrote and theorized under the overwhelming impression that a 'terrible beauty' was born. A new society, 'the industrial society', was in the making, fraught equally with hope and despair. Whether they were struck most by the process of industrialization, or democratization, or rationalization, and whether inspired with more hope or more gloom, the nineteenth-century sociologists conceived their task as the description and explanation of the great transformation taking place before their eyes. And however much they may have been concerned with re-establishing the bases of social order – as Robert Nisbet claims for the whole socological tradition[3] – it was an order seen as lying beyond and based on an acceptance of the current changes. Those changes had to be put in a systematic framework that gave them a past as well as a future.

Their sociologies were therefore pre-eminently evolutionary and developmental. To accomplish their task they had to do two things: they had to give an account both of the mechanisms of change, and of the directions of change. In both areas their accounts became the decisive source for the later conceptualizations of development theorists and futurologists. As to the mechanisms of change, they had recourse to a tradition of thinking as old as recorded Western thought itself. The 'conjectural histories' of the Greeks, the idea of 'the Great Chain of Being', the widespread use of the 'organic metaphor' relating the structure and functions of individual organisms to the structure and functions of society; later the idea of progress, the uniformitarian method in the new geology of the nineteenth century, and finally, a loosely held notion of biological evolution, all these, consciously or not, were compounded into a view of social change that has continued to exert an irresistible fascination for social theorists.[4]

In this conception, change is due essentially to forces intrinsic to the thing changing. Change is constant, cumulative and coherent. It takes the form of evolution by stages, each stage arising out of the preceding one, and, in its turn, being pregnant with the next, and each expressing a 'higher', more developed and more complicated state of the system. Thankfully, not many theorists allowed themselves to be committed to all the implications of this view. In particular, they were interested in only a relatively small number of the stages of social evolution, and especially those that seemed to have been the recent antecedents of their own novel stage. Hence the many dichotomously expressed evolutionary stages: from *gemeinschaft* to *gesellschaft*, 'status' to 'contract', 'folk' to 'urban' etc. But the underlying mechanisms of change still remained the basically organic ones of growth, differentiation and maturation.

As to the directions of change, the nineteenth-century sociologies offered us broadly the 'convergence' thesis: that under the impact of industrialism all societies were moving towards one basic type, 'the industrial society'. Even where, as with Marx, it was felt that the new order had not yet reached its final, stable, form – that was to be the accomplishment of socialism – it was still considered that the destiny of all societies was to tread the path mapped out by the industrial nations, and to incorporate their institutions and culture as a necessary stage in their evolution. As Marx put it in the Preface to the first edition of *Capital*: 'The country that is more developed industrially only shows, to the less developed, the image of its own future.'

Sometime near the beginning of the twentieth century, social change ceased to be the chief preoccupation of social theory. The reasons were many, and cannot be gone into here.[5] At the purely theoretical level, historians and anthropologists attacked the evolutionist character of social change theory as providing bad history and inadequate conceptualizations of the movement from one state of society to another.[6] The weaknesses of evolutionary social thought were traced, by Malinowski and Radcliffe-Brown, to an insufficient concern for how, at any given time, a society actually worked and maintained itself in being. As Radcliffe-Brown put it, 'we cannot successfully embark on the study of how culture changes until we have made at least some progress in determining what culture really is and how it works.'[7] The functionalist approach in sociology and social anthropology was one of the consequences of this view.

But of course the functionalists did not abandon a view of social change. They merely put the topic in cold storage for a time. In fact, their concepts overlapped heavily with some characteristic assumptions of the evolutionists.[8] Their approach represented a sort of 'frozen evolutionism'. Herbert Spencer, after all, had combined a thorough-going evolutionism with a thorough-going functionalism. When the thaw came, and functionalists turned their attention to large-scale problems of historical and societal change, it should not have surprised anybody to find that they reverted almost without modification to the basic form of nineteenth-century evolutionism.[9]

The important point is that no serious revision was made of the classic sociological conception of social change. In the first half of this century the systematic study of social change was left to the philosophers of history, to the Spenglers, Sorokins and Toynbees. Their approaches, for good or bad, did not impinge much on the sociological consciousness.[10] When, therefore, the anti-colonial movements of the post-Second World War era brought into being a host of new states, and the problem of the future development of these societies became too pressing for sociologists to ignore questions of social change, social theory had to fall back on its evolutionary past.

The sociology of development, as it grew from the early 1950s, did represent a return to some of the characteristic concerns of the 'founding fathers', and that, I hold, is something to be welcomed. But the sons imitated their fathers in ways far too automatic and uncritical for the attempts to be reassuring.[11] There was the invoking of the old notion of stages of evolution, with the assumption of each 'undeveloped' society as an enclosed, self-contained entity, propelled upwards through the various stages of growth by some entelechy called 'the will to be modern'. The stages of the earlier evolutionists were bundled together into the two polar types, 'traditional' and 'modern' (or 'undeveloped' and 'developed'), and the process of development or modernization conceived as the movement from the first to the second. Furthermore, there was little doubt from where the model for the ideal-typical modern society came. It was the industrialized, democratized, bureaucratized and rationalized society seen by the earlier sociologists as the ideal-typical 'industrial society', and now almost naturally identified with Anglo-American society of the 1950s.[12]

The resurgence of interest in social change did not, interestingly enough, extend to the societies of the industrial world. Quite the contrary – there seemed, in the social science view of those societies, quite simply the belief that all important structural change had come to an end there. These, the 1950s, were the halcyon days of the 'end of ideology' thesis. Industrial society appeared to have come of age, to have matured with remarkable fidelity along the main lines outlined by the nineteenth-century sociologists. Even the spectre of the unpleasant shuffle at the end, predicted by Marx in the form of the socialist revolution, had ceased its haunting. The conflicts bred of inequality had largely been resolved, and without the need of recourse to revolution. All the industrial societies, of both East and West, had evolved into rational, 'managed' societies, and in doing so had 'got over the hump'. No further major institutional changes should be required in the process of applying the fruits of steady economic growth and a rapidly expanding technology to clear up the marginal pockets of poverty and deprivation.[13]

Views of this sort are still seriously held, of course. But enough happened in the 1960s, in all industrial societies, to shake the firm belief in the consensus, and the view that the industrial societies had resolved all their outstanding problems. The result was a renewal of interest in the future of industrial society: the project known as futurology. Certainly it has not been as widespread an enterprise as the sociology of development, nor so coherent, nor so academically respectable, but it parallels it in some striking respects. It is markedly interdisciplinary in character: more so, perhaps, in that it involves a large number of natural as well as social scientists.[14] It is global in its tendency, both with regard to its field of study and to the organizations involved in that study.[15] More significantly, it has picked up nineteenth-century social change theory in its almost pristine form. Like development theory, futurology was stimulated into existence by pressing developments in the real world. Like development theory, futurology, in casting around for a suitable conceptualization of large-scale societal change, found only the evolutionary schemes of the past to hand and, in some cases, quite consciously adopted these for its own purposes.

In doing so, the futurologists have recommenced the characteristic task and pattern of nineteenth-century sociology. We might call their position the 're-convergence' thesis. They accept that the nineteenth-century scheme in its strict form will no longer do. 'Industrial Society' as it has been known hitherto cannot be taken as the fulfilment and final end of social evolution; but all one has to do is to add another stage to the sequence. The old story is given a new chapter with a new ending, rather as Marx had tried to do, and after him, James Burnham. But formally the pattern remains the same. The present is once more seen as transitional, as metamorphosis: not now from feudal agrarianism to industrialism, but from the industrial society to the 'post-industrial society'. The driving-force of this transformation is also of the same character as in the past. It is technology, 'the great, growling engine of change' as futurologist Alvin Toffler puts it.[16] Instead of the power loom, the steam engine and the railway, we have computers and the electronic media of communications. The futurological enterprise is frankly Saint-Simonian, and a comment by Edward Shils on what he calls 'the generously stimulating tyranny of our classics' seems apposite here:

One of the great difficulties is that we cannot imagine anything beyond variation on the theme set by the great figures of nineteenth- and twentieth-century sociology. The fact that the conception of 'post-industrial society' is an amalgam of what Saint-Simon, Comte, de Tocqueville and Weber furnished to our imagination is evidence that we are confined to an ambiguously defined circle which is more impermeable than it ought to be.[17]

Shils's remark points to one of the main problems associated with the 'post-industrial' idea: the problem of conceptualizing novelty in the terms, and with the basic schema, of nineteenth-century evolutionary social theory. Nevertheless, proponents of the 'post-industrial' thesis are making a number of assertions about current social changes that need to be taken very seriously. Development theorists, in particular, need to examine them because, if true, they have profound implications for strategies of development. I turn now, therefore, to the lineaments of the 'post-industrial' society and its possible consequences for other types of society. As I have remarked before, the futurological literature is particularly thin in treating the issue of the future relations between the industrial and the industrializing societies.[18] Briefly put, the tendency is to think of the future of the industrial societies with optimism, sometimes positively with euphoria, and to be pessimistic about developments in the non-industrial world. We are left largely to infer for ourselves future transactions between these two worlds. But one student at least, Johan Galtung, has applied himself systematically to this issue. In what follows, I have found it convenient to employ Galtung's framework for considering the future of the international system,[19] bringing in other authors and materials by way of elaboration, confirmation and assessment.

II

Galtung distinguishes four societal forms: the primitive, the traditional, the modern and the neo-modern (the last also called the post-industrial) (see table 4.1). Following in the Fisher–Clark–Fourastié tradition, these distinctions are based on the factors of agricultural productivity – i.e. the number of families one family doing farming can feed – and the general distribution of the population in primary (mainly agricultural), secondary (manufacturing or industrial) and tertiary (services) sectors. Behind these, in turn, are the variables that have to do with technology, particularly the technology of production and of communication – the latter added to Marx's emphasis on 'means of production' as a factor of primary importance.

Our concern at the moment is with the neo-modern or post-industrial form. Galtung, along with Kahn and Wiener, Brzezinski, Bell and others, argues that some industrial societies are already clearly in the process of being transformed into the predominantly post-industrial type. The sort of evidence presented to back up this assertion varies a good deal; but the most systematic account has been given by Bell, whose pre-eminence in the elaboration of the post-industrial concept is, in any case, generally acknowledged. Bell identifies five dimensions of the evolving post-industrial society.[20]

1 Economic sector: the shift from a goods-producing to a service society

Colin Clark himself had argued, in *The Conditions of Economic Progress*, that there was a trajectory along which every nation would pass, once it became industrialized, whereby, because of the sectoral differences in productivity and the demand for health, recreation and the like as national incomes increased, the greater proportion of the labour force would inevitably move to the service sector. The first dimension of the post-industrial society is that the majority of the labour force is no longer engaged in agriculture or manufacturing but in services, which are defined residually as trade, finance, transport, health, recreation, research, education and government. This shift, it is generally accepted, is occurring in all the industrial societies. The United States is the only one yet to have actually made it: at some point in the 1950s the United States became the first 'service economy' – 'that is, it became the first nation in which more than half of the employed population was not involved in the production of food, clothing, houses, automobiles, or other tangible goods'.[21]

Table 4.1 Stages of socioeconomic development

Term for the stage	Primitive (P)	Traditional (T)	Modern (M)	Neo-modern (N)
Economic sectors Nature of stratification	Primary	Primary [High / Low] Tertiary	Pri-mary / Sec-on-dary / Terti-ary [High / Middle / Low]	Tertiary [Post-tertiary education / Tertiary education / Secondary education / Primary education]
Term for the transition	Urban revolution	Industrial revolution	Automation revolution	
Population profiles				
Primary sector	100 90	80 75	50 20	5 0
Secondary sector	0 5	5 10	20 30	5 0
Tertiary sector	0 5	15 15	30 50	90 100
Agricultural productivity	1:1 and less	1:1.25 1:1.33	1:2 1:5	1:20 and higher
GNP/capita	Up to $50	$50–$600	$600–$4,000	$4,000 and above
Communication Goods, persons	Walking, running rowing	Animals, wheels sailing	Steam engine Combustion engine	Jet rockets
Information	Eye and ear	Dispatches	Post, telegraph, telephone	Tele-satellite
Economic system	Subsistence economy	Barter economy	Money economy	Credit economy
Domain	Group, clan, tribe	Village, city-state	Nation-state	Region, world state
Magnitude	$10^0–10^2$	$10^2–10^5$	$10^5–10^8$	$10^8–10^{10}$

Source: R. Jungk and J. Galtung (eds), *Mankind 2000* (London, Allen and Unwin, 1969), p. 16. Reproduced with the permission of the publishers.

The service sector there already accounts for more than half the gross national product. By 1975 it is expected to absorb about 60 per cent of the employed population. The evidence from other industrial countries suggests that they too are moving speedily in that direction.[22]

2 Occupational slope: the predominance of the professional and technical class

While the overall growth and predominance of the service sector in the post-industrial economy is important, even more significant is the differential rate of growth of the various occupational groups within the service sector. The fact is that the growth in professional and technical employment has been at a rate twice that of the average. For the United States, in 1940 there were 3.9 million such employees in the society; by 1964 the number had risen to 8.6 million; and it is estimated that by 1975 there will be 13.2 million professional and technical persons, making it the second largest of the eight occupational divisions of the country, exceeded only by the semi-skilled workers. Moreover, within that category of professional and technical employees, a particular group – the scientists and engineers – have been developing even faster. While the growth rate of the professional class as a whole is twice that of the average labour-force rate, the growth rate of the scientists and engineeers is triple that of the working population as a whole.[23]

The distinctiveness of this specialized trend has prompted some students to distinguish between a more narrowly defined tertiary sector and a 'quaternary' sector, and to suggest that the more noteworthy phenomenon in the transition to the post-industrial society is the rapid expansion of the quarternary sector.[24] The tertiary sector is restricted to the area of the classic services, common enough in the capital cities of pre-industrial societies – commerce, financial services, administrative departments. Expansion in this sector seems to be a preliminary phase to a more fundamental phase of expansion of the quarternary sector; indeed, according to the old law of 'the privilege of backwardness' it may be possible for the phase of service expansion to be severely abbreviated or truncated, using the already existing innovations and technology of 'leader' societies. It has been noted that the curve of the explosive expansion of the service sector in the United States is already flattening out, under the impact of better use of management systems and cybernation; while, for instance in Sweden, commerce, finance and clerical occupations account for a much smaller proportion of the overall service sector than in the United States, and a relatively larger share is taken by welfare, health, education and cultural services. Moreover, the share of the routine white-collar services is beginning to shrink more rapidly than in the United States. Thus the key occupational category of the post-industrial society would comprise two main 'quaternary' groups: one concerned with science, research and development, the other with the area of 'human welfare', especially education and cultural services, the health services, social welfare and recreation.[25]

3 Technology: the rise of a new 'intellectual technology'

4 Pattern of change: self-sustaining technical growth
5 Axial principle: the centrality of theoretical knowledge

These three dimensions of the post-industrial society are really all aspects of the final one. The post-industrial society is organized around knowledge, or rather, around a special type of knowledge, since knowledge has been necessary for the existence of any society. 'What has now become decisive for society,' writes Bell, 'is the new centrality of *theoretical* knowledge, the primacy of theory over empiricism, and the codification of knowledge into abstract systems of symbols that can be translated into many different and varied circumstances. Every society now lives by innovation and growth; and it is theoretical knowledge that has become the matrix of innovation.'[26] One can see this in the changing relations of science and technology, for instance. In the nineteenth and early twentieth centuries, the great inventions and the industries that derived from them – steel, electric light, telegraph, telephone, automobile – were the work of inspired and talented tinkerers, many of whom were indifferent to the fundamental laws which underlay their inventions. But if we look at an industry such as chemistry – which has good claims to be considered the first of the 'modern', post-industrial type industries – we find a case where the inventions were based on theoretical knowledge of the properties of macromolecules, which were 'manipulated' to achieve the planned production of new materials. We have here an example of what Radovan Richta has called 'a law of higher priority' in the evolution of the productive forces in the post-industrial era: 'the precedence of science over technology, and of technology over industry'.[27]

Similarly, the development of macroeconomic theory makes it possible for governments, by direct planning, monetary or fiscal policy, to seek economic growth, to redirect the allocation of resources and to maintain balance between different sectors. More generally, the growing sophistication of computer-based simulation procedures – simulations of economic systems, of social behaviour, of decision problems – allows, for the first time, the possibility of large-scale 'controlled experiments' in the social sciences. These, in turn, will allow us to plot 'alternative futures', thereby greatly increasing the extent of our choice and the ability to control matters affecting our lives. All such applications of theory are seen as resulting from the rise of the new 'intellectual technology' – constituted by such techniques as linear programming, systems analysis, information theory, decision theory, games and simulation which, when linked to the computer, allow us to accumulate and manipulate large aggregates of data of a differentiated kind so as to have more complete knowledge of social and economic matters. Such a technology, Bell suggests, 'may by the end of the twentieth century be as decisive in human affairs as the machine technology has been for the past century and a half'.[28] Taken altogether, finally, these developments are making possible continuous, planned technical innovation: partly through the systematic linking of science and technology through the institutionalization of research and development sections in private and public organizations, and partly through the new techniques of technological forecasting, which lay out the future areas of development, and allow industry, or society, to plan ahead systematically in terms of capital possibilities, needs and products. Technical growth in the post-industrial society is therefore self-sustaining.

We may note, in passing, what is considered to be the dominant group and the dominant institutions of this evolving post-industrial society. Bell writes: 'If the dominant figures of the past hundred years have been the entrepreneur, the businessman and the industrial executive, the "new men" are the scientists, the mathematicians, the economists, and the engineers of the new computer technology.' And the dominant institutions will be the institutions they inhabit, in their roles as seekers, elaborators and codifiers of the theoretical knowledge that is the ganglion of the social system of the future: such institutions as universities, research corporations, industrial laboratories and experimental stations. As Bell, again, puts it, no doubt with much satisfaction: 'Perhaps it is not too much to say that if the business firm was the key institution of the past 100 years, because of its role in organizing production for the mass creation of products, the university will become the central institution of the next 100 years because of its role as the new source of innovation and knowledge.'[29] 'Not only the best talents, but eventually the entire complex of social prestige and social status, will be rooted in the intellectual and scientific communities.'[30] Relationships with other groups, especially the politicians, are likely to be problematic, but there seems little doubt about which way the lines of influence will run. The making of decisions, whether to do with business production in the private sector or political goals in the public sector, 'will have an increasingly technical character', shaped and constrained by the 'information' supplied by the masters of the new intellectual technology. The dream of Saint-Simon, of an industrial order ruled in rational, positivist fashion by a 'natural elite' of technocrats, seems at last to be on the point of fulfilment – not, it is true, in the industrial society, but in the 'post-industrial' society.

III

It is in these terms that the future of most current industrial societies is being spelled out. Only the United States is held by anyone to have travelled to any significant extent along the road to post-industrial status. Other industrial societies exhibit aspects of it with varying degrees of clarity, just as they also contain various aspects of 'pre-industrial' life and culture. (Japan is perhaps the best example of the hybrid made out of the simple threefold typology, 'pre-industrial', 'industrial', 'post-industrial'.) But, just as Marx thought that nineteenth-century England showed to less-developed societies the image of their future, so the United States is seen as mapping out the path of development of the industrial societies.

I have followed Bell in specifying only the most novel and, in a sense, pivotal features of the new society in the making. To be more comprehensive, I should have included some account of other, more familiar, trends: continuing urbanization, leading perhaps to the growth of 'megalopolises' ('Boswash',

'Chipitts', 'Sansan' in the United States, for instance); continuing increase in affluence and leisure, with continuing uneven distribution of both; continuing secularization and 'rationalization' in all areas of cultural and moral life. These trends which Kahn and Wiener identify as the 'Basic Long Term Multifold Trend' of Western civilization[31] – are continuities – expansions and intensifications – of processes which brought about the first set of industrial societies in the West; whereas there is a real sense in which the changes selected by Bell express fundamental discontinuities with the earlier processes of industrialization.

This is not the place to attempt a detailed critique of the post-industrial idea.[32] It is, as I have already suggested, basically utopian in conception, closely akin to the industrial utopias of St Simon and Fourier. It is grounded in the belief in the primacy of technology and administration, and hence disdains the autonomous claims of politics. It does not ask what might be the private interests or the political ideologies of the technocratic group it singles out as the emergent elite: such a group is regarded as the neutral and disinterested servant of the new order. More concretely, it takes the fact of an increase in the number of scientists *in* government and industry as an expression of the influence of science *on* government and industry: a dubious inference even were there not such ready examples as Concorde, or the siting of the third airport in Britain, to create suspicion. It may even be the case, as suggested in different ways by Jean Floud and Noam Chomsky, that the features of American society picked out by Bell as indications of an emerging post-industrial society may be no more than the expressions of the abnormal growth forced upon the United States by its massive military commitments.[33] At any rate, so long as politics within and between nations continues, as still seems true, to be dominated by the struggle for power between competing interests, we might fairly expect the next thirty years to be more rather than less like the previous thirty years of this century – only, as it were, writ large.

But it is perfectly possible to be sceptical about the claims for the emergence of a new form of society while remaining impressed by the importance of the trends identified by Bell and company. So far as the 'Third World' is concerned, the effects of these trends are not diminished by their being refused the title 'post-industrial', and the Third World has reason to be concerned about those trends, for they are not reassuring (when, for the Third World, have trends ever been?). Summarily, they point to an increasingly integrated and increasingly autonomous industrial and post-industrial sector of the globe, more or less able to determine its future irrespective of the wishes or requirements of the non-industrial world. Conversely, for the Third World they indicate a situation analogous in many respects to that of the American blacks within American society: that is, of a population desperate but dispensable, in an economic sense. If the future promises the industrial societies the self-sustaining, self-sufficient economy of post-industrial civilization, it seems to condemn the Third World to the limbo of 'global ghetto-ization'.[34]

This stark divergence is not the only possibility nor, of course, is it inevitable. It is simply a strong possibility if we extrapolate from current trends, and if nobody does anything about them. To consider these trends in the context of the broader international system, and the varying responses that might be expected to them, we can return now to Galtung's framework.[35] Having distinguished the four societal forms – primitive, traditional, modern and neo-modern or post-industrial (see table 4.1, above) – Galtung adds two assumptions for the purposes of analysing changes in the world system of states. The first is the assumption of development – that primitive societies tend to develop into traditional ones, traditional into modern and modern into neo-modern (although the development may take place in jumps and, while not necessarily linear, is more linear and more rapid the higher the level of communication between societies at different levels of development). The second assumption is that of the nation-state as a general pattern – that the surface of the world is divided into generally contiguous territories called nation-states, and that some nation-states are composed of societies at various levels of development, and thus have dual or triple economies; others may coincide with one social order at a particular level of development; and still others are segments within one society comprising more nation-states.[36]

These two assumptions lead, says Galtung, to 'what we see as the basic structural condition for change in the international, or global, system: the consequences of the incompatibilities between state and society, between the nation-state and the social orders it contains or is contained in'.[37]

Furthermore, it is not just any nation-state that has become the norm of the international system: it is a nation-state formed in principle according to the model of nations that are societies at the level of development characterized as 'modern'. In order that interaction between nations can take place, certain uniformities of structure come to be impressed upon them. In particular, as Galtung points out,

they have to be organized in a relatively equal manner at the top to respond to at least some of the demands made by international interaction, to participate in the international game. This will facilitate the emergence of modern and even neomodern segments at the top of many nations, which in turn has the consequence that the 'internal development distance' between the least and most developed segments is higher, the less developed the nation is . . . making the less developed nations less cohesive.[38]

Since all nations have to have at least some modern segment, and since all nations contain at least some segments at different levels of societal development, the typology of four types of society can be translated into two types of nation-states. There is type PTM which has primitive, traditional and modern segments, and hence is *less developed*; and type TMN, which has traditional, modern and neo-modern segments, and hence is *more developed*. (Using such indices as the percentage not working in the primary sector, which also correlates highly with per capita GNP, this distinction corresponds essentially to the familiar division between rich and poor, developing and developed nations.)

We can consider now the trends in the 'more developed' and the 'less developed' worlds, and the likely future interaction between them. Characteristic of the more developed world, says Galtung, is the manner in which societies with increasing development are *growing out* of their nation-states 'which even become like strait jackets for them'. This pattern follows basically from the post-industrial development surveyed earlier. For an increasing fraction of the nation, especially those employed in the quaternary sector, the nation-state becomes perceived as being of decreasing relevance. Their typical cast of skills, education, culture and political ideology militates against national identification. When we consider the key occupational groups of the post-industrial sector – the educationists, teachers and students; the specialists in health, welfare and recreation; the professionals of the communications industry; the experts in world welfare (Galtung predicts particularly rapid increases in 'international peace specialists' and 'international development engineers'); above all, the scientists, mathematicians, economists and engineers of the new computer technology – it is clear that these are the groups that are least likely to find the nation-state a satisfactory arena for their activities. As professionals of a particular kind, they will share more in terms of interests, values and lifestyles with similar professions in other countries than with other groups in their own.[39] To a degree never before attained, their skills will be 'universalistic', valid in all post-industrial segments in any country. Finally, the fact that these groups belong to the 'top' of the nation, located in its most advanced and creative areas, means that their influence will offset the nationalism of other groups whose interests still call for a national identification.

The post-industrial groups will, therefore, look for forms of non-national identification: although, for some time to come, the limits to their internationalism may well be set by the area of the more developed world. Evidence for this trend comes at a number of levels. At the lowest level there is the rapid growth of the multinational business corporation, with a 16 per cent growth rate, and, as Peter Drucker has stressed, increasingly multinational in its management personnel and in its scientific and technological foundations.[40] Next comes the growth of the non-profit international non-governmental organizations (INGOs), which, at present, number about 1,600 and have a growth rate of about 10 per cent. Examples of these are the international professional organizations, international political/ideological movements, such as the anti-Vietnam war movement, and international age-set movements, created by the rapidly increasing conflict between the generations in the post-industrial society (due to obsolescence of skills, rapid rate of social change). Finally, there is the growth of the international governmental organizations (IGOs), of which there are about 600 at present, 'with a very high growth rate'. Examples of these are the economic IGOs, such as the EEC, co-production schemes, military alliances and various institutions of the United Nations.[41]

It would be easy to overstate, and to idealize, the internationalism of these developments. There is a strong whiff of the international jet-set in the accounts given by Galtung and others; and the 'internationalism' of development experts and 'international peace specialists' seems closer to David Frost than to the average professional of the 'post-industrial' sector. Moreover, it should not be unexpected if calculations of national self-interest, however misguided, continue to interrupt the process of integration among the developed nations. De Gaulle may have been archaic, but no sociological law seems to prevent political atavisms. Nevertheless, it does not seem unrealistic to interpret the evidence as pointing to a growing interpenetration of the advanced industrial nations; although it is an internationalism of a self-interested, military-industrial type, rather than of the more disinterested UN type.[42] Conversely, we should note the tendency for the more developed world to become not merely integrated and inclusive, but autonomous and exclusive. The corollary of the growing attraction of the industrial nations for each other is their repulsion of the non-industrial Third World.

This would follow from the long-term projection of some familar trends. First is the changing pattern of world trade. As Andrew Shonfield has said, 'the most notorious divergence from the historic norm is the vast increase in trade between advanced industrial countries selling each other manufactured goods.'[43] For more than half a century the greater part of the increase in the sales of capital goods was taken up in trade between the industrial and the non-industrial countries. In the early 1950s there first occurred a reversal of this pattern. Primary products (food, fuel and raw materials) which accounted for 54 per cent of world trade in 1953–4 had fallen to 42 per cent in 1965–6, only a dozen years later. Moreover, *within* the total trade of primary products, the Third World's share has fallen from 45 to 40 per cent. The counterpart of this has been the dramatic expansion of trade in manufactures between industrial countries. As Dudley Seers says, 'even in the short period from 1953 to 1969, world trade has become predominantly trade between rich countries. In these sixteen years, internal trade within the bloc of rich countries quadrupled, while trade between rich countries and poor doubled.'[44] There seems no good reason to expect an interruption of this trend and, given the developments within the industrial nations already noted, we may well expect an intensification of them.

The changed patterns of trade have been made possible through the industrial societies' improved techniques in manufacturing and agriculture (which have meant an increasing economy in the use of raw materials), and the substitution of synthetics for many natural products. Kenneth Boulding has put the position as follows:

One by-product of the technological revolution is a diminution in the bargaining power of the poor countries as against the rich. The whole impact of technology in these days is towards self-sufficiency of smaller areas. There is a tremendous increase in the number of substitutes for practically everything. The only economic bargaining power which the tropical belt possesses in relation to the developed temperate countries lies in its ability to withhold supplies of tropical products. These, however, seem to be becoming less and less essential to the economic systems of the temperate zone. We now have synthetic rubber, synthetic camphor; synthetic coffee and cocoa may be just around the corner, and the tropical belt may be left with very little in the way of comparative advantage.[45]

The industrial societies, comments Boulding, have learnt the lesson that 'the highest pay-offs in these days come from staying home and minding one's own business successfully.'[46] This results not so much from exasperation at the unbusinesslike ways of foreigners, nor of a late conversion to Cobdenism, but from an awareness of the changed environment for economic activities in the industrial world. The Third World is, quite simply, becoming less relevant to those activities. In an economic sense, it is becoming dispensable, something to be cast away once its riches have been plundered and its cultures smashed, like a child throwing away a ruined toy. As the industrial societies take on increasingly post-industrial features, their characteristic interests, concerns and problems will make them even more decisively inward-looking. Their demands will be framed in the context of the tertiary and quaternary sectors, not that of manufacturing. Their focus will be on personal services, education, science policy, leisure; their problems will be pollution, noise, crowding, bureaucracy. In none of these things will the Third World seem relevant – except perhaps as an area for tourism, or for the siting of some of the more polluting industries of the industrial world.[47]

This development throws some doubt on some of the more firmly held beliefs about the relationship between the industrial and the non-industrial world, especially traditional Marxist beliefs. The Marxist category for exploring that relationship has generally been one of exploitation. The Third World was 'underdeveloped' by Western capitalism, its economy and social structure distorted and stunted to provide cheap raw materials for Western industry, and to create a market for Western industrial products. This seems a fair account of what happened in the past.[48] It will not, however, help us to understand the future. The industrial societies of today, and *a fortiori* those of tomorrow, are not those of Marx's day, or even of Lenin's and Luxemburg's day. The chain of exploitation linking exploiters and exploited seems in the process of dissolution, and this largely through the voluntary actions of the beneficiaries under the original scheme of exploitation. Peter Worsley has commented, in this connection, on the attempt to draw Marxist parallels along the lines of 'proletarian' and 'millionaire-capitalist' nations, and to predict a Marxist-style overthrow of the latter by the former. As he says, 'the problem for these "proletarians", increasingly, is that the "millionaires" are less and less interested in exploiting them. Today's "super-profits" are being made in Western Europe, not the Third World.'[49]

We should note, finally, certain other possible developments that would strengthen the tendency towards the creation of a future global system marked by vast 'ghetto' areas (Third World nations), which are less and less capable of affecting the activities of the rich, powerful and increasingly autonomous post-industrial area. Aid and intervention in underdeveloped societies have been to a considerable extent an incident of the Cold War. The relaxation of that war, taken with the other changes already noted, may make that involvement both less necessary and less attractive. The political instability of many areas of the Third World makes foreign investment precarious, and so may discourage involvement of the purely profit-making sort. The prospect may then be that feared by the Algerian delegate to the UN Economic and Social Council, when he commented at its Geneva meeting in 1966: 'Even as the détente in the Cold War has permitted an attenuation of the conflict between blocs with different social systems, one must fear that the East–West opposition will revolve on its axis and become an antagonism of North against South.[50] Boulding, along with many others, has expressed the same apprehension: 'Perhaps one of the greatest dangers we face today, assuming that the East–West relationship can be solved and that the Cold War is put in permanent cold storage, is that the developed nations will form in effect an alliance against the underdeveloped against which the poor countries of the tropical belt will be powerless for many generations to come.'[51]

IV

The less developed world, although it could well be ignored by the more developed, cannot but be affected by it. Just as in the earlier process of industrialization the progress of some societies acted to constrain, retard or distort the development of others, so as the rich societies move into a newer phase of their evolution will they continue to have an impact on the rest of the world, athough their sins may now be those of omission rather than of commission. The international system imposes some measure of interaction on all nations. At the same time it is strongly hierarchical in structure, in a form that Galtung has termed 'feudal'.[52] That is to say, there is a high degree of interaction at the top (between the wealthy and powerful TMN nations), a lesser degree between top and bottom (the less-developed PTM nations). The future of the less-developed world turns to a considerable extent on the implications of that structure. Since the relevant features are very well known to developmentalists and many others, I shall review trends in the less-developed world only briefly, and mainly as a corollary of the changes in the industrial nations.

Galtung suggests that characteristic of the less developed world is the manner in which the societies are *growing into* their nation-states, at the same time as societies of the more-developed world are growing out of theirs. The use of the comforting organic metaphor, which is consistent with the apolitical evolutionism of most futurology, disguises the fact that societies of the Third World are being beaten, battered and bludgeoned into nationhood (as, at the very least, any Kurd or Biafran knows). Moreover these are, and are likely to continue to be, nations marked by a high degree of incohesiveness and unbalanced development, as compared with the past of Western nations. These features are strengthened by the fact that the 'leader' societies in the global system, as they go their own way, continue to cast their long and baleful shadow.

First, it is likely that the problem of the 'dual economies' of the less-developed world will get worse. We might, by the end of the century, reach a situation of massive unevenness: the large cities exhibiting many features of post-industrial society, borrowed from the post-industrial world, with a trend towards tertiary and quaternary occupations; while the rest of society, especially the rural areas, will be slowly moving out of what Kahn and Wiener call 'modified sixteenth century' – modified by the addition of the bulldozer, electric lights, the transistor radio etc. The 'over-development' in the cities, particularly as regards the impact of automation and cybernation, will produce post-industrial style problems (e.g. the displacement of large numbers of routine white collar bureaucrats), but will be exacerbated by the lower level of development of the society as a whole.

Next, we can expect an intensified feeling of frustration and resentment on the part of certain key groups, as a result of the revolutionizing of the 'subjective environment' of the Third World, mainly through the rapid spread of education and communications. As Brzezinski has put it:

In a world electronically intermeshed, absolute or relative underdevelopment will be intolerable, especially as the more advanced countries begin to move beyond that industrial era into which the less developed countries have as yet to enter. It is thus no longer a matter of the 'revolution of rising expections'. The Third World today confronts the spectre of insatiable aspirations.[53]

This, again, will strengthen other familiar tendencies. There will be more dissatisfied graduates and other trained personnel, unable to find work compatible with their expanded expectations. There will, more significantly, be the deepening phenomenon of the formation of alienated elites in Third World societies. 'Foreigners at home, foreigners abroad' – as Alexander Herzen described a much earlier Westernized elite in nineteenth-century Russia – they will have been socialized into the culture, life-styles and aspirations of the ruling classes of the industrial and increasingly post-industrial societies. Their tendency will be to emigrate, either vicariously, into the 'post-industrial enclaves' of the developed parts of their society, or directly, in pursuit of a variety of political, economic, cultural, or scientific values which they feel they can satisfy only in the metropolises of the industrial world.[54]

While there is this movement from the top of the less-developed (PTM) nations to the more developed (TMN) ones, at the same time there is the movement from the bottom levels of the PTM nations, whereby cheap labour is shunted into the lower echelons of the TMN society (as unskilled labourers, domestic servants etc.) left empty by the general upward mobility in these societies. In both these transactions the PTM nations may gain something, but they are clearly losing in terms of national cohesion, potential for future growth and autonomy in relation to the TMN nations. The PTM nations may respond by trying to put collective pressure on the TMN nations: by selling their cheap labour at a higher price, requiring many and very cheap experts in return for brain drainage etc. But clearly their success in pursuing this strategy will depend on how far the TMN nations need this type of resource from the less-developed world; and the indications are that they do not. As Herman Kahn has said of the brain-drain and foreign labour phenomenon in the United States: 'This does not mean, as the Europeans think, that the United States is depending on this importation, but it does mean that we are benefiting; we are getting a subsidy from the rest of the world. This is a subsidy that is not too important to us.'[55]

The third main trend to note is the continuing low level of interaction between nations of the less-developed world. This follows directly from the feudal structure of the international system. All the indicators of international interaction, from plane flights to the volume or value of trade, confirm the feudal hypothesis, and point to the pattern whereby PTM nations are much more closely linked to particular TMN nations or groups of nations than to other PTM nations.[56] The factors creating this vertical system of dependency are obvious, stemming from the economic specialization first imposed during the colonial period; but recognizing them has proved much easier than changing them. It is indeed in this area that change seems most possible, as well as most desirable. Meanwhile, however, given the low level of solidarity between PTM nations, these nations are sitting ducks, to be taken 'one at a time' by the TMN nations. The more-developed nations are greatly helped here by their high level of both internal and external cohesion. This will lead to a rapid growth in the tendency to deal with the less-developed nations collectively, not necessarily through the UN, but typically through the EEC, the OECD, NATO, etc. Some of this dealing no doubt will have a benevolent purpose. But on current showing the developed nations will use aid and investment programmes primarily to tie individual PTM nations to themselves, in the form of clientage, often for military purposes, or for votes at the UN, etc. An alternative possibility, given the inward-turning tendencies in the developed world already noted, would be for the TMN nations to use their collective organizations to fend off the Third World, as dispensable and a nuisance. In either case the amount of leverage possessed by the Third World is very slight.

Finally we can turn to a consideration of the projections of overall economic growth in the Third World nations. Kahn and Wiener, using a fivefold typology of industrial development in terms of levels of per capita income (this overlaps heavily with Galtung's typology – see table 4.1), present a forecast of the levels achieved by the various societies of the world in the year 2000 (see table 4.2). Summarizing their 'scenario' which they describe as 'on the whole, optimistic', they say:

the year 2000 will find a rather large island of wealth surrounded by 'misery', at least relative to the developed world and to 'rising expectations' . . . The post-industrial societies will contain about 40 per cent of the world's population: more than 90 per cent of the world's population will live in nations that have broken out of the historical $50–$200 *per capita* range. Yet at the same time the absolute gap in living standards, between countries or sectors of countries with developed (industrial, post-industrial, mass consumption) economies and those at pre-industrial level, will have widened abysmally.[57]

Some selected items fill out this prediction of growing inequality between the more- and the less-developed worlds. In 1965 the less-developed world (South America, Asia less Japan, Africa) contained about 68 per cent of the world's population but produced only 14.5 per cent of its output. By the year 2000 the less-developed world will contain three-quarters of the world's population and will account for about the same proportion of output as it did in 1965.[58]

Table 4.2   Six economic groupings in year 2000 (millions of people)

(6) Visibly post-industrial		(3) Mature industrial	
US	320	Union of South Africa	50
Japan	120	Mexico, Uruguay, Chile,	
Canada	35	Cuba, Colombia, Peru,	
Scandinavia and Switzerland	30	Panama, Jamaica, etc.	250
France, W. Germany,		N. Vietnam, S. Vietnam,	
Benelux	160	Thailand, the Philippines etc.	250 ·
	665	Turkey	75
		Lebanon, Iraq, Iran, etc.	75
			700
(5) Early post-industrial		(2) Large and partially industrialized	
United Kingdom	55	Brazil	210
Soviet Union	350	Pakistan	250
Italy, Austria	70	China	1 300
E. Germany, Czechoslovakia	35	India	950
Israel	5	Indonesia	240
Australia, New Zealand	25	UAR	70
	540	Nigeria	160
			3 180
(4) Mass consumption			
Spain, Portugal, Poland,		(1) Pre-industrial or small and	
Yugoslavia, Cyprus, Greece,		partially industrialized	
Bulgaria, Hungary, Ireland	180	Rest of Africa	350
Argentina, Venezuela	60	Rest of Arab World	100
Taiwan, N. Korea, S. Korea,		Rest of Asia	300
Hong Kong, Malaysia,		Rest of Latin America	100
Singapore	160		850
	400		

Source: H. Kahn and A. Wiener, *The Year 2000* (New York, Macmillan, 1976), p. 60. © 1967 by the Hudson Institute Inc.

Again, at the beginning of the period, 1965, the per capita product of the industrial world exceeded that of the less-developed nations by a factor of about twelve times. By the year 2000 this factor will approach a difference of eighteen times; this means that the gap between the two worlds will increase by 50 per cent in favour of the developed world by the year 2000.[59]

GNP, it is true, is only one indicator of a nation's health, and by no means necessarily the most important. But it is a good indicator of a nation's military–industrial power and, on that count, the projected trends[60] point to an overwhelming weakness of the less-developed as against the more-developed world for many decades to come. In this, they only confirm the general picture already sketched. On current trends, the future of the Third World seems to be this: internally, within each nation, a lack of cohesion due to the great 'internal development distance' between the more- and the less-developed sectors, and between the nationalist elites and other groups, giving rise to internal conflicts of all kinds (revolutions, *coups d'état*, separatist movements); externally, competition and conflict between Third World nations, because they all produce similar basic commodities, because they are placed in a parallel and competitive orientation towards the top ranks of the international system, and because they are mostly run by elites who are bourgeois nationalists. In relation to the developed world their bargaining power, always slight, seems to be declining further, due largely to developments within the industrial nations, who now seem increasingly to be in a position to turn their backs on the Third World.

As against these gloomy prognostications, some students have discerned hopeful signs of a move towards Third World solidarity.[61] Individual revolutions within particular countries are seen to be of limited effect so long as the international system is constituted as it is: Cuba simply substitutes the Soviet Union for the United States as the indispensable purchaser of her sugar. More significant, therefore, are considered the collective organizations of the underprivileged: such phenomena as the Bandung-, Beograd-, Cairo-Conferences; caucus groups of the Afro-Asians in the UN and its agencies; the more or less concerted initiatives by the less developed nations in the United Nations Conference on Trade and Development (UNCTAD); and, most of all, the Tri-Continental Organization (OSPAAAL) which brings together most of the revolutionary movements of the Third World.

It is unnecessary here to go over the long list of obstacles to the achievement of Third World solidarity. But supposing some sort of real integration does take place, either at the bourgeois-national level or at the revolutionary party level, one can imagine two strategies. Following Galtung's suggestion of the analogy of domestic trade union history,[62] we might expect Third World 'unions' to try 'collective bargaining' first. This means such things as putting higher prices on raw materials (but this assumes that the developed nations will not invent synthetic substitutes for most raw materials very quickly, nor indeed be prepared to exploit their own resources of raw materials, even though costly); and it means attempting to persuade or force the implementation of international welfare state policies (which assumes that the developed world will be willing or compelled to accept some form of heavily progressive taxation, both direct and indirect, which may slow down their own development. At the moment none of the major political parties of the developed world seems prepared to put this to their electorates). Failing this, and given effective international organization on both sides, the scene is set for international class war. It is possible that the poorer nations would chance the likely disastrous consequences of a major war, or at any rate exploit the great social and technological vulnerability of the specialized and interdependent post-industrial nations: although direct appeals to the underprivileged of the developed societies seem likely to be unavailing. The developed nations, for their part, will try various strategies of conciliation and subterfuge to avoid all-out conflict. But to an important and perhaps increasing extent they will rely on preventive military and paramilitary operations to maintain their superiority.

There will be many chances to intervene, given the predicted high amount of intra- and inter-state conflict within the less-developed world; and the developed nations will increasingly take the opportunity to install and maintain 'peace-keeping' forces in the Third World – in the long-term interests of the developed world.

The future remains always open, despite the attempts of some futurologists to close it. In projecting some of the important structural forces of today to look at the future, we are relying on persistencies from the past for our map of the future. Such persistencies would mark out a future existence so depressing for the Third World that we are almost justified in ignoring them and concentrating, however quixotically, on what we perceive as the agencies of change. But we need to remember Bacon's dictum, that nothing that has not yet been done, can be done, except by means that have not yet been tried. Certainly any fundamental change in the relations beween the developed and the underdeveloped worlds will require, as a priority, equally basic changes in the structure of the societies of the developed world. No one can say that that is a thing that has seriously been tried. If it is not, there are good grounds for thinking that, so far as the Third World is concerned, the future *will* be more rather than less like the present, and the past – only, again, writ large.

NOTES

1 The number of institutes, organizations and individuals currently engaged in systematic analysis of future trends runs into thousands; but the bulk of these are concerned with fairly short-term technological forecasting. Among the main bodies one would want to mention: the *Futuribles* project, under Bertrand de Jouvenal; the Commission on the Year 2000 of the American Academy of Arts and Sciences, chaired by Daniel Bell; the Institute for the Future (Middletown, Conn.), which publishes *Futures*; the Institut fuer Zukunftsfragen, directed by Robert Jungk; the Committee for the Next Thirty Years of the British Social Science Research Council, directed by Michael Young. Fairly comprehensive listings can be found in the PEP Survey of Future Studies (C. De Houghton, W. Page and G. Streatfield, ...*And Now the Future*, London, PEP, 1971); the annotated bibliography in W. Bell and J. A. Mau, *The Sociology of the Future* (New York, Russell Sage Foundation, 1971); and E. Jantsch, *Technological Forecasting in Perspective* (Paris, OECD, 1967).

2 For Bell, see note 20 below. References to the others mentioned are, in order: A. Etzioni, *The Active Society* (New York, The Free Press, 1969); K. Boulding, *The Meaning of the Twentieth Century: The Great Transition* (New York, Harper and Row, 1964); H. Kahn and A. Wiener, *The Year 2000* (New York, Macmillan, 1967); P. Drucker, *The Age of Discontinuity* (London, Pan Books, 1971); Z. K. Brzezinski, *Between Two Ages: America's Role in the Technetronic Era* (New York, The Viking Press, 1970); R. Dahrendorf, 'Recent changes in the class structure of European societies', *Daedalus*, 93 (1964), no. 1. This list is, of course, far from exhaustive. Bell has said that he has catalogued eighteen different versions of terms expressing 'transition'.

94   *Continuities and Discontinuities*

3 R. Nisbet, *The Sociological Tradition* (London, Heinemann, 1967).
4 For a recent review of these influences on sociological theories of change, see R. Nisbet, *Social Change and History: Aspects of the Western Theory of Development* (London, Oxford University Press, 1969).
5 The intellectual currents bringing about the reorientation of social thought are well discussed in H. Stuart Hughes, *Consciousness and Society: The Reorientation of European Social Thought 1890–1930* (New York, Vintage Books, 1958).
6 For a summary of the various critiques of social evolutionism, see E. Gellner, *Thought and Change* (London, Weidenfeld and Nicolson, 1964), ch. 1.
7 A. R. Radcliffe-Brown, 'The present position of anthropological studies', *The Advancement of Science: 1931* (London).
8 See especially, K. Bock, 'Evolution, function and change', *American Sociological Review*, 28 (1963), no. 2.
9 See, for instance, T. Parsons, *Societies: Evolutionary and Comparative Perspectives* (Englewood Cliffs, NJ, Prentice-Hall, 1966).
10 It is significant that when Ossip Flechtheim coined the term 'futurology' in 1943, he had no immediate sociological tradition to which he could link his projected enterprise for large-scale social forecasting, and had to rely instead on discussions of Toynbee et al. See his essays of the 1940s and later, reprinted in O. Flechtheim, *History and Futurology* (Meisenheim am Glan, Verlag Anton Hain, 1966).
11 There now seems to be a number of good general critiques of mainstream sociology of development. I have found especially useful: R. Bendix, 'Tradition and modernity reconsidered', *Comparative Studies in Society and History*, XI (1966–7); H. Bernstein, 'Modernization theory and the sociological study of development', *Journal of Development Studies*, 7(1971), no. 2; J. Gusfield 'Tradition and modernity: misplaced polarities in the study of social change', *American Journal of Sociology*, 72 (1967). I have also benefited greatly from an unpublished paper by J. Hilal, 'Sociology and underdevelopment' (University of Durham).
12 It seems, by now, conventional to cite the following warnings: G. Almond and J. S. Coleman (eds), *The Politics of Developing Areas* (Princeton, NJ, Princeton University Press, 1960), especially Almond's Introduction; D. Lerner, *The Passing of Traditional Society* (New York, The Free Press, 1958); W. W. Rostow, *The Stages of Economic Growth* (Cambridge, Cambridge University Press, 1960).
13 For example, Raymond Aron's remark: 'In a sense it would not be wrong to define the advanced countries as those in which the Left and the Right are no longer opposed to each other on the question of development, because development can take place without any further fundamental changes' (*The Industrial Society*, London, Weidenfeld and Nicolson, 1967, pp. 45–6). A similar view, that the industrial society, once created, can 'manage' the stresses to which it gives rise, underlies the argument in Gellner, *Thought and Change*.
14 Surveys of those involved in 'future studies' have indicated a particular prominence of workers in engineering, economics and the physical sciences. See the report in *Futures*, 24 (1970), no. 4, pp. 383–5.
15 See note 1 above. Especially noteworthy here are the attempts to set up international organizations of futurology, e.g. 'The First International Future Research Conference' held in Oslo in 1967, and whose proceedings are published in R. Jungk and J. Galtung (eds), *Mankind 2000* (London, Allen and Unwin, 1969).

For some idea of the coordinated study in the Communist states, see my 'Futurology – the view from Eastern Europe', *Futures*, 4 (1972), no. 1.

16 A. Tofflcr, *Future Shock* (New York, Random House, 1970), p. 25. This work of popular synthesis seems to differ from that of the more sober futurologists only in its greater explicitness.

17 E. Shils, 'Tradition, ecology and institutions in the history of sociology', *Daedalus*, Fall 1970, p. 825. From a rather different point of view, John Goldthorpe has also argued that futurology has taken over much of the logical and conceptual apparatus of the nineteenth century. See Goldthorpe, 'Theories of industrial society: reflections on the recrudescence of historicism and the future of futurology', *European Journal of Sociology*, 12 (1971), no. 2.

18 For instance: in the whole of the massive report by Richta and his team a mere six pages is given to the topic 'The scientific and technological revolution and the "Third World"' (R. Richta et al., *Civilization at the Crossroads: Social and Human Implications of the Scientific and Technological Revolution*, 3 vols, Prague, Czechoslovak Institute of Arts and Sciences, 1967, vol. 1, pp. i-lxxi, and i-lxxii), and doom is written fairly clear there. Daniel Bell has not, to my knowledge, discussed the matter seriously anywhere in his many writings on the post-industrial society.

19 J. Galtung, 'On the future of the international system', in Jungk and Galtung, *Mankind 2000*.

20 Bell, in 'The post-industrial society: the evolution of an idea', *Survey*, 17 (1971), no. 2, p. 168, promises us a forthcoming book on the subject; meanwhile we have some sizeable articles to be going on with: 'The study of the future', *The Public Interest*, Fall 1965; 'Notes on the post-industrial society', *The Public Interest*, I, no. 6, II, no. 7, 1967; 'The measurement of knowledge and technology', in E. Sheldon and W. Moore (eds), *Indicators of Social Change* (New York, Russell Sage Foundation, 1968); 'Technocracy and politics', *Survey*, 16 (1971), no. 1. Bell also provided the theoretical 'baseline' for the Commission on the Year 2000, and edited the volume of its papers, *Toward the Year 2000* (Boston, Mass., Houghton Mifflin, 1968).

21 V. Fuchs, 'The first service society', *The Public Interest*, 1966, no. 2, p. 7.

22 See Dahrendorf, 'Recent changes in the class structure . . .', where he claims (p. 262) that 'Europe is well under way toward a service class society'; also Richta et al., *Civilization at the Crossroads*, vol. III, *Statistical Tables*, tables 2 to 4; and the comparison by continent and region in Bell, 'Measurement of knowledge and technology', p. 153, table 1. Japan shows the interesting and significant phenomenon of having supplanted the primary sector, not first, as had been the rule, with the secondary sector, but with the tertiary sector: the secondary sector expanded fast with industrialization, but the tertiary sector expanded even faster *at the same time*. See K. Tominaga, 'Post-industrial society and cultural diversity', *Survey*, 16 (1971), no. 1, and for further speculation on the future of Japan's spectacular economic development, see H. Kahn, *The Emerging Japanese Superstate* (Englewood Cliffs, NJ, Prentice-Hall, 1970).

23 For US figures, with projections, see Bell, 'The measurement of knowledge and technology', p. 155, table 2. International comparisons are in Richta et al., *Civilization at the Crossroads*, vol. III, *Statistical Tables*, tables 2-6 to 2-9.

24 Kahn and Wiener, *The Year 2000*, pp. 62–3.

25 Richta et al., *Civilization at the Crossroads*, vol. I, pp. 32–6.

26 Bell, 'Notes on the post-industrial society', I, pp. 28–9.

27 Richta et al., *Civilization at the Crossroads*, vol. I, p. 28.

28 Bell, 'The measurement of knowledge and technology', pp. 156–7. Cf. the comment of Kahn and Wiener: 'If the middle third of the twentieth century is known as the nuclear era, and if past times have been known as the age of steam, iron, power or the automobile, then the next thirty-three years may well be known as the age of electronics, computers, automation, cybernation data processing, or some related idea' (*The Year 2000*, p. 86).

29 Bell, 'Technocracy and politics', p. 15.

30 Bell, 'Notes on the post-industrial society', I, p. 30. The idea of a 'knowledge society', focused on the society's intellectual institutions, as the central form of the future society, appears in various guises in most of the writings of futurologists. See, for instance, Peter Drucker, *The Age of Discontinuity*, p. 9: 'Knowledge during the past few decades has become the central capital, the cost centre and the crucial resource of the economy.' And cf. the following echo of Bell: 'While the *Grosstadt* (the industrial city of the nineteenth-century industrial society) was founded on the industrial worker, the megapolis (of post-industrial society) is founded on, and organized around, the knowledge worker, with information as its foremost output as well as its foremost need. The college campus rather than the factory chimney is likely to be the distinctive feature of the megapolis, the college student rather than the "proletarian" its central political fact' ('Notes on the post-industrial society', p. 52). See also Robert Lane, 'The decline of politics and ideology in a knowledgeable society', *American Sociological Review*, 31 (1966), no. 5, and – but drawing different inferences from the centrality of knowledge – Alan Touraine, *La Société Post-industrielle* (Paris, Éditions Denoël, 1969).

31 For the full characterization of this basic long-term trend, see Kahn and Wiener, *The Year 2000*, table 1. The specific expressions of this trend in the full picture of post-industrial society is shown by them on p. 25, table 9. For another, fairly similar, summary characterization of what he prefers to call neo-modern society, see Galtung, 'On the future of the international system', p. 37, n. 15.

32 Some forceful critical comments are made by Jean Floud in 'A critique of Bell', *Survey*, 16 (1971), no. 1. I have tried to trace the ideological origins of the concept in my 'Futurology', *The Listener*, 18 February 1971.

33 N. Chomsky, 'The welfare/warfare intellectuals', *New Society*, 3 July 1969; Floud, 'Critique of Bell'.

34 The phrase is Brzezinski's (see *Between Two Ages*, pp. 33ff).

35 Galtung, 'On the future of the international system'.

36 Ibid., pp. 15–17.

37 Ibid., p. 17.

38 Ibid., pp. 18–19.

39 For some evidence, rather impressionistic, of the international life-style of the 'future people', see Toffler, *Future Shock*, pp. 36ff.

40 For an account of some of these developments, see Drucker, *Age of Discontinuity*, pp. 118ff.

41 For INGOs and IGOs, see Galtung, 'On the future of the international system', pp. 20–5.

42 Cf. the corroborative view of Robin Jenkins that, in the more-developed parts of the world 'there is every reason to believe that regional integration will become a more dominant political and economic force than the integration of nations', (*Exploitation: The World Power Structure and the Inequality of Nations*, London, Paladin Books, 1970, p. 53). Additional evidence comes from the pattern of integration of world regions: while 'regionalization' has been a global phenomenon, it is most marked in the industrial parts of the world. See B. M. Russett, *International Regions and the International System* (Chicago, Rand McNally, 1967).

43 A. Shonfield, *Modern Capitalism*, rev. edn (London, Oxford University Press, 1969), p. 23: see also appendix 1, 'The industrial countries as a market for capital goods', pp. 428–9.

44 D. Seers, 'Rich countries and poor', in D. Seers and L. Joy (eds), *Development in a Divided World* (Harmondsworth, Penguin Books, 1971), pp. 19–20.

45 Boulding, *Meaning of the Twentieth Century*, pp. 113–14.

46 Ibid., p. 115.

47 It was not altogether surprising to hear this last suggestion actually proposed by some Third World countries at the UN Conference on the Environment at Stockholm.

48 This view is presented, simply and powerfully, in Jenkins, *Exploitation*.

49 P. Worsley, *The Third World* (London, Weidenfeld and Nicolson, 1964), p. 261.

50 Brzezinski, *Between Two Ages*, p. 51.

51 Boulding, *Meaning of the Twentieth Century*, p. 23. Cf. the similar view of Galtung's, that 'East and West will rapidly disappear as meaningful contradictions, not because of any complete convergence in socioeconomic systems, but because of the de-ideologization and technification of the economies and a relatively complete mutual interdependence' 'On the future of the international system', p. 25.

52 J. Galtung, 'East–West interaction patterns', *Journal of Peace Research*, 1966, no. 2.

53 Brzezinski, *Between Two Ages*, pp. 35–6. For media development in the different countries, see W. Schramm, *Mass Media and National Development* (Stanford, Ca and Paris, UNESCO, 1964), pp. 90–113, and especially the tables in the appendices. Developments in education are summarized in Brzezinski, ibid., pp. 42–3.

54 It has been noted that the underdeveloped countries supplied almost exactly one-half of the total number of engineers, scientists and medical personnel who emigrated to the United States in the year ending June 1967: 10,254 out of 20,760. It is expected that this proportion will actually rise in the years to come. See Brzezinski, *Between Two Ages*, p. 45.

55 Herman Kahn, commenting in discussion in 'Toward the year 2000: work in progress', *Daedalus*, Summer 1967, p. 962.

56 For patterns of trade among Third World societies, see tables in Worsley, *The Third World*, p. 240. Other indicators of interaction are discussed by Jenkins in *Exploitation*, pp. 139ff.

57 Kahn and Wiener, *The Year 2000*, pp. 60–1.

58 Population assumptions are made as follows. For 1965, the population of the less-developed world was 2,267.9 million, that of the developed world, 1,080.9 million (world total 3,348.9 million); in 2000, the population of the less-developed world will be 4,777.0 million, that of the developed world 1,612.0 million (world total 6,389.0 million). See Kahn and Wiener, *The Year 2000*, p. 142, table 5.

59 Kahn and Wiener, ibid., p. 142.
60 On this there seems to be general agreement, however variously evaluated. See, for instance, the table (based on Kuznets) in the Club of Rome report (H. D. Meadows et al., *The Limits to Growth*, London, Earth Island, 1972, p. 40).
61 For example, Jenkins, *Exploitation*, pp. 148ff.
62 Galtung, 'On the future of the international system', p. 38.

ADDITIONAL BIBLIOGRAPHY

The book by Daniel Bell referred to in note 20 appeared as *The Coming of Post-industrial Society* (New York, Basic Books, 1973; Harmondsworth, Penguin Books, 1976). For some of Bell's later thoughts on the subject, see his *The Cultural Contradictions of Capitalism* (London, Heinemann, 1976) and *Sociological Journeys: Essays 1960–1980* (London, Heinemann, 1980). Bell's views are discussed at length in Krishan Kumar, *Prophecy and Progress: The Sociology of Industrial and Post-industrial Society* (Harmondsworth, Penguin Books, 1978), ch. 6. See also Jonathan Gershuny, *After Industrial Society?* (London, Macmillan, 1978); J. A. Hall, *Diagnoses of Our Time* (London, Heinemann, 1981), ch. 4; R. Badham, *Theories of Industrial Society* (New York, St Martin's Press, 1986).

Herman Kahn's later thoughts can be followed in Kahn, *The Coming Boom* (London, Hutchinson, 1983) and J. Simon and H. Kahn (eds), *The Resourceful Earth: A Response to Global 2000* (Oxford, Basil Blackwell, 1984).

On developments in the industrializing or 'Third' World, the vast literature can conveniently be sampled in H. Bernstein (ed.), *Underdevelopment and Development*, 2nd edn (Harmondsworth, Penguin Books, 1976), and H. Alavi and T. Shanin (eds), *Introduction to the Sociology of Developing Societies* (London, Macmillan, 1982). A good general account is T. Kemp, *Industrialization in the Non-Western World* (London, Longman, 1983).

There is less on the relationship between the industrial and the industrializing worlds, and noticeably less of the kind of thing that I have attempted here, to consider likely *future* interactions between the developed and the developing societies. An effective and much-debated review of trends is the so-called 'Brandt Report': Willy Brandt and others, *North–South: A Programme for Survival* (London, Pan Books, 1980). Marxists have continued to refine the relevant concept of 'underdevelopment' introduced by A. G. Frank, in his *Latin America: Underdevelopment or Revolution* (New York, Monthly Review Press, 1969). See especially Samir Amin, *Accumulation on a World Scale: A Critique of the Theory of Underdevelopment* (New York, Monthly Review Press, 1974), and *Unequal Development: An Essay on the Social Formations of Peripheral Capitalism* (New York, Monthly Review Press, 1976). Equally interesting have been the contributions of Immanuel Wallerstein: *The Modern World System*, 2 vols (New York and London, Academic Press, 1974 and 1980), and *The Capitalist World Economy* (Cambridge, Cambridge University Press, 1980). See also P. Worsley, *The Three Worlds: Culture and World Development* (London, Weidenfeld and Nicolson, 1984). The theme of interaction is also strongly marked in discussions of the new 'international division of labour', which has the merit of seeing 'post-industrial' trends in the developed world as an aspect of capitalist world development as a whole. See especially F. Fröbel, J. Heinrichs and O. Kreye, *The New International Division of Labour: Structural Unemployment in Industrial Countries and Industrialization in Developing Countries*, translated by P. Burgess (Cambridge, Cambridge University Press, 1980); also A. Portes and J. Walton, *Labor, Class and the International System* (New York, Academic Press, 1981).

Johan Galtung, who supplied a helpful framework for this essay, has developed his ideas at length in *The True Worlds: A Transnational Perspective* (New York, The Free Press, 1980). His collected essays, far wider in scope than the title suggests, also contain much of relevance for the theme of this chapter: see Johan Galtung, *Essays in Peace Research*, 5 vols (Atlantic Highlands, NJ, Humanities Press, 1980).

5
The Limits and Capacities of Industrial Capitalism

> Revolutionaries sometimes try to prove that there is absolutely no way out of a crisis [for the ruling class]. This is a mistake. There is no such thing as an absolutely hopeless situation.
>
> Lenin, Report to the Second Congress of the Communist International, 19 July 1920

THE DECLINE OF WESTERN CAPITALISM?

The 'decline of the West' has been pronounced at regular intervals since Oswald Spengler's gloomy prognostications of 1918. It was a favourite theme of Marxist and other literary intellectuals such as Christopher Caudwell and Ortega y Gasset in the 1930s. Later in the 1970s it reappeared in the wake of the oil crisis and a rude awakening to the problem of the world's future supplies of energy. Ecological critiques were now joined to more traditional Marxist analysis to proclaim the bankruptcy of Western capitalism. Capitalism, as the dominant form of industrialism, seemed incapable of escaping the logic of its growth process. As an ecological, economic and social system, it was reaching its limits. Once more the choice seemed to be that posed by Rosa Luxemburg at the beginning of the century: socialism – of *some* kind – or barbarism.

As the millennial year 2000 beckons, such eschatological speculations are bound to grow. Every civilization known to us – and *a fortiori* every one we don't know – has after all declined. Often, like the Hittites or the Mayas, they have disappeared altogether, leaving only a few material remains. Or they go into a state of frozen or suspended animation, like the Polynesians. Of the twenty-six civilizations identified by Arnold Toynbee, sixteen are dead and five 'arrested'. Of the five remaining one of these, Western civilization, is rapidly swallowing up the rest. Is there any reason to think that Western civilization will prove an exception to the law of decay and breakdown? And as it turns itself into the only remaining civilization, a world system or world civilization, does not its own downfall now threaten the downfall of the whole species?

Most theories of civilizational decline emphasize internal factors, or 'internal contradictions'. Suicide, not murder, is the general verdict. In Toynbee's case, this takes the form of a process whereby a civilization's ruling 'Creative Minority' becomes a coercive 'Dominant Minority', losing its ability to bind the 'Internal Proletariat' to its culture and so unleashing class war. The 'External Proletariat' of barbarians beyond its borders, previously kept in check with little difficulty, can now successfully invade a system fatally weakened by internal strains.[1] Max Weber too, in his account of the decline of the Roman Empire, picks out the internal contradictions of the slave-based economy of the ancient world as the principal cause. The barbarians overran an imperial system that was already pointing their way, away from a centralized empire based on slave labour towards a manorial system based on family serfdom. 'The Empire had ceased to be what it once was, and the barbarian invasions simply concluded a development which had begun long before . . . When, after one and a half centuries of decline, the Western Empire finally disappeared, barbarism had already conquered the Empire from within.'[2]

But such theories of decline, with their concentration on internal social mechanisms of contradiction and conflict, have always had to contend with others that emphasize extraneous or natural factors. Social Darwinists have looked to military fitness, in an environment of predatory and competitive states, as the key to survival or servility. International war is the testing agency that elevates some societies and enslaves others. Malthusians, from an even more cosmic perspective, have pitilessly observed the levelling of human societies as they come up against the blank wall of starvation. Population increase continually outstripping food supply, successful and growing societies are punished by their own progress, as if for hubris. Nature, in the form of plagues and famines, jerks them sharply back to their primitive starting-points. The sorry cycle then starts all over again. What latter-day doomster has been able to match the Old Testament thunder of the Reverend Malthus himself?

The power of population is so superior to the power in the earth to produce subsistence for man, that premature death must in some shape or other visit the human race. The vices of mankind are active and able ministers of depopulation. They are the precursors in the great army of destruction; and often finish the dreadful work themselves. But should they fail in this war of extermination, sickly seasons, epidemics, pestilence, and plague, advance in terrific array, and sweep off their thousands and ten thousands. Should success be still incomplete, gigantic inevitable famine stalks in the rear, and with one mighty blow levels the population with the food of the world.[3]

Decline and downfall, all theorists agree, can however inevitable take a very long time. Weber, as we have seen, speaks of the decline of the Roman Empire stretching over a period of at least a century and a half. Toynbee for his part considers the whole Roman Empire as but the penultimate stage in the decline of a larger entity, Hellenic Society, as it vainly attempts to rally within the framework of a 'universal state'. Hellenic Society had in fact been in decline since the convulsions of the Peloponnesian War of the fifth century BC. 'The Roman Empire itself was a monumental symptom of the far-advanced decline of a Hellenic Society of which this empire was the universal state . . . this empire was already doomed before it was established.'[4]

This is *la longue durée* indeed, taking in more than a thousand years; and one wonders how far such a long-breathed perspective is useful to anyone but the most philosophically minded historian. Certainly from the point of view of a comparative historical sociology, centuries rather than millennia might seem a more appropriate time dimension – for instance, the four or five centuries, from the fourteenth to the eighteenth centuries, that Braudel takes as the period of the 'economic civilization' of commercial capitalism in Western Europe.[5] What such a time horizon would sufficiently suggest is that societies can live with their 'contradictions', if not comfortably at least tolerably, for long periods. The signs of decay may be observable only retrospectively, as to an eighteenth-century European like Gibbon musing on Roman history amidst the ruins of the Capitol. Or the persistence of old forms and old values may be so powerful and pervasive as to hide for a long time the seeds of decay. Joseph Schumpeter was convinced that 'there is inherent in the capitalist system a tendency toward self-destruction', and that for those with the eyes to see the signs were becoming evident. But he could also see all around him the evidence of a still confident and prosperous bourgeoisie. 'The middle class is still a political power. Bourgeois standards and bourgeois motivations though being increasingly impaired are still alive . . . The bourgeois family has not yet died', etc. These may, he conceded, be thought of as surface, short-run factors. But

from the standpoint of immediate practice as well as for the purposes of short-run forecasting – *and in these things, a century is a 'short run'* – all this surface may be more important than the tendency toward another civilization that slowly works deep down below.[6]

If a century can be considered a 'short run', then it would clearly be no contradiction to expect, say, the eventual demise of industrialism through the exhaustion of fossil fuels and mineral resources, while at the same time remaining relatively optimistic about its forseeable future over the next century or so. The same can be said about the Marxist notion of 'the falling-rate of profit' as an inherent long-term tendency of capitalism, and one that will compass its doom. So long as there are fresh fields for capitalism to conquer – and this could, without being too fanciful, now include other worlds than our own – it may be only of theoretical interest to deduce from its working some distant point in time when the accumulation crisis will reach revolutionary proportions.

Still, it is one thing to stave off the ultimate, the terminal crisis. There may be other problems in the meantime scarcely less pressing. While to the out-and-out Darwinian survival may be the only thing that matters, human societies have generally also been concerned with the terms of that survival. Those inmates who survived the Nazi concentration camps endured in conditions that few would describe as human. To have remained alive was certainly a triumph of individual ingenuity and resilience, but many would question whether, if whole societies came to resemble concentration camps, survival on these terms and in these conditions could ever be worth fighting for. Similar things have been said of some of the slave societies of the past. Social survival is the necessary premise of all human values and purposes, but it is not synonymous with them.

This is perhaps to put the matter too alarmingly. Few societies are so intolerable that some space for humanly valued activities cannot be found. The point is simply that there can be questions about the 'limits' to social development short of the stage where limits become absolute. Societies can throw up a range of problems that suggest, not catastrophe, but systematic failures and lesions of various kinds. Life can be made so unpleasant and uncomfortable, so threatening and debilitating, that people withdraw from society, or seek to escape it. Society may have gone beyond some point – never easy to fix with precision – at which its institutions still function relatively harmoniously, can still deliver a relatively fulfilling life to the bulk of the population. The system survives, but shows increasing signs of wear and tear. It is just as important – in the short run, more important – to consider these relative limits and incapacities as to speculate on the long-term capacity for survival of the system as a whole.

In the following sections I consider views of this kind as well as those concerned with long-term survival. I make no attempt, of course, to be comprehensive. I have merely selected some examples which are useful for opening up questions about the future development of industrial societies, and for suggesting some of the newer sources of strain within them.

CAPITALISM AND THE WORLD SYSTEM

Despite, or perhaps because of, its origins in nineteenth-century evolutionary social philosophies, sociology has shown little interest in the transformations of whole social orders, and the mechanisms that bring this about. Following Weber, there has been some concern with origins – at least, the origins of capitalism, although even there the field has largely been left to sociologically minded historians such as R. H. Tawney and Christopher Hill. But to scan the literature on revolution, the concept most directly relevant to breakdown and renewal, is to be struck by the paucity of serious sociological contributions (and one Skocpol does not make a summer[7]). To repeat the old but still accurate charge: sociology has been good at explaining order; it has been far less successful in dealing with change.

The exception of course is Marxism. Marxism is the most powerful modern theory of revolution and social transformation. But its limitations as such have also been widely exposed, both in its treatment of past transformations – for example, from feudalism to capitalism – and its anticipation of future ones. Most pertinent to the present concern, it remains true to say that while Marx provided a compelling anatomy of capitalist society, his account of its transformation and supersession in a socialist revolution is, as all admit, incomplete and unsatisfactory.

Marx gives an unrivalled account of the rise of modern society. His writings on the origins and development of capitalism are the best part of his work, and better than anything else yet offered on the subject by anyone. In the *Grundrisse* and *Capital*, in the occasional writings on European politics and society, Marx provides a comprehensive sociology of bourgeois capitalist society that is still unsurpassed, and off which modern sociology still lives.[8]

On the future development of capitalism, the case is less clear. Marx's contempt for futurology – 'I don't make recipes for the cookshops of the future' – is to his credit. To have seen something of the barrenness of contemporary futurology must make us grateful that Marx did not indulge in detailed prediction and prophecy (although the attack specifically on utopianism, a different enterprise, was unfortunate and misplaced).

Nor is it true to say that Marx's account does not contain much valuable material on the future of capitalist society. Any developmental or evolutionary theory, as in essence Marxism is, must embody some notion of emergent properties or processes. Of this there is a good deal in Marx, on both general and particular matters. The analysis of technological innovation, de-skilling and the general proletarianization of labour needs very little to add to it to bring it up to date, as Harry Braverman so vividly demonstrated.[9] So too with the account of the concentration and centralization of capital, and the projected rise of managerial and monopoly capitalism.[10] Marx had from the first seized on the world character of capitalism; hence the massive growth in the internationalization of capital and the international division of labour would have come as no surprise to him.[11] In a celebrated passage in the *Grundrisse*, even the fully automated society is anticipated, at a time when mechanization had barely got under way.[12] In the late twentieth-century world of multinational corporations, the North–South divide, automation, technological unemployment and a growing underclass of casual, unskilled workers, Marx would have found little reason to think that his analysis of more than a century ago was fundamentally mistaken. What might surprise him, and what surely ought to astonish us, is how little he would have to change or add to his original prognosis.[13]

Would he also have felt the same way about his ultimate prognosis, that capitalism must eventually collapse and give way to socialism? Again, the evidence of the past century would have given him some grounds for reaffirming his belief. The instability of capitalism as a system shows little sign of abating. The 'great thunderstorms' in which the economic contradictions of capitalism express themselves[14] have blown up often enough. Crises and depressions, the upswings and downswings of the business cycle, the 'long waves' of growth and recession, have continued with remarkable regularity since the time of Marx's *Capital*.[15] Mass unemployment has been once already, in the 1930s, and returned half a century later to show that Keynesian recipes may not be enough. Technological unemployment, a spectre raised by Keynes himself, threatens a not too distant future of 20–25 per cent unemployed among the adult populations of the industrial countries.[16] The growth and internationalization of capital have brought with them new sources of vulnerability. As the oil-producing countries showed with striking effect in the 1970s, a small group of countries in control of a strategic industrial resource can now exert something like blackmail on even the most powerful capitalist nations. With many new countries – Israel, India, Pakistan – now joining the nuclear club, the possibility of other kinds of pressure on the guardians of the world capitalist order increases further.

And yet the oil crisis itself is a good example of how capitalism can weather even the roughest storm. The OPEC countries increased the price of oil fourfold in 1973–4, and doubled it again in 1979, amounting to more than a tenfold rise in the price of oil in the 1970s. This was at a time when Western countries had become increasingly dependent on oil: in 1973, oil imports were more than seventeen times their 1950 level, and oil represented half of total energy consumption, compared with a quarter in 1950. The oil shock produced simultaneously recession and inflation. Capitalist world production fell by 10 per cent in less than a year, and the average annual price increase in Western countries in the mid-1970s was 12–13 per cent. Unemployment rates too began to climb, rising from an average of 2.5 per cent in 1973 in the Western countries, to 5.5 per cent in 1980. Following the dizzying growth rates – an annual average of 5.5 per cent – and virtually negligible unemployment of the 'Golden Age' of 1950–73, the post-1973 period saw the capitalist countries in the worst recession since the 1930s.[17] In a series of trenchant essays written in the 1970s, the contemporary historian Geoffrey Barraclough proclaimed 'the end of an era'. 'We stand at a watershed in world history ... The days of neo-capitalism are numbered ... Neo-capitalism, with its pretensions to have found the answer to Marx, was the expression of a temporary situation, borne along not by its own dynamic but by the upward wave of the economic cycle.'[18]

In the upshot the prophecies of collapse seemed wide of the mark. The West rallied under the leadership of the United States and brought about a remarkable re-stabilization – or at least 'normalization' – of the international economic order. The first step was to separate the non-oil-producing Third World nations from the OPEC cartel, thus heading off a potentially threatening anti-Western coalition and a strategy of 'collective self-reliance'. This was done through a typical mixture of threat, bluster and bribery. The non-OPEC LDCs (least developed countries) were warned that they, not the West, would suffer most from 'trade union' tactics against the capitalist bloc. They were, it was pointedly remarked, critically dependent on the West, especially the United States, for food and technology. Their best hope for economic development lay in a relationship of 'interdependence' with the West, not one of confrontation. The speedier the West's recovery, the likelier the improvement in the LDCs' own prospects.

The pill was sweetened somewhat by the decision to increase lending quotas to the LDCs through the International Monetary Fund, and by the establishment of a 'Common Fund', underwritten by the developed countries, to stabilize the prices of raw materials – which made up more than 80 per cent of the LDCs' export earnings – if they fell too far on world markets.

But the balance – or rather imbalance – of power was clear. The LDCs' demand for 'indexation' – the tying of the price of raw materials to the price of manufactures – was decisively rejected by the West. So too was a request for an easing of the debt to Western banks. As Barraclough observed, in a somewhat more chastened vein, it was shown 'that if recession is notoriously a bad time for trade unions to fight for wage increases, it is also a bad time for the less developed countries to fight for NIEO [the New International Economic Order]'.[19]

For their part, the OPEC countries were co-opted into the capitalist bloc through the recycling and absorption of petrodollars into the capitalist economies. Direct and portfolio investment gave the OPEC cartel an increased stake in the United States and other capitalist countries. If Western capitalism was hostage to OPEC, OPEC soon became hostage to capitalism. Vast amounts of technology, machinery, arms and spare parts were purchased by OPEC from the West. OPEC increasingly found its future, both as supplier and customer, annexed to the capitalist bloc. Under pressure from Saudi Arabia and Brazil, the Third World retreated from the radical strategy of 'collective self-reliance' and reverted to the traditional pattern of 'trade and aid'.

Even more effectively the United States asserted its leadership over the capitalist bloc and tightened the integration of the capitalist world. The United States, of all the major capitalist countries the least dependent on oil imports, emerged with greater power than ever before. It had been largely instrumental in separating the OPEC cartel from the non-oil-producing LDCs, and had master-minded the policy of setting the enormous power of the organized capitalist nations against the threats of trade union action by the LDCs.[20] It had made it clear that the New International Economic Order demanded by the Third World would be only marginally different from the old. The NIEO would remain, as Michael Harrington said at the time, 'impeccably capitalist'.[21]

There can be nothing very comforting about this recovery, either in its manner or in its prospects for future stability. It tightens the screws even more on the LDCs. At the same time it does not secure the capitalist bloc from future attempts at pressure by other nations sitting on key industrial resources. The secret is now out, and the rich capitalist countries will be faced with demands for Danegeld at fairly regular intervals from now. The capitalist world system may become more integrated, but by the same token it becomes more vulnerable to pressure at its weakest points. Moreover, as the world recession continues, it intensifies rivalries and stimulates beggar-your-neighbour policies within the developed world. Such divisions may once more dissolve the unity of the rich countries *vis-à-vis* the Third World. The United States, Western Europe and Japan, not to mention the East European states, may see their future, in the short run at least, not as part of an integrated bloc of developed nations – the 'North' – but as separate superpowers pursuing separate strategies of survival and self-interest. Barraclough, tracing at intervals the process of re-stabilization during the 1970s, indeed finally came to see this as the likeliest outcome of the experience of these years.

The liberal world economy, as it had existed for a quarter of a century after 1945, was on its way out.

What we have to expect in its place ... is something approximating to a world of regional blocs or superblocs – that is to say, of exclusive trading areas, hedged in by protective tariffs, in which groups of developed and underdeveloped countries are linked together by mutual interests and stand opposed to other groups of developed and developing countries similarly linked.[22]

The point is that, as Barraclough himself admits, such a system of closed trading blocs worked 'relatively well' in the 1930s (the world war was not a product of this system), and there is no reason why it should not work as well today. That it has certain disorderly and inefficient features is not in question. But then the capitalist system has never been stable, if by this we mean orderly and harmonious. Its history is punctuated by alternating phases of progress and regression, growth and depression. What rather is at issue is its resilience, its capacity for survival as a system in the face of such vicissitudes. On present evidence there is little to indicate that it has reached the end of its viable existence.

There is certainly not the remotest sign of a successor (and in this respect at least, Wallerstein's characterization of the East European states as 'collective capitalist firms',[23] participating willy-nilly in the capitalist world economy, seems quite right). What is to come, that is, so far does not look like socialism, though to many it increasingly looks like barbarism.[24] The lesson that Stephen Rousseas, for instance, draws from the response to the oil crisis is that capitalism is quite capable of surviving in the new environment, but at the cost of some prosperity and many liberal freedoms. 'Unplanned advanced capitalism' will give way to 'a planned post-capitalist state' under the control of 'cartelized big business' fused with a strong government. Low growth rates, high unemployment and high inflation will be the norm for a considerable time to come. In the scramble for scarce raw materials and declining energy sources, a new mercantilist world order will emerge (perhaps on the lines of the regionalized world envisaged by Barraclough).

Capitalism has shown over the course of its entire history a remarkable ability to adapt to changing circumstances, and is already beginning to show a similar, though somewhat strained, flexibility in adapting to its biggest challenge of all – effective domestic planning in a finite mercantilist world of increasingly limited resources ... Planned capitalist society's legitimation would be achieved via media control, surveillance, and a co-optation of the masses through a growth based on the predatory exploitation of weaker nations held firmly under political and military control – the 1973–7 scenario replayed with a vengeance.

The descent into barbarism that Luxemburg so feared could become a reality in a world in which capital accumulation will be severely limited. But the 'barbarism' Luxemburg foresaw as a possibility not to be automatically ruled out by a mechanical dialectic will most probably not entail the 'catastrophic' collapse of capitalism but rather its dialectical transormation into an advanced, planned technocratic capitalism operating within newly defined boundary conditions.[25]

MARXISM AND THE COLLAPSE OF CAPITALISM

It is worth remembering that Marx himself opposed the idea that capitalism would collapse as the result of a mechanical working out of its 'objective' logic. In a famous footnote in *Theories of Surplus Value*, he associated himself with Ricardo, as against Adam Smith, in the view that a fall in the rate of profit due to 'an overabundance of capital' posed a temporary and transitory, not a permanent, check to capital accumulation. 'Permanent crises do not exist.'[26] Crises of overproduction indeed seem to function for Marx much as they later appeared to Schumpeter: as 'gales of creative destruction', providing the opportunity for the clearing out of obsolete and unwanted capital stock and a re-stocking with newer and more productive technology. Marx, that is to say, was not a 'breakdown theorist'. Bottomore fairly expresses what now seems to be the general consensus on this.

None of Marx's partial analyses embody a conception of crises as leading to an ineluctable 'economic breakdown' of capitalism ... On the contrary, Marx's general view seems to have been that crises, in purely economic terms, are a means of countering disequilibrium and re-establishing the conditions for further capitalist development.[27]

Rudolph Hilferding put the Marxist position correctly when he stated that 'the idea of a purely economic collapse makes no sense', and that the collapse of capitalism 'will be political and social, not economic'.[28] It was the growing indignation, power and confidence of the proletariat, stimulated by the life conditions of capitalism, that would ultimately bring down capitalism, not some technical economic malfunctioning of the system. This was the view even of those Marxists, such as Rosa Luxemburg, who modified Marx to the extent of postulating an ultimate and irresolvable crisis of capitalism caused by over-accumulation. Marx, Luxemberg pointed out, had assumed for analytical purposes a fully formed, fully developed world system of capitalism. She quotes the relevant footnote from *Capital*:

In order to examine the object of our investigation in its integrity, free from all disturbing subsidiary circumstances, we must treat the whole world as one nation, and assume that capitalist production is everywhere established and has possessed itself of every branch of industry.[29]

This 'theoretical premise' can be misleading. It relates to an abstract, formal model of capitalism. In reality, says Luxemburg, capital accumulation depends on the existence of non-capitalist strata and non-capitalist countries, both as consumers and as suppliers of certain kinds of commodities and of fresh groups of proletarianized labour. Only when capitalism has completely eliminated all internal and external non-capitalist pockets – and this crucially includes the epoch of imperialism – does stagnation set in and push the system to its limits in a crisis of profitability.[30] This is, however, only a *theoretical* limit to the system. It is indeed a 'theoretical fiction, because capital accumulation is not just an economic but also a political process'. Well before the outer theoretical limit is reached, Luxemburg expects capitalism to be overthrown. Its bloody progress through the world increasingly provokes 'an endless chain of political and social catastrophes and convulsions'. These, together with periodic economic crises, 'make continued accumulation impossible and the rebellion of the international working class against the rule of capital necessary, even before it has economically reached the limits it set for itself'.[31]

So Luxemburg too pins her expectations on the development of a revolutionary working class as capitalism enters its 'final phase', the age of imperialism. Final? We have seen enough of capitalism's energy and expansiveness in the past half century to be wary of such eschatologies. Even the bouts of destructiveness, as in the two world wars, have not spelled the end but, confirming Schumpeter's wartime speculations,[32] have actually been the springboard of renewed growth. In an unevenly developed world, with vast areas still available for capitalist penetration and exploitation, it was on the face of it hardly probable that capitalism would be in its final phase in the early part of this century. That being so, it has retained a considerable capacity for staving off a revolutionary crisis by the co-optation of its own proletariat and the exploitation of the 'external proletariat' of the Third World.

What else indeed should one have expected from a system endowed with such unique dynamism by Marx? In the *Communist Manifesto*, the *Grundrisse* and *Capital*, Marx in some well-known passages depicts a force for growth and change whose only limits appear to be the stars. Capitalism, he says, is a stage of society 'in comparison to which all earlier ones appear as mere *local developments* of humanity and as *nature-idolatry*'. Its 'great civilizing influence' comes from its 'universal appropriation of nature as well as the social bond itself'. It penetrates to the heart of nature and society, exploring both in theory and exploiting both in practice to the fullest possible extent.

For the first time, nature becomes purely an object for humankind, purely a matter of utility; it ceases to be recognized as a power for itself; and the theoretical discovery of its autonomous laws appears merely as a ruse so as to subjugate it under human needs, whether as an object of consumption or as means of production. In accord with this tendency, capital drives beyond national barriers and prejudices as much as beyond nature worship, as well as all traditional, confined, complacent, encrusted satisfactions of present needs, and reproductions of old ways of life. It is destructive towards all of this, and constantly revolutionizes it, tearing down all the barriers which hem in the development of the forces of production, the expansion of needs, the all-sided development of production, and the exploitation and exchange of natural and mental forces.[33]

What could stop such a juggernaut? Evidently no non-capitalist force but only its own 'internal contradictions'. Yet their working out demands a world scale and world dimension to history, both of which seem far from exhausted. In its progress capitalism consumes both history (time) and nature (space). It deals with temporal barriers to its growth by smashing down all pre-capitalist residues – peasants, craftsmen, small traders, local markets etc. It deals with spatial barriers by its world-wide expansion and reconstitution of the earth's people and resources. In this aspect its development takes the form of geographical differentiations, which are not 'mere historical residuals' but 'actively reconstituted features within the capitalist mode of production'.[34]

Capitalism tends to integrate the world into a single system characterized by an international territorial division of labour. The accumulation process 'spreads its net in ever-widening circles across the world, ultimately enmeshing everyone and everything within the circulation process of capital'.[35] This brings in its train new forms of inter-regional competition and conflict. Some regions boom, others decline. But this very source of new strains in the system contains, as David Harvey explains, compensating mechanisms of stabilization.

The different regional rhythms of accumulation may be but loosely coordinated because the co-ordinations rest on the variegated and often conflicting mobilities of different forms of capital and labour. The timing of upturns and downturns in the accumulation cycle can then vary from one region to another with interesting interaction effects. The unity to the accumulation process presupposed in earlier versions of the crisis theory fragments into different regional rhythms that can just as easily compensate each other as build into some vast global crash. The very real possibility exists that the global pace of accumulation can be sustained through compensating oscillations within the parts. The geography of uneven development helps convert the crisis tendencies of capitalism into compensating regional configurations of rapid accumulation and devaluation.[36]

It may be true that, as Harvey says, the process of uneven geographical development and expansion will not ultimately solve anything, that 'there is . . . no "spatial fix" that can contain the contradictions of capitalism in the long run.'[37] But the difficulties faced by Marxists in envisaging and explaining the end of capitalism are greater than they are apt to realize. It is not simply that the 'contradictions' must take much longer to express themselves than they usually allow, not simply that – perhaps as a result of this – the international proletariat has so far shown scant willingness to play its allotted part as capitalism's executioner.[38] There is the more serious difficulty of the uniqueness of capitalism's origins, and the corollary of this, the problem that arises in contemplating its outcome. Both Marx and Weber showed that though there was material progress in many societies above the hunting-and-gathering level, in only one place – Western Europe – was there a 'break-through' to the higher level of capitalist industrialism. From there the new system went on to conquer the rest of the world. Elsewhere inertia, social structural or superstructural forces prevented or counteracted tendencies towards autonomous material growth.

What this means is that the materialist conception of history is reduced to explaining a special case, the once-and-only rise of Western capitalism. This poses a question, as Hobsbawm notes, not just about the origins of capitalism but about its expected course of development and final destination. It casts doubt in particular on the inevitability of the clash between the forces and relations of capitalist production. For 'if it can be shown that in other societies there has been no trend for the material forces to grow, or that their growth has been controlled, sidetracked or otherwise prevented by the force of social organization and superstructure from causing revolution in the sense of the 1859 *Preface*, then why should not the same occur in bourgeois society?'[39] This makes the end of capitalism not only 'conjunctural' but, to a large extent, conjectural. Capitalism's end must remain as open, as undetermined, as its beginning. This certainly gives it no permanent or everlasting lease of life. All civilizations, as we have already noted, like all natural species, are marked out for extinction from the moment of their birth. But, as with species, the when and the how of it remain matters more for soothsayers than for sociologists.

'DISORGANIZED CAPITALISM'

There can be other kinds of 'system failures' than those that end in self-destruction. Societies may build up such an array of problems as to make their effective functioning increasingly difficult and costly. There may be no new system on offer, no victory for any party, but simply an enervating and wearisome stalemate. Temporary patching-up and specious palliatives become the order of the day. Alienation and ennui seize considerable sections of the population, leading to attitudes of cynicism and *ohne mich*. There is no recorded instance of a civilization dying of boredom, but plenty of instances – for example, from late Hellenistic civilization – of populations quietly withdrawing their moral support from systems in clear need of renewal.

Capitalism, in the eyes of many contemporary critics and analysts, has become increasingly 'disorganized'.[40] It does not function as it is supposed to, according to its own self-understanding and self-proclaimed principles. Formal parliamentary democracy has been undermined by the rise of the powerful party-state and the policy-making bureaucratic agency. The principle of majority rule, once an instrument of progress, has become regressive by virtue of its 'equal treatment of the unequal', in an environment increasingly characterized by 'minority' areas and interests related to such divisions as sex, age, ethnicity, region and family status. Trade unions, far from being associations of the great mass of oppressed workers, have become the bastions of a privileged core of securely employed male workers, indifferent to the claims and interests not just of the unemployed but of more 'marginal' workers such as women, the young and members of minority ethnic groups.[41] Work itself, the uniquely privileged source of ethic and identity in industrial societies, has for much of the population lost its ability to convey meaning and give shape to an individual's life. It has come to occupy a shorter period of our lives, due to longer schooling and earlier retirement.[42] It tends to become intermittent, interrupted by bouts of unemployment. As an experience it has become unfulfilling, shaped by the dictates of the large bureaucratic organization or the capital-intensive factory.

Even at its most successful, capitalism as an economic system runs the risk of undermining its own cultural and political props. Its emphasis on pecuniary goals and 'possessive individualism' steadily drives out all the pre-capitalist residues of moral restraint that are an essential part of its effective functioning.[43] Its reduction of all relationships nakedly to the 'cash nexus' releases in particular the full energy of the organized working class – but in a capitalist rather than a socialist direction. The working class, schooled by the capitalist ethic and capitalist practice, comes to feel increasingly uninhibited in the use of its industrial power in the market place. It demands its due; the strike weapon is its bargaining counter. The result is endemic industrial conflict and, with leap-frogging wage settlements, endemic inflation.[44]

In the context of an expanding economy, growth can be a surrogate for redistribution. That, as Charles Maier puts it, has been 'the great conservative idea of the last generation', no less so for being espoused by many social democrats.[45] When growth cannot keep up with expectations, as has been the case recently, inflation can for a time disguise the lag. But ultimately its effect is to intensify distributional struggles. Low growth in fact converts all social and political choices and decisions – over environmental pollution, energy use, levels of unemployment – into 'zero-sum' conflicts: ones in which every gain by one group must be suffered as a loss by others, and so all decisions are stalemated. Society achieves stasis.[46] The state, originally drawn into the marketplace to stabilize capitalism and to secure its orderly growth, now finds itself having to adjudicate between competing claims without the economic wherewithal to leave the losers on any issue reasonably satisfied. Capitalist economic growth is in itself destabilizing, but at least while steady it provides the wealth to pay off claimants and still the demands for equality. Periods of stagnation not only do nothing to lessen the destabilizing tendencies of capitalism but actually reinforce them by bringing to the surface tensions and divisions temporarily submerged by capitalism's success.

The most serious problem had already been forseen long ago by Marx. The French Second Republic of 1848 introduced, for the first time in modern history, universal male suffrage. But in conceding political democracy, Marx argued in *The Class Struggles in France* (1850), the bourgeoisie had entrenched a fundamental contradiction between the political and the socioeconomic realms of capitalist society.

The comprehensive contradiction of this constitution ... consists in the following: the classes whose social slavery the constitution is to perpetuate, proletariat, peasantry, petty bourgeoisie, it puts in possession of political power through universal suffrage. And from the class whose old social power it sanctions, the bourgeoisie, it withdraws the political guarantees of this power. It forces the political rule of the bourgeoisie into democratic conditions, which at every moment help the hostile classes to victory and jeopardise the very foundations of bourgeois society. From the ones it demands that they should not go forward from political to social emancipation; from the others that they should not go back from social to political restoration.[47]

For most of the nineteenth and early twentieth centuries, capitalism was legitimated by the persistence of a 'protective cover' of religious and other pre-capitalist moral conceptions: *noblesse oblige*, economic success as the reward for the moral virtues of industry and frugality and so on.[48] The contradiction between the political and the economic realms was masked, not just by the slow and uneven growth of democracy itself,[49] but by the operation of customary restraints that inhibited the full impact of the democratic principle on the capitalist economy. Increasingly, two things have happened. The restraints have dropped away, leading to a politicization of the economy – or, what comes to the same thing, the commercialization of politics. The political victors in the electoral struggle have come to regard the economy as fair game: a fit object of manipulation and a source of spoils for their supporters.[50] More positively, the democratic principle of the state is used to counterbalance the unequal and coercive sphere of the private capitalist economy. In either case, the separation of state and 'civil society', critical to the liberal capitalist order, increasingly breaks down.

This has the effect of inducing 'crises' of various sorts, whose precise definition depends largely on political perspective. For liberal individualists, such as Samuel Brittan and Daniel Bell, the politicization of the economy, and of society generally, generates excessive and 'unfulfillable expectations' on the part of all social groups.[51] There is government 'overload', and an unholy scramble among organized groups for political influence as the state becomes 'the arena for the fulfilment of private and group wants'.[52] For left-wing thinkers, the crisis is primarily one of legitimation, caused by the now evident contradiction between the private character of the capitalist economy and the public character of liberal democracy.[53] The capitalist economy takes its stand on property rights. It promotes an ethos of individual acquisitiveness at the expense, if need be, of society. Its structural principle is inequality – the vast divide between property-owners and the propertyless. Liberal democracy enshrines the universal rights of persons. Its key concept is citizenship, and its structural principle is equality – the equal rights of all citizens, and their effective embodiment in democratic practice. Kept separate, as they were for more than a century, the two spheres can function more or less autonomously, with only occasional clashes. Brought together, as they have been with the politicization of society, their irreconcilable principles create 'a contradictory totality' which sends shock waves throughout the system.[54]

The basic problem, from the point of view of capitalism, is what Claus Offe calls 'the largely irreversible framework of the welfare state and competitive democracy'.[55] The liberal 'nightwatchman' state of the nineteenth century has become the democratic welfare state of the twentieth. The inter-war slump and the national mobilization of the Second World War supplied the main impetus. So far as possible there was to be no repeat of the 1930s. Keynes and Beveridge showed the how and the why. Since the Second World War the state has stepped in as guarantor of an adequate level of demand in the economy. It has accepted the principle of full employment; and the practice of 1950–70, when full employment was substantially achieved, has built this into the expectation of the mass of the population. The state has also committed itself to minimum levels of welfare. Moreover, in conceding welfare as a right of citizenship and not simply an entitlement in return for contributions paid, it has established the principle of a 'social' or 'citizen' wage which has brought about 'the partial de-proletarianization of wage labor',[56] and which signifies 'a partial de-commodification of social relations'.[57] Welfare capitalism is still capitalism; but it is capitalism modified by a welfare ethic and a democratic practice which confront it awkwardly with principles drawn from other, non-capitalist, traditions.

By its own expenditure and employment, the state has seen to it that these welfare goals have been achieved for much of the post-war period. State expenditure accounts for between 40 and 60 per cent of Gross Domestic Product in Western European countries, and state employment for between 25 and 30 per cent of total employment. Since the 1970s, moreover, welfare expenditure and employment have come to predominate in the state sectors of all advanced industrial societies, amounting to about one-half of all public expenditure and of all public employment. Thatcherism and Reaganism have had, despite official rhetoric, remarkably little effect on this general pattern. Public expenditure in the Reaganite United States rose from 35.4 per cent of GDP in 1980 to 38 per cent in 1982: 'Reaganomics' unrolled a vast carpet of public borrowing and spending that left the Federal government with the biggest budget deficit in America's history and made the United States, for the first time since 1914, a net debtor to foreign nations. In Thatcherite Britain public expenditure went up from 42.6 per cent of GDP in 1978 to 46.5 per cent in 1982, dropping only to 43.2 per cent in 1986. And while there has been some shift in the composition of public expenditure – towards 'law and order' spending – it remained the case that 60 per cent of Conservative state spending in Britain in 1986 was on social security, health and personal social services, and education and science.[58]

Welfare state capitalism is 'the integrating principle of the modern economic era' . . . 'The era of the welfare state is synonymous with the era of advanced capitalism.'[59] This suggests, as indeed is clearly the case, that whatever ideological difficulties this may pose are more than off-set by the real degree of stabilization and regularization that the welfare state confers on capitalist development. Private capital clearly benefits from state unemployment and sickness insurance, public housing, a national health service and a national education system – as well as, more obviously, from state subsidies to industry and state infrastructural projects such as motorways. It fares even better if in addition it can 'socialize' the expenses of clearing up the industrial waste and pollution for which it is largely responsible. All this contributes to capitalism's well-being by providing valuable social capital investment as well as the 'social consumption' that is necessary to secure the satisfactory reproduction of the labour force. It also aids capitalism's legitimation by substantially softening the blows of *laissez-faire* capitalism of the older kind.[60]

But the integration of welfare and capitalism is, equally clearly, not an effortless process. There is a genuine conflict of principles at stake. The welfare state is the product not just of capitalist needs but also, perhaps more so, of the political struggles of working-class parties and movements.[61] Hence the possibility and prospect of a 'fiscal crisis', a growing gap between state expenditure and state revenue, caused by the escalation of working class demands on the capitalist state. State expenditure may be necessary to capital accumulation in the twentieth-century world, but by the same token, it may inhibit capital accumulation by reducing the quantity of surplus-value available for reinvestment. While this is not necessarily an insuperable problem – much state expenditure is fed back into the capitalist sector[62] the full generalisation of the welfare ethic in the context of political democracy has appeared to some thinkers on the Left to pose a major potential challenge to capitalism. It would mean the starkest opposition of 'person rights' to 'property rights'. 'Demands posed as universal rights and movements constituted by the universal discourse of liberal democracy are prone to become class demands and class movements.'[63] In such a development a key role is marked out for public sector employees. They have grown with the welfare state, and have a vested interest in its expansion. They are powerfully unionized, and have been among the most combative and politically conscious of all organized workers in recent years. Of all social groups, they are the ones most imbued with the 'service ethic' and most hostile to the calculative rationality of capitalist accumulation.[64]

Lenin thought that 'a democratic republic is the best possible political shell for capitalism' and that, 'once capital has gained control of this very best shell', its rule becomes unshakable.[65] What Bowles, Gintis and others seem to be saying is that the democratic shell, far from being a protective cover, has the potentiality to crack the capitalist kernel – or, to change the figure, that democracy is a dagger pointed at the heart of capitalism. Democracy can indeed be uncomfortable for capitalism. Hitler and Franco, not to mention Napoleon III and, in a somewhat different way, Stalin, all show that capitalist development can proceed at a brisk pace when unhampered by democratic constraints. Capitalism can certainly consort with democracy; but at various times and places it has shown that it may find dictatorship a more congenial 'political shell'.

But discomfort is not the same thing as danger. Capitalism may be able to do without democracy, but this does not mean that democracy, through its regular operations, can displace capitalism. The limits of democratic intervention are tragically illustrated in the case of Allende's Chile. Without the accompaniment of an organized revolutionary movement – of which, to repeat, there is no sign in the contemporary capitalist world – democratic pressure on capitalism may be no more than an inconvenience, easily containable. This has been strongly put by James O'Connor, who was the first to raise in an influential way the possibility of a 'fiscal crisis of the state' in the era of the democratic welfare state. 'Budgetary needs may remain unsatisfied and human wants may go unfulfilled, but if those who are dependent on the state do not engage in political struggle to protect or advance their well-being, the fiscal crisis will remain relatively dormant.'[66]

Nothing in O'Connor's analysis in fact suggests an inevitable or insupportable crisis. On the contrary, what emerges as the dominant tendency is the reconstruction of capitalism around what O'Connor calls the 'social–industrial complex'. The most advanced sectors of monopoly capital have already envisaged a 'revision of the social contract' in response to the demands of welfare and other reformers, such as the environmentalists. Since the business community best understands the capitalist system's problems, David Rockefeller urged in the *Wall Street Journal*, it must 'share in designing the solutions. So it is up to businessmen to make common cause with other reformers . . . to prevent the unwise adoption of extreme and emotional remedies . . .'.[67] Monopoly capital can accommodate itself quite comfortably to the new social environment. Basing itself on the customer–contract model, capitalism can carry out, to its own profit, many of the requirements of the welfare state: for health services, housing, recreation, education, scientific and technical research, and armaments (for the welfare state is also the 'warfare state'). It can even become a partner in law enforcement and social control, in the provision of private police forces and private prisons. In the social–industrial complex, private capital does; the state sanctions and pays.

There will, no doubt, be budgetary pressures and crises all the time. This will not, however, give rise to a horizontally linked, self-conscious class, rather to vertically integrated groupings of service suppliers and their respective clients and customers. The tendency, in other words, will be to segment and subdivide a potential mass opposition. Only a 'mass socialist movement', O'Connor concludes, can overcome this divisive effect of the emerging social–industrial complex.[68]

'STRUCTURAL HELPLESSNESS'

O'Connor wrote more than a decade ago. Today the tendencies might seem to be going the other way. In 1980s Britain, under Conservative rule, widespread 'privatization' of state enterprises and state services is taking place. Private home ownership, at the expense of both the public and private rented sectors, has been achieved by two-thirds of all households. One-fifth of the population owns some equity shares, largely through the sale of public enterprises. There is much talk of a 'welfare backlash' and a decisive breakdown of the Keynesian welfare state that was the linchpin of the political consensus of the post-war period.[69]

But do not many of the elements also point to the very 'social–industrial complex' that O'Connor projected? Are not many of them examples of the state's farming out activities to monopolistic sections of private capital? 'Privatization' takes place generally without any corresponding increase in competition. The degree of monopolistic control remains as high after 'privatization' as before (e.g., British Telecom, British Gas, British Airports Authority). The market remains as rigged and regulated by state policies – on such matters, for instance, as consumer credit and currency rates – as it has been since the war. State handouts to industry remain a ready recourse, as in the large public subsidies to British Shipbuilders, British Steel, British Leyland.

There are other, more direct indications of the continuing strength of the state–business nexus. Private industry is invited to fund special schools for achieving 'scientific and technical excellence', with a remit from the state to oversee critical aspects of the curriculum and staff recruitment. Universities and polytechnics are directed to establish customer–contract relationships with private industry as well as government departments. Welfare services are not abandoned – and it is clearly recognized that it would be electorally damaging to do so, given the strong support for the welfare state among the population at large.[70] The state even boosts, and boasts about, its spending on some of the most popular parts, such as the National Health Service. But with noisy self-advertisement it farms out to private enterprise certain ancillary activities, such as hospital catering and cleaning. In all this Conservative spokesmen make great play with the language of the market and 'the spirit of free enterprise'. What they do not point out is how dominant the state remains by virtue of its continuing high level of expenditure and employment. Nor do they remind us – although some Opposition parties have done so – that what the state gives away it can also take back.

It is easy, in the midst of events, to overestimate their importance. This is the journalistic fallacy. The move to the 'Radical Right' in several democracies marks important changes in the moral and ideological climate of those societies (and no one should underrate these 'non-material' factors). Part of the appeal of the New Right is the nostalgic evocation of the past: past glory – 'putting the "Great" back in Great Britain', making America 'stand tall' again; and past values – reviving authority, regenerating the family, marriage and religion. But, however important the past as a storehouse of cultural symbols, there can be no real going back to the political economy of the past – no 'rolling back of the frontiers of the state', no 'dismantling of the welfare apparatus'. The marriage of large-scale monopoly capital with the state has gone too far, and is far too important to both, to be annulled by party rhetoric and short-term party manoeuvring. This has been implicitly acknowledged by New Right leaders, as the level and direction of state spending – noted above – make clear.

Thatcherism and Reaganism are both populist, and draw on anti-state sentiment; but they are also both authoritarian.[71] This leaves the state with a wide discretion, and undiminished power, to intervene according to the perceived needs of the time. At one moment it may be largely the area of ideology and social control – the educational system, the media, local government, police and prisons, and all the paraphernalia of the warfare state (arms spending, internal and external surveillance etc.). At another moment it could take a turn towards corporatism – always, despite current ill-favour, a temptation for all power groups in the zero-sum conditions of advanced industrial societies. The strength of 'apple-pie authoritarianism'[72] indeed lies in its expansive capacity to blend old and new: anti-state rhetoric with massive centralization, *laissez-faire* individualism with organic Toryism, nostalgic patriotism with a hard-headed wooing of foreign multinationals.

As many have pointed out, the political economy of authoritarian populism is distinctly unhelpful and profoundly frustrating to certain sectors of capital – notably, in the US as much as the British case, manufacturing.[73] This suggests that when the necessary 'restructuring' has taken place, longer-term tendencies will re-assert themselves and the continuities with the 1960s and 1970s will be more evident. A Japanese-style corporatism, rather than either the divisive Social Darwinism of the Right or the more statified European corporatism, may well then appear to monopoly capital the most attractive political form. The Reagan–Thatcher phenomenon has the appearance of a temporary holding operation, a hiatus between one phase of capitalism and another, 'post-industrial', phase. In the interregnum, as Gramsci noted, 'a great variety of morbid symptoms appears'.

The strains imposed upon society by the New Right experiment will not necessarily be repaid by a new, streamlined, effective capitalism. The costs in terms of unemployment and social divisiveness may be too high. The new international division of labour may make it more difficult for any but the most powerful capitalist nations to prosper, pushing many erstwhile leaders, such as Britain, further and further down the economic slope. But it need hardly be said these days that such stresses will not necessarily benefit the Left either, whether we consider the prospects for old-style socialism or the newer, greener, vision of a 'sane, humane, ecological' future.[74] Where the Red and Green critiques remain important, however, is in providing an insistent counterpoint to the erratic, crisis-strewn progress of capitalism. They raise questions about the kinds of 'contradictions' that may not necessarily lead to breakdown but rather reflect a certain 'structural helplessness'[75] in the face of accumulating problems and frustrations within the capitalist world order.

How, for instance, will the capitalist (or any other) world deal with the now visible 'energy gap' that by common expert consent will confront industrial civilization early in the next century?[76] How far can nuclear power, with its attendant risks and danger, supply the want and at what costs to political freedoms? What of the continuing environmental destruction and depletion of natural resources? How practicable though are alternative sources of energy or alternative, 'low-energy' life-styles? The current answers are not reassuring.[77]

What also of the continuing moral, social and psychological costs of capitalism? A growing literature points to the insufficiency of capitalism to satisfy consumption wants and human needs at anything but the crudest material levels. The 'dizzy pirouette of wants and commodities' created by advanced capitalism has led to the fragmentation and homogenization of needs, and 'the dissolution of the commodity into an unstable network of characteristics and messages'.[78] Not only are needs and wants thus no longer satisfied by commodities, but needs themselves are distended and distorted by capitalist requirements to the point where some of them inflict physical and psychological damage on individuals while others – such as the needs for community, care and respect – receive no recognition whatsoever.[79]

Disraeli thought that modern society had mistaken comfort for civilization; to this Tibor Scitovsky adds the equally penetrating criticism that affluent Western society has mistaken comfort for pleasure – or rather, allowed active pleasure to be displaced by mere comfort.[80] In a similar vein Hirsch points to the disappointments of consumers who fail to get the quality (or 'positional') goods and services that they had legitimately expected as they progress economically;[81] while Hirschman adds the melancholy twist that inevitable disappointment and disillusion are in store if and when those consumers get the very goods they have set their hearts on.[82]

Market mechanisms and mentalities invade every sphere of life – not simply work and politics, but recreation, friendship, family and marriage. All are subjected to the capitalist rationality of 'least cost' and 'utility maximization'. But the market is a poor mechanism for handling the non-material and the social spheres of human life. It cannot easily deliver 'positional' and public goods, and it is inefficient in its own self-professed goal of maximizing personal well-being and happiness. Discontent and divisions among many are the other side of material abundance for some.[83]

The end of societies is as slow as their beginning, frequently more so. Revolutionary cataclysms may hasten it, though they may also, as Tocqueville noted, give existing social orders a new lease of life. If, as many historians from Marx onwards have suggested, capitalism took three or more centuries to emerge from feudalism, why expect its decline and demise to take so much less? Industrial capitalism was established, on a reasonably general scale, only by the end of the nineteenth century. In the course of this century it has extended its reach and intensified its hold. The very novelty of its full operation, and the dynamism intrinsic to its mode, have misled some into seeing the emergence of a 'post-industrial' society – barely half a century after industrial society itself had in any real sense come of age. This would be rapid change indeed and, one might add, unprecedented. Social orders change somewhat more slowly than intellectual fashions. Post-industrial theorists have sought to foreshorten capitalism's past and foreclose its future every bit as roughly and arbitrarily as revolutionary socialists.[84]

Some thinkers indeed have been pointing to signs of the renewal rather than the replacement of capitalism. Those convinced of cyclical phenomena such as Kondratieff 'long waves' have suggested that far from facing long-term decline we may be on the threshold of a new upswing in the economy. 'Information technology' and its associated cultural infrastructure will provide the spur to a new swarm of technological innovations which will revitalize the world economy, just as cars and electrical goods pulled the economy out of the global recession of the 1930s.[85] Other thinkers, also depending to some extent on a hopeful view of the new technology, have discerned a 'second industrial divide' marking the long-term evolution of capitalist society. Computer-controlled 'flexible' production in small 'high-tech cottage indu-stries', as in the new industrial districts of central and north-eastern Italy, is bringing about a regeneration of the work environment and may allow capitalism to go beyond the alienating 'Fordism' of classic large-scale mass production.[86]

Marx wrote, with a significance still often unappreciated, that 'the bourgeois period of history has to create the material basis of the new world'.[87] Driving the point home in his account of the continuing world-wide expansion of capitalism, David Harvey remarks that 'the "historical mission" of the bourgeoisie is not accomplished overnight, nor are the "material conditions of a new world" created in a day.'[88] We can expect, as ever before, massive disruptions and bloody turmoil as capitalism continues to transform the world. It remains the case that, half a century after Keynes warned us of it, 'avarice and usury and precaution must be our gods for a little longer still'.[89] The discontents and disappointments of industrial life can be expected to increase *pari passu* with world industrialization. But whether, when and from where the new society will emerge as the fruits of this travail are questions clothed in obscurity.

NOTES

1 A. Toynbee, *A Study of History*, vol. 4: *The Breakdown of Civilizations* (Oxford, Oxford University Press, 1962).
2 M. Weber, *The Agrarian Sociology of Ancient Civilizations*, trans R. I. Frank (London, New Left Books, 1976), p. 389.
3 T. Malthus, *An Essay on the Principles of Population* (Harmondsworth, Penguin Books, 1985), pp. 118–19.
4 Toynbee, *Breakdown of Civilizations*, p. 61.
5 F. Braudel, 'History and the social sciences: the long term', *Social Science Information*, 9 (1970), 145–74.
6 J. Schumpeter, *Capitalism, Socialism and Democracy*, 5th edn (London, Allen and Unwin, 1976), pp. 162–3. My emphasis.
7 T. Skocpol, *States and Social Revolutions* (Cambridge, Cambridge University Press, 1979).
8 See T. Bottomore, *Marxist Sociology* (London, Macmillan, 1975); H. Davis and R. Scase, *Western Capitalism and State Socialism* (Oxford, Basil Blackwell, 1985).
9 H. Braverman, *Labor and Monopoly Capital: The Degradation of Work in the Twentieth Century* (New York and London, Monthly Review Press, 1974).
10 P.M. Sweezy, *Modern Capitalism and Other Essays* (New York and London, Monthly Review Press, 1972); R. Heilbroner, *The Nature and Logic of Capitalism* (New York and London, W. W. Norton, 1985).
11 'The modern history of capital dates from the creation in the sixteenth century of a world-embracing commerce and a world-embracing market' (Marx, *Capital*, vol. I, trans. S. Moore and E. Aveling, Moscow, Foreign Languages Publishing House, p. 146). Elsewhere in *Capital* Marx writes that with the development of capitalism there takes place 'the entanglement of all peoples in the net of the world market, and with this, the growth of the international character of the capitalist regime' (p. 763). It is curious, though, that Marx nowhere develops an economic theory of imperialism, despite – as A. O. Hirschman points out in 'On Hegel, imperialism and structural stagnation', *Journal of Development Economics*, 3 (1976), 1–8 – almost certainly having seen it sketched in Hegel's *Philosophy of Right*.
12 K. Marx, *Grundrisse*, trans. M. Nicolaus (London, Allen Lane, 1975), p. 705.
13 Braudel suggests one reason for Marx's success in prognosis: 'The genius of Marx, the secret of the continuing power of his thought, resides in his having been the first to construct real social models, based on an essentially long-term view of history' (Braudel, 'History and the social sciences', p. 172).
14 Marx, *Grundrisse*, p. 411.
15 A. Maddison, *Phases of Capitalist Development* (Oxford, Oxford University Press, 1982), pp. 64–95.

16 G. Merritt, *World Out of Work* (London, Collins, 1982).

17 Maddison, *Phases of Capitalist Development*, pp. 142–57.

18 G. Barraclough, 'The end of an era', *New York Review of Books*, 27 June 1975, p. 20, 'The Great World Crisis I', ibid., 23 January 1975, p. 24; 'The haves and the have nots', ibid., 13 May 1976, p. 31.

19 G. Barraclough, 'Waiting for the new order', *New York Review of Books*, 26 October 1978, p. 47.

20 The central role of Henry Kissinger in this, as Secretary of State during the Nixon and Ford administrations, is well brought out in the accounts by Barraclough, 'Waiting for the new order' and 'The struggle for the Third World', *New York Review of Books*, 9 November 1978, pp. 47–58, and by S. Rousseas, *Capitalism and Catastrophe: A Critical Appraisal of the Limits to Capitalism* (Cambridge, Cambridge University Press, 1979), pp. 86–93.

21 Cited in Barraclough, 'Waiting for the new order', p. 49; and for the general account, see Rousseas, *Capitalism and Catastrophe*, pp. 76–93.

22 Barraclough, 'The struggle for the Third World', p. 56.

23 I. Wallerstein, *The Capitalist World-Economy* (Cambridge, Cambridge University Press, 1979), p. 68.

24 See, for example, R. Heilbroner, *Business Civilization in Decline* (Harmondsworth, Penguin Books, 1977); T. Bottomore, *Sociology and Socialism* (Brighton, Wheatsheaf Books, 1984), p. 160.

25 Rousseas, *Capitalism and Catastrophe*, pp. 93, 96–7.

26 K. Marx, *Theories of Surplus Value* (Moscow, Foreign Languages Publishing House, 1968), p. 497n.

27 T. Bottomore, *Theories of Modern Capitalism* (London, George Allen and Unwin, 1985), p. 13. Cf. G. A. Cohen: 'Marx was not a breakdown theorist . . . There is no economically legislated final breakdown' (*Karl Marx's Theory of History: a Defense*, Princeton, NJ, Princeton University Press, pp. 203–4). Maddison also notes: 'Though Marx expected capitalism's ultimate collapse in favour of socialism, his breakdown hypothesis is basically socio-political rather than economic. He expected increasing polarization of the interests of workers and capitalists, and the breakdown was expected as a result of the victory of the workers' interest' (*Phases of Capitalist Development*, p. 18). See also Rousseas, *Capitalism and Catastrophe*, pp. 11–14, and the discussion in E. Hobsbawm, 'Marx and history', *New Left Review*, no. 143 (Jan.–Feb. 1984), pp. 44–8; E. M. Wood, 'Marxism and the course of history', *New Left Review*, no. 147 (Sept.–Oct. 1984), pp. 102–7; Heilbroner, *Nature and Logic of Capitalism*, pp. 178–9, 194–208; A. Shaikh, 'Economic crises', in T. Bottomore (ed.), *A Dictionary of Marxist Thought* (Oxford, Basil Blackwell, 1985), pp. 138–43 and J. O'Connor, *The Meaning of Crisis: A Theoretical Introduction* (Oxford, Basil Blackwell, 1987), pp. 49–107. And cf. also Marx's caution that the 'law' of the falling rate of profit 'acts only as a tendency', and that 'it is only under certain circumstances and only after long periods that its effects become strikingly pronounced' (*Capital*, vol. III, ed. F. Engels, Moscow, Foreign Languages Publishing House, 1959, p. 233). For a more 'determinist' view of the economic contradictions of capitalism, see however, Marx, *Grundrisse*, pp. 411ff, 748–50.

28 R. Hilferding, *Finance Capital: A Study of the Latest Phase of Capitalist Development*, trans. M. Watnick and S. Gordon (London, Routledge and Kegan Paul, 1981;

122   *Continuities and Discontinuities*

first published 1910), p. 366.
29 R. Luxemburg, *The Accumulation of Capital – An Anti-Critique*, trans. R. Wichmann (New York and London, Monthly Review Press, 1972), p. 58.
30 'Capital accumulation progresses and expands at the expense of non-capitalist strata and countries, squeezing them out at an ever faster rate. The general tendency and final result of this process is the exclusive world rule of capitalist production. Once this is reached, Marx's model becomes valid: accumulation, i.e. further expansion of capital, becomes impossible. Capitalism comes to a dead end, it cannot function any more as the historical vehicle for the unfolding of the productive forces, it reaches its objective economic limit' (Luxemburg, *Accumulation of Capital*, pp. 145–6).
31 Ibid., p. 146. 'Here, as elsewhere in history, theory is performing its duty if it shows us the *tendency* of development, the logical conclusion to which it is objectively heading. There is as little chance of this conclusion being reached as there was for any other previous period of social development to unfold itself completely. The *need* for it to be reached becomes less as social consciousness, embodied this time in the socialist proletariat, becomes more involved as an active factor in the blind game of forces. In this case, too, a correct conception of Marx's theory offers the most fruitful suggestions and the most powerful stimulus for this consciousness' (ibid., pp. 146–7). This was Luxemburg's riposte to Otto Bauer's attack on her for an allegedly mechanistic theory of the collapse of capitalism. As quoted by her, Bauer had concluded: 'Capitalism will not collapse from the mechanical impossibility of realizing surplus value. It will be defeated by the rebellion to which it drives the masses' (ibid., p. 149). This is also Luxemburg's position, as it was Karl Kautsky's: 'We consider the breakdown of the present social system to be unavoidable, because we know that the economic evolution inevitably brings on conditions that will compel the exploited classes to rise against this system of private ownership' (K. Kautsky, *The Class Struggle*, trans. W. E. Bohn, New York, W. W. Norton, 1971, p. 90).
     Georges Sorel made an even stronger stand against the idea of the historical inevitability of the demise of capitalism as a result of its economic contradictions. Socialism was for him primarily a moral, not an economic doctrine. It 'brings to the world a new manner of judging all human acts'; it 'confronts the bourgeois world as an irreconcilable adversary, threatening it with a moral catastrophe much more than with a material catastrophe' (quoted in Bottomore, *Marxist Sociology*, p. 33). Cf. Adam Przeworski: 'Socialism was originally an invention of a morally sensitive bourgeoise', in 'Proletariat into a class; the process of class formation from Karl Kautsky's *The Class Struggle* to recent controversies', *Politics and Society*, 7(1977), 343–401.
32 Schumpeter, *Capitalism*, p. 163 n.7.
33 Marx, *Grundrisse*, pp. 409–10, emphasis in original.
34 D. Harvey, *The Limits to Capital* (Oxford, Basil Blackwell, 1982), p. 416.
35 Ibid., p. 148.
36 Ibid., pp. 427–8.
37 Ibid., p. 442.
38 For a helpful critical discussion, with copious citation, of the immense literature on proletarian class consciousness, see especially Przeworski, 'Proletariat into class';

S. M. Lipset, 'Whatever happened to the proletariat?', *Encounter*, 56 (1981), 18–34; and G. Marshall, 'Some remarks on the study of working-class consciousness', *Politics and Society*, 12 (1983), 263–301. On the British working class specifically, and the sectional divisions, fragmentation and privatization that many have discerned in its recent development, see E. Hobsbawm, 'The forward march of labour halted?', in E. Hobsbawm and others, *The Forward March of Labour Halted?* (London, Verso/NLB, 1981); G. Marshall, D. Rose, C. Vogler and H. Newby, 'Class, citizenship and distributional conflict in modern Britain', *British Journal of Sociology*, 36 (1985), 259–284; H. Newby, C. Vogler, D. Rose and G. Marshall, 'From class structure to class action: British working class politics in the 1980s', in B. Roberts, R. Finnegan and D. Gallie (eds), *New Approaches to Economic Life* (Manchester, Manchester University Press, 1985); R. E. Pahl and C. Wallace, 'Neither angels in marble nor rebels in red: privatisation and working-class consciousness', in D. Rose (ed.), *Social Stratification and Economic Change* (London, Hutchinson, 1988). And cf. R. Williams: 'there is no real point in pretending that the capitalist social order has not done its main job of implanting a deep assent to capitalism, even in a period of its most evident economic failures. On the old assumptions it would have been impossible to have 4 million people unemployed in Britain, and most of our common services in crisis or breaking down, and yet for the social order itself to be so weakly challenged or political support for it to be so readily mobilized. Yet that is where we are', *The Year 2000* (New York, Pantheon Books, 1983) (published in Britain as *Towards 2000*), p. 254.

39 Hobsbawm, 'Marx and history', p. 45. For a spirited rejoinder to this objection, see Wood, 'Marxism and the course of history'. Wood argues that while capitalism 'offers less than an absolute *promise* of socialism', it 'offers more than a mere *possibility*'. 'Capitalism has created conditions in which the freedom from exploitation and class can be more than an abstract ideal or a vague aspiration. It has created conditions in which socialism can be the concrete and immediate object of class struggle. It has placed socialism "on the agenda"' (ibid., p. 107).

This is at least better than Wallerstein's casual, almost careless, formulation, which while wishing to retain historical openness still wants to hang on to historical inevitability: 'There are secular developments in the structure of the capitalist world-system such that we can envisage that its internal contradictions as a system will bring it to an end in the twenty-first or twenty-second century' (*The Capitalist World-Economy*, p. 67). Capitalism promotes short-term profit maximization and, in pursuit of this, stimulates mass consumer demand. This leads to a process of 'rising expectations' and resulting social conflicts. Such a 'contradictory' development makes 'co-option' ever more costly and will eventually undermine capitalism (ibid., pp. 35, 83).

For Sweezy, the 'principal contradiction' of capitalism is not so much one lying *within* the developed capitalist nations – state welfare and warfare expenditure can take care of this for a long time – but that between the developed and underdeveloped nations in the world system of capitalism. 'National liberation struggles', on the lines of China, Cuba and Vietnam, indicate the manner in which capitalism is likely to be defeated in the long run (*Modern Capitalism*, pp. 13–14, 48–51, 143, 165). This follows the Luxemburg line: conflict born of exploitation will overthrow capitalism long before it reaches its 'theoretical limit'.

It is Harvey who suggests the most cataclysmic end to capitalism – though neither socialism nor anything else appear 'on the agenda' as its successor. Military expenditures, as he notes, have increasingly been capitalism's means of absorbing surpluses of capital and labour power. In recent years especially, capitalism has been stabilized through the defence budget. This idea has 'dreadful' implications: 'Not only must weapons be bought and paid for out of surpluses of capital and labour, *but they must also be put to use*. For this is the only means that capitalism has at its disposal to achieve the levels of devaluation now required' (*Limits to Capital*, p. 455; my emphasis).

40 C. Offe, *Disorganized Capitalism: Contemporary Transformations of Work and Politics* (Oxford, Polity Press, 1985); F. Block and L. Hirschhorn, 'New productive forces and the contradictions of contemporary capitalism', *Theory and Society*, 7 (1979), 363–95; Williams, *The Year 2000*.

41 The proportion of the workforce that is unionized averages about 30 per cent for the major countries of Western Europe (the main exceptions are Belgium and the Nordic countries, which are higher, and France, which is lower) (Offe, *Disorganized Capitalism*, p. 336, n. 13; G. Therborn, 'The prospects of labour and the transformation of advanced capitalism', *New Left Review*, no. 145 (May–June 1984), p. 11). In the United States, with a historically low rate, the proportion in 1984 was under 20 per cent (M. Davis, *Prisoners of the American Dream: Politics and Economy in the History of the US Working Class*, London, New Left Books, 1986, p. 147); in the UK, with an historically high rate, the proportion is now close to the European average – 31 per cent in 1985 (Department of Employment, 'Membership of trade unions in 1985', *Employment Gazette*, 95 (1987), no. 2, pp. 84–8). And on the problematic relationship now of the unions to the 'general interest' of the working class, see Williams, *The Year 2000*, pp. 160–72.

42 'In the Federal Republic of Germany, for example, every second worker and every third white-collar employee is retired from gainful employment before reaching the age limit, and every sixth worker and every tenth white-collar employee becomes chronically incapable of gainful employment before reaching the age of 50' (Offe, *Disorganized Capitalism*, p. 329, n. 23).

43 F. Hirsch, *Social Limits to Growth* (London, Routledge and Kegan Paul, 1977) and see also ch. 2 of this volume.

44 A. Fox, *Beyond Contract: Work, Power and Trust Relations* (London, Faber, 1974); J. H. Goldthorpe, 'The current inflation: towards a sociological account', in F. Hirsch and J. H. Goldthorpe (eds), *The Political Economy of Inflation* (London, Martin Robertson, 1978); M. Gilbert, 'A sociological model of inflation', *Sociology*, 15 (1981), 185–209; J. O'Connor, *Accumulation Crisis* (Oxford, Basil Blackwell, 1984).

45 C. Maier, 'The politics of inflation in the twentieth century', in Hirsch and Goldthorpe, *Political Economy of Inflation*, p. 90.

46 L. C. Thurow, *The Zero-Sum Society: Distribution and the Possibilities for Economic Change* (Harmondsworth, Penguin Books, 1981).

47 K. Marx, *The Class Struggles in France*, in K. Marx and F. Engels, *Selected Works in Two Volumes* (Moscow, Foreign Languages Publishing House, 1962), vol. 1, p. 172. Cf. V. I. Lenin, 'The state and revolution', in *Selected Works* (Moscow, Foreign Languages Publishing House, 1960), vol. 2, p. 358.

48 K. Polyani, *The Great Transformation* (Boston, Mass., Beacon Press, 1957), pp. 130–50; D. Bell, *The Cultural Contradictions of Capitalism* (London, Heinemann, 1976), p. 224; I. Kristol, *Two Cheers for Capitalism* (New York, Mentor Books, 1979), p. 245.

49 G. Therborn, 'The rule of capital and the rise of democracy', *New Left Review*, no. 103 (May–June 1977), pp. 3–41; A. J. Mayer, *The Persistence of the Old Regime: Europe to the Great War* (New York, Pantheon Books, 1981).

50 S. Brittan, 'The economic contradictions of democracy', *British Journal of Political Science*, 5 (1975), 129–59.

51 Ibid., p. 156.

52 Bell, *Cultural Contradictions*, p. 232.

53 J. O'Connor, *The Fiscal Crisis of the State* (New York, St Martin's Press, 1973); J. Habermas, *Legitimation Crisis*, trans. T. McCarthy (London, Heinemann, 1976); A. Wolfe, *The Limits of Legitimacy: Political Contradictions of Contemporary Capitalism* (New York, The Free Press, 1977). So we might say that while liberals emphasize 'the economic contradictions of democracy', radicals emphasize 'the political contradictions of capitalism'.

54 S. Bowles and H. Gintis, 'The crisis of liberal democratic capitalism: the case of the United States', *Politics and Society*, 11 (1982), 51–93, and *Democracy and Capitalism: Property, Community and the Contradictions of Modern Social Thought* (London, Routledge and Kegan Paul, 1986).

55 Offe, *Disorganized Capitalism*, p. 145; see also Therborn, 'The prospects of labour', p. 25. Cf. Bell: 'The historical watershed is the fact that a normative societal commitment [to welfare] has been made, and it . . . is largely irreversible', *Cultural Contradictions*, p. 226; and see Brittan, 'Economic contradictions', p. 130.

56 Bowles and Gintis, 'Crisis of liberal democratic capitalism', p. 88.

57 Therborn, 'The prospects of labour', p. 29; see also Offe, *Disorganized Capitalism*, p. 97.

58 For the figures in this paragraph, and commentary on them, see R. Rose, *Changes in Public Employment: A Multi-dimensional Comparative Analysis* (Glasgow, Centre for the Study of Public Policy, University of Strathclyde, 1980); Therborn, 'The prospects of labour', pp. 27–9, 34–5; *The Times*, 24 January 1985 and 8 November 1986; Davis, *Prisoners of the American Dream*, pp. 235–6; J. Krieger, *Reagan, Thatcher and the Politics of Decline* (Oxford, Polity Press, 1986), pp. 91–101, 159–76; R. Parry, 'Social policy', in H. Drucker, P. Dunleavy, A. Gamble and G. Peele (eds), *Developments in British Politics 2* (London, Macmillan, 1986), pp. 208–9; D. Kavanagh, *Thatcherism and British Politics: The End of Consensus?* (Oxford, Oxford University Press, 1987), pp. 212–30; Central Statistical Office, *Social Trends* No. 17 (London, HMSO, 1987), p. 114.

In view of common misconceptions, a number of things need to be said about 'the Thatcher effect' in Britain in the 1980s. First, the annual average growth in public spending since the Conservatives came to office in 1979 has exceeded that of the Labour government of 1974–9: 1.3 per cent a year under the Conservatives compared with 1 per cent under Labour (*The Times*, 8 November 1986). Second, any changes in the size and composition of public expenditure – which, due largely to increased unemployment, are not great – and such discontinuities in social policy as there are, began under Labour, before the Conservatives took office (I.

Gough, *The Political Economy of the Welfare State*, London, Macmillan, 1979, pp. 131–41: and 'Thatcherism and the welfare state', in S. Hall and M. Jacques (eds). *The Politics of Thatcherism*, London, Lawrence and Wishart, 1983, pp. 148–9; S. Hall, 'The Great Moving Right Show', in Hall and Jacques, *The Politics of Thatcherism*; Krieger, *Reagan, Thatcher* . . ., p. 94). Third, much of the more publicized Thatcherite legislation, such as the 'anti-union' laws, have had little impact on actual practice (on industrial relations see N. Milward and M. Stevens *British Workplace Industrial Relations 1980–84*, Aldershot, Gower, 1987; M. Goldring, 'The Thatcher effect: two nations on the same street', *The Listener*, 2 April, pp. 12–13). Mrs Thatcher has been very successful in altering the moral climate of Britain; she has been less successful in altering its structural continuities. For a balanced assessment, see Kavanagh, *Thatcherism and British Politics*.

For Reagan's parallel difficulties in holding back public expenditure in the United States – due partly to successful Congressional pressure in maintaining domestic social programmes – see G. B. Mills, 'The Budget: a failure of discipline', in J. L. Palmer and I. V. Sawhill (eds), *The Reagan Record: An Assessment of America's Changing Domestic Priorities* (Cambridge, Mass., Ballinger, 1984); D. L. Bawden and J. L. Palmer, 'Social policy: challenging the welfare state', in Palmer and Sawhill (eds), *The Reagan Record*; Krieger, *Reagan, Thatcher* . . ., pp. 154–86; J. J. Hogan, 'President Reagan's fiscal policies: the record of his first term', *Politics*, 7 (1987), 14–20. These show that Federal social programme spending as a proportion of GNP has barely shifted under Reagan from its post-war high of 11 per cent in 1976. Bawden and Palmer's assessment seems fair: 'As it turned out, Congress and the Courts have been considerable moderating forces on the president's intentions. Congress acted to protect many of the Great Society programs and to hold together the bottom tier of the safety net. As a result, by and large, the most ineffective programs were deeply cut or eliminated, while the programs more generally acknowledged as effective were left unscathed or reduced only modestly . . . Somewhat ironically, . . . social spending cuts look like the Achilles' heel of the president's overall budget policy. Because none of the recent program cuts have addressed the basic entitlements and indexed nature of the major social programs, their continued real growth – particularly that of Social Security and Medicare – places more pressure on taxes and defense for solutions to the deficit problem' (pp. 214–15); see also V. Navarro, 'The 1984 election and the New Deal: an alternative explanation' (in two parts), *Social Policy*, 15 (1985), pp. 3–10; 16 (1985), 7–17.

59 O'Connor, *Fiscal Crisis*, p. 72; Gough, *Political Economy of the Welfare State*, p. 74.
60 O'Connor, *Fiscal Crisis*.
61 Gough, *Political Economy of the Welfare State*, pp. 55–74; Bowles and Gintis, 'Crisis of liberal democratic capitalism', pp. 64–84. One could also say that, given the short-term view and blinkered outlook of many individual capitalists, working-class struggles for the welfare state were necessary ('functional') in the long-term interests of capitalism itself. Cf. Gough (following Marx): 'Paradoxically . . . it would appear that labour indirectly aids the long-term accumulation of capital and strengthens capitalist social relations by struggling for its own interests within the state. One could apply this approach to much welfare policy this century' (ibid., p. 55).

Limits and Capacities 127

62 Gough, ibid., pp. 108–17.
63 Bowles and Gintis, 'Crisis of liberal democratic capitalism', p. 92.
64 O'Connor, *Fiscal Crisis*, pp. 236–43; Gough, *Political Economy of the Welfare State*, pp. 141–4; Therborn, 'The prospects of labour', pp. 33–5; Offe, *Disorganized Capitalism*, pp. 139–40.
65 Lenin, 'The state and revolution', p. 312.
66 O'Connor, *Fiscal Crisis*, p. 226.
67 Quoted O'Connor, ibid., p. 227.
68 Ibid., pp. 249–55; Gough, *Political Economy of the Welfare State*, pp. 138–41.
69 See, for example, S. M. Miller, 'New welfare state models and mixes', *Social Policy*, 17 (1986), 10–18.
70 This is shown not just for Britain (P. Taylor-Gooby, 'Citizenship and welfare', in R. Jowell and S. Witherspoon, eds, *British Social Attitudes: The 1987 Report*, Aldershot, Gower, 1987; Krieger, *Reagan, Thatcher* ..., pp. 88–90; Kavanagh, *Thatcherism and British Politics*, p. 217), but also in continuing public support for the social programmes of the New Deal and the Great Society in the United States (Navarro, 'The 1984 election'). Neither in the United States nor Britain is endorsement whole-hearted and clear-cut. As both Taylor-Gooby and Navarro show, public support for welfare is selective and pragmatic, not ideological or 'universalist'. The Thatcher government's practice has echoed this closely: 'government provision of social services within an anti-welfarist ideology, benefit but no beliefs, welfare but no welfare state' (Krieger, *Reagan, Thatcher* ..., p. 89; see also Parry 'Social policy', p. 209).
71 Hall, 'The Great Moving Right Show'; K. Phillips, 'Post-Conservative America', *New York Review of Books*, 13 May 1982, pp. 27–32; T. M. Moe, 'The politicized presidency', in J. E. Chubb and P. E. Peterson (eds), *The New Direction in American Politics* (Washington, DC, Brookings Institution, 1985).
72 Phillips, 'Post-Conservative America', p. 32.
73 B. Jessop, B. Bonnett, S. Bromley and T. Ling, 'Authoritarian populism, two nations and Thatcherism', *New Left Review*, no. 147 (Sept.–Oct. 1984), pp. 32–60; C. Leys, 'Thatcherism and British manufacturing: a question of hegemony', *New Left Review*, no. 151 (May–June 1985), pp. 5–25; Krieger, *Reagan, Thatcher* ..., pp. 159–65.
74 J. Robertson, *Future Work: Jobs, Self-employment and Leisure After the Industrial Age* (Aldershot, Gower, 1985).
75 Offe, *Disorganized Capitalism*, p. 63.
76 And cf. Williams: 'A surprising number of otherwise well-informed people suppose that the systematic crisis has gone away because new oilfields have been discovered, or new energy sources, or new anti-pollution technologies, or simply because the economic depression since 1973 has reduced all the pressures. This is merely foolish. Every quantity and date in *The Limits to Growth* could be amended and yet the radical questions it poses would stand' (*The Year 2000*, p. 17; see also pp. 214ff for the continuing relevance of 'the ecological argument').
77 P. E. Hodgson, *Our Nuclear Future?* (Belfast and Ottawa, Christian Journals Ltd., 1983); J. Edmonds and J. M. Reilly, *Global Energy: Assessing the Future* (New York, Oxford University Press, 1985); United Nations, *Our Common Future: Report of the World Commission on Environment and Development* (Oxford and New York, Oxford

University Press, 1987).

78 W. Leiss, *The Limits to Satisfaction: On Needs and Commodities* (London, Marion Boyars, 1978).

79 Williams, *The Year 2000*; M. Ignatieff, *The Needs of Strangers* (London, Chatto and Windus, 1984).

80 T. Scitovsky, *The Joyless Economy: An Inquiry into Human Satisfaction and Consumer Dissatisfaction* (New York, Oxford University Press, 1977).

81 Hirsch, *Social Limits to Growth*.

82 Hirschman, *Shifting Involvements*.

83 A. K. Sen, 'The profit motive', *Lloyds Bank Review*, no. 147 (1983), pp. 1–20.

84 K. Kumar, *Prophecy and Progress: The Sociology of Industrial and Post-industrial Society* (Harmondsworth, Penguin Books, 1978); R. J. Badham, *Theories of Industrial Society* (New York, St. Martin's Press, 1986).

85 C. Freeman, J. Clark and L. Soete, *Unemployment and Technical Innovation* (London, Frances Pinter, 1982); D. Bell, 'The social framework of the information society', in T. Forester (ed.), *The Information Technology Revolution* (Oxford, Basil Blackwell, 1985); J. Gershuny, 'The leisure principle', *New Society*, 13 February 1987, pp. 10–13. But cf. Hirschman's comment on the Kondratieff cycle, 'whose duration is so long (50–60 years) that, given the limited historical experience with capitalism so far, we cannot be quite sure whether it really exists' (*Shifting Involvements*, p. 4). For a discussion of 'long wave' theory, see T. Kitwood, 'A farewell wave to the theory of long waves', *Universities Quarterly*, 38 (1984), 158–78; and see also, on the 'information society', D. Lyon, 'From "post-industrialism" to "information society": a new social transformation?', *Sociology*, 20 (1986), 577–88.

86 M. Piore and C. F. Sabel, *The Second Industrial Divide: Possibilities for Prosperity* (New York, Basic Books, 1984).

87 Marx and Engels, *Selected Works*, vol. I, p. 358.

88 Harvey, *Limits to Capital*, p. 436.

89 J. M. Keynes, 'Economic possibilities for our grandchildren' (1930), in *The Collected Writings of John Maynard Keynes*, vol. IX: *Essays in Persuasion* (London, Macmillan, 1972), p. 331.

PART II

Politics, Work and Society

6

Class and Political Action in Nineteenth-century England: Theoretical and Comparative Perspectives

> It is the glory of the Socialists ... that they have thrown themselves with enthusiastic zeal into the study of at least one social group, namely the factory operatives; and here lies the secret of their partial success. But unfortunately, they have made the special study of a single fragment of society the basis of a theory which quietly substitutes for the small group of Parisian proletaires or English factory-workers, the society of all Europe – nay, of the whole world.
>
> George Eliot, 'The natural history of German life'

Political sociology has from its very inception had an overriding concern with the nature of political order and stability, and the threats to that stability. Ever since 'the entry of the masses on to the stage of history', at the time of the French Revolution, one source of that threat has regularly been seen as the industrial working class. That has been so, whether the threat was perceived by the liberal Centre and conservative Right; or whether it was converted, by the Left, into a definite promise to overthrow 'bourgeois' stability. In both cases, in the anxious speculations of Mill and Tocqueville as much as the triumphant predictions of Marx and Engels, a key role was marked out for the developing working class of nineteenth-century Europe.

Studies of the European working class abound; and it is not my intention here to add to these, at least in the usual form. The case for returning to a familiar theme of political sociology must rest, not upon the unearthing of new material, but upon the need to reconsider what is in one sense a well-known story. Not a lack of information, or of detailed case studies, bedevil the field, but the imposition of an approach that has distorted the vision of scores of researchers in both history and sociology. I refer here, in general, to the concept of 'class as an agency of social change'; and, in particular, to the view that sees political action as the result, essentially, of the more or less conscious activity of particular classes in pursuit of their perceived class interest. It is in such a view that, for instance, the English Reform Act of 1832 and the repeal of the Corn Laws in 1846 appear as middle-class victories; just as the repeal of the Combination Acts in 1824 and the passing of the Factory Acts of the 1830s and 1840s are seen as victories of the working class, the result of their organization and action. Clearly, the theme is of general significance in the study of the relation between class and political action. It applies to all classes, in most periods of European history. But it has had – largely, of course, owing to Marxist theory and Marxist politics – an unusually strong influence on conceptions of European working-class movements over the past two centuries, in the ways these are perceived and studied.

In this chapter I shall restrict myself largely to the nineteenth-century working class in England, making comparisons with other classes and other countries where it seems appropriate. The reason for this concentration is partly that there exists a particularly rich crop of studies of that class, in that period, which makes it an especially suitable case for illustration. But also these studies have been embodied under the aegis of a whole school, almost a whole philosophy, of left-wing historiography, which has been extremely influential in the study of working-class movements not simply in England, but also on the continent of Europe, and in the United States. In considering the English case, therefore, one may hope to raise questions of a general and theoretical kind that should have relevance for all students of working-class politics and history.

Of these questions, a number suggest themselves on practically any immediate consideration of the material. Does it make sense, for instance, to talk of 'the making of *the* English working class' (or 'the' French or German working class), even if we restrict ourselves simply to the nineteenth century? In examining 'working-class movements' or 'working-class consciousness', in any country in nineteenth-century Europe, *which* working class (or classes) are we referring to? Is it fundamentally the same throughout the century, and, if not, what is the significance of the changes within it? Or, again, how far can we consider the working class (or the middle class) as an autonomous grouping, capable of initiating change out of its own principle of organization and action? What is the relation of the working class to other classes in society, and how important is this in affecting working-class activity? What, for that matter, is the impact on working-class behaviour of developments in the society as a whole, of changes in its national and international character? In discussing the treatment of the English working class, as it developed from the end of the eighteenth century, I hope to be able to comment on these and related questions.

I

Since the view of class in nineteenth-century England derives much of its force from a contrast, implicit or explicit, with the preceding century, it will help to consider briefly class in eighteenth-century England. Here there is an impressive degree of harmony and agreement among historians, not by any means restricted to Marxist historians. If by 'class' we mean the kind of thing we encounter in the nineteenth century, then eighteenth-century England is a 'classless society'.[1] Or, putting the same point another way, it is a 'one-class society', containing 'a large number of status groups but only one body of persons capable of concerted action over the whole area of society, only one class in fact'.[2] Eighteenth-century English society was dominated politically, economically and socially by a single, unified, nationwide, elite, the landed aristocracy, 'standing at the head of all the "interests" of the social pyramid, [and holding] in its hands the strings of connection and dependency which held society together in a hierarchical system'.[3]

In this conception, no other social groups apart from the aristocracy are capable of independent action. They are locked in relationships of dependency with the landed elite, usually in the form of patron–client relationships. The middling groups – tradesmen, merchants and professionals – depend upon the government of the day for financial patronage and upon social elites for place and favour.[4] The lower classes exist in an even greater state of dependency. There is no 'working class' here, in the sense of a group based on a perceived sense of a community of interest, and in common opposition to a class or classes above them. There is instead the plebs, the populace, the crowd, the mob. Vertical ties of 'interest' bind the plebs to powerful patrons – the Court, the Church, the gentry – and submerge any form of horizontal 'class' integration.

The paternalism of eighteenth-century society is indeed qualified, from both directions, the top and the bottom. This is not the paternalism of the southern slave plantation society described by Eugene Genovese. The great had frequently to be compelled to fulfil their paternalist obligations, by the direct pressure of the crowd. Food riots were endemic throughout the century in the countryside and the provincial towns; while the London mob rioted frequently over such matters as the gin tax, foreign labour, Roman Catholics and Jews, and the machinations of Court and government. But the crucial point is the degree of upper-class complicity in these riots. The riots were legitimated by a generally accepted ideology, elaborated especially since the Revolution of 1688, which made possible a continuous series of alliances between disaffected sections of the elite and the plebs. E. P. Thompson speaks of 'the unitary context of class relationships' in this century, of a 'structural reciprocity' between rulers and ruled. Country magistrates frequently accepted the justice of food riots, and the legitimacy of imposing a 'just price' on millers and bakers; they shared in the traditional dislike of 'engrossers' and middlemen. The London crowd, when it was not actually rioting in the name of 'Church and King', still tended to do so on the basis of traditional customs and values, and of traditional liberties sanctified by the principles of 1688.

There was, as a result, throughout the century a complex but never wholly broken connection between the popular movements in the streets, the 'historic' corporate opposition of the City of London, acting through its Court of Common Council and Common Hall, and the upper-class Opposition – now Tory, now Whig – in Parliament. There was, in other words, an intricate and flexible alliance between the official Opposition within the Parliament and the opposition 'without doors', the extra-Parliamentary movement that spilled out on the streets and crowded the hustings. High point of this triple alliance was undoubtedly the Wilkite agitation of the 1760s and 1770s; but there was an even longer-lasting, although less clear-cut, alliance between the 'independent' Tory squires and the plebs, in the form of a popular 'Jacobite' resistance to the Hanoverian Court and the Whig oligarchy. The mob sometimes got out of hand, as in the Gordon Riots of 1780; and in general, as Thompson stresses, the plebeian culture had an authentic vitality and a real degree of autonomy from the patrician society. But for the most part the crowd operated within a framework of expectations between rulers and ruled that was fairly well understood on both sides. A particular failure of duty on the part of the rulers was met by a riot, to recall them to their obligations: this is 'the legitimism of the barricades', in Eric Hobsbawm's phrase. Characterizing eighteenth-century political society as 'class struggle without class', E. P. Thompson sees it as a structure 'which does not preclude resentment or even surreptitious acts of protest and revenge; it does preclude affirmative rebellion'.[5]

So much, as I say, is generally agreed among English historians of class, on the basis of a wealth of evidence that is entirely persuasive. The issue becomes contentious with the period that follows, from the end of the eighteenth to the middle of the nineteenth centuries. For most left-wing historians, this is the period that sees the birth of class, in the true sense, and specifically of course of the birth of the working class. In the stormy struggles for political reform during the French wars, and in the radical agitation and repressive reaction that followed them; in the triumphs of the middle class over electoral reform and the repeal of the Corn Laws, as much as in the defeats of the working class in trade unionism and Chartism, a new combative, class-conscious spirit is discerned. Harold Perkin is the most specific on the change:

It was in the first five years of peace, between Waterloo and the Queen's trial, that the vertical antagonisms and horizontal solidarities of class came for the first time, clearly, unmistakably, and irrevocably, to supplant the vertical connections and horizontal rivalries of dependency and interest. The essence of class is not merely antagonism towards another class or classes but organized antagonism with a nationwide appeal to all members of one broad social level. By this definition the working class almost sprang into existence with the Parliamentary Reform movement of 1816–19.[6]

It is, however, E. P. Thompson, whose work is the inspiration of much of the New Left historiography, who makes the canonical claim:

When every caution has been made, the outstanding fact of the period between 1790 and 1830 is the formation of 'the working class'. This is revealed, first, in the growth of class consciousness: the consciousness of an identity of interests as between all the diverse groups of working people and as against the interests of other classes. And, second, in the growth of corresponding forms of political and industrial organization. By 1832 there were strongly-based and self-conscious working-class institutions – trade unions, friendly societies, educational and religious movements, political organizations, periodicals – working-class intellectual traditions, working-class community patterns, and a working-class structure of feeling.

The conflicts over the Reform Bill during 1831–2 are seen as especially important, the culmination of the process of class formation. The working class was left with a permanent sense of bitterness and betrayal, following its abandonment by the middle class after their common struggle of these years. After 1832,

there is a sense in which the working class is no longer in the making, but has been made. To step over the threshold, from 1832 to 1833, is to step into a world in which the working class presence can be felt in every county in England, and in most fields of life . . . There is no mistaking the new tone after 1832. In every manufacturing district a hundred experiences confirmed the new consciousness of class which the Bill had, by its own provisions, so carefully defined . . . The line from 1832 to Chartism is not a haphazard pendulum alternation of 'political' and 'economic' agitations but a direct progression, in which simultaneous and related movements converge towards a single point . . . There is a sense in which the Chartist movement commenced, not in 1836 with the promulgation of the 'Six Points' but at the moment when the Reform Bill received the Royal Assent.[7]

Thompson here sets not simply the theme (and the tone) of later working-class historiography, but also, in an important sense, the form in which it is conducted. 'The working class' was formed by 1832; what then comes afterwards? How is its subsequent history to be treated? The answer has to be, and has been, to see that history as the progressive evolution of the same substantial entity, 'the English working class', whose formation has been (so it is claimed) definitively chronicled by Thompson. Not that the working class is necessarily seen as going from triumph to triumph, of course. New Left historians reject the older Fabian histories of the Webbs, and Cole and Postgate, in which the working class is represented as arriving at maturity towards the end of the century, with widespread trade unionism and the foundation of the Labour Party.[8] For many of them, indeed, the main problem is to discover why the revolutionary promise of 'the Thompson years', the period from the 1780s to the 1830s, remained so unfulfilled, why the working class faltered, and eventually settled for a quiet life with the Trades Union Congress and the Labour Party.[9] But whether the interpretation is optimistic or pessimistic, the events of the nineteenth century and beyond are still all related to the unfolding of a unified social formation, 'the working class', which is assumed to have structural as well as ideological continuity.

Thus, with varying degrees of enthusiasm, the following events become 'moments' in the further making and re-making of the English working class. After the agitation and defeat over the Reform Bill of 1831–2, there is the retreat into Owenism, then the Ten Hours Movement, the fight against the New Poor Law, the campaign of the radical 'unstamped' press, the rise and demise of Chartism; then comes the 'new model unionism' of the skilled workers of the 1850s to the 1870s, the 'general unionism' of the unskilled workers of the 1880s and 1890s, the formation of the Labour Party, the syndicalist agitation of 1911–14, the shop stewards' movement of the First World War, the formation of the Communist Party, and the post-war strikes culminating in the General Strike of 1926. Things become a bit hazy after that, but mention is usually made of the Labour Government of 1945–51, as an interesting but highly restricted form of working-class politics, and the revival of industrial militancy in the late 1960s and early 1970s.[10]

These are all, it is quite true, events and activities properly associated with the English working class. But *which* English working class, doing what at what times? On what grounds should we accept that the working class that was according to Thompson 'made' by 1832, is in any important structural sense the working class that engaged in the subsequent activities emblazoned in the ceremonial calendar of working-class history? By Thompson's own repeated assertion, the working-class consciousness that he describes is overwhelmingly that of artisans and craftsmen, not of a factory proletariat. In the famous Preface he states clearly: 'I am seeking to rescue the poor stockinger, the Luddite cropper, the "obsolete' handloom weaver, the "utopian' artisan, and even the deluded follower of Joanna Southcott, from the enormous condescension of posterity.' This is attractive, and of course a perfectly warranted historical enterprise. But what is its significance for a general historical sociology of the working class? Throughout his lengthy book Thompson astonishingly fails to connect up this 'moment' with any later tradition of working-class politics, culture, or ideology. Indeed what he has to say about the artisans' ideology implicitly cuts them off from the later, more strictly proletarian movement. So, for instance, stressing the central importance of the weavers to the radical movements up to and including Chartism, he says of their outlook:

They had, like the city artisans, a sense of lost status, as memories of their 'golden age' lingered; and, with this, they set a high premium on the values of independence ... They appealed to essential rights and elementary notions of human fellowship and conduct rather than to sectional interests. It was as a whole community that they demanded betterment, and utopian notions of re-designing society anew at a stroke – Owenite communities, the universal general strike, the Chartist Land Plan – swept through them like fire on the common. But essentially the dream which arose in many different forms was the same – a community of independent small producers, exchanging their products without the distortions of masters and middlemen.[11]

It is difficult to see the direct relevance of this petit-bourgeois Jacobin ideology to the later cooperative, corporative and collectivist ideologies and institutions of the industrial working class. To say that there has been a certain ideological carry-over from the artisan movement is reasonable enough.

Paine, Cobbett and Hunt are indeed important influences in the whole English working-class tradition. But so are John Bunyan, the Levellers, the Diggers and the ancient popular myth of 'the Norman Yoke', not to mention the important contribution of such distinctly middle-class radicals as Locke, Cartwright, Bentham and J. S. Mill. It makes no obvious sense to try to establish a sociological continuity by a piling up of ideological bits and pieces like this. Thompson in fact himself points to a significant possible discontinuity in his explanation of the evident fact that the factory workers of the new textile mills played a negligible part in the radical agitations of the period: 'The radicalism of Cobbett and Hunt, with its emphasis upon the values of economic independence, its emotional hostility to the factory system, and its criticism of the present in the light of an ideal past of mutual ties and economic reciprocity, did not speak for the factory workers' predicament . . . Huntite radicalism had little to say about factory reform, or social questions in general. The main channel for the energy of the factory workers . . . was within their own trade union organisation. Here results were immediate, the issue tangible'.[12] It was indeed because of the vast differences in the conditions of life of artisans and proletarians that Engels refused to recognize the existence of the English working class until the elimination of handicraft workers was (or so he thought) more or less complete.[13]

Engels was wrong in assuming this to have happened by the 1840s, when he wrote *The Condition of the Working Class in England in 1844*. The supersession of the handicraftsmen by a factory proletariat took a long time – far longer than is usually realized. A co-existence, and a struggle, between the two types of workers was still going on well towards the end of the nineteenth century.[14] It is this which ultimately makes nonsense of John Foster's claim to have discovered a revolutionary class conscious proletariat in Oldham in the 1830s and 1840s.[15] The Oldham cotton spinners were indeed factory workers; but they were of a very distinctive kind, that separated them by a world from the general condition of the unskilled proletarian. For one thing they were composed predominantly of adult males, in an industry which relied to an unusual degree on the labour of unskilled females and juveniles.[16] More importantly, they had fought for, and gained, the status of a craft occupation from a very early stage. The Lancashire cotton spinners' unions, established towards the end of the eighteenth century, were the best organized and most powerful unions in the country for much of the nineteenth century. They had enabled the male cotton spinners to achieve a form of craft control within the factory directly comparable to that achieved by traditional artisans in their trades. Adult male cotton spinners controlled all the operations of the mules – generally one on each pair – and themselves employed on an internal sub-contract basis two or more assistants to do the lesser tasks. These assistants were usually children, juveniles or women. The male cotton spinner's authority, and his usefulness to his employer, indeed derived largely not from any special technical skill as from the fact that he could exert a type of patriarchal control over the juveniles and women in his employ (sometimes, of course, that authority was literally and directly familial).[17]

This privileged position was both the source of, and the main strength in, the struggles of the 1830s and 1840s. The introduction of the 'self-acting' mule in cotton spinning was a direct assault on the spinners and their craft claims. It threatened to reduce them to the condition of common labourers, possibly to displace the adult male operatives altogether in favour of unskilled female and juvenile machine-minders. The spinners' trump card was their already existing organization, and the very real benefits, in terms of work discipline, accruing to the employers from the sub-contract system. The spinners could not prevent the introduction of self-actors, but they ensured that they maintained a monopoly on the new occupation of 'minder' that succeeded the older spinners. 'Minding' was less skilled than spinning. The significant thing, however, was that the minder inherited from the spinner the supervisory role over his own mules (again, generally, a pair of self-actors) and his own sub-contracted assistants. There was, in other words, a re-assertion of craft control not different in any major respect from the earlier system, and one which persisted to the end of the century and beyond.[18]

The Lancashire cotton spinners' struggle was, therefore, not essentially of a different kind from that engaged in by other groups of threatened or displaced handicraft workers in the first half of the nineteenth century. It belongs to that era of artisan radicalism, and was characterized by the same, increasingly desperate, defensive action. This showed itself in the ideology of the Oldham radicals which, despite Foster's dogmatic but quite unsubstantiated insistence,[19] remained within the mould of advanced Chartism rather than anything approaching revolutionary socialism. That indeed was what made it possible for the radical leadership to include small manufacturers, publicans, shopkeepers, smallholders and doctors, as well as weavers and spinners.[20] All shared the same mental world, which was 'still much closer to that of the radical artisan than the modern factory proletariat'.[21]

The 'break' in working-class radicalism – or, as we might say, the un-making of the English working class – after the mid-century has been frequently noted, although less often satisfactorily explained. A popular theory is that of 'working-class incorporation', although by itself this is hardly an explanation, more a description.[22] More hard-headed is the concept, derived from Engels and developed by Lenin, of a 'labour aristocracy', which postulates the rise of a group of skilled and articulate workers who separated themselves off from the mass of the unskilled, and so deprived the working class of radical leadership until the final years of the century.[23] While this has the merit of pointing to a precise agency of the change, it lays excessive and unconvincing weight on the internal divisions within the later working class, many of which – as with the cotton workers – in any case long preceded the era of social quiescence.[24]

The taming, or 'de-radicalization', of the English working class after Chartism becomes less of a mystery when we realize that effectively we are talking about at least two working classes, rather than one. A historic succession of strata took place whose consequence could be found in every area of working-class life. The increasing presence of factory workers as components of the working class meant that the class formulated its problems and attacked them in ways very different from the period when artisans predominated. One fundamental difference was that the new working class accepted the capitalist industrial system to an extent quite unthinkable to the earlier generation. The widespread decay of the apprenticeship system, and the slow but steady advance of mechanization,[?] made it clear that the new order was here to stay, for the forseeable future at least. The demoralizing defeats of Chartism, coupled with the fact that employers were in several industries at last succeeding in breaking craft control over the organization and pattern of work, produced a largely apolitical factory workforce which saw its best hopes for the future in industrial, trade union, terms.[26] The 'labour aristocracy' of these years of social peace had little in common with the first labour aristocracy of handicraftsmen. It was above all an aristocracy of and among modern factory workers, possessing some skills and jealously guarding its privileges from the mass of unskilled workers, but tied inescapably to the pace and purpose of the machine. In cotton and engineering, Stedman Jones notes, 'the new forms of skill were based upon a quantum of literacy and technical instruction, and often included quasi-supervisory functions. They did not possess the direct purchase over the production process enjoyed by handicrafts, and were unusable except in the factories for which they had been acquired.'[27]

The new working class was indeed divided, as it has often been before and since.[28] The skilled workers busied themselves, often under the guidance of employers and middle-class philanthropists, with trade unions, the Co-op, adult education, the Sunday school and temperance; the unskilled, with gambling, the pub and the music halls.[29] But neither was capable of, nor interested in, producing a political culture of the kind that characterized the radical artisanate in the first half of the century. As Victor Kiernan says, 'a new labour aristocracy might grow up to succeed the artisans, but a labour intelligentsia such as they were, political to the fingertips, has never been born again.'[30] We can go further: a politicized working class comparable to that which existed before 1850 has never again been seen in the kingdom. In that sense Chartism was truly, as Stedman Jones says, 'the end of an epoch'.[31]

II

Comparisons with – and between – the working classes of continental Europe during the nineteenth century are more than usually problematic, given the very great differences in the timing and rate of industrialization in the various countries. But it has already become clear, as a general strategy, how important the job of 'dis-aggregating' the working class must be, in understanding the character of working-class movements in the course of the century. This is an operation, it should equally be stressed, in which for this period at least a recognition of the *historical* layering and overlap of strata composing the working class takes precedence over the investigation of purely synchronic internal divisions, in the customary manner. Already well known are the studies of the French workers in the revolutions of 1830, 1848 and 1871.

Here the petit-bourgeois, 'artisanal' character of working-class especially Parisian working-class, radicalism, has been shown to be crucial in forming working class aspirations, to the point where more strictly proletarian (not to mention peasant) interests might be disregarded altogether.[32]

Even more directly relevant to the purposes of the present paper is Barrington Moore jnr's recent inquiry into the German working class from 1848 to 1920.[33] Moore is chiefly concerned to explode an image – that of the great militant German working class, growing to revolutionary strength and character before the First World War under the leadership of the Social Democratic Party. This image has always made the capitulation of the SPD in 1914 something of a mystery. It also makes puzzling the failure of the German working class to seize the initiative when a manifest opportunity presented itself during the revolutionary years of 1918–20.

The puzzle is resolved by the realization that the radical activities of the working class of this period were the accomplishment of different groups, with characteristically different problems at different times. In both interests and outlook these groups were often epochs apart. Thus Moore's analysis of the 1848 German revolution emphasizes – in conformity with much recent research – the extent to which it was the work of artisans reacting against capitalism, and against proletarianization, in defence of an existing pattern of life and work. It was the threats to the guild system, and in particular the increasing difficulties, in an era of rapid population growth, of making the move from journeyman to master, that provided the fuel for the fire. The artisans rejected both the individualistic, competitive, ethic of nascent capitalism as well as the egalitarian appeals of socialists and Communists. They wanted 'fair treatment as subordinate members' of the existing order; and, not for the first or last time in European history, they risked destroying that order in attempting to re-affirm their position within it. 'A revolution for the sake of respectability', is how Moore sums up the significance of 1848 for the artisan groups, the main working-class actors. He notes in passing that the admittedly fairly small proletariat, 'the stratum that Marx posited as the spearhead of revolution, was in fact the most quiescent of all'.[34]

Proletarians were active enough in the great miners' strikes of 1889 and 1905 in the Ruhr: but the basis of those strikes was almost the opposite of what we would expect, at least on conventional Marxist grounds. The miners' action shows in fact a striking similarity to the radical activity of the Lancashire cotton spinners discussed earlier. Moore stresses the legitimist and traditionalist norms which governed the miners' indignation and struggle throughout the period before the First World War. The Ruhr miners – like many others in Europe – had had a privileged and honoured position among workers stretching well back into the pre-industrial past. As members of the *Knappschaften* they enjoyed a guild-like, corporatist status hallowed by tradition and protected by a paternalist state. The institutional reflection of this was to be found in such practices as the *Gedinge*, a system of informal collective bargaining over wage contracts and work rules which was officially sanctioned by the *Berggesetz* (Mining Law). The result of this favourable arrangement was that the Ruhr miners were model workers, with no tradition of dissent or revolt.

They were precipitated into action by the deterioration of their position after 1850. The Prussian state 'liberalized' the laws on mining and unleashed market forces in the mines. But expansion took the form of an increase in the labour force rather than through technical innovation. This meant that much of the social organization of the old guild system was carried over into the new capitalist era: 'The miners carried their past with them into the new age.' The mix was explosive. Attempts to rationalize work organization along capitalist lines produced a long series of bitter conflicts from the 1860s onwards, culminating in the great strikes of 1889 and 1905. And the miners' rationale for that conflict, the criteria of judgement and condemnation of the mineowners' action, were drawn from the traditional institutions of the *Knappschaften*, the *Gedinge* and the *Berggesetz*, now under severe attack. Moore once more draws an instructive contrast with the activities of the proletarians proper of the same region: the iron and steel workers of the Ruhr. Despite having 'objective' grievances similar in most respects to the miners, they remained for the whole period up to 1914 'docile and stubbornly refractory to attempts at unionization . . . The general story [is] one of political apathy coupled with patriarchal dependence on firms.'[35] Why? Precisely, says Moore, because they *were* a proletariat proper, an uprooted mass of workers brought into being by the industrial revolution. Unlike the miners, or the artisans of 1848, they lacked the set of 'standards of condemnation', drawn from the past, which would have suggested to them reasons for discontent and legitimized any action springing from that perception. 'The iron and steel workers were, so to speak, a historical creation from scratch – without customs, collective experience, or memory.'[36]

The analysis of these particular episodes brings Moore to the First World War, and the revolution of 1918–20. His conclusion is clear: there was no such thing as a unified, homogeneous, industrial proletariat in Germany in 1914, let alone a revolutionary, class-conscious one. In the new conditions of capitalist industrialism, groups of workers struggled to maintain a decent existence, often on the basis of traditional norms and expectations, and often in isolation from and even conflict with each other. Their overriding concern, then as now, was not politics or theoretical ideas, but family, leisure and private life generally (Adolf Levenstein's survey of 1912 is a valuable source of information on this). Less than half of the industrial workforce was unionized in 1914. The socialist unions found their main support in the smaller firms, and made hardly any inroads into heavy industry, where the new proletariat was being formed. Perhaps most importantly, Moore shows how relatively small and undeveloped the industrial workforce was in 1914. Industrial workers made up at most a quarter of the total workforce; of these, about two-thirds worked in typically modern industries, and far fewer were concentrated in large firms, and large towns and cities. More than three-quarters of all industrial workers were in the rural areas or small-to-middling towns and cities.

It has often been charged, at the time and frequently since, that in 1914 the German SPD betrayed a potentially revolutionary working class. Moore fairly comments:

> The evidence . . . fails to reveal the existence of any massive proletariat of the 'classic' type whose interests the leaders came to ignore. In the light of evidence about the occupational and geographical composition of the industrial working class – its provincial character still flavoured by the artisans' traditions – as well as what evidence we have been able to muster about the workers' life situations and the way they felt about them, the SPD leadership with its cautious policies and occasional outbursts of rhetorical anger at the propertied classes appears reasonably representative . . . A revolutionary policy would have lacked a popular basis and would have been easily crushed.[37]

The failure of the revolution of 1918 was largely premised on this fact, helped by the fervent wish for peace among all sections of the working class, in the wake of a devastating war.

III

Moore is so good, indeed exemplary, in dealing with the first of our main questions – 'which working class?' – that it is disappointing to find him so weak on the second: the relation of the working class to other classes, and to society as a whole. His painstaking anatomy of the German working class takes place in a vacuum. We can see clearly enough from his analysis that the working class did not develop a revolutionary consciousness, and that the question, 'Why no revolution in Germany?,' is therefore in one sense answered. But only by invoking a tautology. For *why* did the German working class act and think as it did? The answer can only partly, and that superficially, be found by investigating the consciousness of its members, as revealed by questionnaires, diaries and the like. At least as important is the need to look at the movement of German society as a whole during this period, to examine the character of the ruling groups and the various strategies adopted by them towards subordinate groups. The working class was formed as much by these things as by its direct experience of work and community life. It was, in other words, at least as much German as it was working class.

We would need, in examining this side of the question, to consider such matters as the accommodation of the SPD to German bourgeois society in the era of the mass industrial state. There would indeed not be much that would have to be added to Michels' brilliant account of this process,[38] although Michels may have exaggerated the influence of the party leaders in the 'de-radicalization' of the working class. But other forces were in any case working in the same direction. Bismarck had already pointed the way by basing the new German Empire on a system of universal suffrage, thus conceding at a stroke what radicals were still painfully fighting for elsewhere. This stealing of the radicals' clothes was followed by a turning out of the socialists' wardrobe, with the introduction of a comprehensive scheme of social insurance in the 1880s: measures that were described shortly afterwards by the English historian William Dawson as 'the largest and most original experiment in constructive social reform ever attempted'.[39] To the liberals' charge that this was 'state socialism', Bismarck happily avowed it, and had the pleasure of seeing the socialist leaders subsequently endorse his measures despite their fierce initial denunciation of them in the Reichstag. After his fall, it was a commonplace to say that Bismarck had failed in his attempt to balk the socialists, as was witnessed by the massive growth in the electoral support of the SPD. But in the long run he can be seen to have succeeded, at least to the extent of adding substantially to the security of working class life, and so making the workers less inclined to favour revolutionary politics. If we add to these reforms from on top, the very real improvement in the standard of living of most German workers in the half century before the First World War, the pride in German achievements and the growth in nationalism among the working class,[40] it becomes easier to understand the 'capitulation' of 1914, and the lack of a revolutionary will in 1918–20.

To go down to the grass-roots, to write 'history from below', is a heart-warming thing, and a necessary corrective to traditional accounts. But it runs the very great danger of producing what Eric Hobsbawm has called 'an esoteric version of history', 'a certain self-isolation of labour movement history from the rest of history'.[41] E. P. Thompson says of his own study that he is seeking 'to break down the Chinese walls which divide . . . the history of working class agitation from the cultural and intellectual history of the rest of the nation'.[42] This is good, but we need to put it more strongly. We will never understand the dynamics of working-class history by an investigation, however sympathetic and acute, of the working class itself. All social action partakes of the nature of the whole society; and it is particularly important to recognize this when considering the action of subordinate groups and classes, which by their position in society are peculiarly limited and inhibited as to their capacity for social action. Working-class action, and *a fortiori* working-class revolutionary action, is an affair of the society as a whole. As Hobsbawm puts it, 'the history of labour is part of the history of society . . . Class relationships, whatever the nature of class, are relationships *between* classes or strata, which cannot adequately be described or analysed in isolation, or in terms of their internal division or stratifications. This implies a model of what societies are and how they work.'[43]

Moore's failure on this count is mirrored by Foster's. As many commentators have pointed out, the latter's account of a putative revolutionary working class in Oldham ignores not simply national politics in general, but even the national political movement of Chartism, which as a working-class movement might surely be expected to figure in any serious argument for a class-conscious proletariat. Insofar as we see them through Foster's eyes, the Oldham cotton spinners organized and agitated with a remarkably high level of local political awareness, but with an indifference to movements and events elsewhere that strikes the observer as equally remarkable. In fact, as Morris says, Oldham 'lay like some cotton-spinning Cuba in the foothills of the Pennines, plotting revolution but receiving little welcome when its delegates ventured into the wider society of Britain'.[44] Since Foster does not venture much into this wider society, he is spared the need to explain this.[45]

What is less excusable is that Foster presents a sociologically undernourished account even when concentrating on the local level. He accepts that there were many middle-class participants – not, obviously, *grands bourgeois* but small traders and small manufacturers – in Oldham's radical movement.[46] But such is his concern to assert the pure working-class autonomy of the movement that these middle-class adherents have to be seen as cowed and coerced members, the fruits of successful working-class pressure on street corner shops and pubs. He gives almost no evidence for this claim; and Gadian has in fact shown that the radical action of the 1830s and 1840s involved, indeed rested upon, close collaboration between working-class and middle-class radicals, acting together not on the basis of coercion but of a shared ideology and a shared interest in opposing the larger manufacturers and landowners with their more cosmopolitan orientation.[47] As Gadian remarks, this alliance was very similar to the radical alliance in Birmingham during the first half of the century, and had very much the same economic and social basis. Compared to other Lancashire towns, Oldham's industrial structure was small-scale and diffuse. There existed a large number of small cotton mills, employing on average below eighty workers each (compared to more than 200 for many of the other major towns). As in Birmingham, relations between employers and workers were often very close, and interests often identified. Gadian aptly comments on this situation that

where the working and middle classes were not yet deeply divided economically their fruitful co-operation in reform movements was a real possibility ... Support for alliances with middle-class reformers should not be regarded, necessarily, as evidence of the retarded growth of working-class consciousness. As in Oldham, alliances based round the realisation of the interdependence as well as the divergence of separate class interests might well reflect the advanced political consciousness of those who participated in them.[48]

As we would expect from at least one of the stated intentions of his book, Thompson is far less guilty of the 'esoteric' approach. One of the best things in the book is indeed his demonstration of the extent to which the whole working-class movement in England was shaped by the response of the middle and upper classes to the French Revolution.[49] But, once having shown this, he seems to forget the lesson in theory which it teaches, and his general treatment suffers at many crucial points from just that overidentification with his subject which is the most serious weakness of 'esoteric history'. A good example is provided by his account of the reform agitation of 1830–2. Thompson makes the claim that 'in the autumn of 1831 and in the "days of May" Britain was within an ace of revolution which, once commenced, might well ... have pre-figured, in its rapid radicalisation, the revolutions of 1848 and the Paris Commune.'[50] The evidence he refers to for this is a fairly familiar catalogue of events in these years: the 'Captain Swing' riots in the countryside, the Bristol and Nottingham riots, the effect of the July Revolution in France, the mass demonstrations accompanying the presentation of the

Reform Bill and, even more, those following its repeated rejection by the Lords, the spread of Political Unions on the model of Attwood's Birmingham Political Union, and the formation of Doherty's National Association for the Protection of Labour. His conclusion is equally familiar: that, swayed by the skilful arguments of such Radicals as Place and Brougham as to the likely consequence of rejecting the Bill, the landowning ruling class gave way sufficiently to satisfy the middle class, leaving the working class to lick its wounds and reflect even more bitterly on the perfidy of its allies. In this view, reform from on top was a concession to the threat of revolution from below.

The very familiarity of this story should make us suspicious of it. In the first place, the appearance of concerted radical or revolutionary activity is deceptive. As George Rudé says, 'the protest movements of 1830–1 ran separate courses, were conducted for different ends, were engaged in by different sorts of people, and were separated in both time and place.'[51] But more important is the general form of analysis adopted. It throws all the emphasis on the *protesting* groups – the middle and working classes – and none on the established ones, the landowning aristocracy and gentry. This is a very peculiar procedure. In effect it ignores the whole structure of politics, and the political context of action, in early nineteenth-century England. W. L. Guttsman reminds us that 'the government which passed the Reform Bill was paradoxically enough one of the most aristocratic the country had ever seen'.[52] The paradox is only apparent. The pre-Reform constitution was aristocratic through and through. During the course of the eighteenth century the aristocracy had consolidated its hold on the state, easily defeating the only attempt – that by George III – to shake that dominance. The aristocratically controlled Parliament could not entirely ignore the agitation 'out of doors', and indeed it often played the risky game of stirring this up for its own purposes. But its position at the centre of state power ensured that it could usually deal with this pressure on its own terms and in its own interest. It had weathered the radical years of the French Revolution and the Napoleonic Wars with relative ease; if anything, the reform movement slackened and lost steam in the period after 1815. If, therefore, reform was once more an issue in 1830, we can be reasonably certain that the dominant groups were active participants and not simply passive respondents. Unless we are to assume that the most experienced and most powerful ruling class in Europe at the time simply sat back and accepted a dose of unpalatable medicine, its behaviour in 1830–2 must be of crucial significance in explaining both the success of reform and the nature of the reform settlement.[53]

We know, in fact, from the work in particular of D. C. Moore,[54] that the ruling class was extremely active not simply in the reform period, but in the reform movement itself. What is especially striking is the role of a section of the Tory party, the 'Ultra-Tories' or Country Party, led in these years by the Marquis of Blandford, and energetically supported by the Tory *Blackwood's Magazine*. The Ultra-Tories, unexpectedly, were among the most fervent proponents of Parliamentary reform. Indeed before 1830, as Moore shows, they largely monopolized the reform agitation. The most radical proposals for reform came in these years not from Cobbett or Place, but from Blandford in Parliament and various Ultra-Tory contributors to *Blackwood's*. And it shows something of the complexity of the forces contending that, of all the possible outcomes, it was a version of Blandford's scheme that emerged finally as the central feature of the Reform Act.

Wellington's Tory government, which had set itself firmly against reform, thus came up against vigorous and at times violent opposition from within its own ranks. What was the basis of this *fronde*, this dissent within the ruling group? It represented a reaction from the shires, as groups of traditionally Tory squires and landowners saw their influence and interests sacrificed, as they thought, by their own government, in favour of newer commercial and liberal constituencies. The era of 'liberal Toryism' of the 1820s, under the leadership of 'new men' such as Huskisson, Canning and Peel, had profoundly alarmed the traditionally protectionist Tory landowners. They had had to swallow a policy of deflation, a relaxation of the Corn Laws, and, an especially bitter pill, Catholic Emancipation. It appeared that the Tory leadership had converted irrevocably to the principles of the new liberal political economy, to the detriment of the landowning interest. The 'apostasy' of the Duke of Wellington himself over Catholic Relief was the last straw. The Country Party became convinced that only a thoroughgoing reform of Parliament could break the basis of Ministerial power, established as it was largely on the system of 'rotten boroughs'. They feared a reassertion of the bid for centralizing state power, of the kind that an earlier generation of county members in 'the economical movement' had defeated in the last century. 'It was,' says Harold Perkin, 'the decision of the High Tories, led by Sadler, to oppose Wellington's Government and let in the Whigs which decisively opened the doors to Reform.'[55]

In the autumn of 1829 the Country Party took to the field. Using the language of Burkean conservatism, they launched a wide-ranging attack on the centralizing and 'despotic' tendencies of the Tory Ministers. With this went a criticism of liberal economic doctrines which were blamed for causing acute economic distress both to the urban poor and in rural areas. It was on the basis of economic and fiscal theory that they were able to make an alliance with the newly formed radical Political Unions, pioneered by Thomas Attwood's Birmingham Political Union. Attwood believed profoundly in currency reform, and was as hostile to the deflationary policies of the Tory government as the Ultra-Tories. He too put his faith in Parliamentary reform as the means to re-direct economic policy. The Country Party members hastened to join the Political Unions; 'indeed, of the initial leaders of the Union movement, the majority were anti-Ministerial Tories.'[56] Thus was first cemented the Tory-Radical alliance which, with different groups at different times, was to be of immense significance in the social movements of the 1830s and 1840s.

Of all the groups whose combined activities produced reform, the Whigs were probably the most cautious and least enthusiastic. Wellington's declaration against reform forced them, as the official Opposition, to revive their old commitment. Having been offered a heaven-sent opportunity to oust the Tories they set about exploiting it. But the Whigs were not only the

Parliamentary opposition and, as such, the most immediately relevant political force. They were first and foremost landowners, the greatest in the land. They favoured reform, therefore, in very much the terms that the Ultra-Tories urged it, as a means of strengthening the landowning interest in Parliament, and of restoring its influence in the country districts. Over the years, many county constituencies had become dominated by urban middle-class free-holders who, based in large manufacturing towns lacking Parliamentary representation, had usually been able to outvote rural free-holders in county elections. Ironically it was just such a normally worrying situation that helped the Ultra-Tories to force reform on Parliament. On the strength of the alliance with the urban Political Unions, urban free-holders were widely employed in the 1831 election to return pro-Bill candidates in the county seats. But such a coalition was always tactical. Ultimately what both the Ultra-Tories and the Whig aristocrats wanted was a separation of the urban and rural areas, and in particular a return of the rural areas to the 'natural' leadership of the landowning classes. Underlying this striving was a social theory of 'natural society', one based on the expression of 'legitimate influence' and the representation of corporate interests rather than isolated individuals.

Backward-looking such a view may have been and, in the long run, overtaken by the liberal-utilitarian conception of representation. But present politics do not turn on future outcomes. What matters is the constellation of forces at the time, and the beliefs of the parties engaged in the action. The corporatist or paternalist view of society was widely shared by upper-class groups in the first half of the nineteenth century. So far as they could, in the Reform Act they gave it a new lease of life, in practice if not in theory. By the terms of the Act, the large towns were given their own representation, and the urban middle class vote thereby absorbed. This meant that eighty-two seats previously often dominated by urban freeholders were returned to the safe care of rural leaders. At the same time the Act also created sixty-two new county seats, thus giving the landed interest a clear predominance over the urban middle class interest in Parliament. The addition of the 'Chandos clause', enfranchising tenants-at-will in the counties, further confirmed the influence of the landowners in the country areas. As Palmerston had pointedly observed in urging the Reform Bill upon the House of Commons, it 'went to *restore* to the landed interest that influence which he thought indispensable . . . to the safety and prosperity of the country'. The results were at all events clear enough in the decades succeeding the Act. Reform could then be seen to have ensured half a century of aristocratic domination of Parliament.[57] If this was indeed a 'concession' to popular pressure from below, it was of a kind unusually favourable to the conceders. But it is clear that, given the character of the social forces involved, and the nature of the political techniques employed, this would in any case be a grave distortion of the process by which reform came about. Grey may have exaggerated somewhat when he called the Reform Bill 'the most aristocratic measure that ever was proposed in Parliament',[58] but his remark underlines the point that the Whigs intended reform to preserve and not destroy the landed influence. As Allan Silver remarks, from the point of view of the landed Whig oligarchs who sponsored the Bill, it 'represented a fundamental continuity in the older political society; the very mechanisms that made reform possible were those of the unreformed political order . . . Elite adaptiveness [in 1830–2] resulted from the encounter with forces of change of those elites whose political and family biographies constituted a relatively integral past, an experience of success in dominating English society and politics in all phases of the aristocratic role . . . It depended on an interpretation of present crisis as a meaningful extension of past experience.'[59]

At just the time that the Whigs were steering the Reform Bill through Parliament, Richard Oastler met the workers of Huddersfield and formed what was to become known as the 'Fixby Hall Compact' (1831). This effectively launched the Ten Hours Movement, otherwise known as the Short-Time Movement or, simply, the Factory Movement. For over twenty years the movement laboured to achieve a ten-hour working day for children, young persons and women, it being clearly recognized by all parties that, strictly interpreted and implemented, this would also entail in practice a ten-hour day for adult male workers. Partial success came with the Factory Acts of 1833 and 1844, and victory seemed assured with the passage of Fielden's Ten Hour Bill in 1847. Factory owners exploited a loop-hole in the Act to evade its intent, and a compromise was reached with a ten-and-a-half-hour day in 1850, the final achievement of the ten-hour day being delayed until 1874.

Still, the movement could reasonably claim success by 1850, at a time when other mass movements, such as Chartism, had conspicuously failed. For many the Ten Hours Act of 1847 is indeed the great working-class triumph of these decades of struggle, the by no means negligible compensation for the failure to make direct political gains. Tom Burns says of the Act that 'it was the first legislative reform carried through by popular agitation among industrial workers, and formulated in direct response to their demands.'[60] Here he echoes Marx's well-known verdict, expressed in the Inaugural Address of the Workingmen's International Association, that 'the Ten Hours Bill was not only a great practical success; it was the victory of a principle; it was the first time that in broad daylight the political economy of the middle class succumbed to the political economy of the working class.'[61]

But Marx had earlier taken a somewhat different line:

The landed aristocracy having suffered a defeat from the bourgeoisie by the passing of the Reform Bill of 1831 . . . resolved to resist the middle class by espousing the cause and claims of the working men against their masters, and especially by rallying around their demands for the limitation of factory labour . . . The landed aristocracy having received a deadly blow by the actual abolition of the Corn Laws in 1846, took their vengeance by forcing the Ten Hours Bill of 1847 upon Parliament.[62]

If the first view expresses the Radical conception of the Factory Movement, this comes close to the Liberal convention, originated in the bitter Parliamentary debates of the time, according to which the Factory Acts were the result simply of a Tory plot aimed at stirring up the workers against free-trade Whig manufacturers. There is clearly something in both these views; but to put it

like this is to miss the essentially *unitary* nature of the movement for factory
reform. It suggests, at most, tactical and opportunist class alliances, when in
fact the Factory Movement embraced a wide spectrum of social groups within
a unified social outlook. We may, for want of a better term, call this outlook
'traditional' or 'paternalist', even nostalgic; but we should not forget Cecil
Driver's reminder that 'if assent to yesterday's acceptances breeds the
complacency of the obtuse, the nostalgia for remoter days may generate the
protest of the rebel'.[63]

Whom do we find prominent within the Movement? There are the two
undisputed leaders from Yorkshire: Michael Sadler, the Tory MP who
introduced the first Ten Hours Bill in the Commons, and Richard Oastler,
the Ultra-Tory 'Factory King', the central organizing figure for more than
twenty years, who established an extraordinary relationship of trust and
affection with the workers of the northern counties. Both came from solid
commercial middle-class backgrounds, and Oastler himself was a successful
cloth merchant before becoming steward of a large country estate (Fixby Hall)
just outside Huddersfield. To these can be added other manufacturers long
active in the movement, such as John Wood and William Walker of Bradford,
and the Lancashire cotton masters Charles Hindley, Joseph Brotherton and
John Fielden. These last three all became MPs and were strong proponents
of the movement in the Commons; and although they took the Radical
appellation, they shared with Sadler, Oastler and Wood a conviction of the
traditional responsibilities of employers to their workers, together with a
profoundly Christian repugnance to the degrading conditions of the workers
in the factories (characterized by Oastler as 'Yorkshire slavery'). Joined with
these middle-class protagonists were more predictably 'traditionalist' elements,
drawn from the established institutions and classes of British society. Such
were the campaigning Anglican vicar 'Parson Bull', and the ex-Wesleyan
preacher J. R. Stephens, who developed a fiery brand of Tory Radicalism
which had rather more in it of Old Testament prophecy than Carlton Club
philosophy. In general the Church of England, especially in the North,
supported the movement throughout, and was a vital factor in its history.
Then there was the Tory gentry, of whom Ashley (later Lord Shaftesbury)
was the outstanding figure, taking over the Parliamentary leadership for more
than two decades after the death of Sadler. With him we can link Oastler's
sympathetic landed employer, Thornhill, and the Yorkshire squire William
Ferrand, together with a host of county magistrates who were hostile to the
new system of *laissez-faire* and clung to paternalist philosophy and practice.
The Parliamentary representatives of this group included the dashing figures
of the 'Young England' movement, led by Benjamin Disraeli and Lord John
Manners. We should note, too, the continued support of influential sections
of the provincial and national press. The Tory *Leeds Intelligencer* was Oastler's
champion throughout, but the columns of Hetherington's *Poor Man's Guardian*
and Feargus O'Connor's *Northern Star* were equally and readily open to him.
From London, *The Times* throughout the 1830s and 1840s vigorously supported
the Ten Hours Movement, and the related movement of resistance to the
New Poor Law. It did so through its editorials and reports, and espcially

through the personal activities of its proprietor, John Walter, a close friend of Sadler's and Oastler's, and an active MP for the cause.[64]

All this, of course, is enough to dispose of the view that the Factory Acts were primarily a working-class achievement. The leadership and organization were quite clearly middle class, with strong support from certain sections of the upper-class Tory gentry and clergy. Working-class participation there undoubtedly was, on a large scale, mostly among the textile workers of the North, the only ones for whom regulation was considered relevant or necessary. But here too the striking thing is the extent to which working-class agitation was based on the attempt to preserve existing patterns of work and family organization. The textile workers certainly wished to reduce their hours of work, so long as there was no loss of pay; but they were unwilling to accept any measures which at the same time had the effect of breaking up the kin-based work group of the early factory system, and depriving the adult male worker of his traditional control of family members, at home and at work.

Thus when Althorp's Act (1833) restricted the hours of children's labour to *eight* (instead of the expected ten), thereby allowing the factory owners to work children in relays while keeping adults on for the customary long hours, many adult male workers collaborated with employers to evade the act. They connived at the falsification of age certificates, so that children under nine continued to be worked more than the statutory hours. This satisfied both employers, who did not then have to hire adolescents at higher wages, and workers, in that it maintained the direct economic link between parents and children. There was even the apparently paradoxical spectacle of workers' leaders after 1833 pressing for a ten-hour, or even twelve-hour day for children, provided that this would reduce the work-day for all other factory workers. This position (which 'troubled the humanitarian promoters of factory legislation in Parliament') was, however, quite consistent with the workers' main aim. Smelser, linking the Ten Hours Movement with the great 'structural' strikes in the cotton industry from the 1820s to the 1840s, thus summarizes their goal:

The ten hours' movement, in the operatives' minds, would have achieved much the same results as the strikes against improved machinery – to halt the flood of children and to protect the traditional economic relationships between parent and child by linking their hours and consequently maintaining the existing conditions of work. The element common to the structural strikes and the ten hours agitation was a desire to maintain or revert to the less differentiated structure of the family economy ... The ten hour act [as proposed in Sadler's failed bill of 1832] would have reduced labour of adult and child, restricted the number of children, and continued to link the labour of adult and child. The Factory Act of 1833, with its relay system and its eight-hour limitation, achieved almost the opposite.[65]

The factory workers in the end had to settle for a different division of family tasks: the men at work, the women and children at home, and at school. But until this became a new lever of demands, for 'leisure' and family time, the workers' actions reflected a broadly common conception of their rights and obligations with their middle- and upper-class leaders. It was this that made it possible to put the identical alliance formed in the Factory Movement at the service of the movement to resist the New Poor Law, above all in the northern factory districts. All commentators stress the continuity of personnel (Oastler, Bull, Ferrand, Fielden), organization (the Short-Time Committees) and newspaper support (the *Leeds Intelligencer*, the *Northern Star*, *The Times*). 'Membership of the Ten Hours Movement almost automatically implied hostility to the Poor Law, and resistance tended to be strongest where the campaign for factory reforms had struck deepest.'[66]

The New Poor Law was an even more direct assault on the traditional practices and outlook of workers, gentry and clergy, than the unregulated factory system. For the workers, it threatened the normal practice in the textile regions whereby support from the poor rates tided over the bad times of the trade cycle for unemployed factory workers and under-employed handicraft workers. 'No workhouse could possibly accommodate the thousands of able-bodied men thrown out of work by the downward swing of the trade cycle.'[67] For workers to be taken into the workhouse meant that their homes would be broken up, their tools and other possessions sold, and their chance of employment rendered negligible when economic conditions improved. Northern magistrates and clergy were fully in sympathy with this view of the matter. In addition they deeply resented the centralizing tendency of the New Poor Law, the elevation of bureaucratic Commissioners over local overseers and justices of the peace. The New Poor Law struck at the heart of the Tory conception of English society as 'an infinity of self-governing republics under one, controlling, limited, constitutional monarchy'.[68] It quite clearly attacked the power of parishes and the local gentry to handle their own affairs, specifically their own poor. Resistance to its application in the North was therefore bitter, determined and long drawn out. In this resistance magistrates played an especially crucial role, since as *ex officio* members of the new Boards of Guardians they were in the perfect position to ignore or obstruct the wishes of the 'bashaws of Somerset House'. 'The difficulties to be feared from almost any degree of popular excitement are not so great as those to be encountered from an adverse and factious Board of Guardians,' complained Alfred Power, Assistant Commissioner in Lancashire and the West Riding, in 1839. The movement of resistance to the New Poor Law largely died out in the 1840s; but this had at least as much to do with success as with failure, since for many decades the administration of the Poor Law in the North continued on traditional, pre-1834 lines, with a large element of outdoor relief.[69]

One last example, the repeal of the Corn Laws in 1846, will illustrate the complexity of class alliances and political behaviour in early nineteenth-century England. There is no more celebrated instance in recent English history of an allegedly clear-cut, one-class, victory. Engels's unequivocal statement, that 'the repeal of the Corn Laws was the victory of the manufacturing capitalists ... over the landed aristocracy',[70] has been repeated by practically every commentator since the 1840s, whether of Left, Right or Centre. It is a view apparently confirmed by the attitudes of the dominant political actors of the time: the Chartists, who distrusted and attacked the Anti-Corn Law League, the Whigs and Liberals who supported it, and the Protectionist Conservative

Party which fought repeal bitterly and was eventually destroyed by it. The leaders of the League, Cobden and Bright, employed all their brilliant organizational and oratorical skills in stirring up middle-class feeling against the landed upper class. 'During the long battle for Repeal,' says Asa Briggs, 'middle class consciousness was forged as it never had been before.'[71] 'We were a middle class set of agitators,' said Cobden, and the campaign was conducted 'by those means by which the middle class usually carries on its movements.' After the battle had been won in 1846, Cobden urged Peel to put himself at the head of the middle class, as now the real governing group of the country: 'The Reform Bill decreed it: the passing of the Corn Bill has realised it.'[72]

Peel's refusal to follow Cobden's advice can, however, be taken as indicating a shrewder awareness of the forces that went to make repeal possible. No-one would deny the importance of the League's activities in mobilizing public opinion against the Corn Laws. But, as with reform in 1832, 'public opinion' had to be translated into political influence in Parliament if it were to have much chance of achieving its ends.[73] And this was a Parliament still dominated by landowners. Without some support for repeal from the landowning interest, a protectionist Parliament could continue to defy middle-class opinion for as long as it had done so over electoral reform. As it happened, there were within both the Whig and Tory parties influential landowners who were beginning to be convinced of the need for repeal. And as it also happened, Peel himself was in the best position to appreciate their reasons, and to coordinate landowning support in Parliament on behalf of repeal when the circumstances warranted it.

Peel was the son of a wealthy cotton manufacturer, but he had himself adopted the life of a country gentleman and farmer. He was in fact a model farmer, a leader in 'high farming', interesting himself in all the latest scientific improvements in agriculture and animal husbandry. In 1838 he was a founding member of the English Agricultural Society, set up to improve agricultural technology and to propagate the attitude reflected in its motto, 'Practice with Science'. Peel therefore was in a good position to realize that for the landed classes as a whole, protection might be more of a curse than a blessing. The Corn Laws allowed the inefficient and less progressive landowners to benefit without the need to improve, and so acted as a barrier to the growth of agricultural productivity. Improving landlords and farmers needed no such protection, as they had clearly demonstrated in the period 1815–40. Kitson Clark comments that 'it is germane to remember that the very remarkable revolution that was going forward in British agriculture in the nineteenth century was the work not only of practical farmers and scientists, but also of squires and noblemen'.[74] For these men, whether Whigs or Tories, the hostility of the urban middle classes over protection was an unnecessary political burden. What they needed was not protection, but the removal of customary and legal impediments to the fuller capitalistic development of agriculture.[75]

Peel failed to carry the Conservative Party with him over Corn Law repeal. But the voting in the House of Commons shows clearly that he had an important section of the Party on his side, and that overall there was nothing like an urban middle class–rural gentry division. In every borough where aristocratic influence predominated, the votes were cast in favour of repeal. Generally, within both the Whig and the Tory parties, a split can be seen between the big landowners, those who were benefiting from improvements and so favoured repeal, and the smaller squires and tenant farmers who had kept to the older ways, socially and economically, and who regarded protection as a life and death issue.[76] It was this latter group, led by Disraeli and Lord George Bentinck, who drove Peel from office and put the Tories in the wilderness for more than twenty years. But they lost the struggle over the Corn Laws, and that defeat cannot be put down simply to some mysterious 'conversion' on the part of their leader, nor to the brilliance of the Anti-Corn Law League's propaganda. It was because Peel's views accorded with those of some of the most powerful figures in the landed establishment that, with the backing of the urban vote, they were able to force repeal on a House of Commons in which the county interest still predominated. Repeal was, in any case, only one objective. In the same speech that he proposed it, Peel also put forward a series of measures reducing the duties in animal feed and similar items, and, most importantly, providing for readily available loans for drainage. By these means Peel sought to encourage experimentation and improvement in agriculture.

In later years, it was claimed that Peel by his action had saved the aristocracy; and undoubtedly, the continued prosperity of English agriculture without the benefit of protection was of immense value politically to the landowners. But as Kitson Clark points out, Peel could not have done what he did 'if the passions, or opinions, or interests of the great aristocracy, or of those who really governed the country, had really been hopelessly committed to the other side'.[77]

IV

It must be evident from these examples – the Reform Movement, the Factory Movement, the Anti-Poor Law Movement and the movement for the repeal of the Corn Laws – that a wider sociological configuration underlies the particular conflicts described. Put most generally, these cases question the idea, advanced for instance by Thompson and Perkin, that there is a radical break in the principle of political action at the beginning of the nineteenth century, that the horizontal solidarities of class replace the vertical ties of 'interest' as the basis for action. It may be appropriate to use the terminology of class for nineteenth-century movements; but if so, we need to be very aware of the welter of class relationships which underlie them. It was possible for classes to attempt independent action: Chartism comes nearest to this, for this period.[78] But the well-nigh total failure of that movement confirms the view that to have any chance of success, social movements require the involvement of social groups close to or at the centre of power. Short of revolution, which seems never to have been seriously contemplated in nineteenth-century England, any movement of the subordinate classes can be contained for an indefinite period provided that the ruling class remains united. Success will depend on the break-down, however temporary, of that united front, and the making of alliances between sections of the upper classes and other disaffected groups. A 'vertical dimension', in other words, is always present and always necessary in successful social movements. Given the persisting political dominance of the aristocratic landowning class in England for much of the nineteenth century, this means that *both* the working class and the new manufacturing middle class needed upper-class allies in their struggle to establish themselves in the emerging industrial society.

The opportunity for the creation of such alliances was provided by the deep divisions within the landowning class, and especially that section of it that was the historic basis of Toryism. From the 1820s to the end of the 1840s, the Tory party was convulsed by a series of internal conflicts that eventually destroyed it in its traditional form, and led to the major realignment that emerged as modern Conservatism in the 1860s and 1870s. The central line of the split ran between the 'country party', representing the traditional squirearchy and tenant farmers, who had throughout the last century been the mainstay of the opposition to the Whig oligarchy; and the Tory leadership, representing the larger landowners and those elements in the aristocracy who had traditionally taken charge of the political fortunes of the party at Westminster.

Early in the 1820s, the Tory leadership began to move towards acceptance of the new political economy and many of the principles of Benthamite administration. This was a long-drawn-out process, inhibited periodically by the propensity of their rivals, the Whigs, to advance precisely in the same direction. But the general line of the development was clear. ('A sound Conservative government,' mocked Disraeli in *Coningsby*: 'I understand: Tory men and Whig measures.') It thoroughly alarmed the country party, both as a betrayal of their traditional social philosophy and as a slighting of their economic interests. Over these decades therefore the country party repeatedly, and dangerously, threw in its lot with men and opinions it would normally have regarded with abhorrence. This formed the basis of the alliance between Blandford and Attwood over Parliamentary reform; between Oastler and the northern workers over factory regulation and the resistance to the New Poor Law; and between Disraeli and the Chartists in the opposition to the repeal of the Corn Laws. The same split within the Tory Party affected the strategy of middle-class leaders like Cobden and Bright. Rather than directing all their energies at the Whigs, they saw that it would be possible to appeal to the Tory leadership over the heads of its recalcitrant followers. In gaining the support of Peel and Wellington for Corn Law repeal, they repeated the combination that had won Catholic Emancipation in 1829. It was perhaps fitting that the same two men, Peel and Wellington, who had opened the first serious breach within the party in 1829, were there to deliver the *coup de grâce* in 1846.

In many of these alliances, especially those connecting 'Tory Radicals' with working-class groups, one can discern the elements of a paternalist philosophy and practice, of an old and wide-ranging kind. Paternalism was, of course, throughout the nineteenth century direly threatened by the new philosophy of utilitarianism and *laissez-faire*. It had succumbed in many areas by the later part of the century, until revived in its closing years by the concept of 'the welfare state' and socialistic philosophies of various sorts. But it was no mere vestige in the first half of the century. It was indeed powerfully revived, as an ideology, by the writings of Burke and Coleridge, Scott and Southey. In many parts of society, in country districts, in northern factory towns and villages, it provided the common framework of reference for all classes.[79] For those groups most threatened by the new forces of capitalist industrialism – the old-fashioned Tory squires and landowners, country magistrates, Anglican clergymen, handicraft workers and the early factory workers – paternalist practice acted as a necessary and unifying defence, an insistence on the vertical ties of integration as against the pull towards 'horizontal solidarities' and vertical antagonisms.

It may be going too far to speak of 'the unitary context of class relationships' in nineteenth-century England, in the way Thompson speaks of the eighteenth century. A general process of mutual repulsion and insulation of the classes was taking place, which had the effect of drawing the lines more sharply between the major social groups. This was a consequence as much of urbanization as industrialization, and could be seen equally in the cultural divide that came to separate the classes as in the conflicts in the workplace. But for the subordinate classes at least, so far as political action was concerned it was never possible to conduct this on the basis simply of their own class culture and community. A link with the wider political society, where the higher social groups dominated political life at the centres of national and local power, was always necessary if action were not to be self-frustrating and futile. Indeed Richard Sennett has suggested that part of 'the tragedy of nineteenth-century politics' lies in the rise of insulated class communities which, in their concern to preserve their 'collective personality', actually diminished their capacity for collective action: 'the shared imagery becomes a deterrent to shared action'.[80] This goes some way to explaining the decline of working-class politics in the later part of the century (as well, perhaps, as its revival in certain forms of industrial action in the 1960s and 1970s). But for the earlier part of the century things had not yet gone so far. Various forms of militant political action, by working-class and middle-class groups, were possible in the context of a society in which structures of feeling as well as of interest maintained an intimate connection between social groups of widely differing kinds. It may be correct, in the end, to endorse the familiar sociological generalization about 'industrialization and the rise of class society'. But if we mean by this the separation of spheres, the creation of separate class universes within the general body of society, we should note that in England, the oldest industrial society, this was nowhere near accomplishment for much of the nineteenth century. Moreover by the time there was a greater definition of classes in industrial society, the rise of new professional and technical groups was making possible a new set of class alliances, and creating new vertical linkages, in such institutions as the labour and socialist parties.

These considerations lead us back to the main theme of this chapter, the treatment of English working-class history and politics in 'New Left' historiography. There is a feature of this treatment that is particularly relevant here. For the period up to 1850, when the working class is seen to be growing and developing in political consciousness, the attraction of the 'esoteric' approach to its history seems to be irresistible. The baby has just been born; it seems to be doing exactly what its fond parents hope and expect of it. How fascinating therefore to concentrate, to the exclusion of all else, on its first movements, and its first smiles. A worm's-eye view, an understanding from within, seems the natural counterpart to this period. After 1850 a new sobriety, even sourness, takes over. The infant does not live up to its promises; the parents, unwilling to blame either the baby or themselves, look around for the forces that have corrupted its ideals and stunted its growth. They show, in other words, a newly displayed realism in analysing the developments in capitalist society which have impinged on working-class consciousness and action. We then have disquisitions on the 'de-radicalization' and the 'incorporation' of the working class; theories of a selfish 'aristocracy of labour' proliferate.[81]

The whole purpose of this chapter has been to question this view of the development of the English working class. I have tried to show that the presumption of a historical and sociological continuity is based on the normative 'collapsing' of a complex and non-linear historical evolution. As is well demonstrated for France and Germany, assertions and hypotheses about the political potential of the working class have to take into account the varying social content and diverse ideological outlooks of the working class over the past two centuries. 'The English working class' may no doubt for certain purposes be treated as a timeless unity, rather as the triune God in Christian theology. But for most mundane purposes we need to recognize the many disparate parts, from different times and different experiences, which go to make up its body.

Even more important, if we wish to get the method right as well as set the story straight, is the need to reject the 'esoteric' approach to working-class history and working-class sociology. It clearly only mystifies the explanations of working-class action in the episodes we have looked at. If misleading for nineteenth-century England, is there any reason why it should be less so for other times and other places? The rise of various forms of 'segmental history' – 'labour history', 'black history' and so on – have had readily understandable origins and motivations. But it is less easy to sympathize with the narrowness of vision, and restricted terms of analysis, imposed by the method of considering events predominantly from the participants' point of view, as 'their history'. As Brian Harrison has said, reviewing the first seven volumes of the journal *History Workshop*, 'the long-term aims of segmental history – "labour", "socialist" or "women's" – will not in fact be achieved until they have collapsed into "total" history, and so have thereby ceased to exist.'[82] It is no help in the realization of particular goals of justice or equity to treat deprived or oppressed groups, now or in the past, as if they operate in a social and political vacuum. This is dangerously to confuse ends with means, and method. The history of working-class action, and not simply in the nineteenth century, demonstrates the significance of complex inter-class interaction. This may be deplored, from some points of view. But it does seem to be, persistently, an aspect of industrial as well as pre-industrial and non-industrial societies; and a principle so well attested, in an area noticeably thin in general principles, surely should not be disregarded by either students of working-class politics, or indeed workers themselves.

NOTES

Earlier versions of this paper were given in seminars at the State University of New York at Stony Brook, the University of Massachusetts at Amherst, and the Center for European Studies at Harvard. I should like to thank the participants for the many helpful comments I received.

1 Harold Perkin, *The Origins of Modern English Society 1780–1880*, (London, Routledge and Kegan Paul, 1969), p. 37.
2 Peter Laslett, *The World We Have Lost*, 2nd edn (London, Methuen, 1971), p. 24.
3 Perkin, *Origins of Modern English Society*, p. 37.
4 Cf. E. P. Thompson: 'In general, the middle classes submitted to a client relationship . . . For at least the first seven decades of the century we can find no industrial or professional middle class which exercises an effective curb upon the operations of predatory oligarchic power', 'Eighteenth-century English society: class struggle without class?', *Social History* (1978), no. 2, p. 143. See also Lucy Sutherland, 'The City of London in eighteenth-century politics', in R. Pares and A. J. P. Taylor (eds), *Essays Presented to Sir Lewis Namier* (London, Macmillan, 1956), pp. 49–74. Sutherland writes (p. 53): 'the City, in the sense of its monied interest, was throughout the period a broken reed for the purposes of party politics, for the good reasons that the prosperity of all its members depended on their being on terms with the Government of the day, and that, even if it might have paid them to hold out for a short time, they were much too competitive among themselves to do so.'
5 E. P. Thompson, 'Patrician society, plebeian culture', *Journal of Social History*, 7 (1974), p. 388. And for this general view of class and class action in eighteenth-century England, see also Thompson, 'Eighteenth Century English Society'; E. P. Thompson, 'The moral economy of the English crowd in the eighteenth century', *Past and Present*, no. 50 (1971), pp. 76–136; Sutherland, 'The City of London'; George Rudé, *Wilkes and Liberty* (Oxford, Oxford University Press, 1962); Rudé, *The Crowd in History 1730–1848*, (New York, John Wiley and Sons, 1964); Rudé, *Paris and London in the Eighteenth Century* (London, Collins, 1970); E. J. Hobsbawm, *Primitive Rebels*, (Manchester, Manchester University Press, 1959), ch. 7, 'The city mob'.
    Adam Smith expressed a typically eighteenth-century view of the workers' capacity for political action which still squares remarkably well with the current view of the eighteenth-century plebs: 'Though the interest of the labourer is strictly connected with that of society, he is incapable either of comprehending that interest, or of understanding its connection with his own. His condition leaves him

no time to receive the necessary information, and his education and habits are commonly such as to render him unfit to judge even though he was fully informed. In the public deliberations, therefore, his voice is little heard and less regarded, except upon some particular occasions, when his clamour is animated, set on, and supported by his employers, not for his, but their own particular purposes', *The Wealth of Nations* (Everyman edition, 1910), Book I, ch. 8.

6 Perkin, *Origins of Modern English Society*, p. 209. The classic statement of this view is Asa Briggs, 'The language of "class" in early nineteenth century England', in Asa Briggs and John Saville (eds), *Essays in Labour History* (London, Macmillan, 1960), pp. 43–73. See also Briggs, 'Middle-class consciousness in English politics', *Past and Present*, no. 9 (1956), pp. 65–74.

7 E. P. Thompson, *The Making of the English Working Class*, (London, Gollancz, 1963), pp. 194, 807, 825–6. And cf. Paul Richards: 'The 1832 Reform Act hurried the transition between the old and new radical politics by conveniently defining a working-*class* opposition to it. Almost as soon as the landed aristocracy and industrial middle class had sealed their political marriage they demonstrated how they regarded working-class interests to be incompatible with their own by rejecting the Ten Hours Bill, obstructing the handloom weavers, attacking trade unionism, and passing the New Poor Law which was interpreted as a measure to grind down wages in town and country' (Richards's emphasis), 'The state and early industrial capitalism: the case of the handloom weavers', *Past and Present*, no. 83 (1979), pp. 96–7.

8 Morris, speaking of 'the Whiggish dimension' to these histories, says that in them class was recounted as 'a series of key events': the publication of Paine's *Rights of Man*, the Nore mutiny, the Luddites, Blanketeers, Peterloo and so on to the end of the century. 'The events listed here appear like the battle honours of the working class movement .... Each event raised the level of working class consciousness, driving the working class towards an institutionalised, constitutional-ised, and powerful place in British society', R. J. Morris, *Class and Class Consciousness in the Industrial Revolution 1780–1850* (London, Macmillan, 1979), p. 30. An important renewal of the Fabian tradition – but from the perspective of Parsonian functionalism – is N. Smelser, *Social Change in the Industrial Revolution* (London, Routledge and Kegan Paul, 1959). And see also B. C. Roberts, 'On the origins and resolution of English working-class protest', in H. D. Graham and T. R. Gurr (eds), *Violence in America: Historical and Comparative Perspectives* (Washington, DC, US Government Printing Office, 1969), pp. 197–220.

9 For one of the earliest and fullest statements, see P. Anderson, 'Origins of the present crisis', *New Left Review*, no. 23 (Jan.–Feb. 1964), pp. 26–53. Reprinted in P. Anderson and R. Blackburn (eds), *Towards Socialism* (London, Fontana, 1965), pp. 11–52. And cf. Tom Nairn's lament: 'The great English working class, this titanic social force which seemed to be unchained by the rapid development of English capitalism in the first half of the century, did not finally emerge to dominate and remake English society. It could not break the mould and fashion another. Instead, after the 1840s it quickly turned into an apparently docile class. It embraced one species of moderate reformism after another, became a consciously subordinate part of bourgeois society, and has remained wedded to the narrowest and greyest of bourgeois ideologies in its principal

movements', T. Nairn 'The English working class', in R. Blackburn (ed.), *Ideology in Social Science* (London, Fontana, 1972), p. 188.

10 Few are rash enough to take all these on board in a general treatment, although Anderson and Nairn (note 9, above) cover most of the ground between them. For a comprehensive view of the nineteenth century, see F. Hearn, *Domination, Legitimation and Resistance: The Incorporation of the Nineteenth-Century English Working Class* (Westport, Conn., Greenwood Press, 1978). See also N. Young, 'Prometheans or Troglodytes? The English working class and the dialectics of incorporation', *Berkeley Journal of Sociology*, 12 (1967), 1–43; William Lazonick, 'The subjection of labour to capital: the rise of the capitalist system', *Review of Radical Political Economics*, 10 (Spring 1978), 1–31; and D. Kynaston, *King Labour: The British Working Class 1850–1914* (London, Allen and Unwin, 1976). For particular periods and episodes, see J. Foster, *Class Struggle and the Industrial Revolution: Early Industrial Capitalism in Three English Towns* (London, Weidenfeld and Nicolson, 1974); G. Stedman Jones, *Outcast London: A Study in the Relationship Between Classes in Victorian Society* (Harmondsworth, Penguin Books, 1976); B. Holton, *British Syndicalism 1900–1914* (London, Pluto Press, 1976); J. Hinton, *The First Shop Stewards' Movement* (London, Allen and Unwin, 1973). Many of the guidelines for later New Left historiography were set by E. Hobsbawm, *Labouring Men: Studies in the History of Labour* (London, Weidenfeld and Nicolson, 1964), and R. Harrison, *Before the Socialists* (London, Routledge and Kegan Paul, 1965). The lack of a systematic historical treatment of the English working class in the twentieth century is notable and interesting.

11 Thompson, *Making of the English Working Class*, p. 295. Answering Thompson's critics, Donnelly has argued that, qualitatively and quantitatively, 'Thompson's concentration on the craftsmen, artisans and domestic outworkers is entirely justified: they are the groups crucial to the emergence of the class movement of the 1830s.' Quite so – but that is precisely what makes their relationship to the later movements of factory workers so problematic. See F. K. Donnelly, 'Ideology and early English working-class history: Edward Thompson and his critics', *Social History*, 2 (May 1976), 211–38. For the importance of handloom weavers in Chartism, see Donald Read, *The English Provinces, c.1760–1960* (London, Edward Arnold, 1964), pp. 124–5; Hearn, *Domination, Legitimation and Resistance*, pp. 184–5.

12 Thompson, *Making of the English Working Class*, p. 645. For the low significance of factory workers in the working-class political movements of this period, see Perkin, *The Origins of Modern English Society*, pp. 178–9. The prominence of handicraft workers in Chartism must make us especially careful of the inferences we draw from the frequent assertion that 'Chartism was the first independent movement of the British working class', (Rudé, *The Crowd in History*, p. 179).

13 F. Engels, *The Condition of the Working Class in England in 1844*, trans. and ed. W. O. Henderson and W. H. Chaloner (Oxford, Basil Blackwell, 1958), pp. 24–5.

14 The position is even more complicated than this. Raphael Samuel has shown how the British pattern of industrial development in the nineteenth century not only remained dependent on many kinds of traditional handicraft workers, but actually stimulated the creation of a vast number of new types and grades of

handicraftsmen. Handicraft work was not merely a vestigial, pre-industrial, hangover into the nineteenth century, but a structural requirement of the industrial revolution, and so continued to flourish until late in the century. 'Steam power and hand technology ... were two sides of the same coin ... The industrial revolution rested on a broad handicraft basis, which was at once a condition of its development and a restraint on its further growth', R. Samuel, 'Workshop of the world: steam power and hand technology in mid-Victorian Britain', *History Workshop*, no. 3 (Spring 1977), pp. 6–72, at pp. 58–60. I have discussed the implication of this persistence for the Marxist concept of a revolutionary proletariat in K. Kumar, 'Can the workers be revolutionary', *European Journal of Political Research*, 6 (1978), 357–79.

15 Foster, *Class Struggle and the Industrial Revolution, passim*. Three good reviews containing detailed historical as well as theoretical criticisms are A. E. Musson, 'Class struggle and the Labour aristocracy 1830–1860, *Social History*, (1976), 335–56; J. Saville, 'Class struggle and the Industrial Revolution', in R. Miliband and J. Saville (eds), *The Socialist Register 1974* (London, The Merlin Press, 1974), pp. 226–40; and G. Stedman Jones, 'Class struggle and the Industrial Revolution', *New Left Review*, no. 90 (1975), pp. 35–69.

16 In 1835, adult male workers of all kinds accounted for 27 per cent of all cotton workers, the rest being women, juveniles and children. Male spinners accounted for 15 per cent of cotton workers – by 1886 this had declined to 5 per cent (Perkin, *Origins of Modern English Society*, p. 144; Hobsbawm, *Labouring Men*, p. 282).

17 On this see especially William Lazonick, 'Industrial relations and technical change: the case of the self-acting mule', *Cambridge Journal of Economics*, 3, (1979), 231–62; see also Stedman Jones, 'Class struggle and the Industrial Revolution', p. 51. On the long persistence of customary work norms based on craft practice, see Hobsbawm, 'Custom, wages, and work-load in nineteenth century industry', in his *Labouring Men*, pp. 344–70. There is an interesting comparison with the American cotton industry, where spinners were not able to establish craft control on the British pattern, in W. Lazonick, 'Industrial relations, work organization, and technical change: US and British cotton spinning', paper given at the Cliometrics Conference, University of Chicago, 15–17 May 1980.

18 Lazonick, 'Industrial relations and technical change'; Samuel, 'Workshop of the world', p. 19. The spinners' relative success would partly explain why they became among the most conservative of workers, even among the 'labour aristocracy', in the later nineteenth century. Smelser also sees the conflicts of these years in terms of a defence of the spinners' traditional rights and status (*Social Change in the Industrial Revolution*, pp. 231–35). It is interesting that Foster notes this aspect of the spinners' struggle but does not apparently feel the need to relate it to his main interpretation: 'more dangerous in the long run ... were attempts to dilute the labour force, cut down the number of well-paid jobs, and substitute women and children for men. This was the real threat to the spinners' position. The 1830s and early 1840s saw a protracted struggle against the attempt to introduce an "automatic spinning mule" which would do

away with the need for skilled labour altogether' (*Class Struggle and the Industrial Revolution*, p. 83).

19 For example, Foster states the theme of his study to be 'the development and decline of a revolutionary class consciousness in the second quarter of the century', *Class Struggle and the Industrial Revolution*, p. 1, see also pp. 74 and 125, where he states: 'Some sort of move from trade union to class consciousness did take place in Oldham during the 1830s and early 1840s.' Foster repeats his claim that a revolutionary class-conscious proletariat developed in Oldham in his reply to Musson in *Social History*, 1 (1976), 357–66. An earlier essay of Foster's is even more explicit, in describing Oldham's radical leaders as a 'coherent and stable group of social revolutionaries . . . working for the overthrow of the existing pattern of ownership and production', Foster, 'Nineteenth century towns: a class dimension', in H. J. Dyos (ed.), *The Study of Urban History* (London, Edward Arnold, 1968), p. 285.

20 See the tables in Foster, *Class Struggle and the Industrial Revolution*, pp. 132, 151–2, 154–9, listing the radical leadership in Oldham from the 1790s to the 1840s.

21 Stedman Jones, 'Class struggle and the Industrial Revolution', p. 60.

22 For a critical discussion of the theory, see H. F. Moorhouse, 'The political incorporation of the British working class: an interpretation', *Sociology*, 7 (1973), pp. 341–59; J. M. Cousins and R. L. Davis, '"Working class incorporation" – a historical approach with reference to the mining communities of S. E. Northumberland 1840–1890', in F. Parkin (ed.), *The Social Analysis of Class Structure* (London, Tavistock, 1974), pp. 275–97.

23 See F. Engels, 'England in 1845 and in 1885', in Karl Marx and Frederick Engels, *Articles on Britain* (Moscow, Progress Publishers, 1975), pp. 386–92; E. J. Hobsbawm, 'Lenin and the "aristocracy of labour"', *Marxism Today*, July 1970, pp. 207–10; and, for a re-statement of the Leninist conception, Martin Nicolaus, 'The theory of the labour aristocracy', *Monthly Review*, 21 (1970), pp. 91–101. The 'neo-classic' statement is E. J. Hobsbawm, 'The labour aristocracy in nineteenth-century Britain', *Labouring Men*, pp. 272–315; see also Hobsbawm, 'Trends in the British Labour Movement since 1850', pp. 316–43. Among those who make the concept central to their accounts are Royden Harrison, *Before the Socialists: Studies in Labour and Politics 1861–1881* (London, Routledge and Kegan Paul, 1965), pp. 1–39; Robert Q. Gray, 'The labour aristocracy in the Victorian class structure', in Parkin (ed.), *The Social Analysis of Class Structure*, pp. 19–38; Foster, *Class Struggle and the Industrial Revolution*, ch. 7; Foster, 'British imperialism and the labour aristocracy', in J. Skelley (ed.), *The General Strike 1926* (London, Lawrence and Wishart, 1976), pp. 3–57. There is a detailed critical discussion of the literature in H. F. Moorhouse, 'The Marxist theory of the labour aristocracy', *Social History*, 3 (1978), 61–82; and see also the exchange between Moorhouse and Alastair Reid in *Social History*, 3 (1978), 347–61, and 4 (1979), 481–90.

24 See especially Musson, 'Class struggle and the labour aristocracy 1830–1860'.

25 On the increasing 'homogenization' of the workforce after 1850 as a result of these changes, see H. Pelling, 'The concept of the labour aristocracy', in Pelling,

162   *Politics, Work and Society*

Popular Politics and Society in Late Victorian Britain (London, Macmillan, 1968), pp. 37–61.

26 One interesting way of considering the change is to see it in 'geo-political' terms: the intensely political, secular, rationalist artisan culture of London gives way, for a time, to the more inward-looking, chapel-based, Dissenting culture of the factory workers of the northern industrial towns. See Hobsbawm, 'Labour traditions', in his *Labouring Men*, pp. 371–85. A similar theme is touched on in G. Stedman Jones, *Outcast London: A Study in the Relationship Between Classes in Victorian Society* (Harmondsworth, Penguin Books, 1976), pp. 337ff.

27 Stedman Jones, 'Class struggle and the Industrial Revolution', p. 65. He points up the relevance of this to the 'labour aristocracy' theory of de-radicalization: 'It was not so much the privileged position [of certain groups of workers] as the vulnerability of that position that changed their industrial outlook.' See also *Outcast London*, pp. 338–9.

28 This division is, however, for purposes of explaining differences of political outlook, greatly exaggerated by proponents of the theory of the labour aristocracy. For the common shaping influences and links between all grades of factory workers, at work and in the life of the community as a whole, see Patrick Joyce, 'The factory politics of Lancashire in the later nineteenth century', *The Historical Journal*, 18 (1975), 525–53. For an outrightly sceptical statement on the concept of the labour aristocracy, see Harold Perkin, '"The condescension of posterity": the recent historiography of the English working class', *Social Science History*, 3 (Fall 1978), 87–101.

29 There is an excellent account of this transformation of working-class life, as far as London workers are concerned, in G. Stedman Jones, 'Working class culture and working-class politics in London, 1870–1900: notes on the remaking of a working class', *Journal of Social History*, 7 (1974), 460–508. For developments among skilled workers in Oldham, see Foster, *Class Struggle and the Industrial Revolution*, pp. 203–50. On middle-class guidance and encouragement of 'respectable' working-class activities in this period, see Trygve R. Tholfsen, 'The transition to democracy in Victorian England', *International Review of Social History*, 6 (1961), 226–48; and Tholfsen, 'The intellectual origins of mid-Victorian stability', *Political Science Quarterly*, 86 (1971), 57–91.

30 V. Kiernan, 'Victorian London: unending purgatory', *New Left Review*, no. 76 (1972), p. 76. And cf. Mayhew's observation of the same contrast: 'In passing from the skilled operative of the west-end to the unskilled workman of the eastern quarter of London, the moral and intellectual change is so great, that it seems as if we were in a new land, and among another race. The artisans are almost to a man red-hot politicians. They are sufficiently educated and thoughtful to have a sense of their importance in the state ... The unskilled labourers are a different class of people. As yet they are as unpolitical as footmen, and instead of entertaining violent democratic opinions, they appear to have no political opinions whatever; or, if they do, ... they rather lead towards the maintenance of "things as they are", than towards the ascendancy of the working people', H. Mayhew, *London Labour and the London Poor* (1861), quoted in Thompson, *Making of the English Working Class*, pp. 240–1. For a study of some proverbially 'red-hot politicians' among the artisans, see E. J.

Hobsbawm and J. W. Scott, 'Political shoemakers', *Past and Present*, no. 89 (1980), pp. 86–114. The authors comment pointedly that shoemakers played no significant part in the later mass political movements among industrial workers.

31 Stedman Jones, 'Class struggle and industrial revolution', p. 60.

32 See especially William H. Sewell Jnr, *Work and Revolution in France. The Language of Labor from the Old Regime to 1848* (Cambridge, Cambridge University Press, 1980). For a brief survey of the material, Charles Tilly, 'The modernization of political conflict in France', in E. B. Harvey (ed.), *Perspectives on Modernization: Essays in Memory of Ian Weinberg* (Toronto, University of Toronto Press, 1972), pp. 50–95; Roger Price, *The French Second Republic: A Social History* (Ithaca, NY, Cornell University Press, 1972), esp. pp. 56–82.

33 Barrington Moore jnr, *Injustice: The Social Bases of Obedience and Revolt* (London, Macmillan, 1978). Moore's subject, as the title of his book indicates, is of course wider than the study of the German working class; but the latter nevertheless is the heart of the book, and the best thing in it. Moore himself suggests that his study of German workers can be taken as a parallel enterprise to Thompson's account of the English working class (*Injustice*, pp. 379n, 474n).

34 Ibid., pp. 126–67. Moore's analysis is fully supported by, for example, T. S. Hamerow, *Restoration, Revolution, Reaction: Economics and Politics in Germany 1815–1871* (Princeton, NJ, Princeton University Press, 1958).

35 Moore, *Injustice*, p. 261.

36 Ibid., p. 272.

37 Ibid., p. 217. A review of the recent German literature on the subject generally supports Moore's conclusion: Dick Geary, 'The Ruhr: from social peace to social revolution', *European Studies Review*, 10 (1980), 497–511. For the view that Moore underplays the revolutionary character of the German working class, see Jonathan M. Wiener, 'Working-class consciousness in Germany, 1848–1933', *Marxist Perspectives*, Winter 1979/80, pp. 156–69.

38 R. Michels, *Political Parties* (1915).

39 W. H. Dawson, 'The turn from laissez-faire', in T. S. Hamerow (ed.), *Otto von Bismarck: A Historical Assessment* (Boston, Mass., D.C. Heath, 1962), p. 74.

40 For a good discussion of these factors in German working-class life, and a comparison with other contemporary workers, see P. N. Stearns, *Lives of Labour: Work in a Maturing Society* (London, Croom Helm, 1975), esp. pp. 241ff.

41 E. J. Hobsbawm, 'Labour history and ideology', *Journal of Social History*, 7 (1974), 373.

42 Thompson, *The Making of the English Working Class*, p. 102.

43 Hobsbawm, 'Labour history and ideology', p. 379.

44 Morris, *Class and Class Consciousness in the Industrial Revolution 1780–1850*, p. 42. Musson, Saville and Stedman Jones (see n. 15) all comment on this aspect of Foster's account.

45 It is fair to point out that in the final part of his book, in dealing with the 'liberalization' of English society after 1850, Foster's range is very much wider, and his account of the 're-stabilization' of bourgeois society, whether or not we accept it, considers many of the necessary relationships and developments at both local and national level.

46 Foster, *Class Struggle and the Industrial Revolution*, pp. 132ff.

47 D. S. Gadian, 'Class consciousness in Oldham and other north-west industrial towns 1830–1850', *The Historical Journal*, 21 (1978), 161–72.
48 Ibid., pp. 171–2. For the social basis of Birmingham's radicalism, see the articles by Briggs cited in n. 56 below.
49 Thompson, *The Making of the English Working Class*, *passim*, esp. pp. 196–8.
50 Ibid., p. 817. Thompson's view is not as novel as it is sometimes made out. It was shared, among others, by historians such as G. M. Young, G. M. Trevelyan, G. D. H. Cole, R. Postgate and W. W. Rostow – not to mention a host of frightened aristocrats at the time in question. For a selection of views, see W. H. Maehl (ed.), *The Reform Bill of 1832: Why not Revolution?* (New York, Holt, Rinehart and Winston, 1967). There is a careful assessment in M. I. Thomis and P. Holt, *Threats of Revolution in Britain 1789–1848* (London, Macmillan, 1977), pp. 85–99.
51 G. Rudé, 'Why was there no revolution in England in 1830 or 1848?', *Studien Über Die Revolution*, Zweite, durchgesehene Auflage (Berlin, Akademie-Verlag, 1971), p. 241. See also the same author's 'English rural and urban disturbances on the eve of the First Reform Bill, 1830–31', *Past and Present*, no. 37 (1967), pp. 87–102.
52 W. L. Guttsman, *The British Political Elite*, (London, MacGibbon and Kee, 1965), p. 35.
53 The relative insulation of the political elite from outside pressure, and its ability to determine the timing and form of change, had already been recently demonstrated in the case of Catholic Emancipation in 1829. Allan Silver shows that Peel and Wellington decided on Catholic Emancipation not out of concession to radical pressure or liberal opinion, but out of the exigencies of political control over Ireland. A very eighteenth-century concept of 'reason of state', rather than the more typically nineteenth-century 'influence of public opinion', determined their actions throughout, and kept the debate firmly within the confines of the ruling elite. See Allan Silver, 'Social and ideological bases of British elite reactions to domestic crisis in 1829–1832', *Politics and Society*, 1 (1971), 179–201, esp. 190–1.
54 See D. C. Moore, 'The other face of reform', *Victorian Studies*, 5 (1961), 7–34; also his 'Concession or cure: the sociological premises of the First Reform Act', *The Historical Journal*, 9 (1966), 39–59. Moore has developed his interpretation of nineteenth-century English politics, and especially the idea of 'the deference community', in a further series of articles: see 'The Corn Laws and high farming', *Economic History Review*, 2nd ser., 18 (1965), 544–60; 'Social structure, political structure, and public opinion in mid-Victorian England', in R. Robson (ed.), *Ideas and Institutions of Victorian England* (London, Bell and Sons, 1967), pp. 20–57; 'Political morality in mid-nineteenth-century England: concepts, norms, violations', *Victorian Studies*, 13 (1969), 5–36. Most of the material has also now been presented in his book, *The Politics of Deference: A Study of the Mid-Nineteenth Century English Political System* (Hassocks, The Harvester Press, 1976); but its unwieldiness makes the articles a better source of reference.
55 Perkin, *The Origins of Modern English Society*, p. 252; and see ibid., pp. 237–52, for a good account of the revival of the 'aristocratic ideal' in the 1820s and early 1830s. Perkin quotes *Blackwood's Magazine* (1829) for the view that 'no

change could well give them [the High Tories] a worse House of Commons than the present system gives them, and that the elective franchise could not be in more dangerous hands than those which now hold it' (pp. 251–2).

56 D. C. Moore, 'The other face of reform', p. 21. For the Ultra-Tory Blandford's alliance with the Radical Attwood, see also Asa Briggs, 'Thomas Attwood and the economic background of the Birmingham Political Union', *Cambridge Historical Journal*, 9 (1948), 190–216; Briggs, 'The background of the Parliamentary Reform Movement in three English cities', *Cambridge Historical Journal*, 10 (1952), 293–317, esp. 298–300. Briggs notes that Attwood's radical career 'began by his supporting the Tory Marquis of Blandford's reform proposals'.

57 See Guttsman, *The British Political Elite*, chs 2–3.

58 Quoted by Derek Fraser, 'The agitation for Parliamentary reform', in J. T. Ward (ed.), *Popular Movements c.1830–1850* (London, Macmillan, 1970), p. 50.

59 Silver, 'Social and ideological bases of British elite reactions ...', pp. 200–1.

60 T. Burns, 'Leisure in industrial society', in M. Smith, S. Parker and C. Smith (eds), *Leisure and Society in Britain* (London, Allen Lane, 1973), p. 43.

61 Karl Marx, 'Inaugural Address of the Working Men's International Association' (1864), in Karl Marx and Frederick Engels, *Selected Works in Two Volumes* (Moscow, Foreign Languages Publishing House, 1962), vol. 1, p. 383. Marx elaborates on this view in ch. 10, 'The working day', of *Capital*, vol. 1.

62 Karl Marx, 'The clergy and the struggle for the ten hour day' (1853), in Marx and Engels, *Articles on Britain*, p. 156. Here as so often in these early years of his residence in England, Marx was instructed by Engels on English politics. See Engels, 'The English Ten Hours Bill' (1850), in *Articles on Britain*, pp. 96–108.

63. Cecil Driver, *Tory Radical: The Life of Richard Oastler* (1946; repr. New York, Octagon Books, 1970), p. 32.

64 On all this see Driver, *Tory Radical*, passim; J. T. Ward, *The Factory Movement 1830–1855* (London, Macmillan, 1962).

65 Smelser, *Social Change in the Industrial Revolution*, pp. 231–4; and, generally on the Factory Movement, pp. 225–45, 265–308. It should perhaps be said here that one does not have to swallow the whole of Smelser's theory of working-class behaviour in nineteenth-century England to appreciate the value of his analysis of the Factory Acts of 1833–50. Lazonick, for instance, who generally takes a 'New Left' view, concurs with Smelser's account of the textile workers' motivation: see 'The subjection of labour to capital', pp. 8–10. In a somewhat different way Jane Humphries accepts Smelser's evidence but gives it a radical interpretation: see her 'Class struggle and the persistence of the working-class family', *Cambridge Journal of Economics*, 1 (1977), 241–58. The complexity of the Factory Movement is increased by the observation that not all manufacturers by any means were opposed to 'short-time' working. Many of the smaller manufacturers in particular joined with the workers in pressing for limitations of hours, as a means of controlling over-production. For evidence in Oldham, see Foster, *Class Struggle and the Industrial Revolution*, pp. 136, 176, 207; Gadian, 'Class consciousness in Oldham ...', pp. 166–7.

66 M. E. Rose, 'The anti-Poor Law agitation', in Ward (ed.), *Popular Movements c.1830–1850*, p. 86. See also Driver, *Tory Radical*, pp. 331ff; Ward, *The Factory*

Movement, ch. 7; G. Kitson Clark, 'Hunger and politics in 1842', *Journal of Modern History*, 15 (1953), 360, 370–2.

67 Rose, 'The anti-Poor Law agitation', p. 83; Driver, *Tory Radical*, p. 332.

68 Oastler, quoted Driver, *Tory Radical*, p. 282.

69 In 1844 Sir James Graham, the Home Secretary, admitted that 85 per cent of relief was still given outside, and not inside, the workhouses (David Roberts, *Paternalism in Early Victorian England*, London, Croom Helm, 1979, p. 245).

70 Engels, 'England in 1845 and 1885', in *Articles on Britain*, p. 387.

71 Asa Briggs, 'Middle-class consciousness in British politics 1780–1846', *Past and Present*, no. 9 (1956), p. 71.

72 Quoted by Briggs, ibid., p. 65. Cobden's verdict is endorsed by the League's historian: see Norman McCord, *The Anti-Corn Law League 1838–1846* (London, Unwin University Books, 1968), pp. 213–15.

73. See on this especially Betty Kemp, 'Reflections on the repeal of the Corn Laws', *Victorian Studies*, 5 (1962), 189–204.

74 G. Kitson Clark, 'The repeal of the Corn Laws and the politics of the forties', *The Economic History Review*, 2nd. ser., 4 (1951), 6.

75 See on this D. C. Moore, 'The Corn Laws and high farming'.

76 Kitson Clark, 'The repeal of the Corn Laws ...', pp. 11–12.

77 Ibid., p. 13.

78 Although it is necessary even here to see the important part played by middle-class radicals, such as Attwood, in the early years of Chartism. See Read, *The English Provinces*, pp. 113–22; D. J. Rowe, 'The London Workingmen's Association and the "People's Charter"', *Past and Present*, no. 36 (1967), pp. 73–86; R. S. Neale, *Class and Ideology in the Nineteenth Century* (London, Routledge and Kegan Paul, 1972), pp. 15–40.

79 See especially Roberts, *Paternalism in Early Victorian England*; and the articles by D. C. Moore, n. 54 above.

80 Richard Sennett, *The Fall of Public Man* (Cambridge, Cambridge University Press, 1977), p. 223. Something similar is suggested in Gareth Stedman Jones's account of the London working class, as he shows it developing a culture 'whose prevailing tone was not one of political combativity, but of an enclosed and defensive conservatism ... The distinctiveness of a working-class way of life was enormously accentuated. Its separateness and impermeability were now reflected in a dense and inward-looking culture, whose effect was both to emphasize the distance of the working class from the classes above it and to articulate its position within an apparently permanent social hierarchy' ('Working class culture and working class politics in London 1870–1900', pp. 462, 498).

81 The whole sequence is especially marked in Foster; see also Hearn, *Domination, Legitimation and Resistance*.

82 Brian Harrison, *New Statesman*, 26 October 1979.

BIBLIOGRAPHICAL NOTE

The most directly relevant contribution, one which takes a broadly similar view to that expressed here, is Craig Calhoun, *The Question of Class Struggle: Social Foundations of Popular Radicalism during the Industrial Revolution* (Oxford, Basil Blackwell, 1982). For further discussion of E. P. Thompson's view of the English working class, see Perry Anderson, *Arguments Within English Marxism* (London, Verso, 1980), esp. pp. 16–58; Harvey J. Kaye, *The British Marxist Historians* (Oxford, Polity Press, 1984). A direct attack is Robert Glen, *Urban Workers in the Industrial Revolution* (London, Croom Helm, 1983). See also Zygmunt Bauman, *Memories of Class: The Pre-history and After-life of Class* (London, Routledge and Kegan Paul, 1982), and Harold Perkin, *The Structured Crowd: Essays in English Social History* (Brighton, Harvester Press, 1981). A full-scale exploration of the role of the working class in British history is Richard Price, *Labour in British Society: An Interpretative History* (London, Croom Helm, 1986).

There is a wealth of relevant information in Eric Hobsbawm, *Worlds of Labour: Further Studies in the History of Labour* (London, Weidenfeld and Nicolson, 1984). Also helpful, for their theory as much as their historical content, are R. S. Neale, *Class in English History 1680–1850* (Oxford, Basil Blackwell, 1981), and George Rudé, *Ideology and Popular Protest* (London, Lawrence and Wishart, 1980). Other useful surveys and collections are: John Stevenson, *Popular Disturbances in England 1700–1870* (London, Longman, 1979); Edward Royle and James Walvin, *English Radicals and Reformers 1760–1848* (Brighton, The Harvester Press, 1982); Eileen and Stephen Yeo (eds), *Popular Culture and Class Conflict 1590–1914* (Brighton, The Harvester Press, 1981); A. P. Donajgrodzki (ed.), *Social Control in Nineteenth Century Britain* (London, Croom Helm, 1977); Paul Adelman, *Victorian Radicalism: the Middle Class Experience, 1830–1914* (London, Longman, 1984); Clive Emsley and James Walvin (eds), *Artisans, Peasants, and Proletarians 1760–1860* (London, Croom Helm, 1985). A good detailed study is I. Prothero, *Artisans and Politics in Early Nineteenth Century London* (London, Methuen, 1981). There is now also a comprehensive new study of the Chartists by Dorothy Thompson: *The Chartists* (London, Temple Smith, 1984). The important article by Patrick Joyce has now been expanded into a book: Joyce, *Work, Society and Politics: The Culture of the Factory in later Victorian England* (London, Methuen, 1982). Gareth Stedman Jones has also collected his articles into a book: *Languages of Class: Studies in English Working Class History 1832–1982* (Cambridge, Cambridge University Press, 1984). An interesting contribution to the debate launched by John Foster and Stedman Jones is Neville Kirk, *The Growth of Working Class Reformism in Mid-Victorian England* (London, Croom Helm, 1985).

Following on E. P. Thompson's *Whigs and Hunters* (1975; Harmondsworth, Penguin Books, 1985), and partly in opposition to it, eighteenth-century radicalism is also receiving fresh attention. See John Brewer and John Styles (eds), *An Ungovernable People: The English and their Law in the Seventeenth and Eighteenth Centuries* (London, Hutchinson, 1983); John Brewer, *Party Ideology and Popular Politics at the Accession of George III* (Cambridge, Cambridge University Press, 1981). A thorough-going revisionist account is J. C. D. Clark, *English Society 1688–1832*

(Cambridge, Cambridge University Press, 1985).

On the comparative aspects of this essay, see Louise A. Tilly and Charles Tilly (eds), *Class Conflict* and *Collective Action* (Beverly Hills, Ca, Sage Publications, 1981); Dick Geary, *European Labour Protest 1848–1939* (London, Croom Helm, 1981); Tony Judt, *Marxism and the French Left: Studies on Labour and Politics in France 1830–1981* (Oxford, Clarendon Press, 1986). A particularly interesting study is Mark Traugott, *Armies of the Poor: Determinants of Working Class Participation in the Parisian Insurrection of June 1848* (Princeton, NJ, Princeton University Press, 1985).

See also the notes and bibliography for 'Can the workers be revolutionary?', chapter 8 in this volume.

7

Twentieth-century Revolutions in Historical Perspective

A Frenchman has nothing to renounce in the Russian Revolution, which in its method and procedures recommences the French Revolution.

Lenin, letter to a French comrade, 1920

As a matter of fact the Russian Revolution was the last nineteenth-century revolution. What does one mean by fighting on the barricades? What are the barricades? Something you put up to stop horses. We all know that they raised barricades in Budapest and they lasted exactly one hour. Then the tanks came in . . .

André Malraux, interview in *Encounter*, January 1968

When hungry peasants say 'we want land' or people demand free elections, they leave one in no doubt as to their grievances and what should be done to satisfy them. When people shout 'Down with the tyrant' they want to kill the tyrant . . . But supposing they were to shout, 'Down with alienation'? Where does one find the palace of Alienation and how does one destroy it?

Leszek Kolakowski, *New Statesman*, 27, July 1973

I

In no other modern phenomenon than that of revolution is there more clearly borne out the truth of Marx's observation that 'the tradition of all the dead generations weighs like a nightmare on the brain of the living'. The failure of the 1848 revolutions, especially in France, was traced by him precisely to an inability to throw off the dead hand of the past. Fixated on the pattern of the revolution of 1789 the revolutionaries were incapable of seeing that 'the social revolution of the nineteenth century cannot draw its poetry from the past, but only from the future. It cannot begin with itself before it has stripped off all superstition in regard to the past.' It was a lesson drawn repeatedly in that exemplary tract 'The Eighteenth Brumaire of Louis Bonaparte', from which these quotations are taken; and, if we see its force with respect to the nineteenth-century European revolutions, how much more should we expect and hope to see its spirit informing the theory and practice of twentieth-century revolutions.

Marx's pleading has largely been in vain. Ever since the first modern revolution, revolutionaries, like generals, have gone into battle resolutely facing backwards (as Barrington Moore once observed[1]). The English Puritan revolutionaries of the seventeenth century looked back to the Bible; the French in 1789 to the Greeks and Romans of classical antiquity; the nineteenth-century revolutionaries to the French of 1789. Similarly in our own century: the Russians claimed to be re-commencing the great French Revolution and to be continuing it in the perspective of nineteenth-century Marxism; the Chinese looked back to the Russian Revolution (nearly annihilating themselves in the process) and again to Marx.

Needless to say, the achievements of these revolutions were in despite of their archaic pretensions. The leading actors, notably Lenin and Mao, were adroit at adapting phrases from the old texts to fit novel situations. And revolutionaries no doubt often have good tactical reasons for saying one thing and doing another. But as an habitual practice this procedure has had very damaging, and sometimes near-tragic, consequences for the theory and practice of twentieth-century revolution. At the theoretical level it has meant that the study of contemporary revolution has been dominated by explanatory and conceptual schemata derived from reflection on the European experience up to the middle of the last century. At the practical level it has meant the striving to bring about revolution in the manner and with the materials of past revolutions, under conditions vastly different from those of the past.

The distinctions to be made are those not just of time but of place. The conditions and prospects of revolution differ as between the industrial and the non-industrial regions of the world: an obvious point, but a necessary first one to make in commenting on the inherited models of revolution. For the most striking facts about twentieth-century revolutions are that (a) they have taken place, almost without exception, in the societies outside the urban-industrial West; and that (b) they have been carried out on the basis of ideologies taken over from the West. It is a particular irony, in view of Marx's own warning, that these ideologies have overwhelmingly been of a Marxist kind; for not only do they disguise the actual content of 'Third World' revolutions to the majority of their participants, they serve also to blind the student of these revolutions to the real forces and conditions at work.

Marxism as a theory of revolution has exerted an almost irresistible attraction to those reflecting on twentieth-century revolutions. To the simple-minded inquirer this fact must seem nothing short of astonishing. Marx, it is true, gave us some of the most illuminating analyses of the European revolutions of the seventeenth to nineteenth centuries; and he speculated interestingly on the future of revolution in industrial societies. It is still an instructive exercise to attempt an answer to the question, why have Marx's predictions about the proletarian revolution not been borne out? But the glaring fact remains that the revolutions that have actually occurred in this century have not been in the industrial societies. They have taken place in colonial or semi-colonial societies: societies, that is to say, where there was almost no industrial working class to speak of, where the middle class was a wafer-thin stratum acting as brokers between the local populations and overseas interests, and where the traditional ruling class was either directly dependent on a colonial power or heavily mortgaged to some such power. The rest of the population – somewhere between 80 and 90 per cent in almost every case – has been overwhelmingly peasant. And Marxism simply has no real insight to offer on peasant-based revolutions.

This chapter will in fact mainly be concerned with the conditions and prospects for revolution in the industrial societies. But, by way of comment on the peasant revolutions of this century, it is worth saying just a little on the strange involvement of Marxism with those revolutions.

Marx's attitude to the peasantry as a revolutionary political force is notorious. They were denied representation as that grand agency of social chance, the *class*. Isolated from each other in the conditions of the largely self-sufficient small-holding, they were incapable of developing a common political consciousness and a national political organization. Their natural form of action was reaction. In the face of changes attempted by landowners or the urban classes, peasant political action typically veered between a tenacious passivity and a sort of 'biological', instinctive reflex of protest in the form of the *jacquerie*, violent but short-lived, and always looking backwards to the confirmation or restoration of traditional rights. Peasants made rebellions, not revolutions. Shlomo Avineri has remarked on the absurdity, in Marxian terms, 'of discussing future history in terms of a war of the Villages of the World against the Cities of the World – it was, after all, Marx who talked about the "idiocy of village life" as the major epistemological obstacle for agrarian socialist revolutionary movements.'[2] Avineri's collection of Marx's writings on colonialism and modernization makes it plain that, for Marx, the fate of the largely peasant non-European world was to be dragged brutally into the orbit of a world economic system that was the creation of European capitalism; and the prospects for revolutionary change in the underdeveloped countries were entirely dependent on the success of the revolutionary socialist movement in Europe. The peasantry, even in alliance with the middle-class intellectuals of the towns, could not be counted on as an independent agency of revolutionary change.

European history it was that suggested to Marx this view of the peasantry, and European history subsequently seemed to confirm it. The Marxist hostility to the peasantry broke a long-standing and, as it were, 'natural' radical alliance between the progressive classes of the towns and the exploited peasants of the countryside. Previously peasants, artisans, intellectuals and the professional and commercial middle classes had fought side by side against the power and privileges of Crown, Church, and nobility. To Marx, the French Revolution of 1789 revealed decisively the fragility of that alliance and, in particular, the limits of peasant radicalism. The experience of that revolution suggested to him that once the peasants were secured in possession of the land, untramelled by feudal and fiscal obligations, they became a counter-revolutionary force.

As against the more radical tendencies of the Jacobins, the peasants had become the mainstay of Napoleon's Empire. In 1848 they stood by while the workers of Paris were shot down, and then voted massively in favour of Louis Napoleon's dictatorship. Indeed everywhere in 1848 the course of revolution spoke eloquently on behalf of this view of the peasantry's role.

Thus, in the Marxist perspective the peasantry had no place in the future. They were a doomed class, destined to be reduced by the natural course of capitalist evolution to the condition of an agricultural proletariat, or forced to abandon the countryside altogether to swell the ranks of the urban proletariat. At best they could provide cannon-fodder for the proletarian revolution, supplying, as Marx realistically put it, 'that chorus without which its solo song becomes a swan song in all peasant countries'.[3] The Marxist orthodoxy was put tersely by Plekhanov when he pronounced that 'the peasantry does not exist, historically speaking' – and that in a Russia which was nearly 90 per cent peasant.[4]

The European peasantry naturally reacted accordingly. As the workers moved from liberalism to socialism so the peasants moved from liberalism to conservatism. David Mitrany has shown[5] how the mutual antagonism between the workers and the peasant parties wrecked nearly every left-wing rising in Europe up to the Second World War. It was massive peasant obstructionism that forced Lenin to fall back on the New Economic Policy of 1921. It was the hostility of the countryside that balked the attempt by the workers to secure power in central Europe during the political collapse that followed the First World War. The capital cities conquered for socialism – Munich, Vienna, Budapest – were subjected to a regular boycott by the peasants. In the end it was the Fascist movements of central and eastern Europe, with their 'organic' and racist appeals to peasants, who reaped the fruits of the Marxist contempt for the peasantry.

In rejecting the peasant, European socialism had at least the semblance of a case for its attitude in the general lines of economic and social development in the West: although only by imposing so abstract a model of development as to lead socialist revolutionaries to perpetrate gross and costly errors of strategy. But the generalizations from the European experience were bound to be seriously distorting when applied to the societies of the colonial and semi-colonial 'Third World', with their radically different components of history, culture and social structure. Of these differences perhaps the most important was that created by Western development itself, through its overwhelming impact on the rest of the globe during the course of its continued industrialization and economic expansion. The transformation of social structures brought about by Western colonialism, although undoubtedly revolutionary in its effect, was not necessarily so in the terms conceived of by European Marxism. Marxism, of course, offered some of the best analyses of this general process of European capitalist expansion, notably in the writings of Marx himself, Lenin and Rosa Luxemburg. But paradoxically this led if anything to an even greater unpreparedness, both theoretical and practical, in the face of the 'Third World' revolutions of the twentieth century. For by emphasizing that the dynamic of the process remained in the heartlands of

Western capitalism, Marxism was forced to argue that the only significant revolutions were those brought about in the urban industrial societies, on the basis of the advanced technology and the developed social consciousness of the industrial classes. Essentially, therefore, the fate of the peasantry in the 'Third World' was linked to the fortunes of the proletarian movement in the industrial world. 'The chain of exploitation must break at its strongest link.'[6]

Despite Marxist insistence, peasants have proved in this century that they can make history. As Barrington Moore jnr has said, it is 'no longer possible to take seriously the view that the peasant is "an object of history", a form of social life over which historical changes pass but which contributes nothing to the impetus of these changes . . . the peasant in the modern era has been as much an agent of the revolution as the machine'.[7] Whereas in the industrial societies the working class has scarcely even attempted to bring about the socialist revolution, in the rest of the world no class has been as revolutionary as the peasantry. In a host of major upheavals their support and participation have been essential to the success of the revolution (six of the chief ones might be listed as: the Mexican Revolution of 1910, the Russian Revolution of 1917, the Chinese Revolution which culminated in 1948, the Vietnamese Revolution, one phase of which ended in 1954, the Algerian Revolution of 1954, and the Cuban Revolution of 1958). The fact that the peasants didn't usually start the revolution, and that the leadership of other groups, especially the urban intelligentsia, was indispensable, does not alter the main point: which is that these are rightly called peasant revolutions, in that without massive peasant participation from the earliest stages the revolutions would have been doomed from the start (as was, for instance, the case in central Europe after the First World War). In 1894 the German Marxist Liebknecht had said: 'We do not need the peasants for making the revolution, but no revolution can hold out if the peasants are against it.' In a sense the situation as revealed by the revolutions of this century has been precisely the opposite. The self-evident fact has been that the peasants were indispensable for making the revolution; the crucial problem has been what to do with them afterwards.

The leaders of twentieth-century peasant revolutions have usually been intellectuals, educated in the West or in the Western mode, and steeped in Western ideologies, especially that of Marxism; hence the Marxist ideological colouring to most of their revolutions. At the same time they are practical men and, in response to the realities of the situation, as a matter of basic strategy, they have been forced to modify their Marxism, sometimes to the point where all that remains are verbal incantations and faint echoes of concepts. The Chinese Communists, for instance, made little headway so long as they clung to the orthodox Marxist notion of the urban proletariat as the vanguard of the revolutionary struggle. The turning point can be dated quite precisely, to 1927 and Mao Tse-tung's *Report on the Peasant Movement in Hunan*, a document that has good claim to be considered the first book of the New Testament of Third World Marxism. Here was the acknowledgement that the mode of revolution for China and other semi-colonial countries had to be very different from that of the industrial West. As Mao put it later, in 1938, the appropriate strategy in the case of the industrial societies was a long legal struggle to mobilize the proletariat, followed by insurrection and the taking of the cities, and only then the move into the countryside. But 'in China, it is different. China is not an independent democratic state, but a semi-colonial and semi-feudal country . . . there is no legislative assembly to make use of, no legal right to organize the workers to strike. Here the fundamental task of the Communist Party is not to go through a long period of legal struggle before launching an insurrection or civil war. Its task is not to seize first the big cities and then the countryside, but to take the road in the opposite direction.'[8]

From this followed the basic strategy which, with variations, has been the pattern of so many Third World revolutionary wars of this century: the political penetration and preparation of the countryside by revolutionary activists, the insertion of guerrilla cadres, the formation of a guerrilla army, and, where possible, the establishment of local sovereignty over liberated 'base areas'; finally, the formation of a national liberation army and all-out war. Mao came under heavy fire from the Comintern for his 'left-wing deviationism'; but the unreality of the official Communist views on insurrection can readily be sampled in the Comintern-inspired volume *Armed Insurrection*, published in 1928 as a manual for intending revolutionaries.[9]

Mao never abandoned, in theory at least, the orthodoxy that ultimately the revolution must remain under proletarian leadership, and that all other movements must be subordinated to the interests of the proletarian movement. Others, while retaining a residual Marxism,[10] have generalized from the Chinese, Vietnamese and Cuban experience towards a more or less complete break with orthodox Marxism. For Frantz Fanon, all the urban classes, including the working class, are disqualified as sources of authentic revolutionary action through their inescapable involvement with and infection by the colonial mentality. 'In the colonial countries the peasants alone are revolutionary, for they have nothing to lose and everything to gain. The starving peasant, outside the class system, is the first among the exploited to discover that only violence pays' – and, Fanon would add, purges.[11] Castro too emphasizes the need to build the movement initially without the involvement of urban actors: 'The city is a cemetery of revolutionaries and resources.'[12] And finally we have the bleakest and most desperate conception of all, that of Guevara and Debray, where cities, parties, intellectuals, trade unions, all are rejected, in favour of the mobile guerrilla band. Even the peasantry *qua* peasantry is suspect: as a settled population it is too vulnerable to the counter-measures of the authorities. Peasants are the natural source of recruits, peasant areas the natural base; but only such peasants as join the band can be trusted, and it is unwise to be based too long in one place. With this conception we are back essentially to one of the oldest and most enduring forms of peasant protest: the phenomenon of social banditry, as we know it, for instance, through the activities of a Salvator Guiliano or a Pancho Villa.[13]

Even were there not the tragic fact of Guevara's Bolivian adventure as evidence, the simplicities of this last position are plain to see.[14] There was some sense – partly because of Mao's own illuminating analyses – in taking the Chinese case as some sort of general model for peasant revolutions; this the North Vietnamese to some extent showed. It took a peculiarly ruthless kind of blindness so to see the Cuban Revolution, a special case not simply in the context of the whole of the Third World, but even in relation to the rest of Latin America (not to mention the cities of Europe and North America). As Eric Hobsbawm has said of the Cuban Revolution, 'its conditions were peculiar and not readily repeatable', for reasons to do with Cuba's own peculiarity when compared with the rest of Latin America, and because of an exceptionally favourable international situation.[15] But China too was an exception: it seems highly unlikely that the Chinese Communists would have come to power had they not been able to mobilize the population (and not just the peasantry) against the Japanese invaders, on the basis of a strong nationalist appeal. And so on. Whatever the revolution that was selected as the baseline for a general model of Third World revolutions, its peculiarities have stamped themselves with distorting effect on the model. No acceptable 'general theory' of peasant revolutions yet exists.

The lack of a systematic theory of twentieth-century peasant revolutions *may* have something to do with our nearness to the phenomena in question. But it is much more likely that we are looking for the wrong sort of thing, just as, *a fortiori*, it is absurd to be seeking a general theory to cover every instance of 'revolution' from seventeenth-century England to twentieth-century Vietnam. As there were certain basic structural similarities in the causes and course of the European revolutions from the seventeenth to the nineteenth centuries, so indeed there are structural similarities in the situations of the Third World societies that have undergone revolution in this century. And that makes possible some useful comparative generalizations. But we must remember that, both in the European and Third World cases, we are dealing with phenomena that, however loosely, are bounded by time and place: better, perhaps, bounded by a certain stretch of history and by what one might call a particular 'culture area', in the sense of a group of societies that have had certain historical experiences in common, which in turn have given rise to certain uniform features of culture and social structure (e.g. 'feudalism'). It is this indeed that both allows the comparative generalizations and restricts their universal applicability. One might, for instance, feel, as Victor Kiernan does, that 'the phase of modern history that made socialism through peasant revolution pure and simple a possibility, is a limited phase only, and confined to special areas – just as the period of possible working-class revolution pure and simple was a limited one.'[16] Such a conviction would certainly set limits to the applicability of any uniformities we might observe in even some of the most recent instances.

This is not the place to attempt to formulate such generalizations for twentieth-century peasant revolutions. But, from a cursory look at the historical materials, it is not difficult to pick out the chief constituents of a non-Marxist framework that would lead us in the right direction. Put very schematically these could be said to be:

1 *Nationalism* – the fact that all these revolutions can be seen most centrally as the attempt to restore, maintain, or create independent nation states in

an international system driven by competitive nationalisms.

2   *Westernizing ideologies* – the fact that to accomplish the preceding, all revolutionary movements have to espouse an ideology that will give the Westernizing elites the most direct access to, and the most complete control over, all the individuals that comprise the would-be nation state. For various reasons some form of Marxism ('Chinese Communism', 'African Socialism') seems to be the most efficacious of these ideologies.

3   *The peasantry* – the critical social force of Third World revolutions, since the crisis provoked by the incursions of the industrial societies has affected it most deeply (though by no means evenly: one of the chief tasks of analysis is to identify the most revolutionary groups among the peasantry).

4   *The urban intelligentsia* – the other key social group, whose articulation of the Westernizing ideology and political organization of the peasantry is crucial for revolutionary mobilization.

5   *War* – as a solvent of *ancien régimes* and colonial powers. The revolutionary forces of this century have had to contest against unprecedented concentrations of military power possessed by the incumbent elites. The weakening of this power, which was decisively accomplished in a host of different countries by the two world wars, seems generally to have been an essential condition of the success of revolutionary movements.

6   *The international context* – as never before, revolution in this century has taken the form of international civil war. Success turns upon the ability or willingness of foreign states to aid, intervene or abstain from intervention in the affairs of the society undergoing revolution.

There is, of course, nothing original or surprising in this list of factors. What is surprising is how few general works there are which employ substantially this framework.[17] Why? Partly because so much of the writing on modern revolutions is of the polemical sort, carried on between, and largely for the benefit of, left-wing groups of various descriptions. But at a deeper level perhaps, partly because revolution is the central category of the ideology of Marxism, and since this is the ideology espoused in various forms by at least half the peoples in the world, it seems an impertinence not to consider contemporary revolutions in the terms used by those peoples. Nevertheless it is a serious case of mystification. It directs both theoretical and practical efforts to the wrong places; to agencies and strategies derived from a European ideology generated by a particular period of European history. The smoke-screen thrown up by the practice of the revolutionary elites, of describing their actions in Marxist categories, has to be dispelled. It is no more sensible to try to understand twentieth-century revolutions in terms of the doctrine of Marxism than it is to try to understand the Wars of Religion in terms of the theology of Christianity. And, after all, who better than the Marxists should see this?

II

What then of the industrial societies? How far ought we to consider present prospects for revolution in terms of the revolutionary tradition of the past 200 years? Was Camus right when he said, just after the Second World War, that '1789 and 1917 are still historic dates, but they are no longer historic examples'?[18]

The situation in the industrial societies is almost precisely the opposite of that in the Third World. The latter, lacking a revolutionary tradition – even, according to Hegel and Marx, lacking 'history' in any meaningful sense of the term – has been almost entirely and solely responsible for causing the twentieth century to be designated 'the century of revolution'. By contrast the industrial societies, whose ancestors invented the principle of revolution and bequeathed a rich tradition of theoretical analysis and practical experience, have been relatively quiescent in this century. There has not been a single successful revolution in the industrial societies of the West. More significantly, perhaps, there have been remarkably few attempts to bring about change by means of revolution. The great exception, the anomaly almost, were the 'events of May' 1968 in France. The May events constitute to date the only serious revolutionary challenge, in a time of peace, prosperity and (apparent) stability, to the authority of the state in an advanced industrial society. As such they deserve and will get special consideration, later on in this chapter. This apart, however, so far as the industrial societies are concerned, to reflect upon twentieth-century revolutions is to reflect upon a negative phenomenon.

The picture is complicated by certain occurrences in the Communist world, notably the radical changes of regime in many countries of eastern and southern Europe after the Second World War, the risings in East Germany (1953) and Hungary (1956), perhaps also the 'Czech Spring' of 1968. Many of these events have been designated 'revolutions', particularly and quite naturally by those who participated in them. But there are good reasons for declining to treat these phenomena in the context of a discussion of revolution in industrial society. Partly this is because many of those societies – Czechoslovakia is the main exception – are or were at best semi-industrial, with large peasant and rural sectors. Partly also because, so far as the post-1945 changes were concerned, they took place in a situation where the war and the German occupation had destroyed both the legitimacy and the power of the pre-war rulers, and where, of course, the changes of regime were aided or enforced by Russian troops (Czechoslovakia, again, partially excepted). But even in the most serious cases for consideration – Hungary 1956, Czechoslo-vakia 1968 – it is quite clear that what we are dealing with are basically nationalist risings, struggles for national liberation from the Soviet empire; and while this may give them a certain affinity with, say, the Chinese and Cuban Revolutions (or the eighteenth-century American Revolution), it disqualifies them from being considered alongside revolutions, and in a revolutionary tradition, where the principal dynamic has been the internal conflict of groups. Nationalist and revolutionary movements do often have

certain characteristics in common, mostly to do with the conditions of their
eventual success or failure: but in terms of their causes, and of the nature of
the social forces contending, they are fundamentally different and need to be
analysed separately.

More significant are a number of other candidates that have been offered
as instances of revolutions, or at least revolutionary impulses, in industrial
society. The most important of these are the risings that took place in Central
Europe after the First World War: in Hungary, Austria, and Germany during
1918–19. These were, of course, the countries of the defeated powers; and
so the first point about these failed 'revolutions' is that they can scarcely be
said to have been made by revolutionary forces at all. The power of the state
and the legitimacy of the ruling class were both temporarily but abruptly
weakened by defeat in a major war. For a brief period there existed a power
vacuum which the revolutionaries had done nothing to bring about but which
gave them the opportunity to make their bid. They failed, with a completeness
that was easier to see in retrospect, and which pointed to the slightness of
the revolutionary potential in the situation.

In the case of Hungary and Austria – the latter being anyway no more than
a faint echo of the former – there was an added weakness. The risings in
Budapest and Vienna were directly inspired by the new Bolshevik government
in Russia, and their progress was monitored and impinged upon throughout
by the newly formed Communist International. The revolutionaries, such as
Bela Kun, had many of them been trained in Russia, and were often ex-
prisoners of war who had been picked out for political training. Their relations
with their native socialist parties were therefore always at best ambiguous, at
worst riddled with an enervating suspiciousness. They never won over more
than a small fraction of the working class, who at the critical moment deserted
them. Kun himself in his farewell declaration admitted this:

The proletarian dictatorship ought to have met a different end, if only we had had
self-conscious and revolutionary proletarian masses at our disposal ... The proletariat
was dissatisfied with our domination, already it shouted in the factories, in spite of all
our agitation, 'Down with the dictatorship'.[19]

Relations with the peasantry – a crucial and overwhelming fact in the case
of Hungary – were even more dismal. Whatever Kun had learned from Lenin,
he had not learned his realism about the peasants. Hungarian socialists in
general, both reformist and revolutionary, held to an orthodox Marxist
contempt for the peasantry, and repudiated the idea of parcelling the latifundia
and giving the plots to the peasants. During Kun's Soviet-style dictatorship
the peasants showed themselves willing to respond to a new order, for which
gesture they were milked mercilessly, and their land and crops requisitioned.
Their natural reaction was to withold cooperation and to engage in large-
scale risings against the regime. Thus in the Hungarian case the two principal
potentially revolutionary actors – the urban workers and the peasantry –
turned their face against the revolution.

Germany offered more significant possibilities. With English developments
becoming the despair of the Marxists, Germany at the end of the nineteenth

century represented the fairest hope of European socialism. Despite, or perhaps because of, Bismarck's anti-socialist laws, the German Social Democratic Party was by 1890 easily the largest and best organized socialist party in any country. In the German election of 1890 it polled a million and a half votes, more than any other party, in that of 1912, its poll of $4\frac{1}{2}$ million votes represented a third of the nation. In its Erfurt Programme of 1891 it had reaffirmed its commitment to a revolutionary class struggle. Moreover, Germany's rapid development since 1870 had been a model for the 'take-off' stage of development. The omens appeared favourable for a revolution of the type classically predicted by Marx for a maturing capitalist economy. Thus the German Revolution of 1918 had a special theoretical interest going alongside its practical implications. In the eyes of left-wing intellectuals it represented, as its historian A. J. Ryder says, 'an attempt, the first of its kind, at the conquest of power by a Marxist party in a highly organized industrial country'.[20]

The reality was much less grand. The revolution of 1918 – not to mention the hopes of European socialism – were already blighted by the events of 1914. In the spring of 1914 the French socialist leader Jean Jaurès told a friend: 'Don't worry, the Socialists will do their duty. Four million German Socialists will rise like one man and execute the Kaiser if he wants to start a war.' Less than a week later Jaurès himself was assassinated, and in flagrant disregard of every resolution of the Second International enjoining its members to oppose a war by all possible means, the German SPD voted by an overwhelming majority in support of war credits for the Kaiser's government. The vote of 4 August 1914 symbolized at once the non-revolutionary nature of German socialism and the triumph of German nationalism. It determined the fate and shaped the character of the revolution of 1918. The dissident socialists, increasingly opposed to the government's war policies and frustrated by the SPD's tenacious attachment to the government, were forced into founding their own party, the Independents, in the spring of 1917. None of the socialist parties 'made' the revolution of 1918. The so-called 'October Revolution' was a purely decorative affair. Under pressure of defeat, and hoping to win popular support for negotiating a favourable peace, General Ludendorff imposed on a passive nation a species of parliamentary democracy of which Lloyd George and *The Times* were rightly sceptical. What the SPD leadership had been striving for for decades was handed to them on a plate by an old-style Prussian militarist.

More serious was the 'November Revolution', sparked off, like the Russian revolution of 1905, by a naval mutiny. Once again the socialists followed where war-weary popular forces led. The shop-stewards and the Spartacists (the extreme left-wing of the Independents, represented by Rosa Luxemburg and Karl Liebknecht) had planned a revolutionary strike for 11 November – more than a week after the Kiel mutiny had launched the revolution in Germany. And though the SPD and the Independents strove to direct the movement to their own ends, its course was largely spontaneous. Certainly there was popular support for the revolution: but these were popular forces for peace, not for revolutionary change. As Franz Borkenau wrote, the pacifist movement, in those final months of the war, swept the nation as a whole, carrying with it elements that were neither socialist nor labour nor even progressive; the Bavarian peasants, perhaps the most conservative element in all Germany, expressed this enmity against war and monarchy in particularly violent forms; a few months later they were again the vanguard of counter-revolution. In the last days before the end all Germany seemed to have become revolutionary, because all Germany sympathised with the pacifist and republican programme of the Independents.[21]

The German Revolution failed because an essential condition of revolution, fragmentation and conflict within the ruling class and among the ruling institutions had not occurred. A comparison with Russia in 1917 makes this point clearer. Why could not Liebknecht play Lenin to Ebert's Kerensky? There was no greater agreement between Bolsheviks, Mensheviks, Social Revolutionaries and Anarchists, than there was between Right Independents, Spartacists and shop stewards. The Bolsheviks were not responsible for the overthrow of the Tsar or the Provisional Government any more than the Independents were responsible for the rise of the soldiers' and workers' councils in the German Revolution. The essential difference in the two situations was a long-term one. Well before the war Tsarist administration had been disintegrating, the effect of decades of opposition from the *zemstva*, the provincial gentry, and increasingly large sections of the nobility. What E. H. Carr says of Bolshevism can equally be said of Kerensky's government: both succeeded to a vacant throne.

The same was never true of Germany. Basically the institutions of Bismarck's Reich remained strong, never more so than during the war when all parties rallied to the government in the *Burgfrieden* or civic truce. Defeat in war brought a weakening of the structure of power, a loss of morale and nerve, especially in the higher ranks of the army. But the weakening was superficial, the loss of nerve temporary. The old institutions, especially the civil service, continued to be manned and to function very much as before the war. F. L. Carsten makes the point generally for the central European powers:

One of the most important achievements of the Habsburg and Hohenzollern monarchies was the creation of large and well-functioning bureaucracies; they outlived the disappearance of their masters, in complete contrast with Soviet Russia where revolution and civil war destroyed the government machine totally and irrevocably.[22]

The German Socialists had a breathing space in which to radicalize institutions and, above all, to attempt to build up an army loyal to their government. Something modest like the post-1945 West German government might have come out of this. They did neither of these things, and instead Ebert's SPD government chose the worst possible course in using the old army against the councils. Ebert was therefore directly responsible for rebuilding confidence within the demoralized army; his government became its first prisoner. The revolutionary socialists, for their part, found themselves an increasingly isolated minority: opposed not just by the official SPD (now the government), the army and the vicious and unscrupulous *Freikorps* (given a free hand by the government), but also by the trade unions and the mass of the working men. 'Again and again, when it came to fighting, the majority of the workers remained at home, and small minorities were cruelly destroyed', as in Kiel, Berlin, Munich.[23] Only the Spartacists – a tiny handful in most of the cities – consistently pursued a revolutionary aim; and they found themselves abandoned by the majority of the Independents and even, on occasion, by the newly formed Communist group. The mass general strike which, in 1920, defeated the reactionary 'Kapp *putsch*' of the Reichswehr, may perhaps be seen as the final and most successful act of the German Revolution; but in the lack of any significant positive gains that followed that action, in the utter disunity of the revolutionary groups, and in the combination of forces behind the *putsch*, may be seen the first act of that more far-reaching counter-revolution of 1933.

A brief mention can be made, finally, of the events in Italy following the First World War. No one speaks of 'the Italian Revolution' of 1919–20, and indeed no such revolution occurred. But the widespread occupation of factories throughout northern Italy during these years; the establishment of a system of workers' councils; and the extreme sophistication of the theoretical writing – notably that of Antonio Gramsci[24] – that accompanied this movement: all these things at least allow us to speak *prima facie* of a revolutionary situation. Such a first impression is speedily dispelled on closer examination.

Despite being nominally on the winning side, Italy emerged from the war looking more like one of the defeated central European powers than like a conquering nation. The government's early policy of neutrality had inspired a storm of nationalist agitation, fed by the ex-socialist Mussolini and the poet Gabriele d'Annunzio. From this agitation the Italian socialists, following steadfastly a position of neutrality, gained not at all. Thus from the start the only party capable of leading and coordinating a revolutionary movement set itself against the popular temper. By contrast, the radical right, with its aggressive nationalism blended with elements of socialist policy, had a ready appeal. It is not difficult to see why this combination should eventually win out in 1922, since it threatened no powerful capitalist interest and, moreover, was a deadly weapon to use against the Left.

The appearance of a serious revolutionary challenge from the left in 1919–20 was deceptive. The sackings of shops in the summer of 1919, the movement among the peasants to redistribute the land, even the massive strikes, were unintended and uncoordinated by the socialist party, and therefore could be picked off separately. The occupations of the factories in Turin and Milan in the summer of 1920, and the setting up of factory councils, forced the party to declare its hand. Predictably, and against the advice of Moscow, it opted for negotiations with the employers, through the mediation of the government. It really could have done nothing else, as Gramsci himself acknowledged. The unions were against revolution, and organized the referendum which endorsed the official union policy of negotiation. To have gone against the unions, and the mass working-class membership which in this case they fairly accurately represented, would have been suicidal. As Gramsci later wrote, 'at that time, with the socialist party we had, with the working class still seeing things through rose-tinted glasses and preferring songs and brass bands to sacrifices, we were bound to have counter-revolutionary movements destined to sweep us away, whatever revolution we had achieved.'[25]

Giolitti, the ageing prime minister, also had a shrewd realization of the situation, and throughout refused to take the factories by armed force, banking on the movement failing on its own account. He knew that the movement represented not the beginning but the end of a wave of revolutionary unrest. In this he was right, not just for Italy, but for all the risings in Central and Western Europe after the First World War. They were the tail end of the revolutionary tradition that had started in seventeenth-century Europe and been given definitive expression by the French Revolution of 1789. They still talked and acted on the basis of a theory and a strategy that had been distilled from the experience of past European revolutions: the idea of a revolutionary party; the role of the vanguard; the education of the masses; the urban insurrection; the seizure of power; the revolutionary dictatorship. Even the concept of the council, the *soviet*, went back at least to the popular clubs of the French Revolution, and, more immediately, to the Paris Commune of 1871. There were some observers – Weber, Mosca, Michels, even Engels – who realized that this slavish imitation of, and dependence on, the existing revolutionary model was highly dangerous. With the general and accelerating industrialization of all European societies in the second half of the nineteenth century, developments had taken place which had rendered that model obsolete. But, when the opportunity presented itself, the revolutionaries, even so clear-sighted a one as Rosa Luxemburg, reverted almost without modification to the cherished examples of the past. It was almost as if, with its dying gasp, the European revolutionary tradition wanted to pay a homage to its history.

In fact the First World War had offered an abnormal and artificial opportunity to the revolutionary parties. It cut across those developments which, in the half-century of peace following the Crimean War, had been slowly but massively transforming the context of revolutionary action. By 1918 revolution in the old style was already out. But the defeat of so many states, the collapse of so many historic empires, was bound to disrupt those long-term tendencies. The revolutionary parties, through no efforts of their own, and mostly to their surprise, suddenly found themselves called upon to act. But the disruption was brief. In throwing-over dynastic titles and outworn political forms the European societies showed these to be merely the shells which had surrounded the growth of a remarkably resilient and integrated organism, the industrial society. The revolutionary parties could temporarily disrupt but not seriously disturb its basic patterns of attachment and organization. At best they could run them under different names.

Shortly after the end of the war the long-term tendencies of industrialism picked up again, and were intensified. At the same time revolutionism, as a principle and a practice, almost vanished altogether from the industrial societies of the West. Socialist parties occasionally debated it, but their debates were no more than faint echoes of nineteenth-century ones. The fate of revolution seemed to turn principally on events in the colonial and semi-colonial world; all new theory and strategy came from there. The Second World War might well have repeated the pattern of the first in giving revolutionary parties an opening in the tightly meshed politico-economic structures of the industrial societies. But, apart from the fact that those parties in practice had abandoned a revolutionary strategy and did not really seem to welcome the opportunity, the leading powers in the victorious alliance were no longer prepared to let the defeated countries sort out their own problems. Once more the context of revolutionary action had changed: it had become a matter of the balance of forces on a global scale. The victorious allies of both West and East supervised, with more or less equal degrees of ruthlessness, the political reconstruction of those countries which had been defeated or occupied. In such a constellation revolutionary parties were more impotent than ever, except where they were directly guided and used by one of the external powers. As a longstanding, intrinsic feature of the development of European societies, revolution seemed to have been laid to rest.

III

Compared with the Third World, the question to be put in the case of the industrial societies is not, then, 'what is the pattern of twentieth-century revolutions?', but 'what are the prospects for revolution?' And one way of answering that question is to ask further: 'under what conditions did the "classic" European revolutions of the past two centuries occur, and what reason have we for expecting that such conditions will recur?'

As with the Third World revolutions we can list, in a simple and schematic way, certain basic factors that were present in the pattern of past European revolutions.[26]

1 The agrarian or rural factor – in all cases revolutions occurred in societies in which only a minority, often a very small minority, of the population, lived in towns and cities. While these were not necessarily peasant societies in the strict sense of the term, they were largely agrarian societies; and the support of the rural classes was a necessary ingredient of success.

2 These were societies where the technical means and organization of coercion possessed by the governments were never so totally superior to those of the insurgents that the insurrections were doomed from the start. The arms available to the revolutionaries were, roughly speaking, not so very different from those available to the government – and they were reasonably portable.

3 These were societies where the integration of political authority, even at its best, was never very complete. There were always large areas where the writ of the ruler ran very little, if at all; where the 'opposition', however conceived, could collect its forces and bide its time, waiting for the most favourable conjunction of circumstances or, simply, for a chance opportunity.

4 These were societies which for a variety of reasons were changing in such a way as seriously to divide the traditional ruling groups among themselves. (In other words, Plato's condition was satisfied: 'In any form of government revolution always starts from the outbreak of internal dissension in the ruling class. The constitution cannot be upset so long as that class is of one mind,

however small it may be.'[27]) Quite apart from whether discontent was stirring among the other classes, it was the fact of fundamental discontents within the traditional ruling stratum that seems to have been the main dissolving force in society. There is here a clear relation to condition (3): the rebellious sectors of the upper classes needed time to develop in consciousness and strategy, and the fact of imperfect political integration – or the lack of effective sovereignty – gave them both time and 'space'.

No claim is made here that these conditions are all of the same logical order, or that they are weighted in terms of causal priority, or that they amount to a list of sufficient or even all the necessary conditions. They are simply, and rather loosely, general conditions associated with the successful revolutions of the European past, and they are a helpful starting point.

If we ask now whether revolution of the classic type is still possible in the industrial societies of the present, we have to see which of these conditions still obtain. Three positions – at least – can be held. Either: to argue that most of these conditions still obtain, hence a revolution in the classic style is still possible, no doubt given a number of incidental conditions which would need to be specified. Or: to argue that these conditions have mostly disappeared, so that the achievement of revolution, in anything like its traditional sense, is no longer on the agenda, and that any contemporary group currently pursuing a revolutionary strategy on the inherited model needs to give very good reasons why this course is not suicidal. The third position is of a different order. It agrees that the conditions that gave rise to revolutions in the past no longer exist. But, it argues, this does not matter, because the sort of revolution possible (or inevitable or desirable) in contemporary industrial society is so different – qualitatively different – from anything experienced in the past that quite different conditions and agencies must be discussed in contemplating it. A corollary of this position is that a new concept of revolution is needed.

I shall leave the discussion of this third position for the final section of this paper. So far as the first two are concerned the evidence seems to speak clearly in favour of the second. In the conditions of contemporary industrial societies neither the social forces nor the technical means exist for the occurrence of revolution in the classic European form.

Consider, first, that the industrial societies are now all overwhelmingly urban. Any rising that took place would lack the support of that vast reservoir of rural population and resources that has been crucial to all revolutions to date. In fact there has not been a single successful purely urban insurrection so far. The lesson has been taught repeatedly: on a large scale in 1848, when the urban risings in Paris, Berlin, Vienna, Budapest, Milan and elsewhere, were all defeated, often with peasant support for the counter-revolution; in the failure of the urban insurrections after the First World War; in 1871, when the Paris Commune was crushed after a three-week war with the government, having failed to take an early opportunity to secure itself by taking the struggle outside the city; in the risings in Shanghai and Canton in the late 1920s, when the Chinese Communists were massacred, and which taught Mao to quit the towns for the countryside; and perhaps finally one might instance the failure of the rising in Algiers from 1954 onwards,[28] and the crushing of the Budapest rising of 1956 by Soviet tanks – not to mention the repeated failures of urban riots in the black ghettoes of the United States.[29] Although there is no space to do it here, the reasons for this history of failure of urban insurrections are relatively easy to spell out.[30] But, at any rate, the point is clear enough. Unless supported by non-urban actors, all urban risings have failed. Thus if revolution is to be attempted in societies which are predominantly urban some very convincing arguments have to be produced as to why the risk is worth taking.

Second, as to weapons technology and the associated organization of the agencies of social control and coercion: an obvious starting-off point is provided by Engels's 1895 Preface to a new edition of Marx's *The Class Struggles in France 1848–1850*. Here Engels argues that revolution in the old style, with street-fighting and barricades, has become obsolete. He pointed out that developments in military technology, in communications (especially the railway system), and in such matters as the planning of cities on the principles of counter-insurgency, had all worked in favour of the authorities and against potential insurgents. Arguably the conqueror of the Communards in 1871 was not Thiers but Baron Haussmann. Victory on the barricades, always a precarious matter for even the revolutions of the past, was now a dangerous myth. The point was not simply the increased power and precision of the new weapons technology: that, after all, could work in favour as much of the revolutionaries as of governments. The important thing, as Engels showed, was that most of the new developments depended for their operation on the complicated products of big industry; they could not be manufactured *extempore* with the time and materials commonly available to the population.

Engels was worried about the breech-loading magazine rifle and the percussion shell. What would he say today of the arsenal of weapons conventionally and readily available to the vastly strengthened police and militia forces of all industrial societies: such as helicopters, gases, Stoner assault rifle systems, counter-sniper teams, armoured vehicles, electronic snooper devices and a host of others regularly pressed by eager manufacturers on to equally eager police forces? And one need hardly add here the incomparable technological and organizational superiority possessed by the national armed forces when set against any possible combination of groups in the rest of society. Again, some of these developments, e.g. two-way radio, can benefit insurgents as much as counter-insurgents. But Engels's main point stands even stronger today. The enormous spending by governments on the research and development of counter-insurgency weapons and tactics, the high level of specialization and skill involved in the manufacture of the new weapons, and, perhaps above all, the great increase in flexibility and mobility of police and troops brought about by advances in communication: all these factors tip the balance decisively in favour of the powers that be, to the extent that the civilian populations of the industrial societies are effectively disarmed.[31]

But it is when we turn to the third general condition under which past revolutions have occurred that we see the most fundamental and far-reaching change. This is in the overall framework of political authority and the new constitution of political society. That looseness in political integration which seems to have been a pre-requisite of all past revolutions has disappeared. Political sovereignty, which had existed in theory in most European societies since the sixteenth century, and whose practical deficiencies had made possible the classic European revolutions, has in the course of the last one hundred years become an accomplished fact.

Ironically it was those very revolutions that were largely responsible for bringing this about. Alexis de Tocqueville documented this superbly for the French Revolution of 1789, showing how that revolution had continued and consolidated pre-revolutionary tendencies in the direction of a strengthening of state power and the elimination of remaining autonomous sectors.[32] The same lesson was taught by all revolutions since the eighteenth century. As Marx remarked: 'All revolutions perfected the state machine instead of smashing it. The parties that contended in turn for domination regarded the possession of this huge state edifice as the principal spoils of the victor.'[33] Increasingly the strong centralized state came to be assumed, as much by revolutionaries as others, as the political framework within which aspirations were conceived and demands made. All attempts to change society either assumed the agency of the state in effecting the changes or, despite initial intentions, ended up by relying on the state and expanding its scope and power. Occasionally, as with the risings after the First World War, defeat in a long-drawn-out war could weaken the state temporarily to the point where a power vacuum was created, in which the revolutionary parties postured briefly. But they seemed both incapable and unwilling to tackle the structure and power of the modern state as such, and were crushed as soon as the state recovered its confidence. In any case the revolutionary parties of the Left were as much dazzled by the potentialities of the new state as the conservative parties of the Right. Even where they remained formally revolutionary the programme and strategy of the working-class parties were shaped to a predominant extent by day-to-day bargaining with the institutions of the state, which imposed their own patterns on the parties. Increasingly, as Michels demonstrated, the structure of left-wing parties came to mirror the structure of the state, so ensuring that even if they did make a successful bid for power they would simply substitute the rule of another bureaucratic elite for the existing one.[34]

Political centralization, the rapid expansion of bureaucracy both public and private, and the establishment of larger, professional standing armies, were the developments that offered the most serious obstacles to a recurrence of revolution on the classic pattern. Bureaucratization in particular was the tendency that led Max Weber, its great theorist, to conclude that in modern industrial societies there could no longer be revolutions, only *coup d'état*. It was not simply that centralization and bureaucratization made it harder to defeat the state: more fundamentally bureaucracy had become – or so it seemed – indispensable to the running of an urban and industrial society. Revolutionary parties could no more do without it than any other; any seizure of power by them would simply amount to putting new political figureheads at the top of largely autonomous bureaucratic organizations. The revolutions of the past had depended for their depth and intensity on the gradual but massive disintegration of political power. Such a condition now appeared highly improbable, since continuing bureaucratic functioning seemed a technical necessity of contemporary society, a premise of its very survival.[35]

The point can be put more generally as follows. The centralization and integration of political authority, whether or not itself originally accomplished by revolution, takes away that looseness in the structure of society which previously allowed revolutionary groups to 'take shelter' in the interstices of society, among its uncoordinated parts. Perhaps the most difficult problem for modern revolutionaries is where to find sufficient geographical and social 'space' in urban–industrial societies: areas, activities and organizations, that is, that are uncontaminated by dependence on the bureaucracies of the wider society, and which can sustain themselves for long enough to develop different values, different practices and different authority structures.[36] So far, at any rate, no group seems to have discovered such space. The difficulty is compounded by the problem of finding sufficient 'psychological space' to develop alternative needs and values. As Marcuse has forcefully argued, industrial society has not been content to shape and control men's behaviour simply from the outside; in its later stages, through its cultural institutions, its schools, mass media and advertising systems, it has invaded men's psychic life so totally that they are incapable of conceiving alternatives to the existing order. Their needs, and the demands resulting from those needs, are none other than those the present order has implanted in them, and consequently can be comfortably met within the confines of the existing order.[37]

Modern industrial societies tolerate, indeed encourage, many varieties of 'sub-culture'. It has room for many movements of protest, retreat and withdrawal: communes, bohemian enclaves and the like. It can contain, apparently without much difficulty, large-scale urban riots, of the kind that occurred in the black ghettoes of US cities in the 1960s. Eric Hobsbawm rightly says that 'an intelligent and cynical police chief would probably regard all the troubles in Western cities during recent years as minor disturbances, magnified by the hesitation or incompetence of the authorities and the effect of excessive publicity. With the exception of the Latin Quarter riots of May 1968 none of them looked as though they could, or were intended to, shake governments.'[38] The fact is that the proliferation of sub-cultures is inversely related to the existence of genuine 'counter-cultures'. Consciously or unconsciously, the whole weight of the systems of contemporary industrial societies is thrown against the development of a revolutionary counter-culture.

There remains the fourth and final condition of past European revolutions: a divided ruling class. Of all the general conditions this is probably the most difficult to assess at any given time, and it may be that this is only possible in retrospect. Unquestionably it is an observable phenomenon in the periods leading up to the English Revolution of 1640, the French Revolution of 1789 and the Russian Revolutions of 1905 and 1917 – to name only the best known and studied. But, putting together the relevant evidence, and considering the twentieth century as a whole, a reasonably uncontroversial picture can be presented. And here what appears as initially the most interesting feature is a divergence in the positions of the ruling classes of East and West, of the industrial societies under Communist rule and those under capitalist rule. Somewhat paradoxically it might be that, because of the particular structure of the ruling groups, there is greater prospect for some kind of revolutionary change in the Communist East than in the capitalist West.

In the evolution of Communist rule, a period of concentration, consolidation and unity at the top, has been followed by one which has revealed serious strains and conflicts.[39] This process has paralleled fairly closely the curve of industrialization: the conflicts within the ruling groups are the expression of the difficulties of managing and developing an advanced industrial society with a ruling structure basically adapted to the conditions of a revolutionary seizure of power and rapid industrialization from on top. Especially since the Second World War there has been observable a process of what Parkin calls 'elite differentiation', a certain fragmentation of interests and of ideology within the ruling stratum. The most important divergence is probably that between the 'old guard', the political officers and bureaucrats, exercising an old-style domination based on their control of the military and bureaucratic apparatus of the state; and the more recently developed intelligentsia – cultural, scientific, technical and 'entrepreneurial' – whose claims are based on their control of knowledge and of much of the legitimating symbols of the social order. There is posed here more than simply a struggle of factional interests at the top. There is the possibility of a radical and chronic conflict, with the opposing groups perhaps being prepared to make open appeals for support to the rest of the population, with the acutely destabilizing consequences that such a pattern exhibited before the earlier French and Russian Revolutions. Something of the kind seems to have happened during the 'Czech Spring' of 1968.

But that episode also reveals the limits of the possibilities in Eastern Europe. Empires can and do last for long periods of time despite quite serious 'internal contradictions'.[40] Moreover, a divided ruling class is only one condition of a successful revolution: the absence of the other conditions noted earlier makes it unlikely that any change that takes place would resemble the classic European revolutions. At best, probably the replacement of the old guard by the new would result in a degree of 'liberalization' in the political and economic realms, for reasons of greater efficiency – a very far cry from the aspirations of the men of 1789, 1848, 1871 or 1917.

Still, by contrast the position of the ruling class of Western capitalist societies has been and seems still remarkably secure. There is a homogeneity, a consensus of interests and outlook, that has confidently resisted all attempts to divide it by infiltration or direct intervention. Property ownership, political office-holding, educational and technical expertise, cultural ideals, all have for a long time formed a pattern of concentration and congruence, a dense system of overlapping and thickening circles of common membership and common experience. Such an integrated elite can afford – at least at the objective level – a degree of tolerance, a variety of deviant behaviours and sub-cultures, a level of 'permissiveness' in moral and cultural life, that is quite unthinkable to the elites of Eastern Europe. Rightly, from the point of view of the latter, such behaviour is seen as politically and ideologically sensitive, always liable to become the material or the focal point of opposition by disaffected counter-elites. In the capitalist West, lacking so far any genuine threats from counter-elites, this attitude can only be the result of paranoia, delusions of the lunatic fringe of both Left and Right.

Not only has the capitalist ruling class not had to fear the consequences of fundamental divisions within its ranks. It must, on reflection, be surprised at how local, transient and superficial have been most challenges to its continued domination. The 'historic' class enemy, the proletariat, has been the most quiescent. In actions which the proletariat itself may in some sense be held to have initiated, such as the British General Strike of 1926, or the French Popular Front government of 1936, the rather modest degree of antagonism to the existing order was contained throughout: in the first case by the trade union leadership together with a good number of the members; in the second case by the Popular Front government itself, which was determined to end the wave of strikes and occupations that had accompanied its electoral victory. In those episodes where, through no pressure of their own, working-class parties were forced to play a major role in the exercise of power – as in the participation of the French and Italian Communist parties in the coalition governments after the Second World War – those parties seemed almost embarrassingly eager to demonstrate their non-revolutionary intentions.[41] Generally, at no time since Marx's death has a successful revolutionary 'dictatorship of the proletariat' seemed at all likely in the industrial societies of the West.

Acknowledging this, revolutionary theorists have been driven to seek other groups as the agents, or at least catalysts, of revolution. The working class is seen as 'incorporated', hopelessly enmeshed in and committed to the existing forms of industrial society, accepting its values and striving only to increase their share of the material goods and benefits that the society urges them to consume. '"The people",' says Marcuse, 'previously the ferment of social change, have "moved up" to become the ferment of social cohesion.'[42] Attention is then concentrated on those groups least 'incorporated' in the system: those who, for reasons of opportunity or interest, have least need or concern to be committed to its values and institutions. Marcuse, in his bleakest vision, turns to 'the substratum of the outcasts and the outsiders, the exploited and persecuted of other races and other colours, the unemployed and the unemployable'.[43] Others have added the white radicals of community and professional action groups, students and intellectuals, 'youth as a class', sometimes even the whole 'external proletariat' of the oppressed Third World, as the revolutionary saviour of the soul of modern industrial man.

There is every reason to be sceptical of these claims.[44] The very tone in which they are offered by their various proponents suggests that they are the products of despair rather than of realistic sociological assessment. Certainly such groups can bring about various kinds of social change, and are indeed doing so now. It is still an open question, which I shall touch on in a moment, whether all these activities taken together, along with certain other structural changes taking place in industrial societies, may not be part of a transformation of industrial society such that the word 'revolutionary' is appropriate. But one thing is quite clear. Whatever the form and manner of social change attempted by these groups, it must be of an entirely different order from that brought about by the European revolutions of the past. All the basic conditions for the recurrence of revolution of that kind have disappeared.

IV

In this final section I want briefly to consider the third possibility posed earlier: that although revolution on the classic European model is no longer on the agenda, a new concept and to some extent a new practice of revolution is emerging in the developed industrial societies of the West. Such a discussion even as little as ten years ago might have seemed academic in the worst sense. What has given it a relevance and a concreteness are the 'May events' (literally May–June) in France in 1968.

The sequence of events can be simply told. The first stirrings of what was to become a mass student revolt can be traced to a series of demonstrations, confrontations and occupations at a number of French provincial universities on the issue of dormitory regulations: specifically, on the right to entertain members of the opposite sex in dormitory rooms. In other words, the theme of sexual freedom and sexual oppression, so prominent in the May events, was the original spark that touched off the revolt. The theme also played a central role in the 'Strasbourg affair' of May 1966, when a group of radicals captured the student organization at the university, and used this agency to distribute a pamphlet entitled *On the Poverty of Student Life* ('De la misère en milieu étudiant'). This remarkably sophisticated tract – the first effective public pronouncement of the International Situationists – generalized from the daily routines and daily resentments of student life to a full-scale critique of advanced industrial society. It was a critique compounded of aesthetic surrealism and libertarian Marxism – so, again, sounding the two key-notes of the May revolt.[45] Rightly it has been said that 'most of the themes sprung upon an amazed public during the May Revolt were inspired by the Situationists and had made their first appearance during the events at Strasbourg'.[46]

Situationist influences – partly in the life and thought of Daniel Cohn-Bendit – were again prominent in the events at Nanterre in late 1967 and early 1968. Once again, the campaign for dormitory privileges precipitated the affair. But almost immediately the movement widened out to embrace every aspect of the university's life and organization, and then went on to develop a radical critique of the whole existing social order. The activist 'Movement of 22 March' was formed, occupations took place, the police were called in and the campus was closed.

The events at Nanterre were simultaneously the last act of the 'pre-history' of the May revolt, and the first act of the revolt proper. On 3 May a meeting of students at the Sorbonne to protest against the closing of Nanterre and the disciplining of militants was cleared by the police. Owing partly to a misunderstanding, a pitched battle took place between police and students. Public sympathy, at least in Paris, was clearly on the side of the students. Barricades went up in the Latin Quarter. During the next two weeks there were major battles between students and police, with many hundreds injured. The government re-opened the Sorbonne, which was promptly occupied and declared an 'autonomous people's university'. The Sorbonne became the festive centre of the revolt, dividing its time between the production of materials for cultural and ideological warfare and the elaboration of programmes and strategy. Later too, as an extension of these activities, the national theatre, the Odéon, was occupied, becoming an open and continuous forum of discussion between students and anyone else who wished to join in. The character of the revolt as 'cultural' as much as 'political' in the conventional sense was firmly established.

The students' action triggered off a nation-wide revolt. Workers occupied and took over Sud-Aviation's aircraft plant at Nantes, and Renault plants at Rouen, Flins and Billancourt. The Confédération Générale du Travail (CGT), the Communist-dominated trade union federation, initially caught off guard, threw its weight behind the workers' movement. A more or less complete general strike was called, and within a week over 6 million workers were on strike or in factory occupation – more than the total number involved in the great strikes of 1938. The middle classes joined in. Professional groups of every kind, media workers, actors and writers, shopgirls and professional athletes, set up hundreds of action committees, demanding the democratization and radicalization both of their workplaces and the functions to which their work was directed. 'Self-management' (*autogestion*) became the slogan of the day. Meanwhile the political parties, as usual reacting rather than initiating, struggled to keep control of events. At governmental level, all leadership seemed to have abdicated. De Gaulle and Pompidou committed one tactical blunder after another.

These weeks, the weeks of mid-May, were the high-point of the revolt. After that came swift decline. Pompidou called a conference of government, business and trade union representatives (the Grenelle Conference) which agreed on an economic package. Although initially rejected by the workers, it became the basis of an eventual settlement and constituted the main direct gain of the May events so far as the workers were concerned. What was particularly significant in the negotiations was the CGT's obvious determination to settle within the framework of the existing political and economic system, their belief that a revolutionary situation did not exist and their anxiety to dissociate themselves from the 'irresponsible' student movement. A similar attitude was observable in the behaviour of the other parties of the Left. De Gaulle meanwhile, conferring with his generals, had reassured himself that army support was secure. Returning to Paris, he dissolved the National Assembly and announced immediate elections. At the same time he warned that if the French people were prevented 'by intimidation, intoxication and tyranny' from expressing themselves in the forthcoming elections he would maintain the Republic 'by other means than an immediate vote of the country'. A huge Gaullist demonstration was mounted in Paris. Workers gradually went back to work, although there were some serious incidents, notably at the Renault works at Flins and the Peugeot works at Sochaux. The students, denouncing the elections to the end, found themselves isolated. Police evacuated the Odéon and the Sorbonne. At the elections in late June, the Gaullists came back with an enormous and increased majority; the Communist, Socialist and Radical parties all dropped their share of the vote. The 'May events' were over.

This, then, was the sequence of the May events. What was their significance? Everyone agrees that, in the direct, immediate, 'practical' sense, the achievements were slight. The main effect was to scare the bourgeoisie into returning the Gaullist parties with a decisive majority at the first available elections. The workers got wage increases, modest by comparison with normal settlements made only a few years later. The students got university reforms, wide-ranging on paper but largely nullified in practice by the hostility and inertia of university administration.

Negatively, too, the May events confirmed the argument of the earlier part of this chapter, that a revolutionary seizure of power in the old style is unlikely to recur. There was never a moment when the revolutionary groups – the students and the workers – were in a position to take power. This was partly because the student revolutionaries were divided among themselves, and, crucially, were never able to forge a revolutionary alliance with the workers in the factories.[47] The bolting of the doors by the workers against the students at the Renault Billancourt plant was symbolic of a deep divide throughout: the students wanted revolution (but against 'the system', rather than against the state), the workers wanted economic reforms. More important, the government was always secure in the allegiance of the police and the army. The armed forces might not be willing to force the workers to evacuate the factories, whose occupation was not necessarily a prelude to revolution; but they made it plain that they were entirely reliable against an insurrection.

The only serious threat, the only one that the government feared, came from the Communist Party. With its mass base – consistently a third of the working class and almost a quarter of the total electorate – and its domination of the trade union organization, it was the only political force likely to topple the government. At one point, towards the end of May, when the striking workers had rejected the Grenelle Agreement, and the government seemed to have played its last card; when the CGT had demonstrated its strength in a massive parade through Paris (skirting the Hôtel de Ville, the traditional seat of the proclamation of new republics, and the Elysée), the Communist Party seemed to be presented with an almost irresistible call for action. De Gaulle and Pompidou certainly thought so. The Party refused to answer the call, and its refusal was more than a matter of simply a temporary failure of nerve, or a tactical error. It reflected the fact that, going along with the other tendencies in industrial society, the party had ceased to be revolutionary. Over the years it had established a particular niche for itself in the French political system, as the bulwark of working-class interests. With this went a particular strategy of accommodation to the routines of elections and municipal administration. The students' demands threatened that strategy, as did the call that the party seize the opportunity to set up a Communist-dominated Popular Front government. The Communists certainly wanted such a Popular Front, perhaps hoping to repeat the experiment of the post 1945 government, minus the mistakes. But their whole tradition of caution, of waiting until they were certain that the revolutionary situation was 'ripe', militated against their taking the initiative. As Jean-Paul Sartre said later, Communist policy in May indicated not merely that the Communists were no longer revolutionary, but that they 'were afraid of revolution'.[48] A Popular Front government was wholly unlikely to attempt a fundamental reconstruction of French society, but the Communists did not want to take the risk.[49] They accepted with relief de Gaulle's offer of elections, even though they knew that recent events would allow the government to raise the spectre of 'red-revolution', and trounce them.

So much about the May events is not really in dispute. What is more controversial is the wider significance of the revolt. Generally a sense obtains that, for those who care to look closely, the May events tell more than they appear to. A certain air of inscrutability surrounds them, with the promise of hidden revelations about the nature and future direction of modern societies: a 'revolution without a face' is Edgar Morin's term for May '68. There is the powerfully argued view that the May revolt was important not so much for what it achieved, as for what it promised; for what it pre-figured, rather than for what it performed. In one version the May events are seen as part anticipation, part expression, of a fundamental transition taking place in industrial society: the movement to 'a knowledge society', with a central role reserved for the intelligentsia – students, professionals – and their institutions – universities, the media, cultural organizations generally.[50] Other versions stress the manner and style of the revolt, seeing in it an alternative to the classic model of revolutionary change, and one more appropriate to the needs and structures of advanced industrial society.[51]

What is common to these approaches is that they do not see the significance of the May events as lying in the facts of May themselves. A special 'reading' is given, from the perspective of the emerging future industrial society. The actions, speeches and writings of the revolutionaries are scrutinized, not for the purpose of making a realistic assessment of chances of success, but for the intimations of the problems, patterns of change and possible revolutions of the future society. The very extremism and exaggeration of behaviour and language ('Demand the impossible') are taken as indications that the events of May do not offer themselves as an instance of revolution, but as a rehearsal of possibilities. They are a projection, almost an artistic representation, of styles of life, patterns of organization, forms of social relations, that make up a model of a future social order, in response to the intensified or novel problems of developed industrial society. And the force of the model lies in the very fact of its 'unreality', its presentation in a 'pure' form uncontaminated by the need to depict realistically the transition from the present to the future society. Writing of the student commune in the month of May Edgar Morin declared: 'Precisely because it has been utopian rather than constructive it has been able to envisage a future which embraces the entire society. Because it has refused immediate compromises it is already exemplary.'[52]

No one could possibly argue that such a conception of May '68 takes in the intentions of more than a very small minority of the actors in the May events. In those events, as in all such upheavals, the past jostled the future in a confusing variety of ways. The student *enragés* of the March 22 Movement recalled the Great French Revolution; there was constant homage done to the Paris Commune of 1871, and to the lost *soviets* of 1917, 1919, 1956. Although there was general and passionate rejection of the Jacobin model of a centralized revolutionary dictatorship, the Trotskyist and Maoist groups still thought in terms of breaking the power of the state and replacing it with an alternative power structure. They had not learned, as the Right has done so well, the lesson of the insurrections of the twentieth century, 'that power is seized not against the state, but through the state'.[53]

In all these ways the 'dead hand of the past' maintained its hold. But there were others – the anarchists, the Situationists – who seemed to live so much in a projected humanized and unalienated society of the future that they were almost oblivious of the current realities of power. It was they above all who gave so distinctive a stamp to the May events. Small in number they may have been; but it was their posters, slogans, and poems, their particular style of confrontation and 'contestation', compounded of insult, ridicule and outrage, that gave a novel complexion to May '68. It was their influence that ensured that art and sexuality would be debated as strenuously as work and politics. The International Situationists were not, in origin, a group of conventional political activists or political intellectuals. They were practising architects, artists and urbanists, driven by the degraded conditions of modern art to seek a political analysis and a political solution. They wanted, however, not to politicize art but to aestheticize politics.[54] They made a politics out of Freud and Reich; Marx and Bakunin; Aragon and Breton; Lautréamont and Dali. Dadaism and Surrealism were as important influences as Marxism and anarchism ('Je suis Marxiste – style Groucho'). The resulting synthesis was a new politics, the 'politics of the surreal', a 'cultural politicization' that anatomized political oppression in every routine activity of the life of contemporary industrial society, and forced the concept of revolution to aim at the transformation of the most intimate and personal activities of daily life as a pre-condition of success.[55]

To the traditional concept of a political revolution the Situationists opposed 'the critique of everyday life'.[56] The alienation and oppression of capitalist society had gradually invaded every recess of contemporary life, aided by the vast productivity of modern industry and the influence of advertising and the mass media. Every activity is experienced as inauthentic, as an image manufactured and imposed by others. 'In those societies dominated by modern conditions of production,' writes Guy Debord at the opening of his *Society of the Spectacle*, 'all life appears as an immense accumulation of *spectacles*. All that once was directly lived, is now transformed into representation.' Dazzled by the world of consumption, people had retreated from the world of production.

They did not see that this retreat represented a further instalment of alienation, a further distancing of man from his potential existence as an active creative producer. Against and opposed to an alienated realm of work had been carved out an equally alienated realm of leisure, an illusory world of 'free time' and 'free activity' when man was truly 'himself'. The politics of modern industrial society was the politics of this *total* condition: man as citizen, worker, consumer, spouse, lover, artist, intellectual. Never was it more mystifying to treat men in the fragmented compartments of their different roles, when all roles were so integrated, orchestrated and manipulated by a unified system of domination. All revolution is political at some level; but the only revolution of any value in contemporary conditions must recognize the exercise of political constraint at every level of social activity, 'individual' and 'personal' as well as 'collective' and 'public'.[57] A revolution now must work itself out as the revolution of everyday life. 'The most certain chances of liberation are born in what is most familiar,' writes Raoul Vaneigem. 'Those who speak of revolution and class struggles without referring explicitly to daily life, without understanding the subversive element in sex and the positive element in the rejection of constraints, have a corpse in their mouths.' 'We do not want a world in which the guarantee that we will not die of starvation is bought by accepting the risk of dying of boredom.'[58]

It is not necessary here to go into the details of how the Situationists proposed to deal with this situation. Various traditions provided the elements of both the content and the form of action. From anarchism came the unremitting hatred of bureaucracy, hierarchy, centralization and specialization, and the corresponding stress on small-scale, self-managing councils, and loose federations of local units. State power was not so much confronted as ignored, in the belief that the setting up of alternative structures of production, distribution, education etc. would simply drain that power away, which in any case rested on the stupefied submissiveness of the population. From Dadaism and Surrealism came the emphasis on creativity and spontaneity, and the 'ludic' and festive quality that so marked the activities in the Sorbonne and the Odéon. The elements of play and theatricality were not just the means, still less the diversions, of revolutionary activity; in an important sense they constituted the end of that activity. From the same source came the characteristic tactics of challenge by humour, ridicule and obscenity: particularly marked in the technique of '*detournement*' (roughly, 'distortion'), whereby familiar images or messages, often from advertising etc., are cross-punctuated by brief 'undermining' counter-slogans and images, so shocking the observer into a new awareness and redefinition of meaning. Thirdly, from de Sade and the psychoanalytic tradition, especially the works of Reich, came the awareness of sexual and emotional mutilation as the consequence of political oppression, and the emphasis on liberation of the emotional life as a central component of the revolutionary enterprise.

Something of the mixture of currents at work in the May events can be pictured from the very titles of the innumerable action committees that sprang up: 'the Freud–Che Guevara Action Committee', 'the Committee of Permanent Creation', the '*Comité Revolutionnaire d'Agitation Sursexuelle*'. The sense of a chaotic confusion of tendencies is excusable. But as many have recognized, the elements do fuse together into a coherent pattern. At the most general level they come together in a concept of revolution as the creation of free human activity in which the aesthetic impulse is primary if not paradigmatic. 'Man creates according to the laws of beauty,' says Marx. 'Poetry must be composed by all' was the oft-quoted remark of the Surrealist writer Lautréamont. In the Situationist influence in the May events, we see the attempt to make daily life itself into a work of art, lived and created as a painting is lived and created.[59]

None of this of course adds up to an actual occurrence of revolution in May '68; and it is difficult to know if it was ever intended to. Nor can it ever be a literal model of revolution, insofar as it blatantly ignores the problem of existing state power (international as well as national). Were there no more than the ideologies and practices of the May events to consider, there would perhaps be no point in treating them seriously as the expression of a new concept and style of revolution. But what gives them their significance in this respect is their correspondence with other tendencies and other forms of action in the industrial societies. The utopianism of May appears more appropriate if it is seen, not as the unreal wish to bring about the end of all alienation, nor the nostalgic rejection of all industrial civilization, but as the compressed anticipation of the forces and strategies of social change of an already visible future. The May events were indeed the first 'synoptic' expression of certain material and intellectual currents which since the Second World War have been confronting the industrial societies with the possibility of profound discontinuities in their development.

Brief indications only of these tendencies can be given, and their connection with the May events implied rather than elaborated.[60] The role of students in the May events highlighted the growing importance of intellectual labour to the industrial economies, together with the paradoxical but explosive fact of the 'proletarianization' of much intellectual life. The particularly strong participation of the cultural and technical intelligentsia in those events also underlines this point. Then, the revolt against large-scale technology and the runaway development of a consumer economy chimed in with a widespread realization since the 1960s that such developments were being purchased at an ever-increasing cost to future generations, in social, moral and material terms. The action of the oil-producing states in taking control of the flow of cheap oil had the salutary effect of reminding the industrial societies that such a rethinking was a matter not just of desire but of necessity. It was moreover a constant theme of the analyses of May that much of the lavish expenditure of those societies was not only wasteful and unnecessary but actually debilitating and stupefying to their populations (not to mention being well-nigh ruinous to the populations of the developing societies).

Related to this last development was that other theme of May which has found expression in a significant general movement: the reaction against size, complexity, hierarchy and specialization, much of this summarized in the revolt against large-scale bureaucracy, both public and private. The reaction has shown itself in diverse ways, with varying degrees of significance: from movements for 'pupil power' in the schools, to the setting up of 'alternative' structures of family, educational and professional practice, to factory occupations by workers and the institution of forms of workers' self-management. There is a retreatist and nostalgic character to much of this, no doubt, especially in the renunciation of urban and industrial life in some aspects of the commune movement. But, abstracting from the utopian sentiment in the reaction, there has also been the hard-headed recognition at last of the real 'dis-economies of scale', the waste and inefficiency – again in both material and social terms – involved in trying to achieve goals through the agency of the large centralized organization. Educational institutions are not educating; medical services are compounding sickness instead of aiding health; the tedious and unfulfilling nature of work in factories and offices with a high degree of specialization and division of labour is leading to absenteeism, sabotage and other forms of discontent on a scale large enough to question their whole rationale of organization. It is indeed not the workers but the managements of Saab and Volvo, along with many others, that institute schemes of 'job-enrichment' involving the modification of assembly-line technology and organization, in order to keep their workforce.[61] The most advanced technological developments, in any case, often point to the possibility and the desirability of drastically reducing scale, centralization and hierarchic coordination. As the Situationist analyses repeatedly insisted, automation and cybernation, differently organized, point the way to distinctly federal structures, with great autonomy of parts and reduction in the scale and specialization of work-tasks.[62]

Finally, and perhaps most importantly, there is the matter of the form of social action. The Situationists in May wished to bypass not just the state, but all the official political parties, the trade unions, the official student bodies, the student Marxist political groups (the *groupuscules*), even their own organizations and alliances at any given moment in the past (a group structure is no longer valid an hour after its creation). All such organizations either were or would be part of the 'established' opposition, an established counter-society that would seek to put an end to the free movement of change. As against this they proposed the strategy of the 'exemplary action', a concept whose intrinsic property was fluidity both as regards the level of action contemplated and the nature of the organization contemplating the action. Since repression was both generalized at the highest levels of society and concretized in all the details of its activities, it could not be confronted in an overall way, in a once-and-for-all head-on clash. Instead, seeking allies appropriate to the locality, the institution, or the nature of the activity in question, one had to intervene at any and all levels of the society. The strategy of change is seen as one of endless and unremitting 'contestation', a serpentine movement of exemplary actions in which each action escalates upwards to the higher levels which appear to condition the level at which the action is started, or downwards to establish the necessary basis for change in the concrete activities of daily life. It is a movement in which, snake-like, the head is barely distinguishable from the tail; in which there are no permanent allies or obligations; and in which the characteristic Situationist techniques of confrontation are designed to reveal both the local and the particular, and the general and societal dimensions of the problem to be overcome.

Here too the forms of May have had their presages and echoes. Since the late 1950s, the mode of reaction to the dominant tendencies and structures of industrial society has repeatedly gone outside the established forms of opposition, and has penetrated areas and activities of the society for long thought safely 'outside' politics. In every form of demonstration, direct action, community action, occupation and 'displacement', politics has invaded the family, the community, the school, the university, the factory; political struggles, at every level of society, have taken place over housework, sex, sport, housing, play and leisure amenities, and the nature of knowledge itself. The lesson has been learned that while the various forms of the established opposition are factors to be taken into account, they are not generally agencies of support for radical social change. They can often be used, but too close an embrace is deadly. The way to future transformations lies outside their confines, through the actions of those whose lives are directly affected, and at levels which they can at all times comprehend and control.

There is, of course, absolutely no guarantee that such a strategy will succeed in transforming society to the extent that we might fairly describe as 'revolutionary'. The limits no doubt will be tested as they have always been, by the felt threat to the power of those who already have it, and their consequent attempts to retain it by every means at their disposal. Those means, as we have seen, are formidable. Against this we have to note the structural tendencies and novel needs of industrial society which, in the most general way, have in recent years been moving in favour of the revolutionary enterprise. The revolutionaries of modern society need not only choose the path of the 'Grand Refusal', if by that is meant a blanket rejection of all contemporary developments. If, as Marx said, 'it is not enough that thought tend towards reality, reality itself must tend towards thought', then modern revolutionary theory has at least one foot in reality. But that is not the same thing as saying that history is on the side of the revolutionaries. Trotsky's alternative ends – 'socialism or barbarism' – still seem, in their various forms, to be equivalent possibilities, and nothing in the present can make us certain which will win out.

It is absurd to suppose that there can no longer be revolutionary changes in the industrial societies of the present. But, equally, it would be tragic if revolution were pursued without respect for the fundamental change of historical context. That change, as it has worked itself out in the course of this century, must force on us a re-definition both of the concept and the strategy of revolution. We cannot now storm the Winter Palace; the Palace of Alienation cannot be taken like that. There is no one barricade across which to fight the enemy. There is a myriad of barricades across which to fight a myriad of struggles, in which yesterday's friend is today's enemy. In the conditions of today, revolution must become what it has always striven to be, permanent revolution. The past failed in this, but its revolutions had other successes. The revolution of the future has no choice: the concept and techniques of permanent revolution are all that the conditions of today allow it. The enduring importance of the May events was to give us some glimpse of that concept and those techniques in a form so eloquent with its message that he must be dull indeed who cannot hear it.

NOTES

1 Barrington Moore jnr, *Reflections on the Causes of Human Misery* (London, Allen Lane The Penguin Press, 1972), pp. 168–9.

2 S. Avineri (ed.), *Karl Marx on Colonialism and Modernization* (New York, Anchor Books, 1969), Introduction, p. 30.

3 Karl Marx, 'The Eighteenth Brumaire of Louis Bonaparte' (1853), in Karl Marx and Frederick Engels, *Selected Works in Two Volumes* (Moscow, Foreign Languages Publishing House, 1962), vol. I, p. 340 n. 1.

4 And cf. Trotsky: 'Historical experience shows that the peasantry is absolutely incapable of taking up an *independent* political role . . . Unorganized, scattered, isolated from the towns, the nerve centres of politics and culture; stupid, limited in their horizons to the confines of their respective villages . . . the peasantry is compelled, in the revolutionary epoch, to choose between the policy of the bourgeoisie and the policy of the proletariat', *The Permanent Revolution and Results and Prospects* (New York, Merit Publishers, 1969; first published 1905–6), pp. 72ff.

5 David Mitrany, *Marx Against the Peasant* (New York, Collier Books, 1961).

6 H. Marcuse, *An Essay on Liberation* (London, Allen Lane The Penguin Press, 1969), p. 82.

7 Barrington Moore jnr, *Social Origins of Dictatorship and Democracy* (London, Allen Lane The Penguin Press, 1967), p. 453.

8 Quoted Stuart Schram, *Mao Tse-Tung* (Harmondsworth, Penguin Books, 1966), p. 95.

9 For strategic reasons the volume was attributed to a mythical author, 'A. Neuberg'. It has recently been issued in an English translation (London, New Left Books, 1970).

10 The spell of Marxism over Third World intellectuals is most impressively instanced in Frantz Fanon, the writer who in almost every other way repudiated European political theory. But even he continues to use the concepts and vocabulary of European Marxism. See David Caute, *Fanon* (London, Fontana/Collins, 1970), pp. 75ff.

11 Frantz Fanon, *The Wretched of the Earth* (Harmondsworth, Pengin Books, 1967), p. 86.

12 Quoted in Régis Debray, *Revolution in the Revolution? Armed Struggle and Political Struggle in Latin America*, trans. Bobbye Ortiz (Harmondsworth, Penguin Books, 1968), p. 67.

13 See E.J. Hobsbawm, *Primitive Rebels* (Manchester, Manchester University Press, 1959), pp. 13–29.

14 In addition to Debray's *Revolution in the Revolution?*, see also Robin Blackburn (ed.), *Régis Debray: Strategy for Revolution* (London, Jonathan Cape, 1970); Ernesto Che Guevara, *Episodes of the Revolutionary War* (New York, International Publishers, 1968), and *Guerilla Warfare* (Harmondsworth, Pengin Books, 1969). For a good

critical discussion see the essays in L. Huberman and P. Sweezy (eds), *Régis Debray and the Latin American Revolution* (New York, Monthly Review Press, 1968).

15 Eric Hobsbawm, 'Guerrillas in Latin America', in R. Miliband and J. Saville (eds), *The Socialist Register 1970* (London, The Merlin Press, 1970), p. 52.

16 V. G. Kiernan, 'The Peasant Revolution', in *The Socialist Register 1970*, p. 34.

17 One of the earliest and most lucid efforts was Hugh Seton-Watson, 'Twentieth century revolutions', *The Political Quarterly*, XXII, no. 3 (July–Sept. 1951). Other works which help in various ways in establishing this framework are: Hamza Alavi, 'Peasants and Revolution', in R. Miliband and J. Saville (eds), *The Socialist Register 1965* (London, The Merlin Press, 1965), pp. 291–335; Chalmers Johnson, *Peasant Nationalism and Communist Power* (Stanford, Ca, Stanford University Press, 1962); G. Ionescu and E. Gellner (eds), *Populism* (London, Weidenfeld and Nicolson, 1969); E. Wolf, *Peasant Wars of the Twentieth Century* (London, Faber and Faber, 1971); John Dunn, *Modern Revolutions* (Cambridge, Cambridge University Press, 1972).

18 Albert Camus, *Neither Victims Nor Executioners* (1946), trans. Dwight Macdonald, reprinted by the journal *Liberation* (New York, February 1960), p. 13.

19 Quoted in Franz Borkenau, *World Communism: A History of the Communist International* (Ann Arbor, University of Michigan Press, 1962; first published 1939), pp. 131–2. Borkenau's book remains the most lucid and convincing account of the revolutions in central Europe.

20 A. J. Ryder, *The German Revolution of 1918* (Cambridge, Cambridge University Press, 1967), p. 2.

21 Borkenau, *World Communism*, pp. 134–5.

22 F. C. Carsten, *Revolution in Central Europe 1918–19* (London, Methuen, 1972), p. 19.

23 Borkenau, *World Communism*, p. 148.

24 Gramsci's writings during these years, in the form of articles in *L'Ordine Nuovo*, are translated and reprinted in *New Left Review*, no. 51 (Sept.–Oct. 1968).

25 Gramsci, quoted in Giuseppe Fiori, *Antonio Gramsci, Life of a Revolutionary* (London, New Left Books, 1970), p. 141. For Gramsci's attitude during this period see also Alastair Davidson, 'Gramsci and Lenin 1917–22', R. Miliband and J. Saville (eds), *The Socialist Register 1974* (London, The Merlin Press 1974), pp. 125–50.

26 I have examined in detail the basic pattern of the classic European revolutions in the 'Introduction' to K. Kumar (ed.), *Revolution: The Theory and Practice of a European Idea* (London, Weidenfeld and Nicolson, 1971), pp. 1–90.

27 Plato, *The Republic*, trans. F. M. Cornford (London, Oxford University Press, 1941), p. 262.

28 As poignantly celebrated by Gillo Pontecorvo in his splendid film, *Battle of Algiers* (1968).

29 A number of urban insurrections are instructively analysed, with depressingly uniform conclusions, in M. Oppenheimer, *Urban Guerrilla* (Harmondsworth, Penguin Books, 1970), pp. 93ff – which also leads him to draw the inevitable lesson for black insurrections in the United States.

30 For a particularly incisive analysis of the problems facing urban risings, see *Régis*

Debray: Strategy for Revolution, pp. 63ff. See also Oppenheimer, *Urban Guerrilla*, *passim*.

31 The balance of advantages and disadvantages to revolutionaries as a result of some of these new developments, especially in the planning of modern cities, is interestingly discussed by Eric Hobsbawm, 'Cities and Insurrections', in his *Revolutionaries* (London, Weidenfeld and Nicolson, 1973), pp. 220–33.

32 Alexis de Tocqueville, *L'Ancien Régime et la Révolution* (1856). Translated as *The Ancien Régime and the French Revolution* by Stuart Gilbert (London, Fontana, 1966).

33 Karl Marx, 'The Eighteenth Brumaire of Louis Bonaparte', pp. 332–3.

34 Robert Michels, *Political Parties* (1915). Translated by E. and C. Paul (New York, Collier Books, 1962).

35 Max Weber, 'Bureaucracy', in *From Max Weber: Essays in Sociology*, trans. and ed. by H. H. Gerth and C. Wright Mills (London, Routledge and Kegan Paul, 1948), pp. 228–30.

36 The analogy is with the liberated 'base areas' of peasant revolutions, and is discussed illuminatingly by Barrington Moore jnr in *Reflections On the Causes of Human Misery*, pp. 181ff.

37 Herbert Marcuse, *One Dimensional Man* (London, Routledge and Kegan Paul, 1964), *passim*.

38 Hobsbawm, 'Cities and insurrections', p. 32.

39 In what follows on elite structure I am especially indebted to the discussion in Frank Parkin, 'System contradiction and political transformation', *Archives Européenes de Sociologie*, XIII (1972), 45–62.

40 For a stimulating exchange of views on the possibility of radical change in East European polities, see Zygmunt Bauman, 'Social dissent in the East European political system', and Leszek Kolakowski, 'A pleading for revolution: a rejoinder to Z. Bauman', both in *Archives Européenes de Sociologie*, XII (1971), 25–60; and the further contribution to the debate by David Lane, 'Dissent and consent under state socialism', *Archives Européenes de Sociologie*, XIII (1972), 37–44.

41 For this verdict, following an analysis of these and similar episodes, see Ralph Miliband, *The State in Capitalist Society* (London, Weidenfeld and Nicolson, 1969), pp. 96–117.

42 Marcuse, *One Dimensional Man* (London, Abacus edn, 1972), p. 199.

43 Ibid., pp. 199–200.

44 Realistic assessments and sceptical conclusions are contained in Stanislav Andreski, *Prospects of a Revolution in the USA* (London, Tom Stacey, 1973).

45 The full title of the pamphlet sufficiently indicates its scope: *De la Misère en milieu étudiant, considérée sous ses aspects économique, politique, psychologique, sexuel et notamment intellectuel, et de quelques moyens pour y remédier.*

46 Bernard E. Brown, *Protest in Paris: Anatomy of a Revolt* (New Jersey, General Learning Press, 1974), p. 5.

47 The possible exception was the remarkable episode at Nantes, when students, workers and farmers together formed a Central Strike Committee which largely replaced the official administration of the city. For a brief account, see Brown, *Protest in Paris*, pp. 142–52.

48 Jean-Paul Sartre, *Les Communistes ont Peur de la Révolution* (Paris, Didier, 1968).

49 Alain Touraine commented sarcastically that in May 1968 the French Communist

Party failed not just as a revolutionary but even as a reformist party. Quoted Eric Hobsbawm, 'May 1968', in his *Revolutionaries*, p. 240. Hobsbawm gives a particularly good account of the thinking of the French Communist Party during the May events.

50 See especially Alain Touraine, *Le Mouvement de Mai ou le Communisme Utopique* (Paris, Le Seuil, 1968), and *The Post-industrial Society* (New York, Random House, 1971).

51 For example, Edgar Morin: 'The Paris student commune will become the classic model for all future transformations in Western societies ... The transformation of the Sorbonne into a forum-cum-festival-cum-laboratory of ideas created the image of an open society and an open university where imagination reigns in the place of dismal bureaucracy, where education is open to all and where economic exploitation and domination have been eradicated', Morin, 'The Student Commune', in Charles Posner (ed.), *Reflections on the Revolution in France: 1968* (Harmondsworth, Penguin Books, 1970), p. 127.

52 Ibid.

53 Brown, *Protest in Paris*, p. 189.

54 A characteristic comment from the anarcho-Situationist literature of May put the old and the new as follows. 'The Trotskyists have an *a priori* scenario ... they want to do a re-make of the 1917 revolution instead of inventing forms of struggle that correspond to present-day needs. It's at the level of mental structure that they are not revolutionary. What they need is a good dose of Artaud ...' Quoted Alfred Willener, *The Action Image of Society: On Cultural Politicization* (London, Tavistock Publications, 1970), p. 178.

55 For the significance of the Situationists in the May events, see especially Alfred Willener, *The Action Image of Society: On Cultural Politicization*, who also reprints some illustrative documents. See also Brown, *Protest in Paris*, pp. 80–109. The themes and manner of the Situationist critique are best seen in the writings of two of the most influential Situationists: Guy Debord, *La Société du Spectacle* (Paris, Buchel-Chastel, 1967) (English trans. *Society of the Spectacle*, Detroit, Black and Red, 1970); Raoul Vaneigem, *Traité de savoir-vivre à l'usage des jeunes générations* (Paris, Gallimard, 1968) (English trans. *The Revolution of Everyday Life*, London, Practical Paradise Publications, 1972). Selections from the review, the *International Situationist*, have been edited and translated by C. Gray, *Leaving the Twentieth Century*, (London, Free Fall Publications, 1974).

56 For a parallel and more conventional approach, highly indebted to the Situationist critique, see Henri Lefebvre, *Everyday Life in the Modern World* (London, Allen Lane The Penguin Press, 1971).

57 For a good discussion of the narrowness of traditional concepts of the political, even in classical Marxism, see Anthony Skillen, 'The Statist concept of politics', *Radical Philosophy*, no. 2, (Summer 1972), pp. 2–6.

58 Vaneigem, *The Revolution of Everyday Life*, pp. 11, 12.

59 cf. Debord: 'Dada wanted to suppress art without creating it; and surrealism wanted to create art without suppressing it. The critical position elaborated since by the Situationists has shown that the suppression and the realization of art are inseparable aspects of the same transcending of art', *Society of the Spectacle*, thesis 191. The Situationists are not of course original or alone in holding to this concept

of revolution. It has been a consistent feature of Herbert Marcuse's writing since *Eros and Civilization* (Boston, Mass., Beacon Press, 1955) and more recently has come to predominate. See *An Essay on Liberation* (London, Allen Lane The Penguin Press, 1969) and *Counter-Revolution and Revolt* (London, Allen Lane The Penguin Press, 1972).

60 I deal more fully with these points in a forthcoming book on the future of the industrial societies [see Bibliographical note below].

61 A striking correspondence of managerial and 'May' thinking is revealed in the work of the management consultant Donald Schon, *Beyond the Stable State* (London, Maurice Temple-Smith, 1971), where he argues that 'the Movement' – of students, the 'counter-culture' etc. – exemplifies the organizational tendencies of the most advanced corporations of the industrial world. And as an instance of the concern felt at 'the top', cf. the following letter from the English Conservative Member of Parliament, John Hannam (*The Times* 13 August 1973): 'jobs are now broken down into simple repetitive tasks scarcely worthy of intelligent, trained men and women; factory and even office automation has come to mean not an end to drudgery, but a proliferation of trivial and tedious tasks around the machinery; work has become degraded into a boring and unsatisfactory part of existence.'

62 For example, Vaneigem: 'if seized from its masters, cybernetics could liberate human groups from toil and from social alienation. The project of Charles Fourier is just this, at a period when utopia was still possible. But from Fourier to the cyberneticians, who control the operational organization of technology, there is the distance from freedom to slavery', *The Revolution of Everyday Life*, p. 74.

BIBLIOGRAPHICAL NOTE

On Third World revolutions: in addition to the general references in note 17, see Joel Migdal, *Peasants, Politics and Revolution* (Princeton, NJ, Princeton University Press, 1974); J. W. Lewis (ed.), *Peasant Rebellion and Communist Revolution in Asia* (Stanford, Ca, Stanford University Press, 1974); W. F. Wertheim, *Evolution or Revolution? The Rising Waves of Emancipation* (Harmondsworth, Penguin Books, 1974); J. M. Paige, *Agrarian Revolution* (New York, The Free Press, 1975); James C. Scott, *The Moral Economy of the Peasant: Rebellion and Subsistence in Southeast Asia* (New Haven, Conn., and London, Yale University Press, 1976); Scott, *Weapons of the Weak: Everyday Forms of Peasant Resistance* (New York and London, Yale University Press, 1986); Theda Skocpol, *States and Social Revolutions* (Cambridge, Cambridge University Press, 1979), pp. 112–57; L. S. Stavrianos, *Global Rift: The Third World Comes of Age* (New York, Morrow, 1981); Peter Worsley, *The Three Worlds* (London, Weidenfeld and Nicolson, 1984), pp. 61–167; J. Walton, *Reluctant Rebels: Comparative Studies of Revolution and Underdevelopment* (New York, Columbia University Press, 1984). Studies of particular revolutions which throw light on the general conditions of Third World revolution include: John Womack jnr, *Zapata and the Mexican Revolution* (Harmondsworth, Penguin Books, 1972); Susan Eckstein, *The Impact of Revolution: A Comparative Analysis of Mexico and Bolivia* (London and Beverly Hills, Ca, Sage Publications, 1976); Alan Knight, *The Mexican Revolution* (2 vols, Cambridge, Cambridge University Press, 1987); Theodor Shanin, *The Roots of Otherness: Russia's Turn of Century* (2 vols, London,

Macmillan, 1986); Isaac Deutscher, *The Unfinished Revolution: Russia 1917–1967* (London, Oxford University Press, 1967); Deutscher, *Marxism, Wars and Revolutions: Essays From Four Decades* (London, Verso, 1984); William G. Rosenberg and Marilyn B. Young, *Transforming Russia and China: Revolutionary Struggle in the Twentieth Century* (New York and Oxford, Oxford University Press, 1982); P. Dukes, *October and the World: Perspectives on the Russian Revolution* (London, Macmillan, 1979); E. K. Trimberger, *Revolution From Above* (New Brunswick, NJ, Transaction Books, 1978); Carl Leiden and Karl M. Schmitt, *The Politics of Violence: Revolution in the Modern World* (Englewood Cliffs, NJ, Prentice-Hall, 1968); Peter Calvert, *A Study of Revolution* (Oxford, Clarendon Press, 1970); Jaroslav Krejčí, *Great Revolutions Compared: The Search for a Theory* (Brighton, Wheatsheaf Books, 1983); J. A. Goldstone (ed.), *Revolutions: Theoretical, Comparative and Historical Studies* (San Diego, Ca, Harcourt, Brace Jovanovich, 1986).

On the European revolutions of 1918–21 (see also nn. 19–25): T. Hajdu, 'Socialist revolution in Central Europe, 1917–21', in Roy Porter and Mikuláš Teich (eds), *Revolution in History* (Cambridge, Cambridge University Press, 1986), pp. 101–20 (also contains a bibliography). There are also useful bibliographical entries, for both First and Second World War revolutionary developments, in Robin Okey, *Eastern Europe 1740–1985*, 2nd edn (London, Hutchinson, 1986). See also John M. Cammett, *Antonio Gramsci and the Origins of Italian Communism* (Stanford, Ca, Stanford University Press, 1967); Charles L. Bertrand (ed.), *Revolutionary Situations in Europe, 1917–22: Germany, Italy, Austria–Hungary* (Montreal, Interuniversity Centre for European Studies, 1977); Dick Geary, *European Labour Protest 1848–1939* (London, Croom Helm, 1981), pp. 134–78; R. N. Hunt, *German Social Democracy 1918–1933* (Chicago, Chicago University Press, 1970); G. Braunthal, *Socialist Labor and Politics in Weimar Germany* (Hamden, Conn., Archon Books, 1978); R. J. Evans (ed.), *The German Working Class 1888–1933* (London, Croom Helm, 1981); Barrington Moore jnr, *Injustice: The Social Bases of Obedience and Revolt* (London, Macmillan, 1978), pp. 275–397; Carmen Sirianni, 'Councils and parliaments: the problem of dual power', *Politics and Society*, 12 (1983), 83–123; D. Kirby, *War, Peace and Revolution: International Socialism at the Crossroads, 1914–1918* (Aldershot, Gower, 1987). For post–1945 Hungarian, Czech and Polish movements, see François Fejtö, *A History of the People's Democracies: Eastern Europe since Stalin* (Harmondsworth, Penguin Books, 1974); Alain Touraine, and others, *Solidarity: Poland 1980–81* (Cambridge, Cambridge University Press, 1983). The special case of Portugal, and the extent to which there was a Portuguese Revolution in 1974, is well studied in Martin Kayman, *Revolution and Counter-Revolution in Portugal* (London, Merlin Press, 1987).

On the main theme of the chapter, the prospects for revolution in contemporary Western industrial societies, nothing very much has appeared since this essay was written. This perhaps reflects the fading of the sixties dream, with its revolutionary promise. There are two good studies of the radical thought of the time: Christopher Lasch, *The Agony of the American Left* (Harmondsworth, Penguin Books, 1973); Richard Gombin, *The Origins of Modern Leftism* (Harmondsworth, Penguin Books, 1975). The radical argument can be sampled in D. Cooper (ed.), *The Dialectics of Liberation* (Harmondsworth, Penguin Books, 1968), Richard E. Rubinstein, *Rebels in Eden: Mass Political Violence in the USA* (London, Macdonald, 1970), and R. Aya and N. Miller (eds), *The New American Revolution* (New York, The Free Press, 1971). An important component of New Left thought is discussed in Bruce Brown, *Marx, Freud, and the Critique of Everyday Life: Toward a Permanent Cultural Revolution* (New York and London, Monthly Review Press, 1973). This leads directly to Situationist themes and the events of May 1968, on which see further: H. Lefebvre, *The Explosion: Marxism and the French Upheaval* (New York and London, Monthly Review Press, 1969); Michel Crozier, *The Stalled Society* (New York, Viking Press, 1974); Patrick Seale and Maureen McConville, *French Revolution 1968* (Harmondsworth, Penguin Books, 1968); Daniel Singer, *Prelude to Revolution: France in May '68* (London, Cape, 1970). A key document, by a key participant, is Daniel Cohn-Bendit, *Obsolete Communism: The Left-Wing Alternative* (Harmondsworth, Penguin Books, 1969). The later history of the International Situationists is engagingly documented in Guy Debord and others, *The Veritable Split in the International* (London, B. M. Piranha, 1974).

The trends in industrial society briefly noted at the end of the chapter are elaborated in my *Prophecy and Progress: the Sociology of Industrial and Post-Industrial Society* (Harmondsworth, Penguin Books, 1978). And, for a general discussion of the argument of the chapter as a whole, see P. K. Edwards, R. Penn and K. Kumar, 'Revolution in industrial societies: some comments on Mr Kumar's article', *Sociology*, 12 (1978), 325–331.

One final note. There is obviously much of relevance to this chapter, though indirectly, in the writings of contemporary Western Marxists on the current conditions of Western capitalism. The literature is now so vast that it is pointless to cite particular items. The interested reader is best advised to consult journals such as *New Left Review, Marxism Today, Telos* and *Socialist Revolution*. Some of the relevant writings are mentioned in the notes and additional bibliography to two other chapters in this volume: 'Can the workers be revolutionary?' (ch. 8) and 'The limits and capacities of industrial capitalism' (ch. 5).

8

Can the Workers be Revolutionary?

It is particularly easy to forecast future events in England because in that country every aspect of social development is so plain and clear cut. The revolution *must* come. It is now too late for a peaceful outcome of the affair – the antagonism between the workers and the bourgeoisie – to be possible.

F. Engels, *The Condition of the Working Class in England in 1844*

The revival of Marxism in the intellectual life of Western societies since 1945 hardly requires extensive documentation. It is plain in the books and journals emanating, mainly but not exclusively, from the social science departments of many universities in those countries. The gains too are self-evident. Not only has there been a welcome revival of theorizing about large-scale social change in industrial societies, there have also appeared, largely under Marxist influence, a number of valuable and stimulating synoptic studies of the social and political structure of contemporary Western societies. I refer here – to take only the more recent – to such books as R. Miliband's *The State in Capitalist Society*, H. Braverman's *Labour and Monopoly Capital*, J. Westergaard and H. Resler's *Class in a Capitalist Society*.[1] These re-analyse, re-affirm and massively document the persisting facts of inequality of wealth and power, and the continuing process of degradation and exploitation in the workplace.

There is a side to these works, however, that deserves more comment than it has been getting. Most of them, quite properly given their Marxist orientation, gesture in the direction of a socialist future. Their analyses are predicated on the notion that contemporary capitalist societies are in a predicament. The strains imposed by the inequalities of power and the alienation of work will prove too much. Discontent and frustration will mount in the working-class movements and parties, leading to the eventual displacement of the system. The capitalist societies, says Miliband,

cannot obscure the discrepancy between promise and performance. They cannot obscure the fact that, though these are rich societies, vast areas of bitter poverty endure in them; that the collective provisions they make for health, welfare, education, housing, the social environment, do not begin to match need; that the egalitarian ethos they are driven to proclaim is belied by the privileges and inequalities they enshrine; that the structure of their 'industrial relations' remains one of domination and subjection; and that the political system of which they boast is a corrupt and crippled version of a truly democratic order ... ... A deep malaise, a pervasive sense of unfulfilled individual and collective possibilities penetrates and corrodes the climate of every advanced capitalist society.[2]

Westergaard and Resler similarly see the prevailing 'institutionalization of class compromise' as always vulnerable, in

a capitalism which survives only by its capacity to persuade labour to accept as routine the breach of promises which capitalism itself appeared to offer. The outcome can be in doubt for a long time to come. While it may go to secure business rule today, tomorrow, the day after, that would not settle the future. Class conflict would still be inherent in the order of private capital, its institutionalization always precarious. The threat of dispossession would continue to hang over it.[3]

These are more than rhetorical flourishes. The sense of the possibility of vast changes, more or less impending, informs the whole manner of inquiry of these studies. The dominant political, economic and ideological structures of capitalist societies are seen as engaged in a massive holding operation against an always potentially threatening working class – with or without allies. The increase in welfare and educational provision, and any general upward movement of wages, are variously interpreted either as concessions wrung from a reluctant and tight-fisted ruling class by a militant labour movement, or as diplomatic sops to the masses – who, however, cannot forever be placated. Intensive laundering and patching up of the social fabric is seen as increasingly necessary to stave off radical disaffection.

Moreover, a particular version of the history of the European working class is more or less explicitly contained in these accounts. There are differences of opinion as to whether things were better (i.e. the working class was more radical) in the past, or whether working-class confidence and consciousness have been increasing with the development of industrial society. That is, analyses are conducted on the basis either of the 'de-radicalization' of the working-class movement, or of its making and remaking of a politically conscious class.[4] But there is a basic agreement that the history of the working class must be seen in relation to some central, expected, pattern of development. There is, in other words, a 'natural' or normative history of the working class, in which it appears as the agency of the transformation of capitalist society. The actual history of that class over the past two centuries can then be scrutinized for the evidence of its success or failure – or successes and failures – in living up to its putative role. Indeed for many left-wing historians and sociologists this can be the only real interest for studying the working classes at all.

I am not concerned here to assess the validity of current expectations of revolutionary change.[5] What interests me is the nature of the tradition that treats working-class history and sociology in so particular a way. To say that the tradition originates with Marx and Engels – which is not quite true, but will do for most practical purposes – is of course only the merest beginning of the inquiry. Why did Marx and Engels think that the working class could and would be revolutionary? What were the theoretical grounds of their conviction? What historical episodes, in earlier times, and in their own, acted to suggest or confirm that conviction? Was it, historically and sociologically speaking, a reasonable belief? The following discussion tries to answer some of these questions.

I

European social theory in the nineteenth century was formed in response to a novel fact: the making of industrial society. A special feature of this response was its need to conceptualize the new system as fully as possible, to grasp it in theory almost before it had begun to work itself out in practice. Hegel may be right in some ultimate sense in saying that the owl of Minerva spreads its wings only with the falling of the dusk. In the more immediate sense, however, as a matter of common observation, thought often anticipates reality. Certainly this was true of nineteenth-century social thought. In a more or less systematic way, Saint-Simon, Comte, Tocqueville, Marx, Weber and Durkheim seized the principles of industrial society at a time when it had hardly established itself anywhere in Europe (even in England).[6] Perhaps we might say that sufficient signs of the new order had revealed themselves to give some idea both of its promise and of the historically unprecedented problems it gave rise to. It was a matter not just of theoretical but of practical urgency that the new system should be comprehended in as complete a way as possible.

We are as clearly still living off that intellectual inheritance as we are off the material inheritance bequeathed by the nineteenth century. Witness the number of studies that still get their inspiration, genuinely and not just as a form of ritual incantation, from the analyses and hypotheses of Marx, Weber, Durkheim. But the other side of that legacy needs to be recognized. It established a schematization of European history, powerful but misleading, whose influence is to be found everywhere in the social sciences. Because of the overriding need to give a systematic account of the new industrial order, the intellectual perfection of the social theories of industrialism conveyed also the idea of a historical perfection. The making of industrial society, it became common to assume, was basically a nineteenth-century phenomenon: more or less completed by the mid-century in Britain, rather later in the rest of Europe, but in any case settled and mature by the time of the First World War. (What comes afterwards is therefore 'late' or 'advanced' industrial society, or even 'post-industrial' society.)

This is a historical perspective especially marked in Marxism, as a result of the writings both of Marx and Engels and of the next generation of Marxists. Marxism is particularly fond of the idea of 'the 1848 watershed' in the development of capitalist industrial society. The period before that, roughly from the 1780s in England and 1789 in France, is seen as the 'heroic era' of capitalism, in which a confident bourgeois class throws off the resistance of the declining aristocratic class, and develops the new productive forces vigorously. 1848 marks the parting of the ways. The 'June Days' in Paris symbolize the arrival on the stage of history of the 'the proud, threatening and revolutionary' proletariat,[7] the birth of which has already been discerned in the gentler movement of Chartism in England. Capitalism goes increasingly on the defensive. The rule of the bourgeoisie, in culture and politics, becomes increasingly decadent and desperate. The period culminates in the imperialist scramble of the late nineteenth century and the subsequent world war among the rival imperialist powers.[8] (What comes after *that*, of course, is something of a problem for Marxists – but tends to be labelled the era of 'managerial capitalism', or 'state monopoly capitalism' – in any case, some version of 'late', decrepit and imminently departing capitalism.)

If, incidentally, anyone was perturbed by this rather casual conflation of the histories of different European societies, there was a ready 'philosophic' answer. 'Generally speaking, for the economical development of the bourgeoisie, England is here taken as the typical country; for its political development, France.' So wrote Engels in an innocent footnote to the 1888 English edition of the *Communist Manifesto*. Marx, in an earlier article of 1844, had similarly written of the proletariat: 'It must be granted that the German proletariat is the *theorist* of the European proletariat, just as the English proletariat is its *economist* and the French proletariat its *politician*.'[9]

The dangers, as well as the attractions, of bringing this 'philosophic' approach to bear on the nature and history of the European working class must be apparent from these statements. Such an approach, with its radical foreshortening and schematization of European history, made it likely that the 'proud, threatening and revolutionary' proletariat would be identified and greeted too early, before the main period of its formation as an active social entity. Also, it was a procedure calculated to subsume many disparate occupational (and indeed national) groupings of the working class under the generalized head of 'proletarian', and to see in the political activities of these diverse groups the signs of a growing awareness and political consciousness of 'the proletariat' as a single class.

All the more striking, therefore, is the claim of Marx and Engels that, unlike the 'utopian socialists' or the Young Hegelian intellectuals of the 1840s, the theoretical conclusions of Marxism – 'scientific socialism' – 'express, in general terms, actual relations springing from an existing class struggle, from a historical movement going on under our very eyes'.[10] In the writings of the 1840s and 1850s, in particular, they both assumed the existence of a fast-growing and already highly developed urban industrial proletariat: a revolutionary class of industrial workers without property in the means of production, a class that was in society but not of it.

Engels, it was thought, had given the definitive account of this development in his book *The Condition of the Working Class in England in 1844*, published on the Continent and immediately hailed by European socialists. Fritz Mehring, Marx's celebrated biographer, later called it 'one of the foundation stones of socialism'. Marx himself referred to it extensively in *Capital*; and

Lenin wrote that 'it made a profound impression upon the minds of all who read it. Everywhere Engels's study came to be regarded as the best available contemporary account of the condition of the proletariat; and indeed, neither before 1845, nor after, has a single book appeared that presented an equally striking and true picture of the misery of the working class.'[11]

Following Engels's lead, and as the product of the most developed industrial society, the English proletariat was universally thought to be the most sophisticated and advanced; but the French, fortified by their revolutionary tradition, were not far behind, and events suggested that even in Germany the proletariat might be considered strong enough to take on the task of both a bourgeois and a proletarian revolution. In a host of radical movements of the middle third of the nineteenth century, Marx and Engels thought they saw the clear signs of the growing consciousness of the European proletariat. There was the Chartist movement in Britain in the 1830s and 1840s, which Marx had described as 'the politically active portion of the British working class', and which Engels in 1892 retrospectively blessed as 'the first working-men's party of modern times' – allowing a modern Marxist, respectfully echoing the received tradition, to designate Chartism 'the first proletarian movement in history to reach the level of sustained nationwide organization'.[12] There was the rising of the Lyons silkworkers in 1831, and of the Silesian weavers in 1844. There were the proletarian movements in the revolutions of 1848, above all the insurrection of the Paris workers in the 'June Days'.

To doubters, Marx and Engels pointed to the vigorous political debates and political education taking place among the French and English workers in these decades, to 'the untiring propaganda which these proletarians are making, the discussions which they carry on daily among themselves'.[13] 'There is no need', they jointly wrote in 1845, 'to dwell upon the fact that a large part of the English and French proletariat is already conscious of its historic task.'[14] In the *Communist Manifesto* of three years later they were already sounding the death-knell of the capitalist industrial order. The failure of the 1848 revolutions everywhere, moreover, did little to dampen their optimism. During the 1850s Marx and Engels were seeing in every shift and dip of the trade cycle the pre-echoes of the imminent socialist revolution, led by the industrial proletariat.[15] Given this powerful backing from the founders, it is not surprising to hear a present-day Marxist declaring that 'the formative period of scientific socialism was precisely that in which the proletariat of the major European nations raised its coarse and urgent voice'.[16]

This makes for fair rhetoric; but its attitude to history is largely mythopoeic, as is that of most of this recital of radical proletarian action. Take first Engels's book, *The Condition of the Working Class in England*. It is immensely powerful. It remains a vivid, superbly written and in many ways remarkably accurate account of the social conditions of early industrialism in England. But it is in no sense an account of a class-conscious *proletariat*, in the strict Marxist meaning of that term. Generalizations are made from the experience of Lancashire textile workers to suggest a condition, and a response to it, that was by no means typical of the English working class as a whole.[17] As late as the Census of 1851 the workforce of the most advanced industrial society of its time was still heavily concentrated in agriculture and domestic service. The remainder were mostly employed in the old craft industries. The factory system was still in its infancy.[18] Even in cotton manufacture, by far and away the most advanced sector of industry, almost two-thirds of the units making returns in 1851 employed less than 50 men, while as late as 1050 only about half the workers in the Yorkshire woollen industry worked in factories, and the hosiery industry was still dominated by the system of small master-craftsmen employed, as of a century ago, by capitalist hosiers on a putting-out basis. It was indeed one of the unexpected features of early industrialization, as a result of the demand for new skills and new products, at first to intensify, rather than supersede, the old putting-out system of the merchant capitalist, the craft-shop and cottage industry. Maurice Dobb has pointed out that 'as late as 1870 the immediate employer of many workers was not the large capitalist but the intermediate sub-contractor who was both an employee and in turn a small employer of labour'. And he comments: 'The survival into the second half of the nineteenth century of the conditions of domestic industry and of the manufactory had an important consequence for industrial life and the industrial population which is too seldom appreciated. It meant that not until the last quarter of the century did the working class begin to assume the homogeneous character of a factory proletariat.'[19]

It is a comment that is relevant not just to a consideration of the significance of Engels's book, nor of the English case alone, but to the whole European working-class movement of the nineteenth century. The fact is that the 'coarse and urgent voice' that was raised in the radical movements of the working class for most of that century was not, or not mainly, that of the factory proletariat, but of more traditional groups who pre-dated industrialism: artisans, small traders and small farmers. There really was nowhere, at the time Marx and Engels made their statements and for many decades thereafter, a factory proletariat large enough or sufficiently concentrated to launch a major insurrection, let alone lead the socialist revolution – even supposing it had wanted to. Working-class activity there was in plenty; but for the whole of the first half of the nineteenth century and much of the second, these workers were not proletarians in Marx's sense but groups of workers who can be more accurately called 'pre-industrial' in their skills, work organization and relation to the means of production. Many of them were self-employed, independent craftsmen who owned their own workshops, or at the very least the tools of their trade, and who generally themselves employed other workers.

In France these groups made the running throughout the radical decades of the 1830s and 1840s – including the 1848 'June Days' – and continued to do so up to and beyond the Paris Commune of 1871.[20] In England they were the main force behind the Chartist movement, acting in alliance with, and to a good extent under the leadership of, distinctly middle-class radicals.[21] As late as the 1860s they were the groups which supplied most of the radicals who joined Marx in the founding of the First International Workingmen's Association. It is in fact quite clear, when one examines the kinds of workers Marx was mixing with and championing so enthusiastically in the 1840s, 1850s and 1860s, that these were the very groups he elsewhere often castigated as 'petit-bourgeois', destined to be swept aside by the inexorable march of industrialization. The 'proletarians' he discovered in the working-class movements of these decades were more likely to be self-employed master bricklayers, cabinet-makers, tailors, printers, carpenters and cobblers, than unskilled factory workers.[22]

Speaking of this period, Collins and Abramsky say: 'What is undoubtedly relevant is the fact that in the lifetime of the First International efforts to organize the unskilled majority failed almost completely . . . Paradoxically, the men who allied themselves with Marx in the period of the International came from the privileged stratum of the working class.'[23] This is not, of course, a paradoxical fact at all, but the common experience of all radical and revolutionary movements of the past 150 years in Europe. The truth is that much of the activity of these nineteenth-century movements can be accounted for in terms of a *defensive* action against the forces of industrialism. The movements were the work in the main of men who – as tragically seen in the case that so affected Marx, the rising of the Silesian weavers – did have some small property in the means of production, and who were fighting against those very forces of large-scale industrialism which menaced their mode of existence and threatened to turn them into a proletariat properly so-called. In a study of the contribution of artisans and *sans-culottes* to the revolutionary tradition, Gwyn Williams has made this point eloquently:

The traditions transmitted in both France and Britain were essentially *pre-industrial* in a deeper sense than the merely technical. 'Long have we been endeavouring to find ourselves men', said the sailors of the British fleet in 1797. 'We now find ourselves so. We will be treated as such.' They learned this tone from others. The first *political* statement of this instinct was made by men who, however poor, could not conceive of themselves as 'hands' or a 'labour force', men with the dignity of a skill and the mystery of a craft, men who polished tools and knew the 'fine points', men whose values, even in adversity, were fixed by an earned independence . . . This is the central truth, whose implications for the industrial nineteenth century we have perhaps not thought out deeply enough. The ideology of democracy was pre-industrial and its first serious practitioners were artisans.[24]

One important implication, at any rate, has been drawn out by Victor Kiernan: 'Modern experience seems to show that workers everywhere have been readier to fight against the establishment of industrial capitalism than for its abolition, once firmly established. It may be a fundamental difficulty for Socialism that, since it is avowedly a new thing, men cannot walk into it backwards, eyes fixed on familiar landmarks of the past, as they walked into many earlier revolutionary changes.'[25]

It is sometimes argued, to meet points of the kind set out above, that Marx and Engels abandoned the optimistic view of a revolutionary proletariat developing in their own times, and looked forward to a revolutionary settlement in a much more distant future.[26] From about the 1860s, it is said, they became increasingly aware both of the as yet undeveloped potential of capitalism and of the persisting obstacles to working-class unity and political consciousness. This is a matter for Marxologists to sort out in detail, although

I do not think the evidence is as convincing as is sometimes made out.[27] The position seems to me fairly stated by Bertell Ollman when he affirms 'the essential point that for the whole of Marx's lifetime the situation in the capitalist world was adequate, by his own standards, for the revolution he expected to take place ... Though it is true that Marx became progressively less optimistic (and always took account of other possibilities) he never really believed he was writing for a century other than his own.'[28]

But in any case future events cannot have been consoling to the ghosts of Marx and Engels. There is an irony in later developments that is impossible to miss. In the 1880s and 1890s, with the rapid industrialization of Europe, with the growth of 'general labour unions' of unskilled workers in England, and the mass Social Democratic parties on the Continent, there came into being a factory proletariat on the scale and with the kind of organization that had been the premise of Marx's analysis in the middle decades of the century. (By which time Marx was dead – 1883.) But this proletariat, and its leaders in Western Europe, showed a distinct reluctance to carry out the mission marked out for it. Throughout the European nations revolutionary activity declined in the second half of the nineteenth century, more or less in direct proportion to the growth of the proletariat. The proletariat preferred, or at least were willing to be lead that way, the tactics of trade unionism and parliamentary politics to that of mass insurrection and the revolutionary transformation of society. There were occasionally symbolic gestures in the direction of revolutionism – e.g. the Erfurt Programme of the German SPD in 1891. In England there was an intensification of industrial struggles in the decades prior to the First World War. But with the honourable exception of the Italian Socialist Party, in 1914 every other Western European socialist party showed its true belief and its true nature in joining with its government in fighting what could variously be seen as a nationalist, dynastic or imperialist war. The capitulation of European social democracy in 1914 is often, and rightly, seen as the symbolic end to a century of revolution. There has not been, in the course of this century, any sustained or major effort by working-class movements to take power in the capitalist societies of Western Europe.[29]

II

Marx and Engels not only deployed history, of course, or contemporary events: they made use of certain general conceptions in projecting the rise of a class-conscious proletariat. Curiously, with the exception perhaps of the *Communist Manifesto*, there is no one place where they spelled out systematically the sociological steps in the growth of this consciousness.[30] The impression remains that, as with the very concept of the proletariat, its class-consciousness was a *theoretical* necessity, a requirement of a schema of social evolution that was a not-quite-complete historical and sociological distillation of Hegel's philosophy of history. Something of this is indicated in the famous passage of 1844, on Hegel's *Philosophy of Right*, where Marx links the coming German revolution to 'the emancipation of man. *Philosophy* is the *head* of this

emancipation and the *proletariat* is its *heart*. Philosophy can only be realized
by the abolition of the proletariat, and the proletariat can only be abolished
by the realization of philosophy.'[31]

Nevertheless, it seems worthwhile to consider, from a sociological angle,
what it was in the position of the proletariat that made Marx and Engels cast
them in the role of revolutionary liberators; and to assess the plausibility of
that view. Briefly – and in a sequence derived from Engels's observation of
English working-class history to 1844[32] – the proletariat first goes through a
backward-looking stage of machine-breaking. It is in this condition a dispersed
mass, but is gradually brought together in more coherent groupings by the
bourgeoisie, for its own purposes in its struggles with the old aristocratic
order, so that the proletariat here is fighting 'the enemies of its enemies'.
Next comes a stage of greater concentration of the proletariat, with developing
urbanization and mechanization, and the elimination of craft conditions of
production. Consciousness is here expressed largely in the form of strikes,
trades unionism and mutual aid in a variety of forms. The factory system
brings, in its clearest form, exploitation and alienation. It also eliminates all
relevant distinctions between workers, so that they increasingly see themselves
as sharing a common condition, a common struggle and a common destiny.
The improved communication system of modern industry nationalizes that
consciousness. Finally, with continuing and deepening economic crises
engendered by intensifying competition nationally and internationally, a section
of the bourgeoisie – the intelligentsia – joins a now confident and politically
mature proletariat, 'the class that holds the future in its hands'. The scene is
now set for a revolutionary encounter between proletariat and bourgeoisie.
But since, as in all revolutions, the essential steps, and the essential struggles,
have all preceded the final face-to-face, the outcome of that encounter is not
really in doubt.[33]

Clearly the proletariat, in different degrees in different European countries,
did go through some of the stages of this schematized sketch of the growth
of class-consciousness. Just as clearly nowhere did they go through them all.
The reasons for this are complex, and have been much discussed.[34] Here I
want to consider just a few points.

Take first Marx's assumptions about the consequences of factory work. Let
us, for the sake of the argument, accept that conditions of work there are as
degrading, brutalizing and alienating as Marx and Engels asserted. By virtue
of what social and psychological mechanism do such conditions produce
rationally comprehending, cooperative, fully politically conscious proletarians?
It is on the face of it highly improbable that such will be the outcome.[35] Here
is a powerful account by Engels of the effects of factory labour on the worker.

It is impossible to imagine a more tedious or wearisome existence. The factory worker
is condemned to allow his physical and mental powers to become atrophied. From
the age of eight he enters an occupation which bores him all day long. And there is
no respite from this boredom. The machine works ceaselessly ... It is nothing less
than torture of the severest kind to which the workers are subjected by being
condemned to a life-sentence in the factory, in the service of a machine which never

stops. It is not only the body of the worker which is stunted, but also his mind. It would indeed be difficult to find a better way of making a man slow-witted than to turn him into a factory worker.[36]

The point is a simple one, but needs to be made. How, given the condition of brutish degradation described by Engels, could such a class make a revolution to emancipate humanity? Is it not more likely to show a spirit of 'revolt, sullen revengeful humour of revolt against the upper classes', as Carlyle – quoted with reservations by Engels – feared?[37] Some years later Alfred Marshall was writing about 'those vast masses of men who, after long hours of hard and unintellectual toil, are wont to return to their narrow homes with bodies exhausted and with minds dull and sluggish';[38] and Westergaard and Resler themselves, apparently unaware that it tells against an important part of their argument, speak of 'the dull, hard facts of working class life'[39] – hardly language which suggests the 'collective effervescence', born of shared work and conflict experiences, that is meant to be the crucial step in the formation of a radical working-class consciousness. The working class has proved, time and again, that it is capable of heroic acts of collective solidarity and individual sacrifice. But this is a far cry from that 'hegemonic' consciousness that is necessary if it is to re-shape society in an entirely new mould, on the basis of a new ethic and a new system of social organization. The suspicion must be that here again we are treading in 'philosophic' territory.

This suspicion is heightened by a further, more general, consideration. According to the Marxist conception, the worker in capitalist society is alienated. He feels powerless, isolated, self-estranged. He is a passive creature in a meaningless, reified world, acted upon rather than acting. In a viciously competitive environment, he is driven to compete with his fellow workers. In other words, he plausibly reflects the dominant characteristics of the capitalist order as analysed by Marx (for do not forget that the capitalist too is alienated). Marx himself says this in *Capital*: 'The advance of capitalist production develops a working class which by education, tradition, habit, looks upon the conditions of that mode of production as self-evident laws of nature. The organization of the capitalist process of production, once fully developed, breaks down all resistances ... the dull compulsion of economic relations completes the subjection of the labourer to the capitalist.'[40] He is also well aware that in the social order of capitalism, not only are the different classes but the individuals *within* classes normally in an intense competitive relationship with each other. Thus he says that 'competition makes individuals, not only the bourgeoisie, but still more the workers, mutually hostile, in spite of the fact that it brings them together'.[41] Elsewhere (in volume III of *Capital*) he speaks of 'the infinite distinctions of interest and position which the social division of labour creates among workers as among capitalists and landowners'.

How then does the proletariat break out of the prison of alienation? How does it begin the process of casting off its chains? Mere revolt, riot, or insurrection, born of outrage or frustration, will not do, as Marx often had occasion to reprove would-be revolutionaries. This simply affirms the existing order, affirms it in its own values and terms (like the criminal, the worker wants the same things as the rich capitalist). The proletariat has to develop a qualitatively different set of values, and a new social purpose. There has, in other words, to be a *break* in the system, socially and culturally, such that the proletariat can create the new outlook that will take it beyond the confines of a class – any class, since its consciousness is to be that of and for humanity as a whole.

The answer will come pat. Reality evolves 'dialectically', by the opposition of contraries. Each system contains the seeds of its own contradiction. So it is with society, so it is with each class within society.[42] Hence the proletariat can be conceived as Janus-faced. It has a split consciousness. It can be both the product of capitalist society, bearing its imprint, and its executioner, showing a radically different consciousness and purpose. This might do in some circles, but in a sober gathering of sociologists and political scientists it is surely insufficient. We need to know the precise mechanism by which such a 'system break' can be expected to take place. We need to know in particular what instances of such breaks have been experienced in the past, and what lessons can be drawn from them. Marx, it is well known, had an answer in that direction too. The projected rise to class consciousness of the proletariat is explicitly couched in terms of an analogy with the rise of the bourgeoisie in early modern Europe. As we shall see in a moment, however, the analogy is unfortunate, as the case in question does not bear out the hoped-for comparison.

Before looking at that case, one further point needs to be made about Marx's general assumptions. Marx, as a true child of the Enlightenment, was a terrible rationalist. He seems to have believed that the proletariat would necessarily and inevitably come to a true, objective, understanding of their situation, simply by virtue of their experiences and their reflection upon them – aided no doubt by middle-class intellectuals such as himself. He could see all the obstacles to this being a straightforward and spontaneous achievement, but seems to have taken for granted that there were no fundamental sociological or psychological reasons why this should not happen within a reasonable period of time.

Here he was helped by a further belief. Marx was clear that with the rise of class society – a specifically capitalist accomplishment – a historical threshold had been crossed. There is no sense in which the class society of the bourgeois epoch is anything like the pre-industrial society of estates, ranks and orders.[43] Capitalist industrialism has brought about a *terrible simplification*. It has reduced class to the most naked and explicit criterion of economic interest. Moreover, it has done so in the full glare of a national, centralized, society, in which individuals are massed together, always conscious of each other's lives, always aware of respective gains and losses. Marx's bourgeois industrial society is one in which all the old religious, geographical and even occupational barriers have come down, and 'has left remaining no other nexus between man and man than callous "cash payment"'.[44]

It was part of Marx's rationalist expectation that in this constant process of national (and even international) cross-comparisons, the individual workers would become so conscious of their relatively deprived position that they would naturally band together to secure the full fruits of their labour – with all that followed from this in the way of class consciousness and political organization. The whole nation, to put it another way, would serve as a single 'reference group'. What has become clear is that individuals and groups do not take stock of their relative position in so clear-sighted a way. There is a multitude of reference groups in society, and feelings of contentment or deprivation are dependent on the choice of particular reference groups – which in turn has to do with a variety of factors.[45] Indeed, as against Marx's notion that a national framework for comparison and adjudication would be productive of proletarian class consciousness, a number of sociologists have recently argued, in a sense, exactly the opposite. Parkin, for instance, has suggested that radical working-class attitudes and behaviour tend only to occur when the working-class community is shielded and insulated from the corrupting effects of the wider (bourgeois) society. It is only within the safe confines of a working-class communal enclave that 'deviant', radical, attitudes can take hold.[46]

Parkin is not suggesting that such radicalism amounts to revolutionism. Indeed he explicitly calls it an 'accommodative' response, different from and possibly antithetical to an 'oppositional' or revolutionary one.[47] In other words, Marx is both right and wrong. He is right in his theoretical claim that only when the working class can form a view of society (and history) as a whole, and of its place within it, only then will it be capable of revolutionary action. He is wrong – partly because of his rationalist bias – in expecting as confidently as he did that such a development would follow in practice.

To come finally to the historical comparison with the rise of the bourgeoisie. It was important to Marx, in giving weight to his theory of social change through class consciousness and class conflict, that there should be a clear historical instance of the process. The rise to power of the bourgeoisie, on the basis of new productive powers developing within the womb of feudalism, became the paradigm case. Indeed it is clear that, whether or not reflection on the appropriate historical episodes actually stimulated the theory of social change, those episodes rapidly became the empirical mainstay of the theory. Taking the French Revolution of 1789 as his point of departure, the class analysis that seemed the most satisfying explanation of that event was projected, in a series of brilliant explorations, back to the English Revolutions of 1640 and 1688, and forward to the European Revolutions of 1830 and 1848. Above all his understanding of the Great French Revolution allowed him to undertake the superb history of early industrialization in England which we find in volume I of *Capital*, and, more sketchily but within a wider frame of reference, in the first part of *The German Ideology* and the *Grundrisse*.

What did the case of the bourgeoisie demonstrate?[48] That a humble group of runaway serfs, small tradesmen and small manufacturers, could by diligently exploiting new techniques and establishing new economic relationships gradually form into a more or less self-conscious class, which over a period of time grew in strength and confidence until it eventually accomplished a social and political revolution. It was particularly important to stress the novel and so to speak extraneous character of the new forces and the new men.

The towns which became the spearhead of the bourgeoisie's rise to power were new creations, unincorporated centres of petty manufacturing which were for the most part outside the medieval guild system and, of course, crucially outside the agricultural sector which dominated economic and political life. They attracted all the elements – especially dispossessed serfs – which could not find a secure place within the medieval system of guilds and feudal land tenure. Such towns were, as Michael Postan once put it, 'non-feudal islands in a sea of feudalism'. Neale has similarly stressed that 'it is important that these towns be conceptually distinguished from cities like Paris or London as well as from the cities of Asiatic and ancient societies. Many were really little more than villages and all were urban islands drawing life from the countryside and giving life back to it.'[49] It was in discovering such a conceptual and sociological break within the social order of feudalism that Marx could discern the origins of the new capitalist industrial order. This, once on a course of growth, could move out from its original bases and overrun the whole society. 'The modern age,' Marx declared, 'is the urbanization of the countryside, not the ruralization of the city as in antiquity.'[50]

When applied to the case of proletarian class consciousness, such a model had a superficial plausibility about it. Like the bourgeoisie, the proletariat was a class in society but not of it. It too was created in the womb of the old society. And it was supposed to rise to consciousness and power on the basis of the exploitation of technical knowledge and economic forces for which the old order had no room.

But on closer inspection the analogy breaks down almost completely. The proletarians are not 'outsiders' in capitalist society in the way the bourgeois were in feudal society. They do not represent an extraneous or exogenous force that 'breaks through' the social order of capitalism in the way that the bourgeoisie broke through the social order of feudalism.[51] The true analogy should be, not with the bourgeoisie, but with the serfs and peasants of medieval Europe. The proletariat is locked into the capitalist system of production, the indispensable basis of it, just as the serfs were the basis of the feudal system of production. If it breaks with it, it is to order and develop the economic forces of capitalism differently, not to introduce new forces of production. As Bottomore has said,

industrial workers are not involved in economic relationships different from those established in the existing society; in Marxian terms, they do not 'represent' a higher stage in the development of productive forces ... Marx implicitly recognizes this in his account of the decline of capitalism; for he explains the crisis of capitalism, not by the advent of new productive forces embodied in a new class, but by the inability of the capitalist social system to utilize the existing productive forces.[52]

The serfs and peasants did not of course make the bourgeois revolution (not, at least, as serfs and peasants). So why expect the workers to make the socialist revolution? But the question is more complex than this, in the way Marx handled it. Behind Marx's theory of class conflict there is an influence that is often stronger than that derived from his own historical understanding. It is the influence of the Hegelian dialectic, and in particular the seminal discussion in the *Phenomenology* of the dialectic of the master–slave relationship. The master derives his self-consciousness from viewing himself in the 'other' of the slave; but according to Hegel the slave gets the better of the bargain, because the 'other' from which he derives his self-consciousness – i.e. the master – is worthier by far than the representation he – i.e. the slave – sets before the master. The slave, moreover, does all the genuinely useful and creative work, while the master luxuriates in idle enjoyments. The slave therefore grows in self-consciousness, knowledge and power in direct proportion to the diminution of the master.

The paradigm (or parable) of the master–slave relationship can clearly be made to fit, with appropriate modifications, the capitalist–proletarian relationship rather well. It shows how, through an intense dyadic interaction, the inferior can become the superior, ignorance become knowledge, demoralization become confidence. No 'third force', no *tertium gaudens*, need be conjured up to explain the breakthrough to a qualitatively different order. But once again the circle is squared by a 'philosophic' trick. The logic of the relationship is philosophical, not sociological. It is true that in interpersonal relationships the master–slave dialectic has a certain basic plausibility about it (as witness the general appeal of a story like *The Admirable Crichton*). But to see it as the model for the relationship between classes, and especially of the revolutionary conflict of classes, is to make a quite unwarranted move from the phenomenological to the sociological level. What sociology as well as common sense should lead us to expect is that two groups (classes, nations) locked in a zero-sum conflict are more likely to converge in their values, attitudes and behaviour than to develop new patterns. That, in any case, is what the history of the increasing contact of the classes during the past century seems to teach us. The irony is that Marx saw this, in his careful and convincing account of the bourgeois capitalist revolution: but without seeing how much this told against his account of the proletarian socialist revolution.

III

This chapter may seem excessively negative, and perhaps I ought at the end to say more generally what it aims to do. I am suggesting that the Marxian inheritance concerning a revolutionary proletariat is a dangerous and misleading one. It is based on a myth about the past history of working-class movements. It uses a shaky philosophical method to establish a link between an accomplished historic event and an anticipated future one. This link disappears on examination. It makes sociological and psychological assumptions about the nature of conflict and social change which are not demonstrated, and which go against common knowledge and experience.

This would not matter much if we were simply dealing with a topic in the history of ideas. But it is a more important matter when we consider the dominating influence of Marxism in the present study of social change. Some of that influence is entirely beneficial; Marxism so often asks the right questions, digs away where others see little to inquire about. But as an orientating and organizing approach, the conception of class and class conflict as the major agency of large-scale social change seems to be based on extremely weak theoretical and empirical foundations. This is particularly so of the concept of the proletariat as the agent of transformation of the present social order. Contemporary Marxists of course make all sorts of qualifications, mainly to do with time and place, in advancing this view. But ultimately the central part of their understanding of contemporary social and political structures is pivoted on this belief. It affects the categories through which they see both present and past, and the whole cast of their investigation. This seems to me a serious distortion, and potentially a great waste of valuable talent and intellectual energy. In questioning the validity of this approach, I hope to make it easier to consider both past occurrences and present prospects of social change in a more realistic and fruitful way.

NOTES

1 In order: London, Weidenfeld and Nicolson, 1969; New York, Monthly Review Press, 1974; London, Heinemann, 1975.

2 Miliband, *The State in Capitalist Society*, p. 269.

3 Westergaard and Resler, *Class in a Capitalist Society*, p. 421.

4 For the former approach, following the classic analysis of Michels's *Political Parties*, see, for example, R. Tucker, 'The de-radicalization of working class parties', in his *The Marxian Revolutionary Idea* (London, Allen and Unwin, 1970); F. Parkin, *Class Inequality and Political Order* (London, MacGibbon and Kee, 1971); M. Mann, *Consciousness and Action Among the Western Working Class* (London, Macmillan, 1973). For the latter approach, see R. Miliband, 'Socialism and the myth of the Golden Past', in J. Saville and R. Miliband (eds), *The Socialist Register 1964* (London, The Merlin Press, 1964), pp. 92–103. And cf. this comment of Tom Burns's: 'The claim that the corporate system has licensed its growth in size and power by providing "the masses" with more and more placebos in the form of consumer goods, or that the lower classes have been "de-politicized" by the parallel effort of the Welfare State to safeguard the system by redistributing income does not bear close scrutiny ... The production of goods and services is and always has been an end, not a means; "de-politicization" assumes, against all the historical facts, that "the past" (as against occasional and transient episodes) was a time when the masses were "politicized". It makes at least as much sense to argue, as T. H. Marshall has, that the Welfare State is the product of the growth of the political consciousness of citizenship as of its decline' ('On the rationale of the corporate system', in R. Marris, ed., *The Corporate Society*, London, Macmillan, 1974, pp. 136–7).

5 For a general assessment, see my 'Revolution and industrial society: an historical perspective', *Sociology*, 10 (1976), 245–69. It might be worth, in passing, pointing out how weak are the accounts of Miliband et al. on precisely this point about the contemporary transformation of capitalist societies. The evidence, so strong on the existing patterns of inequality and alienation, becomes distinctly thin when it comes to discussing contemporary working class consciousness and action. It is perhaps

significant that Westergaard and Resler, for instance, devote only 60–70 pages of their 380-page book to the discussion of 'responses' to inequality – an inequality which they document so well in the rest of the book.

6 For a discussion of this point, and its implications, see my 'Industrialism and post-industrialism: reflections on a putative tradition', *Sociological Review*, 24 (1976), 439–78.

7 The phrase is used in an early piece by Marx and Engels, 'German socialism in verse and prose', quoted G. Therborn, *Science, Class and Society* (London, New Left Books, 1976), p. 328.

8 This periodization is particularly powerfully deployed in the writings of Trotsky. See, for example, *Results and Prospects*, published in 1906 (reprinted New York, Merit Publishers, 1969.) It also informs the work of Georg Lukács throughout – see, for example, *Studies in European Realism* (New York, Grosset and Dunlop, 1964).

9 K. Marx, 'Critical notes on "The King of Prussia and Social Reform"', in L. D. Easton and K. H. Guddat (eds), *Writings of the Young Marx on Philosophy and Society* (New York, Anchor Books, 1967), p. 353.

10 K. Marx and F. Engels, 'Manifesto of the Communist Party', in Marx-Engels, *Selected Works in Two Volumes* (Moscow, Foreign Languages Publishing House, 1962), vol. I, p. 46.

11 V. I. Lenin, 'Frederick Engels', in *Lenin on Britain* (London, Martin Lawrence, 1934), p. 19.

12 See Marx, 'The Chartists', in K. Marx, *Surveys From Exile* (London, Allen Lane, 1973), p. 264; Engels, 'Special Introduction' to the English edition of 'Socialism: Utopian and Scientific', in Marx–Engels, *Selected Works*, vol. II, p. 110; G. Therborn, 'The working class and the birth of Marxism', *New Left Review*, no. 79 (May–June 1973), p. 8. Miliband, too, speaks of Chartism as 'the first authentic working-class mass movement in history' ('Socialism and the myth of the Golden Past', p. 93).

13 K. Marx and F. Engels, *The German Ideology*, trans. R. Pascal (New York, International Publishers, 1947), p. 204.

14 K. Marx and F. Engels, *The Holy Family* (Moscow, Foreign Languages Publishing House, 1956), p. 53. And cf. the similar account in the *The Poverty of Philosophy* (New York, International Publishers, 1963), pp. 172–3, where the evolution of the political consciousness of the English working class is discussed.

15 For Marx's constant expectation of a revolutionary crisis in the 1850s, see D. McLellan, *Karl Marx: His Life and Thought* (London, Macmillan, 1973), pp. 281–2.

16 Therborn, 'The working class and the birth of Marxism', p. 9.

17 There are of course other features of Engels's book that we would want to consider in assessing the status assigned to it by the Marxist (and not only Marxist) tradition. There are the points of history and method indicated by W. O. Henderson and W. H. Chaloner in their introduction to their translation of the book (Oxford, Basil Blackwell, 1958), for example, that Engels quotes evidence from dates as widely scattered as 1801 and 1841 as illustrative of the same point. There is also the unsatisfactory way in which Engels builds up his picture of a developing class-conscious proletariat. Minor movements within (different sections of) the working class, isolated crimes against property reported in the daily newspapers, all are

used to paint a quite misleading picture of the development of a 'social war' of revolutionary proportions.

18 See D. Landes, *The Unbound Prometheus: Technological Change and Industrial Development in Western Europe from 1750 to the Present* (Cambridge, Cambridge University Press, 1969), pp. 118–21.

19 M. Dobb, *Studies in the Development of Capitalism*, rev. edn (London, Routledge and Kegan Paul, 1963), pp. 265–6.

20 From a large literature, see P. Amann, 'The changing outlines of 1848', *Journal of Modern History*, 68 (1963), no. 4. A similar tale can be told of the German working-class movements in the 1848 revolution. See T. Hamerow, *Germany: Restoration, Revolution, Reaction* (Princeton, NJ, Princeton University Press, 1966).

21 See D. J. Rowe, 'The London Working Men's Association and the "People's Charter"', *Past and Present*, no. 36 (April 1967), pp. 73–86.

22 This list is but a selection of groups, almost all of the same craft-like complexion, taken from the list of societies affiliated to the first International by 1867. See H. Collins and C. Abramsky, *Karl Marx and the British Labour Movement* (London, Macmillan, 1965), ch. 5, appendix 3, p. 81.

23 Ibid., p. 48.

24 G. A. Williams, *Artisans and Sans-Culottes* (London, Edward Arnold, 1968), p. 114. (Williams's emphases.)

25 V. Kiernan, 'Patterns of protest in English history', in R. Benewick and T. Smith (eds), *Direct Action and Democratic Politics* (London, Allen and Unwin, 1972), p. 33.

26 See, for example, M. Nicolaus, 'The unknown Marx', *New Left Review*, no. 48 (March-April 1968), pp. 41–61.

27 There is the further point that both Marx and Engels often wrote polemical articles and tracts for immediate tactical reasons, so that what they thought in general is not always easy to be sure about. For a comment arising out of a 40-year friendship, cf. this remark by George Harney, the veteran English Chartist, to Engels in a letter of 1892: 'You are the Prince of Optimists. You always see the Universal Revolution just coming round the corner. My sight is not so good, nor my hope so sanguine', quoted S. Marcus, *Engels, Manchester and the Working Class* (New York, Vintage Books, 1975), p. 89n.

28 B. Ollman, 'Toward class consciousness next time: Marx and the working class', *Politics and Society*, 3 (1972), p. 7.

29 This is assertion rather than argument, of course, but space (and time) forbids further elaboration here. For a good general discussion see V. R. Lorwin, 'Working class politics and economic development in Western Europe', *American Historical Review*, LXIII (1958), 338–51. For the later period, see the lively exchange of views in H. Mitchell and P. N. Stearns, *Workers and Protest: The European Labor Movement, The Working Classes and the Origins of Social Democracy 1890–1914* (Itasca, Ill., F. E. Peacock, 1971). For a survey of the English experience, see B. C. Roberts, 'On the origins and resolution of English working class protest', in H. D. Graham and T. R. Gurr (eds), *Violence in America: Historical and Comparative Perspectives* (Washington, DC, US Government Printing Office, 1969), pp. 197–220; and N. Young, 'Prometheans or Troglodytes? The English working class and the dialectics of incorporation', *Berkeley Journal of Sociology*, 12 (Summer 1967), 1–43.

I have briefly examined some instances of attempts at revolution in Europe in the twentieth century in the article referred to in note 5, above.

30 Ollman, 'Toward Class Consciousness', makes an interesting attempt to show what such an exercise would entail, at both the sociological and the psychological level. As he shows, the process so schematically alluded to by the Marxists is one of immense complexity, with no necessary logic at all to its sequence.

31 K. Marx, 'Contribution to the critique of Hegel's *Philosophy of Right*: Introduction', in T. B. Bottomore (trans. and ed.), *Karl Marx: Early Writings* (London, Watts and Co., 1963), p. 59. (Marx's emphases.)

32 See especially the chapter 'Working class movements' in *The Condition of the Working Class in England*.

33 For this sequence, see Marx and Engels, 'Manifesto of the Communist Party', pp. 41–3.

34 See, for example, T. B. Bottomore, *Classes in Modern Society* (London, Allen and Unwin, 1964), ch. 1. For a useful review of theories, see H. Wolpe, 'Some problems concerning revolutionary consciousness', in J. Saville and R. Miliband (eds), *The Socialist Register 1970* (London, The Merlin Press, 1970), pp. 251–80.

35 As borne out by most recent studies of factory workers – see, for example, Huw Beynon, *Working for Ford* (Harmondsworth, Penguin Books, 1973).

36 Engels, *Condition of the Working Class in England* (ed. Henderson and Chaloner), pp. 199–200. Suddenly realizing what he is saying, Engels tries to save the day: 'If in spite of all this the factory operatives have not only managed to save their reason but have actually developed their minds and sharpened their wits to a greater extent than any other class of worker, it is because they have been inspired by violent hatred against their fate and against the bourgeoisie. This and this alone fills the thoughts of the operatives when they are tending their machines.' But in the next sentence he goes on to pick up what is clearly the main thrust of his argument: 'And if they are workers who are not inspired to a fury of indignation against their oppressors, then they sink into drunkenness and all other forms of demoralising vice.' And cf. a similarly powerful passage in the same work (pp. 133–4), where Engels comments: 'It is obvious that a man must be degraded to the level of a beast if he is condemned to work of this kind.'

37 This occurs in *Chartism* (1839). In a later more splenetic vein, Carlyle saw the working class as characterized by 'blockheadism, gullibility, bribeability, amenability to beer and balderdash'. See *Shooting Niagara, and After* (1867).

38 A. Marshall, 'The future of the working classes' (1873), in A. C. Pigou (ed.), *Memorials of Alfred Marshall* (London, Macmillan, 1925), p. 105.

39 Westergaard and Resler, *Class in a Capitalist Society*, p. 105.

40 Quoted Young, 'Prometheans or Troglodytes?', p. 16.

41 Marx and Engels, *The German Ideology*, p. 58. And cf. the more important general point, that 'the separate individuals form a class only insofar as they have to carry on a common battle against another class; otherwise they are on hostile terms with each other as competitors', ibid., pp. 48–9. The first statement is, of course, the loaded one.

42 Cf. a characteristic statement of Marx's of the early period, that the proletariat is 'that misery conscious of its spiritual and physical misery, that dehumanization

conscious of its dehumanization and therefore self-abolishing' (*The Holy Family*, p. 52).

43 Cf. Engels's clarifying footnote of 1885 to a passage in Marx's *The Poverty of Philosophy*: 'Estates here in the historical sense of feudalism, estates with definite and limited privileges. The revolution of the bourgeoisie abolished the estates and their privileges. Bourgeois society knows only *classes*. It was, therefore, absolutely in contradiction with history to describe the proletariat as the "fourth estate" (*Poverty of Philosophy*, p. 174n). It is worth reminding ourselves that when Marx wrote, the classes *were* in much closer contact with each other than they have been since. Cities had not yet gone so far in residential segregation that housing could be seen as 'class on the ground'. Most working-class parents had a daughter, and possibly also a son, in domestic service in the houses of the middle class. Such intimate knowledge of each other's daily lives must have had quite profound effects on consciousness.

44 Marx and Engels, 'Manifesto of the Communist Party', p. 36.

45 For a discussion of reference groups within this context, see W. G. Runciman, *Relative Deprivation and Social Justice* (London, Routledge and Kegan Paul, 1966).

46 See F. Parkin, 'Working class Conservatives', *British Journal of Sociology*, 18 (1967), no. 3. Such a finding has been frequently reported by sociologists. See, for example, C. Kerr and A. Siegal, 'The inter-industry propensity to strike', in W. Kornhauser (ed.), *Industrial Conflict* (New York, McGraw-Hill, 1954).

47 Parkin, *Class Inequality and Political Order*, ch. 3, esp. p. 90.

48 I am not concerned here to argue whether or not Marx was right in his account, simply to show what he derived from it in his conception of the future proletarian revolution. For some stimulating essays on the whole problem, see M. Dobb, *Development of Capitalism*; R. Hilton (ed.), *The Transition from Feudalism to Capitalism* (London, New Left Books, 1976); E. Kamenka and R. S. Neale (eds), *Feudalism, Capitalism, and Beyond* (London, Edward Arnold, 1975).

49 R. S. Neale, 'Property, law, and the transition from feudalism to capitalism', in Kamenka and Neale (eds), *Feudalism, Capitalism and Beyond*, p. 18.

50 Marx, *Grundrisse*, trans. M. Nicolaus (London, Allen Lane, 1973), p. 479.

51 Marx in most of his writings seems to have regarded that breakthrough as necessary for the development of capitalism; as he saw it, any innovatory tendency in feudalism tended to be negated after a time, and be re-absorbed in the old order. For an interesting attempt to see the rise of capitalism as a matter of 'endogenous' growth within feudalism, through *agrarian* capitalism, see Dobb, *Development of Capitalism*.

52 T. B. Bottomore, 'The ideas of the Founding Fathers', *European Journal of Sociology*, I (1960), 45. And cf. a similar point made by R. Aron, *Main Currents in Sociological Thought*, vol. I (Harmondsworth, Penguin Books, 1968), pp. 167–8.

BIBLIOGRAPHICAL NOTE

Nearly all of the many studies of Marxism published in the past decade or so deal at least in passing with the questions raised in this chapter. But there have been few systematic treatments. Among the most useful are: Tom Bottomore, *Marxist Sociology*

(London, Macmillan, 1975); and Bottomore, *Sociology and Socialism* (Brighton, Wheatsheaf Books, 1984); Henri Lefebvre, *The Survival of Capitalism* (London, Allison and Busby, 1976); Robin Blackburn (ed.), *Revolution and Class Struggle: A Reader in Marxist Politics* (London, Fontana/Collins, 1977), Sidney Hook, *Revolution, Reform and Social Justice: Studies in the Theory and Practice of Marxism* (Oxford, Basil Blackwell, 1976); Hal Draper, *Karl Marx's Theory of Revolution*, vol. II: *The Politics of Social Classes* (New York and London, Monthly Review Press, 1978); R. Jacoby 'Political economy and class unconsciousness', *Theory and Society*, 5 (1978), 11–18; R. E. Lane, 'Waiting for Lefty: the capitalist genesis of socialist man', *Theory and Society*, 6 (1978), 1–28; Frank Parkin, *Marxism and Class Theory: A Bourgeois Critique* (London, Tavistock Publications, 1979). There are some interesting suggestions in Anthony Giddens, *Studies in Social and Political Theory* (London, Hutchinson, 1977).

Specifically on Marxist notions of working-class consciousness and action there are: T. McCarthy, *Marx and the Proletariat: A Study in Social Theory* (Westport, Conn., Greenwood Press, 1978); S. M. Lipset, 'Whatever happened to the proletariat?', *Encounter*, 56 (June 1981), pp. 18–34; G. Marshall, 'Some remarks on the study of working-class consciousness', *Politics and Society*, 12 (1983), 263–301; Adam Przeworski, *Capitalism and Social Democracy* (Cambridge, Cambridge University Press, 1985), esp. ch. 2; Adam Przeworski and J. Sprague, *Paper Stones: A History of Electoral Socialism* (Chicago, Chicago University Press, 1986). There are some relevant thoughts in John Clarke, Chas Critcher and Richard Johnson (eds), *Working Class Culture: Studies in History and Theory* (London, Hutchinson, 1979), Anthony Giddens, *The Class Structure of the Advanced Societies*, 2nd edn (London, Hutchinson, 1981) and Zygmunt Bauman, *Memories of Class: The Pre-history and After-life of Class* (London, Routledge and Kegan Paul, 1982). See also Barrington Moore jnr, *Authority and Inequality under Capitalism and Socialism* (Oxford, Clarendon Press, 1987).

Of the more general works on Marx and Marxism, the following contain helpful discussions of the putative role of the working class: Perry Anderson, *Considerations on Western Marxism* (London, New Left Books, 1976); G. A. Cohen, *Karl Marx's Theory of History: A Defense* (Princeton, NJ, Princeton University Press, 1978); Leszek Kolakowski, *Main Currents of Marxism* (3 vols, Oxford, Oxford University Press, 1978); Jon Elster, *Making Sense of Marx* (Cambridge, Cambridge University Press, 1985). On problems concerned with the bourgeoisie and the rise of capitalism see R. J. Holton, *The Transition from Feudalism to Capitalism* (London, Macmillan, 1985) and Randall Collins, *Weberian Sociological Theory* (Cambridge, Cambridge University Press, 1986), part 1.

See also the notes and additional bibliographies to chapters 5 and 6 in this volume: 'The limits and capacities of industrial capitalism' and 'Class and political action in nineteenth-century England'.

9

The Social Culture of Work: Work, Employment and Unemployment as Ways of Life

As soon as we begin to look at this, we see how curiously limited is the vision of human excellence that has got built into our society, and that we have made do with up to now. It is a vision that is inextricably bound up with the market society. And the sad truth is that it is a vision of inertia. It is almost incredible, until you come to think of it, that a society whose keyword is *enterprise*, which certainly sounds active, is in fact based on the assumption that human beings are so inert, so averse to activity, that is, to expenditure of energy, that every expenditure of energy is considered to be painful, to be, in the economist's term, a disutility. This assumption, which is a travesty of the human condition, is built right into the justifying theory of the market society, and so of the liberal society. The market society, and so the liberal society, is commonly justified on the grounds that it maximizes utilities, i.e. that it is the arrangement by which people can get the satisfaction they want with the least effort. The notion that activity itself is pleasurable, is a utility, has sunk almost without trace under this utilitarian vision of life.

C. B. Macpherson, *The Real World of Democracy*

Writing in the *Guardian* of the plight of three unemployed teenage 'punks', Jill Tweedie commented: 'For the first time in history, we have created a society that has given every one of its members aspirations towards individuality and yet is slowly withdrawing the major method whereby such individuality can be expressed – work.' The concern is impeccable; and yet we stir uneasily. The equation between a person's work and his individuality is being made too directly. Certainly it is a conventional one. 'Who am I?' has so often in recent Western society been answered by another question, 'What do I do?'. A man's work was his being. But here, too, an equation of another sort is made. 'Work' equals 'job'. Identity and occupation are seen to go together – an association carried to absurd lengths in Huxley's *Brave New World*, where embryos destined to be rocket maintenance men are decanted upside down:

'They learn to associate topsyturvydom with well-being; in fact, they're only truly happy when they're standing on their heads.' The sets of equations – work: job: identity: individuality – begin to take on alarming features.

The confusions are readily understandable. Work is a social institution; and, like all such institutions, it has a history. How it has seemed to people at one time is not how it seems at another. Once a curse – 'in the sweat of thy brow shalt thou eat bread' – it could come to seem a blessing – 'laborare est orare' – and then again an affliction, 'shunned like the plague'. Nor were these judgements necessarily shared by all the people at any given time. Where work was fulfilment to one man or group it could be seen as defilement to another man or group. As far as work is concerned, the saying 'one man's meat is another man's poison' can carry the sense, not of the relativity of tastes and values, but of the brute fact of exploitation. Work has, in other words, not merely a history but an ideology.

The question is, where do we now stand? What has work come to mean? What is the nature of the connection between work and employment? How far should we be trying to find employment for people, rather than seeking to help them to work? What is now implied by the phrase, 'the necessity of work'? What work, how much and by whom? These are properly questions for a series of essays, not just one. Here I simply want to map out the background to these questions, to suggest the historical and ideological premises that so often lurk unexamined behind them.

I

All societies accept the necessity of work in order to survive. For most societies, for most of the time, work is simply a fact of existence which they must accommodate to. There are always some people who, as rulers, warriors and priests, escape the more burdensome kinds of work by persuading or forcing others to do it for them. Most societies, too, contain collective fantasies of the Garden of Eden or Land of Cockaigne type, where food and comforts abound without the need to work. And there are even some societies, of the hunting and gathering type, where, as Sahlins has shown, economic life is so simple and needs so undeveloped that their members have a degree of 'leisure' unheard of until the era of 'the affluent society' of the West.[1]

But it makes little sense in the case of most of these societies – pre-industrial or non-industrial – to ask our typically modern questions about work, leisure, identity and the like. Such questions presuppose a separation of spheres which does not exist. The life of work, play, family, religion and community forms a continuous or overlapping set of activities, no more to be divided up than the separate cells of a piece of living tissue. This does not mean of course that people work all the time, any more than it means that they play, or pray, all the time. The categories collapse and convert into one another in an almost infinitely flexible way. The Dogons of the Sudan, Keith Thomas tells us, employ the same words to indicate both cultivating the ground and dancing at a religious ceremony, for to them both are equally useful, and equally prayerful, forms of activity. A terracotta from Thebes shows four women rolling dough into loaves to the sound of the flute. Recreational activities flow out of economic needs: horse racing (according to a twelfth-century account) developed out of the practice of allowing the animals at Smithfield market to show their paces in a sort of primitive selling-plate. Or out of kinship and community relations: in friendly form, as with the convivial wakes and ales, or in ferocious competition, as with the bloodthirsty football matches between rival villages in pre-industrial England.[2]

Just as 'leisure' comes out of work, so work itself is heavily impregnated with needs and obligations of a ritual, religious and recreational kind. The clearest example of this is the medieval European guild. 'The model craft guild,' writes Thomas, 'maintaining standards and a sense of professional pride, permitting all to work their way up from apprentice to master, allowing masters and journeymen to work side by side, invoking the comforting patronage of a saint, helping the poor and sick among its members, and combining economic functions with religious and convivial ones, must have produced a very different attitude to work from that to be found today in a large factory or steel works.'[3] Work, moreover, is regulated by the task, with its characteristically irregular rhythms in which labour and leisure are intermingled. 'The working-day lengthens or contracts according to the task – and there is no great sense of conflict between labour and "passing the time of day".'[4] The irregular pattern imposed by the task is heightened by the irregularity of the working week, and the working year. People work for as long as is needed to meet traditionally defined needs, and no more. Many an English artisan honoured 'Saint Monday', and showed a pious disposition to give due homage to 'Saint Tuesday' as well. 'The work pattern was one of alternate bouts of intense labour and of idleness, wherever men were in control of their own working lives.'[5] A standard argument against raising the wages of workers in eighteenth-century England was indeed that they would thereby work less. Their needs being satisfied by less work, they would prefer more leisure to more pay. The priorities still occasionally show themselves among more traditional workers today. A time-hallowed set of values supported the chronic absentee mineworker who, pressed as to why he seemed able to manage only four shifts, replied 'because I can't live on three'.

Given the confusion or conflation of categories, it is neither easy nor particularly profitable to work out how much 'leisure time' is enjoyed by the populations of non-industrial societies. But for at least one reason such an exercise is important. Industrial peoples harbour profound prejudices and illusions about non-industrial peoples, one especially potent one being that they are all bowed down by a lifetime of unremitting toil. What studies there are suggest a quite different picture. Sahlins calculates that the workday of the Australian Aborigines – the time spent in subsistence activities – is about four to five hours of intermittent and not very demanding labour. An even lower figure is arrived at for the South African Bushmen. 'Hunters,' says Sahlins, 'keep banker's hours, notably less than modern industrial workers (unionized), who would surely settle for a 21–35 hour week.'[6] The ancient Romans, following what one student has called 'man's ineradicable tendency to convert his fast days into feast-days', so piled up festival days that it is estimated that in the middle of the fourth century AD Roman citizens had 175 days a year off.[7] For the European Middle Ages, contemporary evidence suggests that agricultural workers spent nearly a third of the year in leisure, while Paris craftsmen, for instance, worked for only about 194 days in the year   that is, nearly half the year was leisure time.[8]

Such figures are not of course to be taken too literally. But they do at least do something towards putting our present position in the industrial societies in perspective. What they suggest in fact, and what is borne out by all else we know about the nature of work in non-industrial societies, is that the coming of industrialism marks a clear watershed in the history and ideology of work. One superficial but still quite telling indication of this lies in the fact that the hours of work actually go up, sometimes startlingly, for the populations of the industrial societies, at least in the early stages. Factory workers in nineteenth-century Europe worked a seventy- and even eighty-hour week. It took a hundred years for them to return to the working hours roughly equivalent to that of the guildsmen who were their medieval forbears. But far more important than these quantitative measurements is the transformation in the very concept and meaning of work brought about by industrialization.

II

The Greeks, we know, had a low opinion of work in the conventional sense. 'A state with an ideal constitution,' wrote Aristotle in the *Politics* (1328b), 'cannot have its citizens living the life of mechanics or shopkeepers, which is ignoble and inimical to goodness. Nor can it have them engaged in farming: leisure is a necessity, both for growth in goodness and for the pursuit of political activities.' It is a mistake, however, to think that the contempt for work was a contempt for manual or bodily labour as such. Physical and manual effort was frequently extolled in the case of both athletes and artists. It was not work *per se* that was degrading but, as Aristotle's remarks suggest, the status of being a *worker*. Being a worker meant having to work for one's living, hence being tied, like an animal, to necessity. Greek thought was consistent throughout in the view that the labour of one's body which is necessitated by its needs is slavish. Hence occupations which did not actually consist in labouring, yet were undertaken not for their own sake but in order to provide the necessities of life, were assimilated to the status of labour.[9] By the same token, the free citizen who had the leisure to devote himself to the truly human pursuit of politics or (later) philosophy, was allowed and indeed encouraged to practise manual skills. The important distinction was always that between work performed as a matter of animal need or necessity, and work freely chosen and executed, the only human way of work.[10]

This attitude partly explains the institution of slavery, and the justification of it, at least in Greek eyes. As Hannah Arendt has argued:

The opinion that labour and work were despised in antiquity because only slaves were engaged in them is a prejudice of modern historians. The ancients reasoned the other way around and felt it necessary to possess slaves because of the slavish nature of all occupations that served the need for the maintenance of life ... The institution of slavery in antiquity, though not in later times, was not a device for cheap labour or an instrument of exploitation for profit but rather the attempt to exclude labour from the conditions of man's life. What men shared with all other forms of animal life was not considered to be human.[11]

But of course needs, such as for shelter and subsistence, which man did inescapably share with other animals, had to be met; and these needs were supplied by the labour of slaves, free artisans and foreigners. Hence in practice, if not in principle, a fundamental wedge was driven between the 'leisured classes', those who did not work for a living, and all those who, however wealthy they became, continued to follow an occupation in the world of work. Freedom, defined as an escape from the sphere of necessity (labour), came to be seen as an aristocratic prerogative. This has been a tradition, corrupted into a prejudice, of extraordinary strength and resilience. It survived both the Roman and the medieval eras. It is to be found, alive and vigorous, among the eighteenth-century Whig aristocracy (not least, no doubt, at Wentworth Woodhouse), as well as among the nineteenth-century planter aristocracy of the southern states of America; and there are many signs of its persistence today.[12] In a peculiarly ironic twist, there was even the invention of the term 'the aristocracy of labour' (in its pre-industrial, not the bastardized nineteenth-century form) to describe those workers who possessed in the world of work a faint echo of the attributes of the 'man of independent means': being their own boss, having their own tools, setting their own pattern and times of work, and so on.

Christianity modified this classical, aristocratic tradition; but in ways which for a long time devalued work even further, making it partake even less of the good life than it had in the eyes of the ancient philosophers. There were, however, contradictory pressures within the Christian attitude to work. In what one might regard as the 'optimistic' strain, there was the view of man's work as a human mimesis of the original act of divine creation. This was a view that gained particular prominence among Renaissance humanists: man as 'the second just creator after Jove', the Prometheus who stole the creative fire from the Gods. As an important subsidiary theme within the optimistic tradition, there was the popular emphasis on the human life of Christ, the humble carpenter who gathered to himself equally humble workers and continued an active life in the world, countering the influences of the rich and powerful. In the right circumstances, such a popular tradition could explode with revolutionary force in peasant rebellions and millenarian movements, with their hopes and demands of a communistic, egalitarian society in which the claims and organization of work were central.

But even within the 'optimistic' tradition there were ambiguities. Christ the carpenter, after all, downed tools in favour of his mission, and drew his disciples away from their crafts. The non-worldly or other-worldly strand in Christianity – what John Passmore has seen as the Augustinian as opposed to the this-worldly Pelagian emphasis[13] – repeatedly came out as the dominant ideological force. It appealed not simply to the mystics, but to the orthodox theologians and the Church Establishment, the more so as it seemed to continue the classical, Platonic tradition. With the decline of the city-state and the rise of the 'cosmopolis', Plato's followers increasingly rejected the older idea of politics as the highest activity of free men. Politics was now also relegated, along with work, to the mundane world of the *vita activa*; the ideal life was the *vita contemplativa*, the life of philosophic contemplation of the 'real forms' that lay behind worldly appearances. Such an approach squared well with the temperament and intellectual outlook of some of the best minds in the Christian world. In the theology of Aquinas, strongly influenced by Aristotle, work is indeed rescued from the contempt in which the Greeks held it. But only, as it were, to be damned even more completely as an activity of the incorrigibly lesser realm of the human world, as compared with the divine order. As an end in itself, Aquinas would have regarded it with even greater incomprehension than the Greeks. At best, work can be a helpful discipline in preparing the individual for a fit state of religious piety. P. D. Anthony thus sums up the orthodox position:

The worker might contribute to the mutal exchange of services for the sake of the good life, but the good life was the end and it was not to be measured in ergonomic or economic terms. The church developed a new doctrine of the importance of work but strictly as an instrument of spiritual purpose. The Benedictine rule emphasised the spiritual danger of idleness and ordered regular work at fixed times of the day in order to reduce it. The church also recommended labour as a penance on good scriptural authority emanating from man's fall. Work was a discipline, it contributed to the Christian virtue of obedience. It was not seen as noble, or rewarding, or satisfying, its very endlessness and tedium were spiritually valuable in that it contributed to Christian resignation.[14]

Protestantism cut across both the 'optimistic' and the 'pessimistic' strands within the Christian attitude to work, and prepared the way for the distinctly modern conception. The legacy of work as a curse put upon Adam and his seed persisted: work was not seen as fulfilment, it was a relentless, joyless activity performed in the spirit of asceticism. But the truly radical innovation was the elevation of the place of work in the life of the individual, and of society. Protestantism broke down the barrier between everyday life and spiritual life, between the monastery and the marketplace. To work diligently and soberly in one's 'calling' became a central requirement of the Protestant way of life. It was a spiritual duty, an expression of one's faith and piety far surpassing any good works that might be performed in an eleemosynary spirit. With the Calvinist doctrine of a predestined elect, work took on even greater urgency. As Max Weber argued, success in worldly life became the sign of election in a world where no action of a conventionally religious kind could be the means of salvation. The psychological need to know whether one was chosen was transformed into an intense, almost neurotic, striving for recognition in the world of men, for such attainment might at least be the outward manifestation of inward grace.

Whether as cause or effect it does not matter here; but at the same time, and in the same places, as Protestantism was giving to work a uniquely spiritualized status, labour was increasingly being discovered as the fundamental factor of production, and a unique source of value. Between the sixteenth and the eighteenth centuries, *Homo rationalis*, the model for pretty well all speculation on the human condition up till then, began to give way to *Homo laborans*. The speed of this historic shift, as well as its momentousness, still seems insufficiently appreciated. In a complete reversal of the traditional ordering, in which man's rational capacity was seen as the faculty that raised him above the beasts, there developed a naturalist conception in which man was defined precisely by the capacity that linked him to the rest of nature, the capacity to labour.[15] The Industrial Revolution was bound to enhance that conception. The fantastic and unprecedented productivity of man linked to machines beggared any other description of him save as producer. Such a description we find pre-eminently in Marx, in whose system labour appears not simply as the source of all productivity but as the expression of the very humanity of man, his 'species-being'.

With industrialism, work is placed at the centre not just of man, but of history. Work is the means by which man makes himself. It is also the means by which he constructs his whole world. Starting with Rousseau's celebration of the craftsman in *Émile*, there develops a tradition of thinking about work in which work is treated with an almost metaphysical pathos and intensity. Work, quite simply, as a philosophy and an activity, becomes a secular religion. No longer, as in the Protestant ethic, does religion sanctify work. Work now sanctifies religion. The claims for work grow in scope and urgency as the nineteenth century progresses, in the writings especially of Schiller, Hegel, Saint-Simon, Fourier, Marx, Tolstoy and Zola. In Ruskin and Morris they reach a culminating point. In the case of Morris in particular one has the feeling that to be deprived of work – fit work – is to be deprived of a soul, to be left in a dark void.[16] It is in this tradition that we get most of our modern humanist definitions of work as 'the first moral category', as Roger Garaudy has stated it. Here, typically, is David Meakin: 'Work – and not least manual work – is an integral part of our humanity and our intelligence. It dictates not only our relationship to nature, to our environment, but thereby also the working and scope of our consciousness itself, for consciousness is born of that active confrontation with nature.'[17] Or Tom Kitwood: 'In a fundamental sense, work may be regarded as the exercise of a person's powers in the constructive transformation of the world: an expression of individuality, an enhancement of the sense of being alive, and the most powerful of social bonds beyond the family.'[18]

The shift to industrialism produced a further emphasis, and a further equation. Not only was a man's being to be defined by his work, but his work was now also increasingly defined and determined by his *job*, his occupation in the formal money economy. The industrial revolution methodically undermined the older system whereby work, family, and leisure life were all of a piece, performed as an undifferentiated whole. Technical changes, together with other such changes as urbanization, took work out of the home and into a specialized setting, the factory (and somewhat later, the office). To be 'at work' was henceforward to be 'in work', to be employed as a 'worker' in the formal economy. This had the unexpected effect of enhancing the status of work even further. For work-as-job was now linked firmly to the economy; and the industrial revolution, for the first time in history, made the economic realm supreme. It was the sphere of activity which was both the central dynamic of the society and the source of its central values. The industrial economy was 'the unbound Prometheus', and all roles and activities linked to it shared in its glory, just as those which didn't, such as that of the priest, shrank in status and significance. Hence the final equation of work with job, following upon that of work with identity, doubly underscored the importance of work. The question, 'Who am I?', which would formally have been answered almost everywhere in terms of religion, family, or place of origin, could now really be answered only in terms of the occupation a man worked in.

III

But here is the paradox. The celebration, the idolization almost, of work, proceeds against a background of its imminent redundancy. As Meakin says, 'looking back from our vantage point, it seems ironic that the industrial revolution leads to a conscious realization of the ethical value of work in all its fullness – and especially those qualities enshrined in the artisanate – at the very moment when those same values are seriously threatened and perhaps doomed by the advent of machino-facture.'[19] It is important to stress that this is not simply an aspect of our own contemporary predicament.[20] The challenge to the ethic of work was implicit in the very phenomenon, industrialism, which provoked the most passionate advocacy of that ethic. From the very start industrialization aimed at eliminating the human factor in production altogether. Eric Hobsbawm notes that, 'the original cotton factory already strove after the ideal of becoming a gigantic, complex and "self-acting" (as it was then called) automaton, and each technical innovation brought it a little closer towards this object.'[21] And where machines did not (yet) actually displace labour, the goal of the early industrialists was to make that labour as routine and machine-like as possible. The main difficulty of the early factory system identified by Andrew Ure in his *Philosophy of Manufactures* (1835), was 'in training human beings to renounce their desultory habits of work, and to identify themselves with the unvarying regularity of the complex automaton'. The more skilled the worker, the more intractable to discipline. The solution must be to organize and mechanize work in such a way as to withdraw any process which required 'peculiar dexterity and steadiness of hand ... from the cunning workman', and to place it in charge of 'a mechanism, so self-regulating, that a child may superintend it ... The grand object therefore of the modern manufacturer is, through the union of capital and science, to reduce the task of his work-people to the exercise of vigilance and dexterity – faculties speedily brought to perfection in the young.' Or, as Josiah Wedgwood more pithily put it, the ideal was 'to make such machines of the men as cannot err'.[22]

The dilemma of the philosophers of work is clear. Objectively, the Industrial

Revolution provided the most eloquent testimony to the truth of the conception of man as worker, or producer. At the same time, in practice it threatened to reduce man's work to a nullity. As industrialism progressed, it ruthlessly undermined the need for all skill and creativity on the part of the worker. It reduced him first to a part of the machine, then, having thus simplified his task to a mechanical routine, eliminated him altogether by a further bout of mechanization. There was thus an inverse relationship between the capacity of the system to provide creative and satisfying work, and the increasingly agonized assertions of the value and need of such work – or even work as such – as the essential basis of all truly human activity. Various strategies were adopted to fend off reality. There were attempts to set up cooperative and communal ventures, usually on a pre-industrial scale and with pre-industrial technology. Nearly all failed.[23] The vanishing world of the medieval craftsman was, in suitably idealized terms, resurrected as the standard of all work, and attempts were made to fuse industrial technology with craft practice. There was, it was recognized, not just *Homo laborans*, but more importantly *Homo faber*. All European languages, it could be shown, had continued to reflect a critical Latin distinction between *laborare* and *facere* (or *fabricari*), between mere 'labour' or 'toil', and true 'work'. For the Germans there was *Arbeit* versus *Werk*, for the French *oeuvre* as against *travail*. In a desperate stand, Ruskin pedantically proposed that we should distinguish between '*opera*' and '*labor*', between joyful, creative work and negative work, 'that quantity of our toil which we die in'. All these efforts, in theory and practice, were of little avail against the increasing tendency of industrial society to reserve interesting work for the diminishing few, and tedious toil for the many.

The circle was squared, temporarily, by Utilitarianism. In a watered-down version of Protestantism, it accepted that industrial work was an intrinsically unrewarding, burdensome necessity. But the alienated character of work was compensated for by high wages, and by increasing periods of 'free time'. In the Benthamite 'felicific calculus', the individual trades off the pain of work against the pleasure of leisure. He accepts the 'homelessness' of the sphere of work as the necessary and acceptable price of his being more truly 'himself' in his non-work sphere. As Peter Berger expresses it:

The typical and statistically normal state of affairs in an industrial society is that people do not work where they carry on their private lives. The two spheres are socially and geographically separate. And since it is in the latter that people typically and normally locate their essential activities, one can say even more simply that they do not live where they work. 'Real life' and one's 'authentic self' are supposed to be centred in the private sphere. Life at work then tends to take on the character of pseudo-reality and pseudo-identity.[24]

But the Utilitarian contract turns out to be fraudulent, in at least two ways. There is firstly the fact that we cannot, in practice, so neatly maintain the separation of 'work' and 'leisure'. Long hours of passive employment at work seem to breed long hours of passive employment in leisure. Dull, monotonous and repetitive work – the normal character of most jobs in industrial society – seems to dampen the capacity for active and enjoyable leisure. Alasdair

Clayre, who notes these findings, rightly comments that 'if nothing can repay a man in leisure for the capacities of enjoyment that depriving work has destroyed, then monotonous work is paid for in a coinage which work itself debases, and the entire notion of a fair wage-bargain for depriving work becomes suspect.'[25]

But even if leisure can in some sense be held separate from work, how far can it be considered genuinely 'free time', that is, time in which the individual re-composes himself, and establishes a significant identity denied him by the standardizing routines of work? The fact is that during the nineteenth century the sphere of leisure was as much 'industrialized' as that of work. As a concept, 'leisure' is indeed an invention of nineteenth-century industrial society, a part of that fragmentation and specialization that was an inherent principle of the industrial way of life. Right from the start, therefore, it carried the hall-mark of industrialism. It was organized, regulated, packaged and sold like any other commodity on the market. As Briggs comments, 'the old adage, well known to the nineteenth century pioneering retailers, that the luxuries of today become the necessities of tomorrow, had obvious implications in the world of *Homo ludens*.'[26] Burns notes that 'the new leisure of the working classes represented a vacuum which was largely filled, even to begin with, by amusement industries.' Drinking, racing, football and boxing were reconstituted and heavily capitalized, to be transformed into mass entertainment industries. The spare-time reading habits of the new urban classes were equally well taken care of by the new popular press. Leisure might in a subjective sense be seen as 'time off' work. But in a deeper sense it was part and parcel of the same system that also included work, and the determining pressures were to be seen equally in both spheres. Later, you might very well be employed as a worker by the same corporation that provided your daily paper and saw you safely across the Channel on your packaged holiday. Burns well makes the point that 'the swamping of everyday life by industrialism has not been succeeded by a mere ebbing, or forcing back, of the flood [i.e. in the form of leisure time won]. Social life outside the work situation has not re-emerged; it has been created afresh, in forms which are themselves the creatures of industrialism, which derive from it and which contribute to its development, growth and further articulation.'[27]

IV

All these dilemmas of nineteenth-century work and leisure are clearly still with us. The currents of industrialism have continued to flow strongly, and to deepen their course. No longer only manual work, but also white-collar and professional work have been subjected to the industrial processes of mechanization and 'rationalization', in the Weberian and Taylorian sense. Higher educational qualifications are demanded for work that is itself increasingly less demanding, in terms of skill, responsibility and the exercise of autonomy. As dependent employees of large-scale bureaucracies, more and more hitherto autonomous professionals find themselves well-paid but relatively impotent actors in an economic and political environment that includes powerful unions and even more powerful multinational elites.[28]

The consequences of all this are equally evident. Work is being questioned on a scale unthinkable to an earlier generation. When at the end of the last century Marx's son-in-law Paul Lafargue produced an attack on the ethic of work entitled *The Right to be Lazy*, he offended both his Marxist friends and his bourgeois critics. Nietzsche's 'Do I work in order to live? No, I live in order to work', was by far the more typical and conventional attitude, as was Freud's response 'love and work' to the question of what were the healthiest activities of the normal balanced person. But today, it is not middle-class drop-outs from the counter-culture but two hard-headed trade unionists, Clive Jenkins and Barrie Sherman, who announce 'the collapse of work', and roundly dismiss the whole ethic of work as bourgeois indoctrination:

We do not believe that work *per se* is necessary to human survival or self-esteem. The fact that it appears to be so is a function of two centuries of propaganda and an educational system which maintained the 'idea' of work as its main objective, but which singularly failed to teach about leisure and how to use it . . . People at present accept that they will be bored if out of work, and so become bored; they believe they will drift, and they drift; they believe that by not working they will become useless, and too many become useless. This need for work is, we would argue, an ingrained and inculcated attitude of mind.[29]

It is not simply of course that people now demand, as a belated counter to the obsession with work, an equal attention to leisure, as an activity with its own valid claims on public policy, and the public purse. These demands have in any case been voiced regularly since at least the 1930s, when 'the leisure society' was first anxiously discerned and discussed. The concern now springs more seriously from the perception that the mounting dissatisfaction with work itself seems to be reaching a critical point. Work in the future – if it has any at all – appears to hold out an unending prospect of alienated and irresponsible activity, a desert of meaningless and trivial tasks in factory, shop and office. What work there is left after the widespread application of microelectronic technology would seem to require of most of us no more than the elementary skills of a junior typist.[30] Such a prospect not surprisingly has begun to keep a few people awake at nights.

In one of the most thoughtful reviews of the problem, two Canadian researchers, Gail Stewart and Cathy Starrs, suggest that our dissatisfaction with work currently reveals itself as a basic anxiety and uncertainty about where we should draw the line between work and non-work:

For the most part the 'line of turbulence' between the old work ethic and an emerging and different work ethic seems to lie within us rather than between us. We may be disturbed or frustrated or alienated or confused as, in one situation after another, it becomes clearer to us that there are different ethical criteria we can apply with respect to work, and that the answers are not so clear-cut as they used to be. Whether it is a son's career plans or perhaps an absence of them; our own early retirement; the legitimacy of using office-time to do community work; the methods we have used to settle competition for positions or for university entrance; the wondering at night at what has really been accomplished during the day, even though mountains of paper may have been processed – all of these may create a turbulence within us that is the surest sign of emerging new concepts of work. Much of this turbulence is not yet visible in public forms but it is readily elicited in personal conversation. While it takes many forms the common theme is a questioning of the old work ethic and the struggle to find a new mode of working which is perceived as both personally and socially productive.[31]

These thoughts take us into the heart of the immediate issue, the relation between 'work' and 'employment'. For the questioning of the ethic of work is not simply negative. It appears that one way out of the dilemma of alienated work and alienated leisure is to re-define, or re-conceptualize, both 'work' and 'leisure', such that any activity which is personally fulfilling and 'socially productive' can be regarded as work – even if, and in current conditions perhaps especially if, it is performed outside the confines of a 'job' in the formal work economy. Given the expected and enforced increase in 'leisure time', leisure (or unemployment) could be converted from a threat into a promise. It could become the sphere of satisfying and useful activity of the kind idealized by the philosophers of work, and now denied precisely 'at work'.

This has many attractions, and has had a good number of advocates. The French sociologist George Friedmann, for instance, foresaw 'in the society of the future, the flowering of a "new man" of the artisan type, devoted to the patient and creative fashioning of materials with the aid of manual tools, a new *Homo faber* resurrected by leisure.'[32] Stewart and Starrs similarly suggest that 'work' can be and is frequently found elsewhere than in the job economy. It's all a matter of what we choose to call work:

What is a job? What does it mean to be employed, to be working? Fundamentally it is to find, reflected back to you in the eyes of other people, that they think that what you are doing is worthwhile. It probably helps if you are being paid for what you are doing, and it probably helps if what you are doing is something that most people would regard as an unpleasant activity, something they wouldn't want to have to do themselves, and something that you yourself probably wouldn't do voluntarily. And it probably helps if it is a visibly exhausting activity with a visible output. But none of these is essential. What constitutes work is decided by social contract, by social agreement. We construct our social agreements – it is we who decide what constitutes work. Work is what we decide it is ... Until very recently we bestowed the legitimacy of 'work' on only a very narrow range of our human activities, carried out in particular times and places ... 'Do you work or are you just a housewife?'[33]

Everyone can see the immediate sense of this. The amount of work to be done is and always will remain infinite: in making, maintaining and re-making ourselves, our families, our homes, our environment, our world. The statistics of employment and unemployment are quite irrelevant to this. It is well known how even in the conventional world of employment, a job can properly be done only if the worker goes, as it were, beyond the formal description of the job, putting into it his own 'informal' resources of intelligence and

238 Politics, Work and Society

creativity. Look what happens when people 'work to rule'. The chaos that results is a measure of the tenuousness of the distinction between work and non-work even in the formal economy.

The anxieties about this position are of a different kind, and are by no means trivial or philistine (there are many of *those*, but not worth the time). Some arise out of a concern for what is lost when the tie between work – conceived as free activity – and employment – conceived as a realm of necessity – is broken. There is a particularly interesting religious tradition here that views this disconnection with grave alarm. The artist Eric Gill constantly inveighed against 'the Leisure State', with its notion 'that matter is essentially evil and therefore work essentially degrading ... Culture, if it is to be a real thing and a holy thing, must be the product of what we actually do for a living – not something added, like sugar on a pill.'[34] The supreme exponent of this tradition is probably Simone Weil, who viewed man's entire being as formed through an 'encounter with necessity' through work: a necessity which he can never in the end escape, and which it is dangerous for him ever to lose sight of. Weil was particularly concerned that, if the increased productivity achieved through automation made men feel free of material needs, they would come to inhabit an illusory world of freedom, the prey of arbitrary fantasies. I quote the passage from *Oppression and Liberty* at length because it seems to me particularly fine:

We have only to bear in mind the weakness of human nature to understand that an existence from which the very notion of work had pretty well disappeared would be delivered over to the play of the passions and perhaps to madness; there is no self-mastery without discipline, and there is no other source of discipline for man than the effort demanded in overcoming external obstacles. A nation of idlers might well amuse itself by giving itself obstacles to overcome, exercise itself in the sciences, in the arts, in games; but the efforts that are the result of pure whim do not form for a man a means of controlling his own whims. It is the obstacles we encounter and that have to be overcome which give us the opportunity for self-conquest. Even the apparently freest forms of activity, science, art, sport, only possess value in so far as they imitate the accuracy, rigour, scrupulousness which characterise the performance of work, and even exaggerate them. Were it not for the model offered them unconsciously by the ploughman, the blacksmith, the sailor who work *comme il faut* – to use that admirably ambiguous expression – they would sink into the purely arbitrary. The only liberty that can be attributed to the Golden Age is that which little children would enjoy if parents did not impose rules on them; it is in reality only an unconditional surrender to caprice. The human body can in no case cease to depend on the mighty universe in which it is encased; even if man were to cease being subjected to material things and to his fellows by needs and dangers, he would only be more completely delivered into their hands by the emotions which would stir him continually to the depths of his soul, and against which no regular occupation would any longer protect him.[35]

Something of the same force, and even of the same criticism, can be seen in Hannah Arendt's objections to Marx's vision of the future society. Marx, it will be remembered, looked forward to a communist society in which abundance was such that material needs, the 'realm of necessity', were totally satisfied. Men would exist primarily in and for the 'realm of freedom', which 'begins ... where that labour which is determined by need and external purposes ceases'. It is a realm, Marx says, in which there takes place 'the development of human potentiality for its own sake'. He goes on: 'The shortening of the working day is its fundamental prerequisite' (*Capital*, vol. III).

If freedom is to consist in an end to labour, what will men actually do in the future society? Marx makes some notoriously vague remarks about hunting and fishing, but it is in fact fairly clear that what he had in mind was largely what most people would call 'leisure activities'. The trouble is that he nowhere indicates how the labouring mentality of pre-communist man would be transformed in such a way as to make his work in the realm of freedom truly creative and productive. Arendt, noting 'the fundamental contradiction which runs like a red thread through the whole of Marx's thought', comments: 'The fact remains that in all stages of his work he defines man as an *animal laborans* and then leads him into a society in which this greatest and most human power is no longer necessary. We are left with the rather distressing alternative between productive slavery and unproductive freedom.'[36] In practice, Arendt suggests, no qualitatively new activities will emerge, no principle appropriate to 'the public realm' of human action as opposed to 'the private realm' of (animal) labour:

Neither abundance of goods nor the shortening of the time actually spent in labouring are likely to result in the establishment of a common world, and the expropriated *animal laborans* becomes no less private because he has been deprived of a private place of his own to hide and be protected from the common realm. Marx predicted correctly, though with an unjustified glee, 'the withering away' of the public realm under conditions of unhampered development of the 'productive forces of society', and he was equally right, that is, consistent with his conception of man as an *animal laborans*, when he foresaw that 'socialized men' would spend their freedom from labouring in those strictly private and essentially wordless activities that we now call 'hobbies'.[37]

It is probable that the 'leisure as work' (or 'work as leisure') theorists can deal adequately with these warnings. They are, however, valuable as a caution against a too careless identification of 'leisure activities' with worthwhile and productive work – quite apart from the force of Weil's worrying insistence on the requirement to keep in touch with 'natural necessity' as a condition of human fulfilment and proper understanding. It is notoriously easy to conceive the society of abundance, or even – what is by no means the same thing – the society of no (formal) work, as a sort of Disneyland of leisuretime pursuits. Those projections which look forward to a future in which work centres on 'the informal economy' or 'the household economy'[38] are less likely to fall victim to these seductions. But they still need to specify carefully and concretely what kind of work will be performed, how it will be organized, and above all what will be the nature and degree of its dependence on the 'formal economy' of alienated labour and advanced technology.

To come finally to a view which most forcibly stresses the need to maintain the connection between work and employment. The basis of this view is Freud's observation that work is man's strongest tie to reality. It follows from this, for many thinkers, that this function is best performed when work is most highly institutionalized. Unemployment, on this view, is unacceptable even if the unemployed are as financially secure as they would be if employed, and despite all the 'free time' that is released for their varied use.

Marie Jahoda, drawing on her own study of an unemployed community in the 1930s – the Marienthal study[39] – stresses the extreme psychological disintegration brought on by unemployment. She considers a wide range of more recent studies of attitudes to work, and they serve to confirm her view that while there is much dissatisfaction with work, for the vast majority 'having a job is better than being unemployed, even beyond the financial implications'.[40] Kitwood's survey of English adolescents similarly shows that 'anxiety about employment prospects has become a major feature of the way adolescents view their future, especially when the time for taking action draws near. Conversely, there is virtually no indication that unemployment would be considered a desirable alternative to having a job, even if the remuneration were comparable to a normal wage.'[41] Both Kitwood and Jahoda are at pains to emphasize what Jahoda calls 'the latent consequences of employment as a social institution, which meet human needs of a more enduring kind'. As Kitwood puts it: 'When a boy or girl personally accepts the label "unemployed", the subjective environment changes, it becomes a state of inactivity and lassitude, where personal powers cannot be adequately used or expressed . . . At least for indigenous, English adolescents, it seems that there are no social life-worlds specifically adapted to the unemployed condition . . . Employment, for all its deficiencies, at least provides an arena for social development, and an acceptable general role.'

Jahoda offers a more elaborate list of the beneficial 'latent consequences of employment':

First among them is the fact that employment imposes a time structure on the waking day; secondly, employment implies regularly shared experiences and contacts with people outside the nuclear family; thirdly, employment links an individual to goals and purposes which transcend his own; fourthly, employment defines aspects of personal status and identity; and finally, employment enforces activity. It is these latent 'objective' consequences of work in complex industrialised societies which help me to understand the motivation to work beyond earning a living; to understand why work is psychologically supportive even when conditions are bad and by the same token, why unemployment is psychologically destructive.

She concedes that other social institutions – schools, clubs and so on – can provide one or more of these psychological supports.

I know of none, however, in our society, [apart from work,] which combines them all and, in addition, has as compelling a manifest reason as making one's living. It is equally true that nobody prevents the unemployed from creating their own time structure and social contacts, from sharing goals and purposes with others or from exercising their skills as best they can. But the psychological input required to do so on a regular basis under one's own steam is colossal.[12]

It may be that we are dealing with a historical time lag here, as both Kitwood and Jahoda accept. Work and employment have been associated, as a matter of necessity, for so long that the effort that will be needed to separate them without seriously damaging consequences is bound to seem enormous. A helpful step in that direction would be to show where, and in what manner, the disconnection has been made on a reasonable scale and for a sufficient length of time to show that it can be done successfully. At any rate perhaps history is catching up with us. If the widely quoted and increasingly widely accepted (even, if press leaks are to be believed, in many government departments) projection of five million (or 20 per cent of the workforce) unemployed by the 1990s in Britain comes about, we will have no choice but to seek to ensure that 'unemployment' can be as fully satisfying a way of life as employment. We are faced with a future in which unemployment will be a normal, not aberrant, experience for the mass of the population. Since we are all potentially among the unemployed, this has now become much more than a matter of pleasant speculation about other people's lives.

NOTES

1 Marshall Sahlins, 'The original affluent society', in his *Stone Age Economics* (London, Tavistock Publications, 1974), pp. 1–40.
2 For these examples, see Keith Thomas, 'Work and leisure in pre-industrial society', *Past and Present*, no. 29 (Dec. 1964), pp. 50–66.
3 Thomas, 'Work and leisure', p. 55. Thomas acknowledges that this is an idealized picture. For a more sceptical account of work in pre-industrial England, see P. Laslett, *The World We Have Lost* (London, Methuen, 1965). The conventional sociologist's view of the pre-modern age is well exemplified by Professor Herzberg and his colleagues: 'Life in primitive societies is hard and filled with backbreaking toil. There is relatively little opportunity for individual growth and development because of the necessity for constant emphasis on sheer subsistence. In a society which spends 70 or 80 per cent of its labour on the mere growing of food there is relatively little left over for the fullest development of the individual', F. Herzberg, B. Mausner and B. Snyderman, *The Motivation to Work* (New York, Wiley, 1959), p. 121.
4 E. P. Thompson, 'Time, work-discipline, and industrial capitalism', *Past and Present*, no. 38 (Dec. 1967), p. 60.
5 Ibid., p. 73.
6 Sahlins, 'The original affluent society', pp. 34–5.
7 H. Wilensky, 'The uneven distribution of leisure: the impact of economic growth on free time', *Social Problems*, vol. 9 (Summer, 1961), p. 33.
8 Thomas, 'Work and leisure', p. 63.
9 On this see Hannah Arendt, *The Human Condition* (New York, Doubleday Anchor Books, 1959), pp. 72–3.

242 *Politics, Work and Society*

10 Arendt writes: 'Historically, it is important to keep in mind the distinction between the contempt of the Greek city-states for all non-political occupations which arose out of the enormous demands upon the time and energy of the citizens, and the earlier, more original and more general contempt for activities which serve only to sustain life – *ad vitae sustentationem* as the *opera servilia* are still defined in the eighteenth century. In the world of Homer, Paris and Odysseus help in the building of their houses, Nausicaä herself washes the linen of her brothers, etc. . . . All this belongs to the self-sufficiency of the Homeric hero, to his independence and the autonomic supremacy of his person. No work is sordid if it means greater independence; the selfsame activity might well be a sign of slavishness if not personal independence but sheer survival is at stake, if it is not an expression of sovereignty but of subjection to necessity', *The Human Condition*, p. 324.

11 Arendt, *The Human Condition*, p. 74.

12 It is not too fanciful to see in many of the claims and practices of the *jeunesse dorée* of the 1960s a reassertion of just this aristocratic principle.

13 John Passmore, *The Perfectibility of Man* (London, Duckworth, 1970), chs 4–6.

14 P. D. Anthony, *The Ideology of Work* (London, Tavistock Publications, 1977), p. 37.

15 I am not denying of course that older conceptions of the *Homo rationalis* persisted for a long time, especially in the period of the Enlightenment. But even then the assumptions were being severely undermined by the psychology of the English and Scottish thinkers – Locke, Hume, Smith.

16 For two useful studies of this tradition, see A. Clayre, *Work and Play: Ideas and Experience of Work and Leisure* (London, Weidenfeld and Nicolson, 1974); and David Meakin, *Man and Work: Literature and Culture in Industrial Society* (London, Methuen, 1976).

17 Meakin, *Man and Work*, pp. 1–2.

18 T. Kitwood (forthcoming study). [Now published as *Disclosures to a Stranger : Adolescent Values in an Advanced Industrial Society* (London, Routledge and Kegan Paul, 1980).]

19 Meakin, *Man and Work*, p. 4.

20 Thus, in a direct echo of Meakin's comment, P. D. Anthony writes: 'Perhaps, just as societies and institutions are said to build their most magnificent monuments when they are in decline, so the ideology of work reaches its most refined state when it becomes redundant', *Ideology of Work*, p. 9. Anthony is writing of current developments. What he says, however, could equally well be applied to the situation at the beginning of the nineteenth century.

21 E. J. Hobsbawm, *Industry and Empire* (London, Weidenfeld and Nicolson, 1968), p. 146.

22 Quoted Meakin, *Man and Work*, p. 22.

23 For a sympathetic account of some of these ventures, see Dennis Hardy, *Alternative Communities in Nineteenth Century England* (London, Longman, 1979).

24 Peter Berger (ed.), *The Human Shape of Work* (New York, Macmillan, 1964), p. 217.

25 A. Clayre, 'Improving the quality of work', *New Universities Quarterly*, 30, no. 4 (Autumn, 1976), p. 441. That people still think in terms of the Utilitarian contract, however, is indicated by E. Chinoy's survey of American car workers in the 1950s. As David Riesman wrote in his introduction to Chinoy's book: 'Chinoy's interviews

show work to be part-time imprisonment, through which one pays off the fines incurred by one's pursuit of the good – or rather the good time – life at home and on vacation', E. Chinoy, *Automobile Workers and the American Dream* (New York, Doubleday, 1955).

26 Asa Briggs, 'The organisation of leisure', *The Times*, 11 October 1969.

27 T. Burns, 'Leisure in industrial society', in M. A. Smith, S. Parker and C. S. Smith (eds), *Leisure and Society in Britain* (London, Allen Lane, 1973), pp. 45–6.

28 For an excellent account of these changes in work, see H. Braverman, *Labor and Monopoly Capital: The Degradation of Work in the Twentieth Century* (New York, Monthly Review Press, 1974); and see also *Work in America*: Report of a Special Task Force to the US Secretary of Health, Education and Welfare (Cambridge, Mass., MIT Press, 1973).

29 Clive Jenkins and Barrie Sherman, *The Collapse of Work* (London, Eyre Methuen, 1979), p. 141. And as further evidence of a shift in trade union thinking, cf. this comment by Len Murray, General Secretary of the Trades Union Congress, on the problem of 'surplus labour' in the industrial economy: 'Looking further ahead, it isn't so much that we need a new policy to deal with the situation, I believe we need a whole new philosophy. This is becoming recognized and accepted throughout Western Europe and throughout the whole of the capitalist industrialized countries. When I say philosophy, I mean we've got to get away from what I have on one or two previous occasions called Old Testament economics: "In the sweat of thy brow shalt thou eat bread", that work is good and non-work is bad, that work is good and leisure is to be deplored ... I see this as an opportunity rather than a threat – to increase the amount of active leisure, or active non-employment, if you like, in society', *The Times*, 24 August 1977.

30 For the impact of microelectronics on work and employment, see Colin Hines, *The 'Chips' are Down* (London, Earth Resources Research Ltd, 1978); Jenkins and Sherman, *The Collapse of Work*; I. Barron and R. Curnow, *The Future with Microelectronics* (London, Frances Pinter, 1979); and, best of all, the CIS Report, *The New Technology* (London, Counter Information Services, 1979).

31 Gail Stewart and Cathy Starrs, *Re-Working the World: a Report on Changing Concepts of Work* (Ottawa, Public Policy Concern, 1973), pp. 19–20.

32 George Friedmann, *The Anatomy of Work: Labor, Leisure and the Implications of Automation* (New York, Free Press, 1961), p. 108. This was an idea already anticipated by William Morris (among others, no doubt). In his essay, *How We Live and How We Might Live*, he suggests that by the use of genuinely labour-saving devices, there could be 'a vast amount of leisure gained for the community ... [and] a great deal of the best work done would be done in the leisure time of men relieved from any anxiety as to their livelihood, and eager to exercise their special talent, as all men, nay, all animals are.' 'Under a happier state of things,' says Morris, 'I should probably use my leisure for doing a good deal of what is now called work', *The Political Writings of William Morris*, ed. A. L. Morton (London, Lawrence and Wishart, 1973), p. 151. On the whole, however, Morris was inclined to distrust leisure. Looking to the future of work, he asked: 'Shall all we can do with it be to shorten the hours of that toil to the utmost, that the hours of leisure may be long beyond what men used to hope for? And what shall we then do with the leisure, if we say that all toil is irksome? Shall we sleep it

244 *Politics, Work and Society*

away? – Yes, and never wake up again, I should hope, in that case' ('The Art of the People').

33 Stewart and Starrs, *Re-Working the World*, pp. 36–7.

34 Eric Gill, quoted Meakin, *Man and Work*, pp. 141, 155.

35 Simone Weil, *Oppression and Liberty* (London, Routledge and Kegan Paul, 1958), pp. 84–5. There is a weak echo of this in the objection of the American sociologists F. Herzberg and his colleagues to 'the leisure society': 'A carpenter's workshop in the basement and a neatly groomed backyard are no substitute for the direct relationship between work and the fulfilment of the individual's needs ... Thus we reject the pessimism that views the future as one in which work will become increasingly meaningless to most people and in which the pursuits of leisure will become the most important end of society. We cannot help but feel that the greatest fulfilment of man is to be found in activities that are meaningfully related to his own needs as well as those of society', Herzberg, Mausner, and Synderman, *The Motivation to Work*, pp. 130, 139.

36 Arendt, *The Human Condition*, pp. 90–1.

37 Ibid., p. 101. This is a necessarily elliptical rendering of her view – see esp. chp. 5, 'Action', for explication. Arendt's criticism of Marx can probably be applied with equal effect to the very similar and equally famous assertion by Keynes that, although the 'economic problem' is not permanent, it must continue to dominate until an abundance is achieved. Only then will freedom be feasible: 'For at least another hundred years we must pretend to ourselves and to everyone that fair is foul, and foul is fair; for foul is useful and fair is not. Avarice and usury and precaution must be our gods for a little longer still. For only they can lead us out of the tunnel of economic necessity into daylight' (J. M. Keynes, 'Economic possibilities for our grandchildren', 1930). This Utilitarian formulation leaves it only too likely that the appetites and aptitudes learned while in 'the tunnel of necessity' will continue to dominate when we at last come out blinking into the light.

38 See, for example, Scott Burns, *The Household Economy* (Boston, Mass., Beacon Press, 1977); Hazel Henderson, *Creating Alternative Futures: The End of Economics* (New York, Berkeley Publishing Corporation, 1978); James Robertson, *The Sane Alternative* (London, James Robertson, 1978); J. I. Gershuny, 'The informal economy: its role in industrial society', *Futures*, February 1979, pp. 3–15; J. I. Gershuny and R. E. Pahl, 'Britain in the decade of the three economies', *New Society*, 3 January 1983, pp. 7–9.

39 Now re-issued: M. Jahoda, P. F. Lazarsfeld and H. Zeisel, *Marienthal: The Sociography of an Unemployed Community* (London, Tavistock Publications, 1972).

40 Marie Jahoda, 'The impact of unemployment in the 1930s and the 1970s', *Bulletin of the British Psychological Society*, 32 (1979), 309–14.

41 T. Kitwood (forthcoming study) [*Disclosures to a Stranger*]. I am grateful to Dr Kitwood for the opportunity to see part of this work.

42 Jahoda, 'The impact of unemployment in the 1930s and 1970s'.

BIBLIOGRAPHICAL NOTE

Work on work has become an academic industry in itself, the more so perhaps as academics themselves fear unemployment. Specifically on the historical and ideological concerns of this paper, however, there is relatively little new. The most useful volume is the wide-ranging collection edited by Patrick Joyce, *The Historical Meanings of Work* (Cambridge, Cambridge University Press, 1987). A stimulating brief contribution is Maurice Godelier, 'Work and its representations', *History Workshop*, no. 10 (Autumn 1980), pp. 164–74. On work in the classical world, there is M. I. Finley, *Economy and Society in Ancient Greece* (Harmondsworth, Penguin Books, 1983); see also G. E. M. de Ste Croix, *The Class Struggle in the Ancient Greek World* (London, Duckworth, 1981). For the medieval period there is Georges Duby, *The Age of Cathedrals* (London, Croom Helm, 1981) and *The Three Orders: Feudal Society Imagined* (Chicago, Chicago University Press, 1982). A useful brief study is S. H. Udy, *Work in Traditional and Modern Society* (Englewood Cliffs, NJ, Prentice-Hall, 1970).

On specific thinkers: R. N. Berki, 'On the nature and origins of Marx's concept of labour', *Political Theory*, 7 (1979) no. 1; on Marx's view of work in Communist society, R. N. Berki, *Insight and Vision: The Problem of Communism in Marx's Thought* (London, Dent, 1983), and Jon Elster, *Making Sense of Marx* (Cambridge, Cambridge University Press, 1985), esp. pp. 513–31. On Ruskin and Morris: P. D. Anthony, *John Ruskin's Labour: A Study of Ruskin's Social Theory* (Cambridge, Cambridge University Press, 1984); E. P. Thompson, *William Morris: Romantic to Revolutionary*, new edn (London, Merlin Press, 1977); Paul Meier, *William Morris: The Marxist Dreamer* (2 vols, Brighton, Harvester Press, 1978). Marx and Weber are interestingly discussed in David Rubinstein, 'Love and work', *Sociological Review*, 21 (1978), 5–25.

Work and its necessity are more philosophically discussed in: M. Canovan, *Hannah Arendt on Work and Labour*, Acton Society Occasional Papers, no. 19 (London, Acton Society Trust, 1980); Sira Dermen, 'Necessity, oppression and liberty: Simone Weil', in Edward Goodman (ed.), *Non-conforming Radicals of Europe* (London, Duckworth, 1983), pp. 172–83; Sean Sayers, 'Work, leisure and human needs', *Thesis Eleven* (Melbourne, Australia), no. 14, 1986, pp. 79–96. There is a good account of the contribution of European philosophers in Richard Norman, *The Moral Philosophers* (Oxford, Clarendon Press, 1984), chs 8–9.

On work and leisure: Stanley Parker, *The Sociology of Leisure* (London, Allen and Unwin, 1976); James Walvin, *Leisure and Society 1830–1950* (London, Longman, 1978); Hugh Cunningham, *Leisure in the Industrial Revolution* (London, Croom Helm, 1980); Eileen and Stephen Yeo (eds), *Popular Culture and Class Conflict 1590–1914* (Brighton, Harvester Press, 1981); Barry Sherman, *Working At Leisure* (London, Methuen, 1986). The original essays by Joseph Pieper (1947) still repay study: *Leisure, the Basis of Culture* (New York, Mentor Books edn, 1963).

The general literature on work, its past and especially its future, grows so fast that any list is out of date before it appears. Still, something should be attempted. Good collections are: Kenneth Thompson (ed.), *Work, Employment and Unemployment* (Milton Keynes, Open University Press, 1984); Craig R. Littler (ed.), *The Experience of Work* (Aldershot, Gower, 1985); Sandra Wallman (ed.), *The Social Anthropology of Work* (London, Academic Press, 1979); G. Esland and G. Salaman (eds), *The Politics of*

Work and Occupations (Milton Keynes, Open University Press, 1980); Rosemary Deem and Graeme Salaman (eds), *Work, Culture and Society* (Milton Keynes, Open University Press, 1985); B. Roberts, R. Finnegan and D. Gallie (eds), *New Approaches to Economic Life* (Manchester, Manchester University Press, 1985). See also R. E. Pahl (ed.), *On Work* (Oxford, Basil Blackwell, 1988).

For particular contributions: Charles F. Sabel, *Work and Politics* (Cambridge, Cambridge University Press, 1982); Elliott A. Krause, *Division of Labor: A Political Perspective* (New York, Greenwood Press, 1982); R. E. Pahl, *Divisions of Labour* (Oxford, Basil Blackwell, 1984) and 'The politics of work', *Political Quarterly*, 56 (1985), pp. 331–45; Larry Hirschhorn, *Beyond Mechanization: Work and Technology in the Post-Industrial Age* (Cambridge, Mass., MIT Press, 1984); M. Rose, *Re-working the Work Ethic* (London, Batsford, 1985); Claus Offe, *Disorganized Capitalism: Contemporary Transformations of Work and Politics* (Oxford, Polity Press, 1985); M. Piore and C. F. Sabel, *The Second Industrial Divide* (New York, Basic Books, 1984). Gershuny has developed his ideas on goods, services and work-time in a number of contributions: Jonathan Gershuny, *Social Innovation and the Division of Labour* (Oxford, Oxford University Press, 1983); J. Gershuny and I. Miles, *The New Service Economy* (London, Frances Pinter, 1983); J. Gershuny, 'The leisure principle', *New Society*, 13 February 1987. On the informal economy, see Alejandro Portes and Saskia Saseen-Koob, 'Making it underground: comparative material on the informal sector in Western market economies', *American Journal of Sociology*, 93 (1987), 30–61.

Harry Braverman's *Labor and Monopoly Capital* (New York, Monthly Review Press, 1974) has been the inspiration for much of the theory of work in the past decade. For a critical discussion, see Stephen Wood (ed.), *The Degradation of Work? Skill, Deskilling and the Labour Process* (London, Hutchinson, 1983). See also Craig Littler, *The Development of the Labour Process in Capitalist Societies* (London, Heinemann, 1982), and Paul Thompson, *The Nature of Work* (London, Macmillan, 1983).

Green, ecological and other non-Marxist radical perspectives on work are presented in: Ivan Illich, *The Right to Useful Unemployment* (London, Marion Boyars, 1978) and *Shadow Work* (London, Marion Boyars, 1981); André Gorz, *Farewell to the Working Class* (London, Pluto Press, 1982) and *Paths to Paradise: On the Liberation from Work* (London, Pluto Press, 1985); James Robertson, *Future Work: Jobs, Self-Employment and Leisure After the Industrial Age* (Aldershot, Gower, 1985). For other thoughts on the future of work, including the impact of the new microelectronic technology, see Barry Jones, *Sleepers, Wake! Technology and the Future of Work* (Brighton, Wheatsheaf Books, 1982); Charles Handy, *The Future of Work* (Oxford, Basil Blackwell, 1984); Howard Davis and David Gosling (eds), *Will the Future Work?* (Geneva, World Council of Churches, 1985); Colin Gill, *Work, Unemployment and the New Technology* (Oxford, Polity Press, 1985); Arthur Francis, *New Technology at Work* (Oxford, Oxford University Press, 1986). More visionary are Alvin Toffler, *The Third Wave* (New York, Bantam Books, 1981); Norman MacRae, *The 2024 Report: A Concise History of the Future 1974–2024* (London, Sidgwick and Jackson, 1984); Robert van de Weyer, *Wickwyn: A Vision of the Future* (London, SPCK, 1986).

Three journals, the *Work and Society Newsletter*, the British Sociological Association's *Work, Employment and Society* and *New Technology, Work and Employment* contain much of interest on current discussions. And see also the references and bibliographical note to 'Unemployment as a problem in the development of industrial societies', chapter 10 in this volume.

10

Unemployment as a Problem in the Development of Industrial Societies: the English Experience

With a job, there is a future; without a job, there is slow death of all that makes a man ambitious, industrious, and glad to be alive.

E. Wight Bakke, *The Unemployed Man: A Social Study*

People sometimes talk as if all that a man wants is regular work. It is nothing of the sort. What they really want is a regular income. Regular work is of no great value to anyone except as a kind of discipline for the young.

William (later Lord) Beveridge, speech of 10 August 1910

When Adam delved and Eve span,
Who was then the *working man*?

Old English rhyme, modified

Unemployment, as a concept and as a structural phenomenon, is a relatively new thing in Western society, even Western industrial society. It was first elaborated and analysed in the 1890s. In the succeeding decades, and especially as a result of the Great Depression of the 1930s, the debate gradually moved from a concern with a subordinate element in social policy to one which saw unemployment as a central feature of the industrial economy, and the linchpin of all future social policy. The old socialist claim of 1848, of 'the right to work', was transmuted to 'full employment' as the goal in principle of all industrial societies. This goal was substantially achieved, virtually irrespective of social policy, in the two decades of rapid economic growth that followed the end of the Second World War.

In the 1970s unemployment returned once more to haunt Western industrial societies. By the end of the decade the rate of unemployment was accelerating so fast as to threaten, in the eyes of many, a 'world without work', a 'workless state'. A whole generation was growing up with the prospect of a jobless future. Full employment was still the almost universally acknowledged goal; but to many, of all parties and political outlooks, the unlikely prospect of achieving this in the foreseeable future was confronting Western industrial societies with their most urgent problem of social welfare and social order.

What light can a historical perspective throw on this predicament? How realistic or desirable is it, in the long-term perspective of the evolution of industrial societies, to erect full employment as the norm by which all policies and options are to be judged? What other possibilities and ideas lie buried in the historical deposit left by developing industrialism? Can we seriously, without irresponsibility, contemplate a 'world without work' – work considered as employment?

The justification of a historical approach is not simply the perspective it allows us on an all-too-pressing matter of current concern. There are also, I suggest, lessons of a more concrete kind to be learned from the past: about the organization of work, of the relation of work to other spheres of 'leisure', family and community life, and of the primacy of values in governing the relations between these. Nothing of the past can be re-lived or restored in a literal sense. Nor is there any intention here to indulge in antiquarian nostalgia. But there are times, critical points, perhaps, in the evolution of societies when the experience and attitudes of past epochs seem peculiarly relevant to considering present problems. 'History does not repeat itself; but historical situations recur.'

In the account that follows, I want to consider, first, the history of the attitude to the 'unemployed', and what this tells us about the conditions of life and work of the labouring population, before the public recognition and definition of the specific status of being unemployed. I then look at the period, roughly the 1890s to the 1940s, in which 'full employment' came to be inscribed on the banner of all industrial societies. Lastly I consider the implications of this account for full employment in the future of industrial societies, and the extent to which we should continue to regard this as a possible or desirable aim. Throughout the centre of interest is in the precarious 'economy of the poor', and the shifting balance of sufficiency and need in the struggle for subsistence.

I confine this discussion to England, for certain obvious reasons of space and relevance, as well as of relative competence. As it happens, the English case is peculiarly well fitted for an investigation of this sort, partly because England was the first country to industrialize thoroughly, but more particularly because the existence of a national system of poor relief afforded a unique point of reference for public debate about the condition of the labouring poor. No other European country possessed such a system. It is largely in the twists and turns of the Poor Laws that the fluctuating fortunes of the poor of England can be seen, as in a mirror.

I

'Unemployment' and the labouring poor under the Old Poor Law,
1601–1834

For more than three centuries – from the Elizabethan Poor Laws of 1597 and 1601 to Lloyd George's unemployment insurance legislation of 1911[1] –

the history of the attitude to the unemployed in England is essentially the history of the Poor Laws. H. L. Beales once said that 'like the House of Commons, the Poor Law provides an institutional microcosm of the English people . . . it is the history of the country's social conscience.'[2] For the greater part of England's modern history, the Poor Law established the framework of a unique system of public provision for all forms of poverty and destitution. Whether from sickness or old age, widowhood or desertion, low wages or unemployment, poverty was relieved, as a right and not simply as a call on charity, in a wide variety of ways by the parish endowed with a statutory duty and authority.

The Poor Law covered all forms of distress due to poverty, however caused. Any member of 'the labouring poor' might be caught by its safety net. The term 'the labouring poor', or simply 'the poor', as commonly used right to the end of the eighteenth century, designated an exceedingly comprehensive category. Besides those in need of relief, for the time-being, because of hardship, it included many artisans and small farmers, as well as all wage-labourers in town and country.[3] The comprehensiveness of the phrase reflected fairly accurately the comprehensiveness of experience. The line between the independent artisan or wage-earner and the pauper on parish relief was always an extremely tenuous one. For shorter or longer periods, through sickness, low wages, high prices, bouts of unemployment, or simply an inconveniently large family, the independent labourer might frequently find himself thrown upon the parish for relief under the Poor Law. Hence the labouring poor, those who actually or potentially fell within the scope of the Poor Law, constituted an enormous group, by far and away the most numerous group in English society. It has been estimated that in the sixteenth, seventeenth, and for the most of the eighteenth century the labouring poor made up at least between 50 and 60 per cent of the total population, and, at various times and places, the proportion could rise to three-quarters. The really poor, those more or less permanently on relief and so below the status of wage-earner, constituted at any one time between a quarter and a third of the population. But it has to be emphasized that in practice the distinction between the independent labourer and the dependent pauper was never firm. Gregory King in 1696 classed almost half the population of the kingdom as 'decreasing' rather than 'increasing' the national wealth, that is, their annual family expenditure was greater than their income and hence they were at least partly dependent on Poor Law relief. D. C. Coleman confirms this with an estimate that 'in Stuart England between a quarter and a half of the entire population were chronically below what contemporaries regarded as the official poverty line'. Jacob Viner, too, on the basis of an estimate that the labouring poor formed well over half of the population of England in the eighteenth century, says: 'The really poor portion of the "poor" I take to have comprised, with their dependents, at a minimum somewhere between 50 per cent at the beginning and 40 per cent at the end of the century.'[4]

This promiscuous classification of the poor, necessary in face of the realities of the situation, was however highly distasteful to the authorities. We can indeed almost say that, from the authorities' point of view, the entire history of the Poor Laws was an attempt to impose a classification upon the undifferentiated poor, and to back up this classification to the utmost by parliamentary statute and rigorous parish administration. One basic distinction that was usually made explicit in every Poor Law amendment and regulation was that between the 'able-bodied poor' and the sick, old and infirm. Another, generally implicit but more or less corresponding to the first, was that between the 'deserving' and the 'undeserving' poor. It is the attempt to make and hold this distinction that runs like a red thread through three centuries of Poor Law policy. And it is the almost total failure to hold the line that constitutes the actual history of the interaction between the labouring poor and the Poor Law authorities on the ground, in the counties and parishes.

Thus, from the very start, the 1601 Act distinguished between those of the poor able to work – the able-bodied – and those who could not – the physically and mentally ill, the old, abandoned or neglected children, and one-parent families (whether headed by widows, deserted wives, or unmarried mothers). About this second category there was no problem, at least in theory. These were the traditional recipients of private philanthropic and charitable gifts and endowments, administered in the past usually by the Church, the official guardian of the poor and distributor of alms. With the Reformation and the dissolution of the religious houses, the state partly took over this function through its Poor Law institutions, supplementing the still very extensive private charities. By means of pensions (regular cash payments), payments of rent, occasional distributions of fuel, food and clothing, the provision of infirmary and other medical care, and apprenticeships for the young, an elaborate system of 'outdoor relief' catered to the needs of the aged, infirm and other dependent poor.

'Indoor relief' was provided in workhouses. The workhouse as an institution was implicit in the 1601 Act, with its provision for setting the poor to work. But for a long time parishes seem to have been reluctant to follow up this suggestion in the form of workhouses, and the workhouse system remained largely unrealized until the later seventeenth century. In 1696 Parliament gave recognition to the Bristol workhouse experiment, and so gave impetus to the workhouse movement, which was widespread by the mid-eighteenth century. Contrary to its ostensible purpose, however, the workhouse rarely provided remunerative work. Workhouses became 'homes for the most needy of the deserving poor: the children, the sick, the insane, and the elderly, those with no homes of their own and no relatives to nurse and care for them. . . In spite of the name, most workhouses were more like hospitals, boarding schools and old people's homes than factories.'[5] In particular, for the whole period up to 1834 able-bodied males rarely found their way into the workhouse.

Parish vestries might grumble about the increasing cost of the poor rates; particular overseers might be unscrupulous and tyrannical; workhouses might attract criticism variously for being too like prisons or too like palaces. But in general, for the category of the traditional 'deserving' poor, the system seems to have worked remarkably well, and with a fair measure of humanity. There was a widespread acceptance of the need for a Poor Law, and of the community's obligation to provide for the dependent or impotent poor. But about the able-bodied poor, whom virtually all thinkers regarded as the crux of the problem, there was no such unanimity, and a considerable confusion of both policy and practice. At the centre of the confusion we can discern, in fact if not in name, a dispute about the nature of unemployment, its causes and its remedies.⁶

In the earlier sixteenth century – as shown, for instance in the Act of 1531 – the authorities followed traditional practice in allowing the 'impotent poor' to beg for alms; but severe penalties and sanctions against begging were laid down for 'sturdy rogues and vagabonds', all of whom were assumed to be capable of finding employment were they not culpably idle and work-shy. As John Pound says, the 1531 Act 'distinguished between the able-bodied vagrant, who was to be whipped, and the impotent beggar who was to be relieved, but it made no provision whatsoever for the man who desperately desired to be employed but had no job to go to'.⁷ An Act of 1572 acknowledged that there were certain groups of workers – such as returning sailors and soldiers, harvest workers and servants who had been turned away – who were genuinely unemployed through no fault of their own. It exempted them from the penalties for vagrancy but made no provision for their relief.

What brought about a change of feeling was a series of four catastrophic harvests between 1593 and 1597. Food prices soared, there were widespread food riots and a large increase in vagrancy. This was the immediate background to the Poor Law legislation of 1597–1601. The government was forced to accept that there were many thousands of men in both the rural and the urban areas who were out of work for reasons beyond their control. It also accepted that there would have to be provision for their relief. But there was to be no blurring of the old line between the able-bodied and the incapacitated. The government wished to discourage begging, seeing it as a threat to public order. The incapacitated poor were therefore to be given relief, in their own homes if that were possible, in almshouses if not. The able-bodied were to be removed to their parish of origin and there set to work. Provision was made for the raising, out of parish rates, of stocks of materials – flax, hemp, wool – on which the poor might be set to work in their own homes.

The 1601 Act set the pattern of thinking about the able-bodied poor for a very long time to come. The goal was the speedy resumption of independence by the head of the family, the able-bodied adult male. It was assumed that, unless incorrigibly lazy and so deserving punishment, most of the able-bodied would be able to find work relatively quickly. Aid would be needed only for short periods, in times of exceptional hardship, to tide over the worker and his family until the return of normal times. In the conditions of a pre-industrial economy for a good deal of the time this was indeed often the case, as we shall see. But there were far too many causes of hardship in the lives of the labouring poor for this ideal seriously to have much chance of attainment in practice. A string of recurrent bad harvests, falling demand for a particular craft skill, chronic underemployment, low wages, or simply the accident of a large family to support: all these could be the cause of persistent and severe hardship for individual families. At a different level there was the kind of distress caused by mass local unemployment due to the closure of a mill during a slump. Although the severity of the distress would clearly vary enormously from region to region, the fact that these were not haphazard but endemic features of the pre-industrial economy meant that the Poor Law authorities were constantly faced with the challenge of what to do with the able-bodied poor. As a problem they simply would not go away.

Setting the able-bodied poor to work at home on stocks of materials, the main hope of the 1601 Act, had turned out to be such a failure that well before the beginning of the eighteenth century the scheme had largely been abandoned.[8] The eighteenth-century policy-makers pinned their hopes on employment in workhouses. In the full flush of the workhouse movement, an Act of 1722 laid down the imposition of a 'workhouse test' whereby relief, including employment, was only to be given in the workhouse. But most workhouses were quite unsuited to providing anything but the lowest level of textile work – spinning, clothes-making and repairing – together with some pig grazing and allotment cultivation: work, in other words, reasonably suited to the women, children and old people who largely made up the workhouse population. Since most workhouses were small,[9] they were in any case incapable of taking in large numbers of unemployed during a depression.

Certain visionaries, such as Josiah Child, John Bellers and Lawrence Braddon, and later Bishop Berkeley and Jeremy Bentham, projected grandiose schemes for the large-scale exploitation of the labour of the able-bodied unemployed. Organized in 'colleges of industry', or set to work by private contractors in 'corporations of the poor', they would not only become self-supporting, but make sufficient profit to support the rest of the dependent poor, and so solve the problem of the poor once and for all. These schemes mostly remained where they rightly belonged, on paper.[10] Had they been tried, they would almost certainly have encountered the main stumbling block that stood in the way of all attempts by the Poor Law authorities to create meaningful work for the unemployed: that, whether in the agricultural or the industrial sector, it simply was not possible to provide profitable work for workers whose skills were the very ones not required – for the time being at least – by commercial employers. All that could be offered were short-term palliatives, of which road-mending increasingly became the most popular towards the end of the eighteenth century.[11]

From the parish's point of view one fact in any case was a dominating consideration throughout: since employment in the workhouse was never self-supporting, it was always cheaper to make cash payments to able-bodied paupers than to bring them into the workhouse.[12] Most parish authorities therefore ignored the 'workhouse test' of the 1722 Act, just as they had largely ignored the injunction of the 1601 Act concerning the provision of work for the poor. Dorothy Marshall has wisely advised that 'to understand the old Poor Law it is necessary to concentrate on administration rather than legislation.'[13] Nowhere is this truer than in the treatment of the able-bodied poor. Despite all the intentions of the national policy-makers, the authorities at the local level responded to the real conditions on the ground and went in for outdoor relief to the able-bodied on a massive scale. Outdoor relief, largely in the form of cash pensions, had become the well-nigh universal remedy by the end of the eighteenth century,[14] helped on by a movement of thought that adopted a distinctly more 'benevolent' attitude to the labourer, and a greater understanding of his problems of work and employment.[15] Gilbert's Act of 1782 gave official recognition of this practice, by sanctioning the granting of aid-in-wages, that is, the supplementing of low wages by payments from the parish rates. This should make it clear that the widespread adoption of the 'Speenhamland system' after 1795 introduced nothing new in principle in the working of the system of poor relief. In supplementing the wages of labourers according to the price of bread and the number of family members to support, the Berkshire magistrates were merely following the practice of most eighteenth-century authorities.[16]

Thus by the end of the eighteenth century it was clear that the attempt to hold the line between the able-bodied poor and the rest, between the 'deserving' and 'undeserving' poor, had resulted in almost total failure. Those lacking work through unemployment, or low on wages through under-employment, were treated in a more or less uniform system of outdoor relief along with most other categories of the poor. Only those too young, too old, or too sick, to care for themselves, and with no one to look after them, were relieved in workhouses. Most others received cash pensions in lieu of or in addition to wages. Depending on the spirit in which these payments were given and received, they could be demoralizing and degrading, or they could be accepted as a right and an entitlement. There seems good reason to believe that, until the end of the eighteenth century, the second attitude was at least as common as the first. Most workers accepted that there would be temporary periods of unemployment in their trades, and that in particular agricultural work depended on a wide series of factors – such as the weather and the seasons – seemingly quite independent of human control. Hence there could be nothing especially degrading about accepting support from the local community to which one belonged, in those periods of distress that were a natural and apparently permanent part of the life of all pre-industrial communities. Certainly employers, who made up the main body of the rate-payers, could not be happy about paying out rates to support the poor. But they could see that there was a reciprocal interest involved in maintaining their unemployed workers, many of whom would be familiar, long-standing members of the community, and whom they would hope to employ again when better times returned. As the eighteenth century progressed, this became an especially strong consideration for the farmers, anxious to stem the flow of labour to the towns. Hence, too, their continued support for the increasingly onerous burden of Speenhamland.[17]

Work, employment and unemployment in the pre-industrial economy

The support of the unemployed worker by the parish becomes even more intelligible when we consider that the links and associations between work, employment and unemployment were very different from what they were to become with the developing industrial economy of the nineteenth and twentieth centuries. Certainly, there is no question that wage labour was the predominant form of labour in seventeenth- and eighteenth-century England. This is clear from the researches of Hill, Macpherson, Macfarlane, Coleman and others.[18] Most workers, moreover, were dependent on wages for the essential part of their subsistence. Adam Smith may, for the sake of argument, have exaggerated somewhat when he said that 'many workers could not subsist a week, few could subsist a month, and scarce any a year without employment'.[19] But we do nothing to aid the understanding of unemployment today by resurrecting the old sociological myth of a pre-industrial subsistence economy of self-employed peasants and craftsmen – least of all for England.

But having said that, it is important to realize that while workers might be dependent on wages, this did not by any means necessarily assimilate their condition to that of modern wage workers in factories and offices. The organization and setting of work for most eighteenth-century workers, wage-earners as much as others, expressed an experience and an ethos of labour a world away from the time-governed discipline of the modern factory. The term and status of 'wage-labourer' was itself ambiguous, carrying diverse connotations. Building workers, for instance, were paid wages on a daily rate; but it turns out that part of these wages were in payment for the cost of training and maintaining the apprentices who worked alongside the building workers, thus suggesting a craft occupation of a kind very different from that of the standard day-labourer.[20] Ashton describes iron workers – nail-makers and the like – in the west Midlands who were wage-earners paid by the piece, and who did their work in little sheds attached to their cottages. At the same time there were other iron workers in the same area who bought their materials from the iron masters and sold their product back to them, often the same master in each case; these thought of themselves as independent producers, not as wage-earners. Hosiery workers of the east Midlands who superficially followed the work pattern of these iron workers were, however, wage-earners. They collected materials and orders from the large merchant hosiers, worked them up at home, and then returned the finished work to the hosiers, for which they were paid wages by the piece.[21] Agricultural labourers often lived-in with the families whose farms they worked, or were provided with a cottage and a small plot of land. Money wages, often paid only at the end of the year, in most cases represented only a very subsidiary part of their subsistence.[22]

The varied pattern of eighteenth-century work allowed for a different 'mix', and a different relation, of 'work' and 'leisure', and of wage-labour and subsistence activities, than was possible later. From this followed a now familiar set of characteristics of work and workers before the coming of the factory system: work was regulated by the task, rather than by time; bouts of intense labour alternated with long periods of idleness; the irregularity of the workday pattern imposed by the task was heightened by the irregularity of the working week and the working year; 'Saint Monday' and often 'Saint Tuesday' were piously honoured; and the summer season of the year, often for as long as from June to October, was given over to agricultural and farming activities as against the manufacturing work carried on during the rest of the year. The keynote throughout is irregularity: of time, of effort, of the payment of wages by employers, who often delayed for two or three months before paying for completed pieces of work. John Rule rightly says, 'it was not the length of the factory day, but its regularity which contrasted with the cottage labour system.'[23]

Irregularity was also a central characteristic of employment. Uncertainty in the demand for labour marked practically every trade and occupation, although the problem seems to have been mainly one not so much of actual redundancy as of under-employment or 'concealed unemployment'. This was a function of the general structure of agriculture and industry, with the seasonal and cyclical fluctuations common to both. But the effects of this lack or loss of regular employment were significantly lessened by two crucial features of the eighteenth-century labourer's position.

In the first place, the eighteenth-century labourer was a 'pluralist' as far as occupation was concerned. When one occupation went cold and slack on him, he could often resort to another. Rule has pointed out that one important consequence of the domestic or 'putting-out' system was to disperse manufacturing to the countryside, while at the same time many rural craftsmen such as blacksmiths, wheelwrights and thatchers were really part of the agriculture 'industry', and probably spent more time mending than making. Not only does this make it very difficult for us to distinguish occupational categories by economic sector, as 'industrial', 'manufacturing' or 'agricultural'. It also meant that for workers of the time various occupational 'mixes' were possible, varying both as to region and as to the extent of the mix. Thus there was 'a continuum from the fully mixed in which a man might be equally dependent upon two occupations, through the seasonally mixed in which he might be employed in one or other of two occupations, depending on the time of the year, to the tending of a garden which added usefully but in a strictly collateral way to the family's comfort'.[24] Manufacturing and mining activities were often inextricably mixed with agricultural ones, so much so that, according to R. W. Malcolmson, 'some historians have spoken of the existence of an economy of dual-occupations: a household economy in which there was such an integral relationship between farming ... and some kind of cottage industry that it may be misleading to speak of "by-employments" at all, for it is often the case that one means of livelihood cannot be clearly identified as predominant and the other as subsidiary.'[25] Prominent examples during the eighteenth century were the weavers, who regularly mixed weaving with husbandry; many communities of coal miners; the small self-employed clothiers of the West Riding of Yorkshire; and the tin miners of Cornwall.[26] Defoe went so far as to describe those regions where the only source of livelihood was agriculture as 'unemployed counties'.[27]

This 'economy of dual-occupations' already points to the second important feature of the eighteenth-century labourer's position: that his work was organized around the home. This in itself reduced the degree of dependence on employment for wages. The household economy could and indeed had to draw on the labour of all its members. Few families could subsist for very long on the earnings of the head of the household alone. The household acted as an integrated subsistence unit, depending variously on contributions in the form of wages, food grown on allotments and cattle grazed on the commons. As Malcolmson says, rather than speak of occupations in this period 'it is better to speak of the work itself – farm labour, weaving, housewifery – and to try and understand how such work contributed to a family's living'.[28] In the weaver's family, for instance, both husband and wife would be involved in 'manufacturing' – he weaving, she spinning – as well as 'agriculture' in the relevant seasons, while the wife would also do the domestic chores and probably also feed the livestock. The children would be employed as helpers in both weaving and spinning and would also do sundry domestic tasks. While it is probably true that for most labouring families the income from wages was the single most important means of support, in most cases it was rarely relied upon as the indispensable contribution to family subsistence. 'As long as domestic industry was supplemented by the facilities and amenities of a garden plot, a scrap of land, or grazing rights, the dependence of the labourer on money earnings was not absolute; the potato plot or "stubbing geese", a cow or even an ass in the commons made all the difference; and family earnings acted as a kind of unemployment insurance.'[29]

It should be clear from all this that 'unemployment', while not exactly welcomed, cannot have been the threat to livelihood that it later came to pose. And this in turn goes a long way to explaining the apparently lax attitude of the Poor Law authorities towards outdoor relief for the able-bodied poor. The loss of employment by the adult male head of the household produced hardship, and needed to be compensated in some way. But apart from the fact that unemployment was usually for intermittent short periods, and so a predictable part of family life, the wages lost made up only one part of the total family economy. The Poor Law overseers and Justices of the Peace were not faced, normally at any rate, with a situation of utter destitution and poverty as a result of unemployment. Hence it made sense, both out of humane consideration, and as a hard-headed financial calculation, to bring families up to a level of subsistence by supplementing their incomings of cash and kind, from whatever sources. By taking into account the total pattern of subsistence of labouring families, including their rights on the commons, the level of subvention would not normally have been very high. It was certainly cheaper for the parish to act in this way than to attempt to bring the labourer and his whole family into the workhouse, even had that been practicable. Aided by modest cash payments, together with what other income the wife and children might be able to bring in, the family was likely to emerge relatively unscathed from spells of unemployment.

There is one further point that should be mentioned in this account of the eighteenth-century labourer's relation to wages and employment. The eighteenth-century labourer did not *desire* income beyond a certain level. The idea of a continuously growing stream of income over the life-span was alien to him. Eighteenth-century commentators are unanimous in the view that workers preferred leisure to increased income. When wages were high, or prices low, they cut down the number of hours of work, as they were able to achieve the expected level of subsistence and comfort with less labour. It was one reason why many eighteenth-century writers argued against high wages, if production were to be increased. In a famous expression of what later economists were gracefully to theorize as 'the backward-sloping supply curve of labour' Arthur Young declared that 'everyone but an idiot knows that the lower classes must be kept poor or they will never be industrious'.[30]

Once more, therefore, the importance of wages was qualified by a set of values and expectations that limited the needs and requirements of eighteenth-century families. The truly fateful change came with the creation of a new set and structure of needs. As early as 1755 Bishop Berkeley threw out the suggestion 'whether the creation of wants be not the likeliest way to produce industry in a people?' Adam Smith was soon to argue that high wages, far from depressing industry, acted as an incentive to increased output, as it brought new standards of 'ease and plenty' within the range of the worker's perceptions, and encouraged him to 'exert his strength to the utmost' in striving to attain them.[31] The importance of money wages was to increase at the very time that the other supports of the family economy were being knocked away, as more and more of the commons were enclosed and the factory system invaded the household economy. From being one among several components of the family economy, wages from employment threatened to be the sole precarious base.

II

The working class and the New Poor Law in the nineteenth century

But not for some considerable time to come – not, in fact, until late in the nineteenth century. This fact is still not sufficiently appreciated. Because of a tendency to antedate the full impact of the Industrial Revolution in England,[32] the pattern of work and employment characteristic of twentieth-century industrial man is read back into the earlier years of the nineteenth century. From this it is inferred, in particular, that unemployment must have had much the same consequences in the last century as in this – and without the support of the social services available today.

It is this, I think, that lies behind the traditional view that the Poor Law Amendment Act of 1834 constitutes a watershed in the treatment of the able-bodied poor – the category that, as we have seen, for most of Poor Law history covered (and concealed) the unemployed. The New Poor Law is seen as making a radical break with the past by abolishing outdoor relief and forcing all the able-bodied poor into the workhouse, on pain of abandonment to destitution outside. It is, on this view, not simply the product of a new toughness towards the poor, in keeping with the generally disciplinarian ideology of an expanding industrial economy, but the response of a society harbouring a different ethic of work, and a different attitude towards poverty and unemployment. It is thus truly the child of Bentham and Senior, Malthus and Ricardo.[33]

The view that the New Poor Law, 'the principles of 1834', marked a sharp break with the past is, however, a mistaken one. Even at the level of theory alone, without considering practice, it is not difficult to show that the Act of 1834 represented a continuation and indeed a culmination of the central philosophy of the 1601 Act. The 'New' Poor Law can in fact be seen as the last and grandest effort of the old order to establish and hold the line between the 'deserving' and the 'undeserving' poor, between the truly destitute – the sick, the old, widows and orphans – and the able-bodied poor, who could find their own means of support if they were not demoralized and pauperized by public subsidies. The 1834 Act wished to make this distinction as hard and thoroughgoing as possible. The 'less eligibility' feature of the Act – the principle that the situation of the pauper in the workhouse 'must cease to be really or apparently so eligible as the situation of the independent labourer of the lowest class' – merely re-affirmed, in a more rigorous form, the 'workhouse test' of the 1722 Act, designed to discourage the able-bodied from applying for relief unless utterly destitute. The ideal remained the same as that of the Elizabethan Poor Law, the same as it had been throughout the last 200 years: the rapid resumption of independence by the labourer, who for whatever reason might be tempted or forced to fall back on the rates. Nassau Senior, the chief architect of the 1834 Act, in a review of Poor Law history in 1841, reserved his harshest condemnation for the 'over-generous' Speenhamland system, whose policy of wage subsidies had driven the labourer into a servile and dependent position not very different from that of the American slave. 'Before the Poor Law Amendment Act, nothing but the power of arbitrary punishment was wanting in the pauperized parishes to a complete system of praedial slavery.'[34] The 1834 Act therefore pinned its highest hopes on the abolition of outdoor relief to the able-bodied, and the re-establishment of the 'workhouse test' with a vengeance. The 'deterrent' element, always latent and often practised under the old Poor Law, was here given its fullest expression in the hope that this would at last realize the long-cherished goal of removing the able-bodied from the sphere of the Poor Law.[35]

Mark Blaug is therefore quite right when he says that 'the Poor Law Amendment Act of 1834 marked a revolution in British social administration, but it left the structure of relief policy substantially unchanged'.[36] The parallels and continuities persist when we move from policy to practice. The 1834 Act had already compromised to some extent on the absolute prohibition of outdoor relief by allowing it to continue in the case of those of the old and the sick who could be relieved in their own homes (those who could not were to be taken into the workhouse). This was meant to be a severely limited provision. But as with so much Poor Law legislation in the past, what the national policy-makers sought after was undermined by the practice of the authorities at the local level. The formidable powers of the new Commissioners proved ineffectual to prevent the erosion of the central aspect of Poor Law policies by a large number of Poor Law Guardians, responding to the realities of the situation in their own areas.

In the northern counties, resistance to the New Poor Law was immediate, long-drawn-out and crowned with an impressive degree of success. All sections of the community recognized the inappropriateness, in that region, of a policy which restricted relief of the able-bodied poor to the workhouse. In the northern industrial areas, the commonest experience of unemployment was of the temporary mass kind, when a slump threw thousands of workers out of work. It was impossible to attempt to relieve numbers as large as this in the workhouse, quite apart from the fact that this would destroy the worker's chances of re-employment when better times returned. A powerful coalition of manufacturers, magistrates, local clerics and local Chartists combined to make the New Poor Law in many northern areas a dead letter for decades, by which time new ideas about poor relief were beginning to emerge. Outdoor relief to the unemployed poor continued to be given on a substantial and regular basis, even frequently in the form most anathematized by the Poor Law Commissioners, that of allowances in aid of inadequate earnings.[37]

The North exhibited the most spectacular resistance to the New Poor Law, but other regions carried out quieter wars of attrition which moved them more or less in the same direction.[38] In 1844 Sir James Graham, the Home Secretary, was forced to admit in the Commons that 85 per cent of relief was still given outside, and not inside, the workhouses.[39] The difficulty of enforcing central policy, and the widespread flouting of it, is shown in the frequent but unsuccessful campaigns of the Poor Law Commission (and later the Poor Law Board and the Local Government Board) to force local Boards of Guardians to abandon their practice of outdoor relief to the able-bodied (the last major campaign seems to have been in the early 1870s). In practice, local Boards of Guardians were able to operate with considerable freedom of the central authority, and they used this freedom to maintain many of the features of the old Poor Law system. As with old Poor Law overseers and vestries, considerations of humaneness were mixed with calculations of cost. In London, for instance, in 1862 it was calculated that a pauper in the workhouse cost the ratepayer 4s. 8d a week as compared to 2s. 3d for an outside pauper. Motives of both kinds, therefore, often pointed in the same direction, in the maintenance of a considerable level of outdoor relief in the form of cash payments. The result was that the workhouse population of the nineteenth century was remarkably similar to that of the eighteenth in composition: that is, it was made up largely of the sick and infirm, the aged, and orphaned or abandoned children. The able-bodied poor, men and women, shunned the workhouse like the plague, and in many cases the Poor Law Guardians were willing accessories.[40]

The economy of the poor in the nineteenth century

Still there remains a large question. The outdoor relief, in the form of cash payments, given to the poor was hardly generous. It was indeed the very meagreness of the dole that, in the eyes of many guardians, made it so attractive an alternative to the provision of relief in the workhouse. What, if any, additional resources did the poor have to draw on? What in particular was the pattern of work and employment that enabled the able-bodied poor to manage in the Victorian era? Did they in fact manage?

One answer, as revealed in the official statistics of the central Poor Law authorities, was that the problem of the poor was being solved by the disappearance of poverty itself. Official statistics showed a gratifying and progressive drop in the number of paupers on relief throughout the century: from 1.26 million (8.8 per cent of the population) in 1834, to 1 million (5.7 per cent) in 1850, to 808,000 (just over 3 per cent) in 1880. By 1900 only 2.5 per cent of the population was estimated to be in receipt of poor relief. It was thought by many professional commentators that the rising standard of living of the working classes, together with improved Poor Law administration, were reducing poverty to a problem of relatively minor proportions.[41]

Such complacency could not, however, stand up to the extent of poverty revealed by the painstaking investigations of Booth, Rowntree, Bowley and others towards the end of the century and in the early years of the new one. These showed, with a striking degree of agreement, that something like 30 per cent of the population were living in poverty. When this is compared with the 2–3 per cent officially on relief in the same period, it is clear, first, that the Poor Law statistics are of little use as a measure of poverty and, secondly, that a significant proportion of the population were living in poverty without having recourse to poor relief.

And yet the Booth–Rowntree–Bowley picture is itself far from unproblematic. For one thing it is not clear how far back into the nineteenth century we can project these turn-of-the-century estimates, although Henry Mayhew's more impressionistic (and more vivid) observations of working-class life at the mid-century reveal something of the same dimensions of poverty. But the real problem is the nature and significance of poverty itself. Who were the poor in the nineteenth century? What part did poverty play in the total picture of working-class life? What aspects of that life, especially of working life, may have begun to change by the time Booth and Rowntree started their investigations?

Booth himself found old age to be the most frequent cause of poverty in the East End of London. The old made up one-third of all paupers in his 1892 study of Poplar and Stepney; while over half of all paupers on outdoor relief under the Poor Laws were aged and infirm. As in the eighteenth century, widows with dependent children constituted a high proportion of Poor Law relief cases. So did the sick; the Royal Commission on the Poor Laws of 1905–9 revealed that 30 per cent of paupers were receiving medical treatment. Large families again, were another major cause of poverty.[42] So far, the picture is one that shows a striking similarity with the eighteenth-century poor, and suggests that many aspects – including some of the grimmest – of eighteenth-century working-class life had persisted well into the nineteenth century.

Is this also true with another major cause, for many, *the* major cause, of poverty – inadequate or irregular earnings? We have seen that eighteenth-century workers frequently lost wages through spells of unemployment, but that these were at least in part compensated for by other resources of the household and local economy. How far was this still true in the nineteenth century? The precise contribution of unemployment to poverty in the nineteenth century is impossible to estimate, since the figures for unemployment before the establishment of labour exchanges in 1910 are notoriously patchy. The Board of Trade figures, based on returns from benefit-paying unions of members in receipt of 'out-of-work' benefit, show that between 1870 and 1912 average unemployment for the trades covered ranged between 3 and 6 per cent, with a rise to between 7 and 10 per cent for the bad years of 1879, 1885–7, 1893–5 and 1908–9.[43] These do not seem excessive, certainly as compared with some later levels. But as against this we have to set, for example, the estimates of Hobsbawm and Foster for the first half of the century. Hobsbawm shows that in the worst slump years, such as those of 1826 and 1839–42, anything between 25 and 75 per cent of particular occupational groups, and in some places of the whole working population, might be unemployed; although he makes the point that at most other times in this period 'underemployment, rather than cessation of work' was the main problem for most trades.[44] In the case of the Lancashire textile workers, Foster calculates that up to 30 per cent of the workforce were unemployed in the worst years of the 1830s and 1840s.[45] And generally it seems that a high degree of casual and irregular employment, and so a marked degree of underemployment, was a feature of the English economy right up to the end of the century, although patterns of stability and security of employment were beginning to be established in several trades.[46]

But of course we have to go behind these figures of 'the unemployed' to know what they meant in the lives of the workers concerned. And here there is sufficient evidence to indicate that, until about the end of the century, conditions of work and subsistence persisted which mitigated the bare fact of unemployment and modified its significance in the lives of workers. It was not merely that, as now, to be out of employment was not necessarily to be without work. More important was the 'undeveloped' state of the industrial economy itself, leaving significant pockets of 'pre-industrial' work organization and attitudes which militated against the complete identification of work with formal employment in the market economy. The statistics of 'unemployment' in the nineteenth century, such as they are, conceal a very considerable amount of remunerative work actually done, and distort the real situation of families in the emerging industrial economy.

Take first the family economy, the traditional arrangement whereby virtually all members of the family contributed to its subsistence. This defensive bulwark against the involuntary unemployment of particular family members persisted throughout the nineteenth century, in the factory districts as much as in domestic industry. Smelser's suggestion that family employment declined in the cotton industry in the 1830s and 1840s has been shown to be untrue by Anderson and Pollard. At the mid-century, 'family employment was still characteristic, and as a result the local labour force was able to show superior resilience and attachment to the industry in depressions, even though wages were not high.'[47] There is even the possibility that early industrialization increased the employment of women and children, at a time when employment opportunities were declining in agriculture and domestic industry. Since, in addition, women and children earned more in the factories than elsewhere, 'with the Industrial Revolution their earnings became central to the domestic economy. They made a significantly larger contribution and they made it to a significantly larger number of families.'[48] Where family members did not actually work for money, they could contribute to family income indirectly, as in the case of grandparents who co-resided with their married children, 'caring for the children and home while the mother worked in the factory'.[49]

Thus the coming of the factory system did not for some time destroy the unity of the family economy. Thompson's remark, that 'the family was roughly torn apart each morning by the factory bell',[50] is misleading with its suggestion of a decisive fragmentation of family life, a radical separation of the spheres of work and family. Families continued to work as well as to live as a unit, a fact acknowledged indirectly by Engels in his appalled middle-class observation on the effects of working wives:

It is inevitable that if a married woman works in a factory, family life is inevitably destroyed ... [However] very often the fact that a married woman is working does not lead to the complete disruption of the home but to a reversal of the normal division of labour within the family. The wife is the breadwinner while her husband stays at home to look after the children and to do the cleaning and cooking. This happens very frequently indeed ... One may well imagine the righteous indignation of the workers at being virtually turned into eunuchs.[51]

Factory employment was, of course, a fact of experience for only a minority of nineteenth-century workers, and least of all for adult males.[52] The persistence of the family economy was naturally even more evident in the small-scale domestic and outwork industries, which far from being extinguished by industrialization, actually expanded enormously as a result.[53] In mid-nineteenth-century Stourbridge, for example, by then a medium-sized industrial town based on iron, 'a good half of the workforce was employed in or about the home', with a family-based, task-orientated, work pattern traditionally associated with domestic industry. This meant not simply the customary observance of 'Saint Monday' and 'Saint Tuesday' – until well into the 1870s and beyond – but the equally conventional interruption of industrial work to go harvesting and hopping (joined by the miners of the area) in the summer months. Children and women worked as a matter of course in these domestic industries – such as nail-making and brick-making – and shared in the long hours and laborious but intermittent toil characteristic of them.[54]

It was the continuation of domestic and outwork industry on an extensive scale that was mainly responsible for concealing from contemporary census enumerators – and later historians – a good deal of the remunerative work actually done in Victorian England, especially by women. This was especially true in a town like London, where few trades were transformed by the factory system until the twentieth century. The commentators and social statisticians tended to concentrate on women workers in factories, and so largely ignored the host of washerwomen, needlewomen, charwomen, landladies, baby-minders, midwives, and other female domestic workers, including those married women who worked with their husbands in their trade. Even less visible to the enumerators were the ill-defined categories of female market workers and street-traders, not to mention street-walkers. Speaking of the

London working class, Sally Alexander says:

Women (and children) of this class always had to contribute to the family income . . .
It was often the household and not the individual worker, or even separate families,
that was the economic unit. A mixture of washing, cleaning, charring as well as various
sorts of home- or slop-work, in addition to domestic labour, occupied most women
throughout their working lives. The diversity and indeterminacy of this spasmodic,
casual and irregular employment was not easily condensed and classified into a Census
occupation.[55]

There was nothing idyllic about the family economy, either in its full pre-
industrial form or in its increasingly attenuated and straitened state in the
nineteenth century. It was nearly always stretched to its limit, with the Poor
Law as a largely feared and disdained safety-net. But it remained, at its most
besieged, a welfare system in miniature, with children, wives and occasionally
grandparents covering as best they could when the man was unemployed or
unable to work. That for a good part of the time the system provided at least
a bare subsistence for the family is suggested by the fact that throughout the
nineteenth century the Poor Law figures consistently show that only a
small percentage of able-bodied paupers were destitute through want of
employment.[56] It is this system that also partly explains the otherwise
extraordinary clinging of many families to handicraft trades where these were
in direct competition with factory production. Pollard refers to the plight of
the hand-loom weavers, 'whose numbers did not decrease as their wages were
inexorably depressed even further below subsistence level', as 'one of the best
known and most puzzling episodes of the industrial revolution'. 'It will be
better understood,' he suggests, 'if it is remembered that many weavers were
now women, often part-time; others combined weaving with farming; and still
others clung to their spurious independence with the help of other members
of the family working in the mills.'[57]

A further perspective on the still 'unmodern' nature of the Victorian
economy is provided by a consideration of the two areas of employment that
dominated throughout the nineteenth century: agriculture and domestic
service. Domestic service did not simply give rise to the second-largest
occupational group after agriculture, it was far and away the most important
source of employment for women. It expanded rapidly in the second half of
the century, accounting for more than forty per cent of all employed women
up to 1901. The denunciation of the conditions of domestic service has
become so common that it is easy to forget that the alternatives for most
women, and for their families, were far worse. It is in fact no idealization of
domestic service to say that 'service provided country girls with a surrogate
home and family', or that 'employment in a good household was akin to
membership of an extended family group'.[58] For women and children, life in
one's own home and family was at least as likely to lead to exploitation as
life in someone else's service. Domestic service was a way out, both for them
and their families; a means of externalizing some of the economic pressures
on poor families living in cramped quarters on low wages, especially in the
country districts. For the girls of these families, moreover, it was a secure,

well-paid and regular occupation for which there was a steady and rising demand throughout the century. The wages of domestic servants rose faster than those of almost all other wage-earners. In addition, 'servants' food and accommodation were in most cases far better than what they could have expected in their parents' home, and there were few workers so likely to receive medical attention paid for by their employers, pay during sickness, and regular paid holidays.'[59]

Nor did the movement out of the family disrupt the basic unity of the family economy. Girls in domestic service, like many of their counterparts in factory work, continued to regard themselves as part of the family enterprise. They regularly sent back much of their wages to their families, and made frequent visits for longer or shorter stays. For both themselves and their families, their movement into domestic service in the towns was no more than an extension, or an expansion, of the traditional contribution of girls to the family economy.[60] Moreover, once married, women workers were similarly occupied in 'domestic' employment – as homeworkers in the textile and dressmaking trades – and continued in a different guise to play their traditional part in the overall domestic economy. It is clear, then, that for this large section of the Victorian workforce – women accounted for about 30 per cent of the total labour force throughout the century – 'unemployment' could be neither as threatening nor as consequential as it was to become when domestic employment declined after the First World War.

Traditionalism, in work practices and attitudes, seems also to have been the hallmark throughout much of the countryside during the nineteenth century. The importance of this for the assessment of the impact of 'unemployment' is obvious when we consider that agricultural workers made up the largest occupational group for practically the whole century. 'Somewhere near mid-century British agriculture employed more workers than at any time before or since.' Agricultural workers then made up almost a quarter of the entire occupied population.[61] British agriculture was certainly being revolutionized, and the proportion of landless wage-labourers, already high relative to other countries, continued to grow throughout the century. But, as with work practices in the factory,[62] so in the countryside there was for long little attempt to 'systematize' and 'regularize' the workforce. Samuel comments that 'occupational boundaries in the nineteenth century countryside were comparatively fluid. They had to be, where so much employment was by the job rather than by the regular working week.' He goes on to echo Alexander's warning about the limitation of census-based accounts, in presenting a realistic picture of employment in the countryside:

There is a whole spectrum of occupations which historians (following the census enumerators) have overlooked, either because they were too local to show up prominently in national statistics, like coprolite digging in Cambridgeshire and Bedfordshire, or because they were too short-lived to rank as occupations at all ... Industrial occupations in the countryside, such as lime-burning, brickmaking, or quarrying, are ignored. So too is the whole range of country navvying jobs which kept the out-of-work farm labourer employed – sand getting and gravel drawing, for instance, clay digging, wood-cutting and copse work, and such locally important alternative sources of employment open to the labourer; the census enumerators largely ignore them. 'Field labour' covers all.[63]

Something of the variety of work carried on in the countryside as late as 1892 comes out in the finding of the Royal Commission on Labour of that year that three-quarters of the farm labourers of Monmouthshire were engaged in wood-cutting, quarrying and mine work. In a surprisingly direct echo of many statements about eighteenth-century workers, they comment: 'With respect to many of them, it is difficult to determine whether they may be styled wood-cutters and quarrymen, coming to the land for hoeing, harvesting, and sundry piece-work, or whether they are in the main agricultural labourers, going to the woods, quarries and mines in the winter months.'[64]

The nineteenth-century farm labourer was clearly no stranger to the 'dual-occupation' economy. In addition he had access, on a declining scale no doubt, to the remaining rights (acknowledged or not) on commons, pasture and woodlands, together in most cases with a small plot of land or allotment.[65] In the grim conditions of the agricultural labourer's life, especially in the South, these features were of inestimable value in gaining a subsistence. They also enabled farm families, even more than urban families, to act in a common enterprise. Women and children played a noticeable part in the family economy, not simply at harvest time but throughout the year, in such activities as laundry work, the keeping of ducks and pigs, poaching and gardening.[66] In such an economic environment, 'unemployment' was decidedly not a meaningless thing – the winter months were especially hard – but it might be difficult to know precisely what it meant, or to assess the true consequences.

We should note, finally, that 'dual occupations' were not restricted to rural workers, but in a general sense involved a large proportion of the Victorian workforce as a whole. Victorian working life still showed a noteworthy 'irregularity' and diversity that in many ways harked back more to the eighteenth-century pattern than it looked forward to the twentieth. Raphael Samuel has shown a cyclical pattern of employment for many urban workers. The cycle, however, was not that of the economy but of the seasons. As the spring approached, families, sometimes in groups, would leave the town to seek employment in the countryside. At the height of the summer season, whole towns would be deserted and certain industries forced to close down temporarily. With the autumn and winter, the drift back to the town set in, with yet another change of occupations. The next spring set families moving again. Samuel makes it clear that the pattern was not really broken until the end of the century, with the 'regularization' of employment in factories and on farms.[67] Certainly the descent of East End London families on the hop fields of Kent in the summer months was still going strong at the turn of the century (and indeed for many decades thereafter).[68]

It is important to stress that the work pattern of these 'wandering tribes' was not something marginal and exotic in the Victorian workforce as a whole. Hobsbawm's examination of the 'tramping' system shows that a period of wandering in search of work – or simply of variety of place – was a normal part of the working lives of respectable artisans. The system combined elements of 'unemployment relief' with primitive labour exchanges and the creation of a mobile labour market. It was, from the point of view of the artisans, a normal way of dealing with the threat of unemployment, setting men in motion from areas of scarcity of work to those where, with the help of local union branches, they could more easily find it. As Hobsbawm says, 'what we may call the non-capitalist sector of the economy long remained large enough, and the capitalist sector localized and diversified enough, to make temporary migration appear a feasible escape from slumps'. In the earlier part of the century, when the system – apparently as much a new growth as a continuation of eighteenth-century practice – was at its height, the General Union of Carpenters commented that of late 'our highroads have resembled a mechanical workshop, or a mighty mass of moving human beings'. Hobsbawm adds that 'some men, in that period of rapid industrial growth, were semi-nomadic, leaving a permanent home for varying periods, or shifting their families from time to time, especially among builders, specialist craftsmen and supervisory workers.'[69]

These are simply glimpses. Many aspects of Victorian working life remain hidden to us by the preconceptions of officials, historians and sociologists. But perhaps enough has been said to back up the main point: which is that work, employment and unemployment in nineteenth-century England still bore many of the hall-marks of the pre-industrial economy and society. Poverty was caused and relieved in much the same way as the previous century. Work was not so specialized that workers could not turn their hand to a variety of occupations in town and country. Urbanization itself had not yet gone so far that most workers and their families could not have some access to the 'free' resources of the countryside. The contingencies of life, including unemployment and underemployment, pressed as hard as ever; but a mixture of outdoor relief, a diversified labour market and mutual aid in traditionally oriented families and communities softened their stark impact.

III

'The unemployed man' and the charter of 'full employment'

All this had begun to change fundamentally by the time Booth, Rowntree, Beveridge and the rest began their researches on the poor. Industrialization was at last delivering up its fruits, and England was becoming the first fully recognizable urban–industrial society. The irregularity that marked work and the workforce was being eliminated in a number of ways, by specialization, mechanization, work organization and a firmer imposition of work discipline. For those workers in the right trades and industries this promised greater security and status. For others, de-casualization was a threat to their livelihood in circumstances where alternative ways of making ends meet were disappearing. For all, the 'right to work' was coming to carry almost exclusively one meaning, 'the right to employment'. The employed status was the only one entitling the worker to a claim on the society's resources; even when out of work, claims for benefits and support turned preponderantly on earned rights through previous employment.[70] Those who could not get employment at all, or for too short periods to build up legitimate claims for support, were faced with a hostile and increasingly unsupportive environment.

The resouces of the family itself, for so long the refuge of the unemployed, were squeezed by the withdrawal of labour of some of its members. The Education Acts of 1870 and later did what many factory acts had failed to do, gradually eliminating child labour on any but the most insignificant scale. The number of working wives also declined. By 1911 only 10 per cent of married women were employed, compared with a quarter in 1851 and probably twice as much as that at the beginning of the century.[71]

It is not surprising, therefore, and far from a coincidence, that this is the period, beginning in the 1880s, in which 'unemployment' as a concept first received formal recognition, and was widely investigated and subjected to theoretical scrutiny.[72] We have often had occasion up to now to refer to 'unemployment' and the 'unemployed' before this period, and of course it is quite proper to do so. But the whole point of the discussion so far has been to stress the different meaning and significance of 'unemployment' in that earlier period, both for the workers themselves and the public authorities which had to deal with their situation. The appearance of a new word or concept, in the social world at least, sometimes does not mark more than a belated recognition of what has for long been going on. But in many cases, as with 'unemployment', it is a good indication that something in the social environment has significantly changed. A new awareness, a first response to a novel challenge, arises in the society. Such a challenge was now, for the first time, seen to be posed by unemployment, as an endemic structural feature of industrial economies, and as a social problem of potentially overwhelming proportions. A new phase of industrial life was signalled by the Minority Report of the Royal Commission on the Depression of Trade and Industry (1886) when it declared that the great problem of the age was not the scarcity and dearness of commodities, but 'the struggle for an adequate share of that employment which affords to the great bulk of the population their only means of obtaining a title to a sufficiency of those necessaries and conveniences, however plentiful they may be'.

Compressing the account somewhat, we may say that it was in the period from the 1890s to the 1940s that the norm – one might almost say the ideology – of 'full employment' was gradually developed and enshrined in the industrial societies. It is, once again, not surprising that England should be the country where the phenomenon was first subjected to the most intense public scrutiny, since it was in England that industrialization had gone furthest. From about 1895, when the concept was first discussed by J. A. Hobson, through to the appearance of Beveridge's *Full Employment in a Free Society* in 1944, some of the most eminent of Britain's economists, social theorists, politicians and publicists addressed themselves to the problem of unemployment. There were the social surveys and investigations of the extent and nature of the problem by Booth, Rowntree, Beveridge, Llewellyn Smith,

Bowley, Reeves and others. There was the voluminous and exhaustive history of the Poor Law by Sidney and Beatrice Webb, designed as the background to their own specific remedies and solutions, many of which appeared in the Minority Report of the Royal Commission on the Poor Laws of 1905–9. There were the European investigations and radical policies of Winston Churchill and Lloyd George, who showed themselves by no means content to be the mouthpieces of the professional Fabian researchers. And there were the theoretical analyses of the professional economists, A. C. Pigou, R. C. Hawtrey, D. Robertson and John Maynard Keynes.

In this development, the First World War marks a clear divide. Before then, from the 1880s to 1914, unemployment was regarded chiefly as a problem of social policy and social administration, not of economic theory and economic policy.[73] Hence the concentration, not on the staple industries of cotton, coal, iron and steel, where there was in fact considerable 'cyclical' unemployment, but on the pool of casual labour in the docks and in the building trades, especially in London. 'When economists, politicians and pamphleteers first talked of "unemployment", they thought above all of the situation in London. "The unemployed" were not the miners of the Rhondda or the millhands of Lancashire but the casual labourers of the capital.'[74] The reason for this selectivity was that unemployment, though clearly a serious issue, was seen largely in terms of the social threat it posed. The teeming mass of casual labour in London, especially in the East End, was the most vivid and visible expression of this threat. The casual labourer, it was felt, was not only himself demoralized and pauperized by the conditions of his trade, and hence a volatile and potentially dangerous actor; he also threatened to 'contaminate' the respectable artisan groups above him by flooding their trades with cheap sweated labour and so undermining their economic positions.[75]

The main strategy for dealing with the unemployed in this period was formulated within this analysis. Immediately, the unemployed were to be segregated from the regularly employed; in the longer term the answer was the de-casualization of their trades. Various kinds of labour colonies, at home and overseas, were the favourite remedy in the earlier part of the period. 'In the early 1900s,' says Harris, 'the creation of farm colonies with a view to restoring workmen permanently to the land was the most widely canvassed solution to the problem of surplus labour.'[76] The failure of most of these schemes, which had also been officially encouraged on a local basis by the Unemployed Workmen Act (1905), led to a more determined attack at the national level. The Liberal Government of 1906 accepted the view that segregation was no solution in the long run, and under the energetic prompting of Churchill, Lloyd George and Beveridge worked towards the more efficient organization of the labour market as a whole. 'The first object of the organisation of the labour market,' wrote Beveridge in 1909, 'is to make possible a policy of "de-casualisation".'[77] From this followed Beveridge's pet solution, the setting up of labour exchanges (1909), with unemployment insurance (1911) coming as the necessary back-up to cope with short-term unemployment.[78]

The First World War eliminated unemployment, more or less, as did the short-lived boom that immediately followed it. Then in the winter of 1920–1 came the start of the long depression, intensified at the end of the decade by the even more catastrophic slump. By December 1921 there were more than 2 million registered unemployed, and for the whole of the inter-war period the number did not drop below 1 million. Between 1921 and 1939 unemployment averaged 14 per cent of the insured workforce, with an early peak of 16.9 per cent in 1921 and a later one of 22.1 per cent (nearly 3 million unemployed) in 1932. Unemployment did not fall below a million until the first year of the Second World War. Long-term unemployment persisted beyond the general recovery of the mid-1930s, being a quarter of all unemployment in 1936 and still 23 per cent in 1939.[79]

Unemployment on this scale necessarily broke through the framework established for the pre-1914 period. The National Insurance Act of 1911 had assumed an average unemployment level of 8.46 per cent among eligible workers, for the unemployment insurance scheme set up by it to work as intended. This made sense within the context of an average annual unemployment level – roughly estimated – of 4.5 per cent between 1880 and 1914.[80] Emboldened by their experience of low unemployment between 1914 and 1920, the government rashly reduced their assumed rate of unemployment to 5.32 per cent in the Unemployment Insurance Act of 1920, which extended unemployment insurance to practically all manual and other low-paid workers. Since the assumed rate turned out to be only about one-third of the rate that actually prevailed in the inter-war period, it is not surprising that the unemployment insurance fund rapidly ran into massive deficit, and had to be bailed out by the Treasury on innumerable occasions.[81]

The unemployment insurance scheme was the most contentious political issue, and the most widely discussed casualty, of the inter-war period. An indication of this lies in the fact that between 1920 and the Unemployment Act of 1934 there were twenty Acts of Parliament on unemployment insurance. This preoccupation reflected the failure of policy. All the governments of the time, Labour as much as Conservative, professed themselves helpless in the face of mass unemployment. They clung to orthodox economic policies in the belief, unaffected by the outcome, that only these would eventually restore economic prosperity. Alternative, Keynesian, offerings by Lloyd George and the Liberals, as well as by Mosley's New Party and the Independent Labour Party, were steadily resisted by the Treasury and most economists and, more to the point, were repeatedly rejected by the electorate at the polls. The resulting disaster forced all governments to fall back on unemployment benefits, eked out with 'Public Assistance' (the new name after 1930 for outdoor relief under the Poor Law), as the principal means of staving off serious discontent. That they were able to achieve this thereby was a testimony not simply to the real value of the benefits, exiguous as they were, but also to the fact that no government could any longer choose to regard unemployment as a residual social problem. Again and again, and contrary to their formal intentions, governments gave way to popular pressure by and on behalf of the unemployed to raise or restore benefits.[82]

Whatever the inadequacies of economic policy in dealing with unemployment in this period, one thing was clear. Unemployment was acknowledged by all to be a central issue of economic theory and economic policy: a matter, in other words, of the working of the economy as a whole. The dispute about the level of unemployment benefits itself forced consideration of theoretical issues upon the protagonists. With the erosion of the actuarial basis of the unemployment insurance scheme, the Treasury as both guarantor of the insurance fund and guardian of public money became directly involved in the unemployment question. The state of the national budget, and the orthodox requirement for tight balances, had obvious relevance to unemployment. Was the attempt to balance the budget by cutting government expenditure deflationary? Did the return to gold in 1925 at pre-war parity wreak further havoc with British industry? Did low wages and reduced benefits lead to a lack of demand through under-consumption? Would a reflationary strategy of budget deficits, involving public works and government subsidies for industry, lead to recovery? Even political movements with more distant goals were forced to relate their advocacy to the issue of unemployment. This was true not simply of Fascists and Communists, but also of such movements as Leo Amery and Beaverbrook's campaign for tariff reform and imperial preference. Addressing themselves to the Treasury's obsession with budgetary stringency, they argued that a system of protective tariffs within the boundaries of the Empire would both give a boost to British industry and raise revenue for the Exchequer. As an alternative to domestic reflation as a solution to unemployment, it clearly had much to recommend it to the Treasury. It also commended itself to the voters, who returned a strongly protectionist Parliament in 1931. This represented a striking change of attitude, corresponding to the new significance of unemployment. A similar campaign with similar arguments had failed decisively under the leadership of Joseph Chamberlain in the early 1900s. Now his son Neville redressed the past, in introducing protection and imperial preference in 1931–2.[83]

There was another obvious reason why unemployment became a central concern of public policy in the 1920s and 1930s. Unemployment was at its highest in those industries that, to all commentators, were the ones that mattered most in Britain's economy. It was the staple industries of the North and West, coal, textiles, ship-building, iron and steel, that were the most serious victims of the depression. These were the ones which, throughout the nineteenth century, had been the glory of British industry and the source of national prosperity, accounting for three-quarters of all exports on the eve of the First World War. In the inter-war period they went into long-term and permanent decline, creating a pattern of 'structural' unemployment that was overlaid by the 'cyclical' unemployment of the slump to produce an employment crisis of devastating proportions. Unemployment could still be treated basically within the framework of Poor Law administration when, as before 1914, it appeared to affect mainly the 'surplus labour' of the casual trades; when it ate into the heartlands of the national economy it was clear that a more drastic re-appraisal was urgently required.

In fact, unemployment in the casual trades in London – the main focus of pre-1914 concern – remained high after the war: the dockland areas of Bermondsey and Poplar registered rates of 11 per cent and 9.5 per cent in 1929, and in 1927 East London had the highest ratio of unemployed claimants for poor relief to total population of anywhere in Britain.[84] But London and the South-East generally, together with the Midlands, were precisely the areas where economic growth on a considerable scale was taking place in the inter-war period, based on the new consumer goods industries: motor cars, electrical goods, processed foods, the products of the chemical industries. Employment in the new industries, and the general prosperity they brought to those regions, tended to 'swamp' the still persisting pools of unemployed casual labour, reducing the social threat they had seemed to pose to the pre-war generation. The South had its black spots, but there was nothing to compare to the situation in the North and West. In 1930, for instance, London and the South-East had an unemployment rate of 8 per cent, half that of the national average of 16 per cent; the North-East at the same time registered 20.2 per cent, the North-West 23.8 per cent, Scotland 18.5 per cent and Wales 25.9 per cent. In the worst years of the depression in the mid-1930s, several towns in these regions, on Tyneside, Clydeside and in the South Wales coalfields, had more than three-quarters of the insured population out of work – 77 per cent at Jarrow in 1933, for instance.[85]

Finally we should remember that the 'Hungry Thirties' created graphic images of unemployment that stamped themselves indelibly on the national consciousness. The pre-war period had also produced some striking literary accounts of the unemployed poor, as in George Gissing's *The Nether World* (1889), Walter Besant's novels of the East End and Robert Tressell's *The Ragged Trousered Philanthropists* (1914).[86] The Victorians and Edwardians too had made their voyages of social exploration into 'darkest England'.[87] But they still conveyed the idea of the poor and unemployed as something apart, as diseased and somewhat exotic colonies encapsulated within the generally healthy body of the nation.[88] The writers of the 1930s by contrast produced portraits of the unemployed as the emblem of the whole society. The social explorers and investigators depicted unemployment as a cancer at the very heart of society, threatening its social stability in the present and its prospects for recovery in the future. A variety of literary forms contributed to a sociological mosaic which delivered a powerful indictment of the current social order. There were the careful social inquiries of E. W. Bakke, *The Unemployed Man* (1933), the Pilgrim Trust's *Men Without Work* (1938) and the Carnegie Trust's *Disinherited Youth* (1943), as well as new studies by Rowntree, the Coles and others. These showed conclusively, among other things, that to the older persisting causes of poverty, such as old age and ill-health, there now had to be added unemployment as a potent new factor.[89] There were the more artfully constructed personal reports, such as J. B. Priestley's *English Journey* (1934) and George Orwell's *Road to Wigan Pier* (1937), the latter originally commissioned as a study of unemployment. There were moving documentary novels, such as Walter Greenwood's *Love on the Dole* (1933).

It was this widely read and widely publicized 'dole literature', more than official statistics of unemployment or the marches of the unemployed, which brought about the general conviction that 'full employment' had to be the central item on the agenda of all political parties and programmes of the future. The slogan was 'never again', and a whole generation of politicians was to be anathematized as 'the guilty men'. On the eve of the Second World War, an impressive body of opinion, formed from members of all parties and of none, had converged on 'the middle ground' of British politics, committed to full employment as an essential part of a planned economy and a national welfare system.[90] Early in 1941 *Picture Post*, aptly registering as so often changes in the national mood, published 'A Plan for Britain'. Included in this special issue was an article by the economist Thomas Balogh, on 'The first necessity in the New Britain: work for all'. It was to be a theme repeated, in many different guises, throughout the Second World War and the post-war period.[91] The Labour Party's election manifesto of 1950 summed up the *credo* of a decade when it declared that 'full employment is the cornerstone of the new society'.

Among the moving forces of these decades one has to pick out William Beveridge. He is, of course, far from being the sole author of the charter of full employment in Britain. But he is a fitting symbol of it. He straddles, and in a sense delimits, the entire period of the 'discovery of unemployment', from the 1890s to the 1940s. Coming at the beginning and the end of the process, he is, as the enormously energetic and industrious policy analyst, civil servant, expert adviser and publicist, the best exemplar of the new attitude. It was his analysis of 1909, *Unemployment: A Problem of Industry*, which was the first systematic treatment of the subject, summing up five years of his own historical and sociological studies of the problem; and it was his unofficial report of 1944, *Full Employment in a Free Society*, which effectively set the seal on the new public policy. He was in charge of the department of the Board of Trade that supervised both the new labour exchanges and the unemployment insurance scheme in 1909–11, and he was Secretary of the Unemployment Insurance Statutory Committee set up under the Unemployment Act of 1934. Even when employed full-time as Director of the London School of Economics in the 1920s and early 1930s, he continued to lecture and publish widely on unemployment.

Beveridge fluctuated considerably in his thinking about unemployment, as his biographer makes clear.[92] Lloyd George's unorthodoxy alarmed him, and he did not join other radical Liberals in the preparation of the famous Lloyd George policy documents, *Britain's Industrial Future* (1928) and *We Can Conquer Unemployment* (1929). Strongly under the influence of Lionel Robbins in the 1930s, he was inclined to be sceptical of Keynesian solutions to unemployment. But for him, as for many others, the far-reaching character of the Second World War had a radicalizing influence and removed inhibiting doubts about the possibility of large-scale economic and social reconstruction after the war. Now fully converted to Keynesian ideas, he went beyond them in a much more full-blooded socialist direction.[93] His report on *Social Insurance and Allied Services* (1942), which laid out the chief features of the post-war welfare state, made it clear that full employment was the indispensable basis of a comprehensive system of welfare. The message was spelt out more fully in *Full Employment in a Free Society*, which proposed largely Keynesian measures to create full employment. It must have been with the greatest satisfaction that Beveridge could write, in the prologue to the 1960 reprint of his *Full Employment*: 'Full employment in Britain has been accomplished.'[94]

A 'world without work'?

'Full employment' was never of course to be taken literally. Beveridge himself accepted that there would always be some 'frictional unemployment' in any progressive economy. In practice this would amount to 3–4 per cent unemployed at any one time. Between 1948 and 1966 unemployment in Britain was generally below 2 per cent. The cause of this may well have had less to do with economic policy than with the worldwide recovery and growth of the industrial economies after the war. But Beveridge would at least have cause to feel that 'full employment' was far from a utopian goal.

Beveridge died in 1963. Had he lived only another decade he would have seen the dream beginning to fade. By the early 1980s Britain was experiencing an unemployment rate of 12 per cent and higher,[95] and most other industrial societies were also experiencing disturbingly high rates. There was virtually no one who expected this to come down significantly for a considerable time to come, and several who were projecting an unemployment rate of 20 per cent in Britain by the end of the decade. Indeed this seems in general the more realistic expectation even on optimistic assumptions. For if and when economic growth resumes, the likelihood is that it will do so on the basis of an even less labour-intensive economy than before. In both manufacturing and large parts of the service sector – offices, banks, shops – microelectronic technology is threatening to reduce the share of labour in production to an infinitesimal part.[96] In other areas – restaurants, hotels, transport, the leisure industries – employment is being eroded by the continued development of the 'self-service economy', based on cheap manufactured goods delivering 'final' services in the home.[97]

As a concept and as a practice, 'full employment' has been both recent and short. 'Unemployment' has been a normal part of life, and even a way of life, for all pre-industrial societies and for a good part of the history of industrial societies. But over time, as part of its general logic, the industrial revolution has undermined the basis of the balance between 'employment' and 'unemployment' in two ways. First, it aimed in principle at ensuring that all incomes were derived solely from the market, and that all goods and services were transacted and allocated through it.[98] Such perfection, such deathly finality, was fortunately in practice never attainable. But the striving towards it had the effect of gradually driving out most of the non-market areas of work and subsistence. Since production for the market increasingly entailed the large-scale organization of work in factories and offices, wage labour came to be indistinguishable from factory or office employment.

At the same time as the industrial revolution imposed the identification of meaningful, remunerative work with formal employment, it threatened, as a next stage, to make this marriage increasingly precarious. For, again in very principle, industrialization was committed to mechanization and rationalization, the goal of which in both cases pointed to complete automation and the elimination of the human worker. Thus both by its ideology (market assumptions) and by its structural evolution (the elimination of work) industrial society has imposed a double-bind on its population. Work is identified with employment in the formal economy, but employment in the formal economy is an increasingly diminishing resource. The crisis of work and unemployment – 'the collapse of work' – is not incidental to the development of industrial society but a creation of its central mechanisms.

Illich quotes Schumpeter: 'In principle, medieval society provided a berth for everyone whom it recognised as a member: its structural design excluded unemployment and destitution.'[99] Since the end of the eighteenth century, full membership of society – 'citizenship' – has been extended to virtually everyone: first all adult males, then all adults, later children (and now, it seems, even animals). But the exercise of that membership in any practical sense came to be pivoted on having an employed status, the only status giving a justified and legitimate claim on society's resources. Hence the first stages of the women's movement everywhere have involved the claim of the 'right to work' equal to that of men. Where work is lacking, people are thrown into an unstructured social and moral void where the only status acorded is that of dependent pensioner. None of the institutions of modern industrial society is geared to dealing with mass unemployment. Even trade unions are associations of the employed, and have largely ignored the problems of the unemployed.

In a situation where a fifth of the adult population may be 'unemployed' this is an absurd position. Something like a return to the medieval principle is necessary. Everyone, by virtue of membership in society, has a right to be provided with 'a berth' (which is not the same thing as saying they should be equal, any more than it was in medieval society). Concepts of 'employment' and 'unemployment' are a hindrance to a recognition of the true situation. To be employed is coming to be largely a matter of luck and accident, having little to do with social contribution. So long as 'full employment' or 'work for all' remains the goal of reformers and critics, so long will the achievement of a 'berth for all' remain unfulfilled. The pursuit of full employment creates increasingly larger 'pockets of unemployed', for whom all sorts of remedial policies have to be invented which preserve them as second-class citizens.

There is no virtue in work *per se*, work, that is, in the sense of formal employment. Much work in the twentieth century, including that of many professionals, has become routine and repetitive, a slur on the concept of 'the dignity of labour'. Insofar as it can be got rid of by further mechanization, this should in itself be no cause for regret. Whatever work in the formal economy will still need to be done should be reduced to a minimum and shared out. For the rest, what is required is not 'employment' – there is plenty of other *work* to be done – but income. Something like a guaranteed minimum income for all adults, an ancient but still serviceable idea, seems the best way of rationalizing and extending the patchwork of supports and benefits now available under the welfare system.[100] This may turn out to be not only more economical than at present, and less baffling to the citizenry, but has the more important advantage of removing the stigma from the unemployed. Since we are all likely to find ourselves among their ranks at one or another point in our lives, this surely is an objective in which we should have a genuine common interest.

NOTES

A first version of this chapter was given as a paper at an EEC–FAST seminar on attitudes to work, Marseilles, 23–26 November 1981. I should like to thank the participants for their comments. Thanks are also due, for help on particular points, to my colleagues at the University of Kent: Richard Disney, John Oxborrow and Ray Pahl.

1 The Poor Laws themselves were not repealed until 1948 (in the National Assistance Act), although the Local Government Act of 1929 transferred the functions of Poor Law Unions and Guardians to the county and county borough councils.

2 H. L. Beales, 'The New Poor Law', *History*, XV (1931), reprinted in E. M. Carus-Wilson (ed.), *Essays in Economic History*, vol. III (London, Edward Arnold, 1962), pp. 179–80.

3 All students of the period agree on this. See especially Edgar S. Furniss, *The Position of the Laborer in a System of Nationalism* (Boston, Mass., Houghton Mifflin Company, 1920), pp. 25n., 93n. Dorothy Marshall notes the large proportion of the population – anyone who did not inhabit a tenement worth £10 or more a year – over whom parish overseers had rights of removal under a clause of the 1662 Act of Settlement: 'This clause in theory affected not only the old, the infirm, the helpless, and the infants, but also all those agricultural labourers who worked for, and were dependent on, their wages; it affected the great class of manual workers of every kind; it affected most of the smaller manufacturers, such as the spinners, the weavers, the dyers, and the shearers; it affected, too, the large class of small craftsmen, the blacksmiths, the carpenters, or the tailors. In short, as the Poor Laws had power not only over those who were actually chargeable, but over those likely to become so, their operation included the greater part of the lower working class under the designation of "The Poor"' (Marshall, *The English Poor in the Eighteenth Century*, London, George Routledge and Sons, 1926, p. 2).

4 Jacob Viner, 'Man's economic status', in James L. Clifford (ed.), *Man versus Society in Eighteenth Century England* (Cambridge, Cambridge University Press, 1968), p. 27. R.W. Malcolmson, using hearth tax returns, suggests that 'at least 75 per cent of England's roughly 5.5 million people in the later 17th century were labouring people. My own judgement is that around 80 per cent of the population were labouring men and women', *Life and Labour in England 1700–1780* (London, Hutchinson, 1981), p. 19. And see D.C. Coleman, 'Labour in the English economy of the seventeenth century', *Economic History Review*, 8 (1956), no. 3, reprinted in E.M. Carus-Wilson (ed.), *Essays in Economic History*, vol. II (London, Edward Arnold, 1962), p. 295. Macpherson also estimates that the

labouring poor (wage earners, cottagers and paupers) constituted over two-thirds
of the adult male population of seventeenth-century England, and that 'alms-
takers' – those dependent on the parish for relief – made up between a quarter
and a third. C. B. Macpherson, *The Political Theory of Possessive Individualism:
Hobbes to Locke* (Oxford, Oxford University Press, paperback edn, 1964), pp. 61,
301 (note T) and, especially, the appendix, 'Social classes and franchise classes
in England c. 1648', pp. 279–92. See also his 'Servants and labourers in
seventeenth century England', in *Democratic Theory: Essays in Retrieval* (Oxford,
Oxford University Press, 1973). Macfarlane notes that in the township of
Killingham, in Kirkby Lonsdale, in 1695 approximately one-third of the population
were listed as being in receipt of poor relief, and that this figure seems to have
been typical for the area (Alan Macfarlane, *The Origins of English Individualism*,
Oxford, Basil Blackwell, 1978, p. 77). For the estimate of the poor in the sixteenth
century, see John Pound, *Poverty and Vagrancy in Tudor England* (London,
Longman, 1971), pp. 25, 79. In her splendid study of the French poor in the
eighteenth century, Olwen Hufton also observes that 'the poor' included 'the
perpetual poor' – the old, sick, orphaned etc. – along with labourers and small
peasant farmers. She estimates that 'both *pauvre* and *indigent* [i.e. the truly
destitute] . . . together in 1789 formed something above a third (and, speculatively,
perhaps as much as a half) of the total population'; and she continues: 'where
one merged into the other was, to say the least, obscure. The closer one looks
at the conditions of existence of this large proportion of the French population
the more difficult it becomes to isolate *pauvre* from *indigent*; for a process of
continual recruitment took place from the higher to the lower category: the
difference between the two was one of degree' (Olwen Hufton, *The Poor of
Eighteenth-Century France 1750–1789*, Oxford, Clarendon Press, 1974, p. 24). Cf.
Mathias on the eighteenth-century English poor: 'in practice a narrow and
fluctuating margin separated the condition of destitution, where people became
a charge upon the public purse, and poverty, where they remained poor but
viable, making their own way in the world' (Peter Mathias, *The Transformation of
England: Essays in the Economic and Social History of England in the Eighteenth
Century*, London, Methuen, 1979, p. 158).
5 Geoffrey W. Oxley, *Poor Relief in England and Wales 1601–1834* (Newton Abbot,
David and Charles, 1974), p. 92. Oxley's book is the most comprehensive recent
study of the old Poor Law. It corrects at various points, in the light of later
research, Dorothy Marshall's older study (note 3, above), which, however, remains
invaluable for its detail and breadth of coverage. Oxley notes that the character
of the workhouse rather accurately reflected its 'stop-gap' provenance, and that
of the Poor Law in general, in filling the space between the almshouses of the
endowed charities on the one hand, and the houses of correction of the vagrancy
laws on the other: hence its own hybrid nature (ibid., p. 80). Garraty remarks
that 'the typical English workhouse became a combination of Bedlam and
Bridewell, a place where idiots and lunatics, thieves and worn-out prostitutes,
dotards and abandoned waifs existed side by side amid filth and chaos, and the
effect was to drive all "idle poor" (read, *unemployed*) out, to make of them
vagabonds and furtive beggars' (John A. Garraty, *Unemployment in History: Economic
Thought and Public Policy*, New York, Harper Colophon Books, 1979, p. 48).

6 Cf. Dorothy Marshall: 'To both 17th and 18th century writers the crux of the problem was the position of the able Poor. . . . The question was, in fact, one of unemployment rather than of poor relief It was thought on all sides that [in Locke's words] "could all the able hands in England be brought to work, the greatest part of the burden that now lies upon the industrious for maintaining the Poor, would immediately cease, for, upon a very moderate computation, it may be concluded, that above one-half of those who receive relief from the parish, are able to get their living"', *The English Poor in the Eighteenth Century*, p. 26. And cf. also Oxley: 'The main achievement of the old poor law was . . . the establishment of an effective, comprehensive and flexible system for the relief of the deserving poor (the aged, sick, etc.). . . Yet this task was only peripheral to what, in 1601, was thought to be its main purpose: to solve the problem of unemployment and its consequential evils by setting the able-bodied poor to work. To be effective this policy required curbs to be placed on begging, which necessitated provision f r those who deservedly obtained their sustenance in this way. Two centuries or so later the failure of the old poor law to deal adequately with the able-bodied poor of the industrial revolution led to its being substantially amended. Thus the able-bodied poor may have been peripheral to the main activities of the old poor law, but they played a very significant part in the evolution of its legislative framework', *Poor Relief in England and Wales 1601–1834*, p. 102.

7 Pound, *Poverty and Vagrancy in Tudor England*, p. 44.

8 Marshall, *The English Poor in the Eighteenth Century*, p. 125. Oxley suggests that the main reason for the failure of the scheme was the difficulty the parish faced in raising the capital sum needed to purchase the materials: *Poor Relief in England and Wales*, pp. 103–4.

9 The 1722 Act gave parishes permission to form unions for the construction of workhouses in common, so that they could be of reasonable size; but few parishes seem to have availed themselves of this provision. Marshall, *The English Poor in the Eighteenth Century*, pp. 128–30.

10 For these schemes see Furniss, *The Position of the Labourer in a System of Nationalism*, pp. 88–95; Marshall, *English Poor in the Eighteenth Century*, pp. 42–7; Viner, 'Man's economic status', pp. 45–6; Karl Polanyi, *The Great Transformation: The Political and Economic Origins of Our Time* (1944; Boston, Mass., Beacon Press, 1957), pp. 105–9; John A. Garraty, *Unemployment in History*, pp. 48–50. Garraty's book contains a good general account of the workhouse movement as a whole in Europe since the seventeenth century: see pp. 44ff.

11 Oxley, *Poor Relief in England and Wales*, p. 117. Ashton notes that 'in the years of depression that followed the wars with the French, thousands of men, women, and children were employed . . . in breaking up rock with hammers, to provide material for use by the turnpike trusts' (T.S. Ashton, *An Economic History of England: The 18th Century*, London, Methuen 1955, p. 113).

12 That is, where a workhouse existed at all in the parish. The 1722 Act was permissive, not mandatory, and many parishes did not take up the sometimes expensive option of constructing workhouses, or modifying other premises to that end. For many parishes cash payments remained the only, and clearly in their minds the cheaper, option.

13 Dorothy Marshall, 'The Old Poor Law, 1662–1795', *Economic History Review*, 8 (1937), no. 1, reprinted in E.M. Carus-Wilson (ed.), *Essays in Economic History*, vol. 1 (London, Edward Arnold, 1954), p. 295.

14 Oxley, *Poor Relief in England and Wales*, pp. 105–6. Cf. Marshall: 'It is interesting to see that giving allowance in relief of wages was no new expedient adopted to meet the emergency of the French Wars, or to deal with the distress at the end of the 18th century. By that time the practice was at least a century old ... It is difficult, indeed, to know why it arose, for it was not contained in the provision of any statute. The overseer was ordered to relieve "the poor and impotent", not able-bodied labourers, however low their wages. Yet it seems to have been a responsibility which the parishes assumed at an early date' (*English Poor in the Eighteenth Century*, p. 104). A parliamentary inquiry of 1776 showed clearly that a large amount of relief consisted of 'allowances-in-aid of wages', even in those parishes which had workhouses (ibid., pp. 154–5). See also Garraty, *Unemployment in History*, pp. 52–3. Furniss notes that the dominant mercantilist theory of the time itself provided a justification for allowances-in-aid of wages. By keeping wages low, knowing that they would be supplemented out of the parish rates, manufacturers would be able to offer their products at lower prices and so compete more effectively in foreign markets. 'Under these circumstances the allowance in aid of wages was a form of bounty given to the export industries, the burden of that bounty being borne by the contributors to the rates', *The Position of the Laborer in a System of Nationalism*, p. 196. See also Mathias, *The Transformation of England*, p. 157.

15 See especially for this change of attitude, A.W. Coats, 'Changing attitudes to labour in the mid-eighteenth century', *Economic History Review*, 11 (1958), reprinted in M.W. Flinn and T.C. Smout (eds), *Essays in Social History* (Oxford, Clarendon Press, 1974), pp. 78–99, and A.W. Coats, 'Economic thought and Poor Law policy in the eighteenth century', *Economic History Review*, 13 (1960), 39–51. The contrast with the earlier 'mercantilist' conceptions of labour can well be seen from Furniss, *The Position of the Laborer in a System of Nationalism*; see also Eli F. Heckscher, *Mercantilism* (2 vols, London, Allen and Unwin, 1955), vol. 2, pp. 112–68; Coleman, 'Labour in the English economy of the seventeenth century'.

16 'It is clear ... that the magistrates of Berkshire, in issuing their notorious bread scale, were acting in accordance with tradition and precedent. They followed the tradition that relief should generally be given in cash to bring insufficient wages up to subsistence level in periods of temporary crisis, and the precedents of other counties in ordering such assistance, both in other crises and in the one with which they themselves were now confronted.' (Oxley, *Poor Relief in England and Wales*, pp. 111–12). This is a needed corrective to the influential view of Polanyi that 'allegedly Speenhamland meant that the Poor Law was to be administered liberally – actually, it was turned into the opposite of its original intent. Under Elizabethan Law the poor were forced to work at whatever wages they could get and only those who could get no work were entitled to relief; relief in *aid of wages* was neither intended nor given' (*The Great Transformation*, p. 79). Polanyi is right about the intent of the Poor Law legislation, wrong about the practice. In fact Gilbert's Act acknowledged that the practice of aid-in-wages had existed on a wide scale for a long time. As with practically all Poor Law legislation from

the sixteenth century to 1834, Parliamentary acts merely consolidated or confirmed what had been going on in various localities, sometimes for decades.

17 See on this Polanyi, *The Great Transformation*, pp. 93–4, 297–9. On the attitude of the poor to cash payments, cf. Furniss. 'By the middle of the eighteenth century, two hundred years of official relief had filled the lower orders with the feeling that the overseers' dole was their right and due, was justice not charity, and could therefore be accepted without shame and without gratitude', *The Position of the Laborer in a System of Nationalism*, p. 231. On the corresponding acceptance by the state and local elites of their obligations to the poor (and the control of disorder thereby), see J. Walter and K. Wrightson, 'Dearth and the social order in early modern England', *Past and Present*, no. 71, May 1976, pp. 22–42.

18 See, for instance, Christopher Hill, *Reformation to Industrial Revolution* (Harmondsworth, Penguin Books, 1969); D. C. Coleman, *The Economy of England 1450–1750* (Oxford, Oxford University Press, 1977); Macfarlane, *The Origins of English Individualism;* Macpherson, *The Political Theory of Possessive Individualism;* B. A. Holderness, *Pre-industrial England: Economy and Society from 1500 to 1750* (London, Dent, 1976).

19 Adam Smith, *The Wealth of Nations* (2 vols, Everyman edition, London, Dent 1910), vol. 1, p. 59.

20 Donald Woodward, 'Wage rates and living standards in pre-industrial England', *Past and Present*, no. 91, May 1981, pp. 28–46, *passim.*

21 Ashton, *The 18th Century*, pp. 101–2.

22 Ibid., p. 206.

23 John Rule, *The Experience of Labour in Eighteenth Century Industry* (London, Croom Helm, 1981), p. 60. Most writers on labour in eighteenth-century England stress these general characteristics. Especially good are: T. S. Ashton, *The 18th Century*, pp. 201–35; Sidney Pollard, *The Genesis of Modern Management: A Study of the Industrial Revolution in Great Britain* (Cambridge, Mass., Harvard University Press, 1965), pp. 160–208; E. P. Thompson, 'Time, work-discipline, and industrial capitalism', *Past and Present*, no. 38 (1967), pp. 56–97; Douglas A. Reid, 'The decline of Saint Monday 1766–1876', *Past and Present*, no. 71, May 1976, pp. 76–101; Rule, *The Experience of Labour*, pp. 49–69. For general characteristics of pre-industrial labour, see Keith Thomas, 'Work and leisure in pre-industrial society', *Past and Present*, no. 29 (1964), pp. 50–66; and my 'The social culture of work', *New Universities Quarterly*, 34, no. 1 (Winter 1979), pp. 5–28.

24 Rule, *The Experience of Labour*, p. 12.

25 Malcolmson, *Life and Labour in England*, p. 38. Malcolmson gives this example: 'In the area of Frampton Cotterell, Gloucestershire, north-east of Bristol, a district that was full of rural industry, many men who were identified in contemporary documents as tailors, masons, weavers and other clothworkers, tanners, cordwainers, feltmakers and coal-miners can be shown from the probate inventories to have retained a substantial involvement in agriculture, in many cases equal in extent to that of yeomen and husbandmen . . . in some cases so much so that, were it not for the indisputable written attribution of their primarily non-agrarian occupation, one would have assumed they were either yeomen or husbandmen.' And he concludes: 'Occupational designations . . . can be seriously

misleading, for in their apparent straightforwardness they often conceal much of the complexity of the household economies from which people supported themselves. A man was not always simply a farmer, or a weaver or a metalworker, or – the most difficult of all to interpret – a labourer, any more than most married women today could be usefully represented as 'simply' housewives. We want to learn about the actual activities in which people were involved', ibid., p. 40. For the integration of manufacturing and rural pursuits, see also Joan Thirsk, 'Industries in the countryside', in F.J. Fisher (ed.), *Essays in the Economic and Social History of Tudor and Stuart England* (Cambridge, Cambridge University Press, 1961), pp. 70–88.

26 Rule, *The Experience of Labour,* pp. 13–15. Woodward shows the extensive involvement in agriculture of a wide range of craftsmen – carpenters, masons, thatchers – in the sixteenth and seventeenth centuries – for example in Lincolnshire agricultural possessions accounted for over 50 per cent of the personal estates of seventy-nine craftsmen of these kinds, in Lancashire and Cheshire over 40 per cent (Woodward, 'Wage rates and living standards in pre-industrial England', pp. 40–1).

27 Quoted Coleman, 'Labour in the English economy of the seventeenth century', p. 302. Coleman, considering the question how far domestic industry might have been able to compensate for underemployment in agriculture, observes that 'the very ease with which an under-employed rural labour force . . . could at once form the basis of a domestic cloth industry and at the same time contribute to increasing national agricultural output suggests that some measure of success must have been achieved' (ibid.). For a remarkably similar mix of agricultural and industrial activities in seventeenth- and eighteenth-century Japan, see Thomas C. Smith, 'Farm family by-employments in preindustrial Japan', *Journal of Economic History* (1969), 687–715.

28 Malcolmson, *Life and Labour in England,* p. 23.

29 Polanyi, *The Great Transformation,* p. 92. Furniss echoes Hammond's view that 'in the open field village the entirely landless labourer was scarcely to be found', and comments: 'Whether the cultivation of his own acres was an incidental or the chief part of his economic activity, the fact that the laborer controlled a portion of the earth's surface introduced a factor of vital importance into his struggle to win subsistence for himself and his family. As a source of income independent of the labor market the land would, it is apparent, become of supreme importance at times when prices were high and wages low. Access to the commons and wastes made possible the ownership of a cow which the produce of the laborer's scrap of land would have been unable to support; sometimes a pig or a few geese could be added to his little stock; fuel, which later became of so large importance in the family budget, could be obtained at odd times by cutting the turf or gathering the dead wood from the wastes. These together with the garden would furnish the foundation for his economic support, the capital which the laborer brought to the assistance of his muscular energy in his struggle for existence. Moreover, here as elsewhere in modern society the family must be taken as the economic unit, and from this point of view the garden patch and common rights acquire additional importance. For they made possible the exploitation of the economic opportunities of every member of the family over

the age of infancy; each could contribute his share to the family income, the wife by her work in the garden, the children by their care of the stock on the commons. A single pair of hands need not attempt to carry the burden of the entire family, nor need the burden grow progressively greater as the family increased in size (Furniss, *The Position of the Laborer in a System of Nationalism*, pp. 213–14). On the quantity and variety of common rights at this time, see Malcolmson, *Life and Labour in England*, pp. 23–35; on the perquisites of particular jobs, see Rule, *The Experience of Labour*, pp. 125–9. On the elimination and 'criminalization' of these rights and perquisites, see Peter Linebaugh in 'Conference Report', *Bulletin of the Society for the Study of Labour History*, no. 25 (Autumn 1972), p. 13; Jason Ditton, 'Perks, pilferage, and the fiddle: the historical structure of invisible wages', *Theory and Society*, 4 (1977), 39–71. For a parallel account of the French poor's 'economy of makeshifts' – including beggary, theft and smuggling – see Hufton, *The Poor of Eighteenth Century France*, passim.

30 The remark occurs in Arthur Young's *Eastern Tour* (1771). An earlier tour had already produced a general law to cover this observation: 'Great earnings . . . have a strong effect on all who remain in the least inclined to idleness or other ill courses, by causing them to work but four or five days to maintain themselves the seven; this is a fact so well known in every manufacturing town that it would be idle to think of proving it by argument', *Northern Tour* (1770).

31 Ashton, *The 18th Century*, pp. 213–14. See also, for the change of attitude, the articles by Coats cited in note 15 above.

32 See on this my *Prophecy and Progress: The Sociology of Industrial and Post-industrial Society* (Harmondsworth, Penguin Books, 1978), pp. 131–49.

33 For such a view, see, for example, Polanyi: 'The New Poor Law abolished the general category of *the poor*, the "honest poor", or "labouring poor"... The former *poor* were now divided into physically helpless paupers whose place was in the workhouse, and independent workers who earned their living by labouring for wages. This created an entirely new category of the poor, the unemployed, who made their appearance on the social scene. While the pauper, for the sake of humanity, should be relieved, the unemployed, for the sake of industry, should *not* be relieved' (*The Great Transformation*, p. 224).

34 [Nassau Senior], 'Poor Law Reform', *Edinburgh Review*, 74 (1841), 1–44, at p. 3, reprinted in A.W. Coats (ed.), *Poverty in the Victorian Age* (4 vols, Westmead, Gregg International Publishers, 1973), vol. II, 'English Poor Laws 1834–1870'. Senior's views on Speenhamland, accepted by generations of historians, were sharply and, it appears, successfully challenged in two important articles by Mark Blaug: 'The myth of the Old Poor Law and the making of the New', *Journal of Economic History*, 23 (1963), 151–84, reprinted in Flinn and Smout, *Essays in Social History*, pp. 123–53, and 'The Poor Law Report re-examined', *Journal of Economic History*, 24 (1964), 229–45. In the second article he summarizes the findings of the first as follows: 'Despite what all the books say, the evidence that we have does not suggest that the English Poor Law as it operated before its amendment in 1834 reduced the efficiency of agricultural workers, promoted population growth, lowered wages, depressed rents, destroyed yeomanry, and compounded the burden on rate-payers. Beyond this purely negative argument, I tried to show that the Old Poor Law was essentially a device for dealing with

the problems of structural unemployment and substandard wages in the lagging rural sector of a rapidly growing but still under-developed economy. It constituted, so to speak, "a welfare state in miniature", combining elements of wage-escalation, family allowance, unemployment compensation, and public works, all of which were administered and financed on a local level. Far from having an inhibitory effect, it probably contributed to economic expansion' (p. 229). A critical review of recent interpretations of Speenhamland concludes largely in favour of Blaug: see J. D. Marshall, *The Old Poor Law 1795–1834* (London, Macmillan, 1968); and see also J. R. Poynter, *Society and Pauperism: English Ideas on Poor Relief, 1795–1834* (London, Routledge and Kegan Paul, 1969), *passim*, and esp. pp. 278ff.

35 Social policy and social thinking throughout the nineteenth century and beyond continued to elaborate on this basic theme. Philip Abrams's account of policy-orientated research in Victorian England shows that, in the eyes of the researchers, 'the problem was to design reforms that would so ameliorate social conditions that individuals would be enabled, or forced, to improve themselves'. This led to 'the distinction that quickly developed as a cardinal analytical principle of this mode of social science, between the steady, industrious, self-reliant, rational and therefore deserving poor on the one hand, and the feckless, weak, drunken, loafing and therefore actually or potentially criminal and undeserving poor on the other' (Abrams, *The Origins of British Sociology 1834–1914*, Chicago, University of Chicago Press, 1968, pp. 31, 41).

36 Blaug, 'The Poor Law Report re-examined', p. 229. The 'revolution' referred to was the new centralized administration of the Poor Law, with a national Poor Law Commission supervising Boards of Guardians in local unions of parishes.

37 On the failure of New Poor Law policy in the North, see Nicholas C. Edsall, *The Anti-Poor Law Movement 1834–1844* (Manchester, Manchester University Press, 1971). For the continuation of the provision of outdoor relief to the able-bodied, especially allowances in aid of wages, see Michael E. Rose, 'The allowance system under the New Poor Law', *Economic History Review*, 19 (1966), 607–20; David Ashforth, 'The Urban Poor Law', in Derek Fraser (ed.), *The New Poor Law in the Nineteenth Century* (London, Macmillan, 1976), pp. 128–48.

38 For the continuity of pre- and post-1834 poor relief policies in the southern agricultural counties, see Anne Digby, 'The labour market and the continuity of social policy after 1834: the case of the Eastern Counties', *Economic History Review*, 28 (1975), 69–83; Digby, 'The Rural Poor Law', in Fraser (ed.), *The New Poor Law in the Nineteenth Century*, pp. 149–70. See also Anthony Brundage, *The Making of the New Poor Law: The Politics of Inquiry, Enactment and Implementation 1832–1839* (London, Hutchinson, 1978). Both Digby and Brundage emphasize the extent to which policies of continued outdoor relief were in the economic and political interests of the gentry and tenant farmer groups who dominated the countryside.

39 The situation did not change much during the course of the century. In Norfolk as late as the 1870s, 87 per cent of the able-bodied poor were receiving outdoor relief: Digby, 'The Rural Poor Law', p. 163. For the country as a whole, Brundage comments that 'the profile of relief policies and the lines of authority remained remarkably constant throughout the 19th century. In towns as well as rural

districts, four-fifths of those supported wholly or partly out of the poor rates were on outdoor relief. The union workhouse was relegated to the status of a general asylum for the very old, the very young, the infirm. It was also useful as a residual deterrent against insubordination', *The Making of the New Poor Law*, p. 184. For urban areas specifically, Ashforth shows that throughout the latter part of the nineteenth century, 'never less than 85 per cent of all able-bodied paupers were in receipt of outdoor relief', 'The Urban Poor Law', p. 131.

40 For the relative cheapness of outdoor as opposed to indoor relief, see Rose, 'The allowance system under the New Poor Law', pp. 613–14. The rarity of finding the able-bodied poor in the workhouse was frequently commented on in the course of the century. As Ashforth says, 'in most years, in most urban unions, somewhere between 6 and 15 per cent of all those who were receiving relief, were receiving it in the workhouse. As a rule, the only able-bodied applicants sent to the workhouse were those considered to be idle, troublesome, morally unsound or Irish. The general attitude was expressed by the chairman of the Burnley board, when he stated that "the house was not a workhouse, it was a poor house. It was for the old and infirm and the destitute poor. It was never intended for able-bodied, hard-working, honest men"' ('The Urban Poor Law', p. 135). As a consequence, workhouses became, for most practical purposes, little more than 'hospitals of sorts; and indeed from the 1860s were described as such in official terminology', Fraser, 'Introduction', in Fraser (ed.), *The New Poor Law in the Nineteenth Century*, p. 5. By 1870, the Poor Law Board could casually record that 'workhouses, originally designed mainly as a test for the able-bodied, have, especially in the large towns, been of necessity transformed into infirmaries for the sick', Ashforth, 'The Urban Poor Law', p. 148. A similar thing was noted of rural workhouses. In 1892 Mr Lockwood, inspector for the Norfolk Union, commented that 'during the last 20 years the rural workhouse has become almost exclusively an asylum for the sick, the aged, and children', Digby, 'The Rural Poor Law', p. 163. In the light of this well-attested position it is curious how strongly the Dickensian workhouse has dominated our image of the Victorian poor. Much of this no doubt has to do with the powerful propaganda of the anti-Poor Law movement, including of course Dickens's own writing.

41 For these figures see Michael E. Rose, *The Relief of Poverty 1834–1914* (London, Macmillan, 1972), pp. 13–15. For a good example of professional social research of the time, and the agreement on the diminishing extent of poverty, see Robert Giffen, 'The progress of the working classes', *Journal of the Statistical Society*, 1883, reprinted in Abrams, *The Origins of British Sociology*, pp. 157–76; see also J. T. Danson, 'The condition of the people of the UK 1839–1847', *Journal of the Royal Statistical Society*, XI (1848), 101–40.

42 For these findings, and a valuable brief discussion of the 'discovery of poverty', see Rose, *The Relief of Poverty*, pp. 20–34. See also E. H. Hunt, *British Labour History 1815–1914* (London, Weidenfeld and Nicolson, 1981), pp. 120–5.

43 See José Harris, *Unemployment and Politics: A Study in English Social Policy 1886–1914* (Oxford, Clarendon Press, 1972), appendix B, 'Unemployment statistics before 1914', table 2, p. 374. See also Sir William H. Beveridge, *Causes and Cures of Unemployment* (1931, Westport, Conn., Greenwood Press, 1976), p. 6.

44 E. J. Hobsbawm, 'The British standard of living, 1790–1850', in his *Labouring Men: Studies in the History of Labour* (London, Weidenfeld and Nicolson, 1964), pp. 72–82. Hobsbawm quotes Henry Mayhew's estimate at the mid-century as 'worth our attention': 'Estimating the working classes as being between four and five million in number, I think we may safely assert ... that ... there is barely sufficient work for the *regular* employment of half our labourers, so that only 1,500,000 are fully and constantly employed, while 1,500,000 more are employed only half their time, and the remaining 1,500,000 wholly unemployed, obtaining a day's work *occasionally* by the displacement of some of the others', ibid., p. 82.

45 John Foster, *Class Struggle and the Industrial Revolution: Early Industrial Capitalism in Three English Towns* (London, Weidenfeld and Nicolson, 1974), pp. 81, 258–9.

46 Hobsbawm, 'The British standard of living', pp. 80–2.

47 Sidney Pollard, 'Labour in Great Britain', *Cambridge Economic History of Europe*, vol. 7, part I (Cambridge, Cambridge University Press, 1978), p. 133. And see Neil Smelser, *Social Change in the Industrial Revolution* (London, Routledge and Kegan Paul, 1959); Michael Anderson, 'Sociological history and the working-class family: Smelser re-visited', *Social History*, 1 (1976), 323–4.

48 Neil McKendrick, 'Home demand and economic growth: a new view of the role of women and children in the Industrial Revolution', in N. McKendrick (ed.), *Historical Perspectives: Studies in English Thought and Society* (London, Europa Publications, 1974), pp. 185–6; Elizabeth Pleck, 'Two worlds in one: work and the family', *Journal of Social History*, 10 (1977), 185.

49 Michael Anderson, 'Household structure and the industrial revolution: mid-nineteenth century Preston in comparative perspective', in P. Laslett and R. Wall (eds), *Household and Family in Past Time* (Cambridge, Cambridge University Press, 1972), p. 230. For the general contribution, material and non-material, of the wider kinship network to family support in nineteenth-century factory towns, see Michael Anderson, *Family Structure in Nineteenth Century Lancashire* (Cambridge, Cambridge University Press, 1971), esp. ch. 10.

50 E.P. Thompson, *The Making of the English Working Class* (London, Victor Gollancz, 1964), p. 416.

51 F. Engels, *The Condition of the Working Class in England in 1844*, trans. and eds, W.O. Henderson and W.H. Chaloner (Oxford, Basil Blackwell, 1958), pp. 161–2.

52 Cf. Chambers: 'The representative Englishman, it has been said, was still a countryman in 1831, and the representative workman was still a handicraftsman in a traditional workshop, working with traditional tools. In 1851, the distribution of the population had changed in favour of the townsman, but the representative Englishman was still far from being a worker directly employed in machine industry. The victory of the factory over the older forms of industrial organization was slow and it was not until the last decades of the century that it became the dominant form of organization in a majority of the industries. In 1851, those employed in the principal non-mechanized categories comprised about five and a half million workers and outnumbered those in the mechanized industries (including coal) by three to one; and of the one and three quarter million in the mechanized groups, half a million were cotton workers. The most numerous group after agriculture were domestic servants. In 1851, their number had risen to over a million and was still twice as large as the cotton workers. At 1,039,000

they were drawing nearer to the agricultural group which now numbered 1,790,000 and together these two groups numbered more than double those engaged in manufacturing and mining. When Britain was the undisputed workshop of the world, the "great industry" on which it was based actually employed 1.7 million out of a total British population of 21 million', (J.D. Chambers, *The Workshop of the World*, London, Oxford University Press, 1961, pp. 21–2). See also John Burnett (ed.), *Useful Toil: Autobiographies of Working People from the 1820s to the 1920s* (Harmondsworth, Penguin Books, 1977), pp. 256–65.

53 R. Samuel, 'Workshop of the world: steam power and hand technology in mid-Victorian Britain', *History Workshop*, no. 3 (Spring 1977), pp. 6–72; Pollard, 'Labour in Great Britain', pp. 128–9; F.F. Mendels, 'Proto-industrialization: the first phase of the industrialization process', *Journal of Economic History*, 32 (1972), 246–7; Pleck, 'Two worlds in one', pp. 181–2.

54 Eric Hopkins, 'Working conditions in Victorian Stourbridge', *International Review of Social History*, 19 (1974), 401–25.

55 Sally Alexander, 'Women's work in nineteenth century London: a study of the years 1820–1850', in Juliet Mitchell and Ann Oakley (eds), *The Rights and Wrongs of Women* (Harmondsworth, Penguin Books, 1976), p. 65.

The concealment of the degree of female employment is, of course, not confined to non-factory areas like London. Andreson notes that 'well over a third of all working wives in Preston in 1851 were employed in non-factory occupations, but were not recorded', *Family in Nineteenth Century Lancashire*, p. 71. See also Hunt, *British Labour History*, p. 345, n. 36. For a good account of the contribution of women's part-time work – among other 'non-quantifiable' items – to family income in another Lancashire area, see Elizabeth Roberts, 'Working-class standards of living in Barrow and Lancaster', *Economic History Review*, 30 (1977), 306–21.

It is his excessive reliance on Census returns that largely vitiates the argument by Richards that women's employment *declined* in the Victorian age. See Eric Richards, 'Women in the British economy since about 1700: an interpretation', *History*, 59 (1974), 337–57. There seems no real evidence to support the view of a *quantitative* decline in female employment – rather the reverse. What is more plausible, however, is the idea of a 'qualitative' decline, a loss of status for women workers as they moved from pre-industrial household production to the factories and slop-shops of the nineteenth century. For this view, see, for example, Thompson, *Making of the English Working Class*, p. 416. In another sphere of women's work, there was also the decline in the status of 'domestic service' itself, as reflected in the changing meaning of the word 'menial': Burnett, *Useful Toil*, p. 165; *Oxford English Dictionary*, 'menial'.

56 Harris, *Unemployment and Politics*, p. 371. Given the relatively high levels of unemployment at various times in the century, this suggests that the unemployed were supported in other ways than by the public system of poor relief.

57 Pollard, 'Labour in Great Britain', p. 132.

58 Hunt, *British Labour History*, p. 106; Burnett, *Useful Toil*, p. 137.

59 For this account of domestic service see Burnett, *Useful Toil*, pp. 135–42; Hunt, *British Labour History*, pp. 19–22, 105–7. See also Teresa M. McBride, *The Domestic Revolution: The Modernisation of Household Service in England and France 1820–1920* (London, Croom Helm, 1976).

60 Joan W. Scott and Louise A. Tilly, 'Women's work and the family in nineteenth century Europe', *Comparative Studies in Society and History*, 17 (1975), 36–64. See also the various autobiographies of domestic servants in Burnett, *Useful Toil*, pp. 175–245. On domestic service as an extension of traditional family (and marital) roles for females, see Leonore Davidoff, 'Mastered for life: servant and wife in Victorian and Edwardian England', *Journal of Social History*, 7 (1974), 406–28.

61 Hunt, *British Labour History*, pp. 26–9. See also Pollard, 'Labour in Great Britain', pp. 139–47.

62 See E. J. Hobsbawm, 'Custom, wages, and work load in nineteenth-century industry', in his *Labouring Men* (London, Weidenfeld and Nicolson, 1964), pp. 344–70.

63 R. Samuel, 'Village labour', in R. Samuel (ed.), *Village Life and Labour* (London, Routledge and Kegan Paul, 1975), pp. 3–5.

64 Quoted Samuel, 'Village labour', p. 4. For a detailed account of the many different ways and means of 'making out' in the countryside in the late nineteenth century, see also R. Samuel, '"Quarry roughs": life and labour in Headington Quarry, 1860–1920', in Samuel (ed.), *Village Life and Labour*, pp. 139–263. Samuel's account, based on oral evidence as with Roberts's similar study of Barrow and Lancaster (see n. 55 above), indicates the importance of local studies of this kind in correcting many of our notions about the nature of work and employment in Victorian England.

65 Samuel, 'Village labour', pp. 6–10; '"Quarry roughs"', pp. 189–94; G. Mingay, *Rural Life in Victorian England* (London, Futura Publications, 1979), pp. 116–17. Urban dwellers in certain regions also continued to eke out family income with the free produce of the countryside; see Roberts, 'Working class standards of living in Barrow and Lancaster', pp. 316–17.

66 See D. Morgan, 'The place of harvesters in nineteenth-century village life', and J. Kitteringham, 'Country work girls in nineteenth-century England', both in Samuel (ed.), *Village Life and Labour*.

67 Raphael Samuel, 'Comers and goers', in H. J. Dyos and Michael Wolff (eds), *The Victorian City: Images and Realities* (2 vols, London, Routledge and Kegan Paul, 1973), vol. 1, pp. 123–60.

68 See Gareth Stedman Jones, *Outcast London: A Study of the Relationship Between Classes in Victorian Society* (Harmondsworth, Penguin Books, 1976), pp. 90–2.

69 E. J. Hobsbawm, 'The tramping artisan', in his *Labouring Men*, pp. 48, 42, 44.

70 For this development see David Macarov, *Work and Welfare: The Unholy Alliance* (Beverley Hills, Ca., Sage Publications, 1980).

71 Hunt, *British Labour History*, p. 18. The change reflected both the decline of domestic outwork and working-class imitation of middle-class family life. Rural areas were as much affected as urban: 'One of the features of Rowntree and Kendall's investigation of rural poverty shortly before the First World War was how little wives were able to contribute to family earnings', ibid., p. 23.

72 See John A. Garraty, *Unemployment in History: Economic Thought and Public Policy* (New York, Harper Colophon Books, 1979) pp. 103ff. The word 'unemployed' did not appear in its modern meaning in the *Oxford English Dictionary* until the late 1880s, and 'unemployment' was not a separate heading in *Hansard* until after the Boer War.

73 'Throughout this period the history of unemployment policy at all levels – voluntary and statutory, local and central – is primarily concerned with problems of social administration', Harris, *Unemployment and Politics*, p. 6. See also Jim Tomlinson, *Problems of British Economic Policy 1870–1945* (London, Methuen, 1981), pp. 62–3.

74 Stedman Jones, *Outcast London*, p.v.

75 Ibid., pp. 281ff.

76 Harris, *Unemployment and Politics*, p. 143.

77 William Beveridge, *Unemployment: A Problem of Industry* (London, Longmans, Green, 1909), p. 201.

78 On the policies of 1905–11, see Harris, *Unemployment and Politics*, pp. 211ff. See also Bentley B. Gilbert, *The Evolution of National Insurance in Great Britain* (London, Michael Joseph, 1966). In view of the tendency to belittle the achievement of the pre-1914 period, it is worth quoting Harris's assessment: 'by 1914 fatalistic acceptance of the inevitability of the trade cycle and doctrinaire prejudice against the relief of mass unemployment seemed to have largely passed away. Unemployment had been transformed from a rather peripheral concern of the Poor Law guardians into a central problem of public administration. The Asquith government was in principle committed to a policy of counter-depressive public works. A department of the Board of Trade was responsible for insuring part of the labour force against irregular employment, penalizing employers who gave work on a casual basis, and finding vacant situations for unemployed workmen. Advanced liberals as well as socialists had endorsed the controversial doctrine of "the right to work"; and both liberal and socialist reformers believed that they were moving towards a "final solution for the problem of the unemployed" [Beveridge]' (*Unemployment and Politics*, p. 5).

79 For these figures, see Stephen Constantine, *Unemployment in Britain Between the Wars* (London, Longman, 1980), pp. 3–4.

80 Sean Glynn and John Oxborrow, *Interwar Britain: a Social and Economic History* (London, Allen and Unwin, 1976), p. 145. The authors warn, however, that this figure – based on trade union returns – probably understates the pre-1914 level, and that figures based on insured workers probably overestimate the proportion of workers unemployed in the inter-war period while underestimating the absolute numbers unemployed.

81 Bentley B. Gilbert, *British Social Policy 1914–1939* (London, Batsford, 1970), pp. 51–86. And on the history of unemployment benefits generally in this period, see *The Evolution of National Insurance*, chs 2 and 4.

82 For economic policies in this period, and the response to them, see K. J. Hancock, 'The reduction of unemployment as a problem of public policy, 1920–1929', *Economic History Review* (1962), 328–45; Constantine, *Unemployment in Britain Between the Wars*, pp. 45–84; Glynn and Oxborrow, *Interwar Britain*, pp. 116–42; John Stevenson and Chris Cook, *The Slump: Society and Politics During the Depression* (London, Quartet Books, 1979).

83 On the 'imperial visionaries', see Tomlinson, *Problems of British Economic Policy*, pp. 106–19.

84 Tomlinson, *Problems of British Economic Policy*, p. 64.

85 Glynn and Oxborrow, *Interwar Britain*, pp. 152–3.

288   *Politics, Work and Society*

86 See P.J. Keating, *The Working Classes in Victorian Fiction* (London, Routledge and Kegan Paul, 1971), pp. 53ff.

87 For a selection, see Peter Keating (ed.), *Into Unknown England 1866–1913: Selections from the Social Explorers* (London, Fontana, 1976).

88 It may perhaps be also that, partly as a result of this attitude, this was the period in which the working class came to see *themselves* as something apart, dependent only on their own kind and their own resources. See Standish Meacham, *A Life Apart: The English Working Class 1890–1914* (London, Thames and Hudson, 1977).

89 Cook and Stevenson, *The Slump*, pp. 76–93. For a good selection of the literature of social inquiry, see John Stevenson, *Social Conditions in Britain Between the Wars* (Harmondsworth, Penguin Books, 1977).

90 See Arthur Marwick, 'Middle opinion in the Thirties: planning, progress and political "agreement"', *English Historical Review*, 79 (1964), 285–98; Paul Addison, *The Road to 1945* (London, Quartet Books, 1977), pp. 23–52.

91 A representative example of the mass of statements of this kind was Michael Young and Theodor Prager, *There's Work For All* (London, Nicolson and Watson, 1945). Later the same affirmation was made, with world-wide reference, in the United Nations' Universal Declaration of Human Rights (1948): 'Everyone has the right to work, to have free choice of employment, to just and favourable conditions of work and to protection against unemployment.'

92 See José Harris, *William Beveridge: A Biography* (Oxford, Clarendon Press, 1977), pp. 313ff.

93 Ibid., p. 433.

94 Lord Beveridge, *Full Employment in a Free Society* (1944; London, Allen and Unwin, 1960), p. 1.

95 With three and a quarter million unemployed – 14 per cent of the workforce – in the autumn of 1982, Britain had reached the unemployment level that was the annual average for this country during the inter-war depression.

96 From a burgeoning literature, see Tom Forester (ed.), *The Microelectronics Revolution* (Oxford, Basil Blackwell, 1980); Trevor Jones (ed.), *Microelectronics and Society* (Milton Keynes, Open University Press, 1980); I. Barron and R. Curnow, *The Future with Microelectronics* (Milton Keynes, Open University Press, 1979); Colin Hines and Graham Searle, *Automatic Unemployment* (London, Earth Resources Research Ltd, 1979); Clive Jenkins and Barry Sherman, *The Collapse of Work* (London, Eyre Methuen, 1979).

97 J. Gershuny, *After Industrial Society? The Emerging Self-Service Economy* (London, Macmillan, 1978).

98 The definitive account of this is Karl Polanyi, *The Great Transformation*.

99 Ivan Illich, *Shadow Work* (London, Marion Boyars, 1981), p. 136.

100 For some interesting reflections on this, see J.R.L. Anderson, 'Has unemployment a future?', *Encounter*, November 1972, pp. 12–18. See also R. Disney, 'Theorising the welfare state: the case of unemployment insurance in Britain', *Journal of Social Policy*, 11 (1982), 33–58.

BIBLIOGRAPHICAL NOTE

On the economy of the poor under the Poor Law, and on much else of relevance besides, see K.D.M. Snell, *Annals of the Labouring Poor: Social Change and Agrarian England 1660–1900* (Cambridge, Cambridge University Press, 1987). Another major study, concerned largely with social thought and ideology, is Gertrude Himmelfarb, *The Idea of Poverty: England in the Early Industrial Age* (New York, Alfred A. Knopf, 1984). Also interesting, in the same vein, is E.P. Hennock, 'Poverty and social theory in England: the experience of the eighteen-eighties', *Social History* (1976), 67–91. On the Poor Law itself there is Peter Dunkley, *The Crisis of the Old Poor Law in England, 1795–1834: An Interpretive Essay* (New York, Garland Publishing, 1984), and J.D. Marshall, *The Old Poor Law 1795–1834*, 2nd edn (London, Macmillan, 1985). See also John Knott, *Popular Opposition to the 1834 Poor Law* (London, Croom Helm, 1986), which supplements Nicholas Edsall's book mentioned in note 37. A wide-ranging comparative study is C. Lis and H. Soly, *Poverty and Capitalism in Pre-industrial Europe* (Brighton, Harvester Press, 1982).

On the social and economic conditions of working-class life in nineteenth-century England, there are: James H. Treble, *Urban Poverty in Britain 1830–1914* (London, Methuen, 1983); Paul Johnson, *Saving and Spending: The Working Class Economy in Britain 1870–1939* (Oxford, Clarendon Press, 1985); Pat Thane, 'Women and the Poor Law in Victorian and Edwardian England', *History Workshop*, no. 6 (1978), pp. 29–51; Pat Thane (ed.), *The Origins of British Social Policy* (London, Croom Helm, 1978); Ursula R.Q. Henriques, *Before the Welfare State* (London, Longman, 1979). Two surveys of earlier work are still valuable: Duncan Bythell, 'The history of the poor', *Economic History Review*, no. 351 (1974), pp. 365–77; Arthur J. Taylor (ed.), *The Standard of Living in Britain in the Industrial Revolution* (London, Methuen, 1975). A splendid study is David Vincent, *Bread, Knowledge and Freedom: A Study of Nineteenth-century Working Class Autobiography* (London, Methuen, 1982). There is also much food for thought in Maxine Berg, *The Age of Manufactures 1700–1820* (London, Fontana, 1985). See also the journals *History Workshop Journal* and *Social History* for many articles of relevance.

On current concepts and discussions of unemployment, the literature is now so vast that any selection can only be illustrative. See M. Jahoda, *Employment and Unemployment* (Cambridge, Cambridge University Press, 1982); B. Crick (ed.), *Unemployment* (London, Methuen, 1981); Adrian Sinfield, *What Unemployment Means* (Oxford, Martin Robertson, 1981); Brian Showler and Adrian Sinfield (eds), *The Workless State* (Oxford, Martin Robertson, 1981); Bill Jordan, *Mass Unemployment and the Future of Britain* (Oxford, Basil Blackwell, 1982); Giles Merritt, *World Out of Work* (London, Collins, 1982); Jeremy Seabrook, *Unemployment* (London, Quartet Books, 1982); J. Richardson and R. Henning (eds), *Unemployment: Policy Responses of Western Democracies* (London, Sage Publications, 1984); Doreen Massey, *Spatial Divisions of Labour* (London, Macmillan, 1984); K. Hawkins, *Unemployment*, new edn (Harmondsworth, Penguin Books, 1984); Peter Kelvin and Joanna Jarrett, *Unemployment: Its Social Psychological Effects* (Cambridge, Cambridge University Press, 1985); S. Allen, K. Purcell, A. Waton and S. Wood (eds), *The Experience of Unemployment* (London, Macmillan, 1985); Göran Therborn, *Why Some Peoples are More Unemployed Than Others* (London, Verso, 1986).

See also the references and bibliographical note to 'The social culture of work: work, employment and unemployment as ways of life', chapter 9 in this volume.

11

Thoughts on the Present Discontents in Britain

> By far the greatest obstacle to the progress of science and to the new undertaking of new tasks ... is found in this: that men think things impossible ...
>
> Francis Bacon, *Novum Organum*, Book I, xcii

It can hardly have escaped anyone's attention that what Carlyle called 'the condition of England' question is with us again. But what a difference. When commentators wrote about the condition of England in the early nineteenth century they were discussing the social consequences of England's pioneering leap into industrialism, her revolutionary turning of the course of world history. Growth, not stagnation, was the cause of the concern of moralists and sociologists. Now the situation is precisely the opposite. The country's problems seem to be the product of illness and senescence, rather than youth and vigour. An acute case of 'the British disease' is pronounced (re-termed 'Englanditis' by Her Majesty's Ambassador to Washington, Peter Jay[1]). Its symptoms are economic inefficiency, antiquated attitudes and institutions, national complacency, and a general and deep-seated inability to pull ourselves out of a growing pit of declining standards in all areas of the society. All in all, the situation is widely glossed as a 'crisis'.

The British themselves have taken the lead in breast-beating. Not surprisingly, much foreign opinion echoes this judgement, and gleefully propagates it. But there is a group which thinks quite differently. This includes such distinguished foreign observers and residents as John Kenneth Galbraith, Arthur Koestler and Ralf Dahrendorf. These see in many of the symptoms of the 'disease' the signs of a national strength which other industrial countries might well come to envy and even to imitate.

'Your real problem,' says Galbraith, 'is that you were the first of the great industrialised nations, and so things happen here first. You are living out the concern for some more leisurely relationship with industrial life that other people have been discussing for fifty years or more.'[2] Dahrendorf, commenting on a *New Society* opinion poll which seemed to confirm the charge of national complacency, proposes that 'the desire to "live a pleasant life" rather than "work as much as one can for as much money as one can get" is a source of strength, not of weakness in Britain.'[3] The American physicist Robert Socolow is even more definite:

It seems likely to this visitor that the world's developed countries will be emulating Britain within a decade or less. The limits of nature's resources and the limits to our own cleverness in protecting ourselves from our own mischief put severe constraints on the level of activity any developed society will freely choose. As these limits are faced more and more squarely, developed countries will acknowledge the vigour attained by a mature society that cherishes the past, cares for its physical surroundings, socializes in pubs and changes houses reluctantly ... When the next round of industrialization – which will emphasize durability, quality and community level systems – arrives, you will more quickly recognize how well matched its demands are to your national strengths.[4]

In the nineteenth century, eminent foreign observers such as Marx and Tocqueville came to Britain to see and study the marvels of the new industrial society. In this century, some at least seem to be watching with close interest the emergence of the first post-industrial society.

Is this mere flattery? Is it just a gracious sop to a nation in decline, Britain playing Athens to America's Rome? We should at least acknowledge the appeal of a view that recognizes the long-term, historical nature of the current predicament. Britain was the first industrial society in the history of the world. From having this head start over her competitors she reaped great rewards. But she has long been losing out in the race to stay among the leaders of the industrial nations. Parallels with past civilizations would suggest that it is difficult and dangerous for a society to strive to regain the leadership in the same race. Better by far to start a new one, with different rules. First in, first out.

This is a view which gets intermittent airing in Britain, but hardly serious public discussion. I shall be returning to it later. Here it simply serves to indicate the breadth of the options open to British society. It seems a healthy working premise, to put it no more strongly than that, at least to start from the position that the choices can be cast more imaginatively, and far more widely, than is implied in the conventional exhortations to 'put Britain back on its feet', or to make Britain a great manufacturing nation again, or to speed up economic growth. Many of these injunctions are indeed highly ambiguous. It is rare for their proponents to spell out what might be entailed in pursuing these traditional goals in an environment that has for so long been unreceptive to them. Before advocating any particular strategy, therefore, it seems necessary to consider some of the more widely held views on the nature of the current crisis, together with any remedies offered.

I

Is there a crisis of British society, and, if so, what kind of a crisis is it?

We need not dwell on the purely semantic aspect of this. There is a strong, and strongly expressed, sense in many areas of British society that its traditional social institutions and practices are failing it, and that the consequences are serious and long-term. As Peter Jay says, 'the causes of the crisis are deep-seated and general, embedded in the very organization of our society.'[5] The corollary of this is that change needs to be conceived in a radical way, and that is perhaps sufficient to justify the term 'crisis'. Remarkably, and perhaps unprecedentedly, there is scarcely a single thinker from any part of the political spectrum who is prepared to argue positively (rather than by default) that really there is not much wrong with British society, and that the best thing is to sit tight and to leave things alone for a while.[6] All conservatives are now radical conservatives.

The prevailing assumption in most of the current political debates is that there is a crisis, and that it is centrally an economic one. Economics has come to dominate political discussion to an extent surprising even in a nation of shop-keepers. This is perhaps inevitable – it is, after all, where the shoe pinches – and it is right too in the sense that some answer to the economic question is crucial to any strategy. But at the level of Parliamentary and media discussion the conception of economics is woefully narrow. Occasionally even academic commentators endorse this. So Lawrence Silverman, a political scientist, argues that 'Britain's crisis is neither a social nor a political crisis. There is nothing in the condition of British society or the British polity that can conceivably justify speaking of a crisis. Only the economy is in such a condition.'[7] Get the economy 'going' again, so the argument runs, and most of the other problems can then be attended to. Class inequality, education, social welfare, public transport, the environment – thought and action on these must, regrettably, follow the solving of Britain's economic difficulties. I am over-simplifying the approach, but something like it undoubtedly exists – indeed it seems to express a weary consensus in public life, and as a political force it is very strong.

The remedies suggested reflect this narrow basis of analysis. Here are to be found all the conventional exhortations to regenerate British industry: to increase investment and worker productivity in manufacturing, to cut public spending and employment, to hold the unions to an incomes policy, to force the banks and insurance companies to invest in British industry rather than abroad, and so on. The revenue from North Sea oil is seen as a providential helping-hand to this end; but an opportunity of strictly limited duration.

Recommendations of this kind can be found repeated a hundred times in press and Parliament, and from all political quarters.[8] That, to the extent that they have been tried, they have so far had negligible effects on the fortunes of the British economy, seems not to silence the chorus of politicians, businessmen and trade unionists which continues to voice them. It is not only that the short-sighted utilitarianism and philistinism of the approach is so depressing. There is also the failure to see that the insufficiency of any or all of these remedies turns on their quite manifest dependence on other political and cultural factors. Thus, for instance, as John Goldthorpe pointed out some time ago, an incomes policy or any other feature of a 'social contract' is scarcely likely to work very long given the palpable inequalities that still exist in British society.[9] Without (social) justice, what is the social contract but a great robbery? Similarly, bright graduates are hardly likely to be attracted into industrial management so long as British society awards it such low status as compared with the professions and public service.

There is naturally a wider focus, and a more precise understanding, in the economic analysis of the Marxist or *marxisant* kind which seeks to explain 'the crisis of British capitalism'. The milder version has been expounded in Stuart Holland's *The Socialist Challenge*,[10] which is offered as a long-term party programme from the left-wing of the Labour Party. Here it is argued that current public policy and current economic institutions, which were formed in a Keynesian mould, have ignored the rise to dominance of national and multinational monopolistic corporations in the world economy. These have created a new 'mesoeconomic' sector, which seriously challenges the state's power to direct the economy by the traditional macroeconomic Keynesian techniques of demand-management. As a result there can be no economic recovery arising out of the existing structures of the mixed economy, with a weak public sector supporting and to a large extent subsidising a powerful, profit-seeking private sector. Only public ownership on a massive scale, including the banks and other financial institutions, will allow the degree of control necessary to stimulate technical innovation and industrial investment, and so reduce employment and speed up economic growth.

In the more radical Marxist version, as expounded for instance by Glyn and Sutcliffe,[11] the crisis is seen as deeper, and less conventionally soluble. Organized working-class movements have steadily pushed up wage levels, so that the share of national income going to labour as against capital has been increasing throughout the century. Employers have for their part not been able to raise prices correspondingly, owing to intensified competition between capitalist countries in the world market. Hence there has been a dramatic and profound decline in the profitability of capitalist firms, threatening their survival at the most basic principle of operation.[12] The crisis is a general one, affecting all capitalist countries. But it is being experienced at its most acute in Britain because Britain is the oldest of the capitalist societies. 'Britain, as the "maturest" capitalist country, is both the weakest part of the system and gives an example of the path which other capitalist economies might quite rapidly follow. The profit share is being maintained in the strongest countries while it falls elsewhere.'[13] So far as Britain is concerned, then, the scene is set for a class war of revolutionary proportions, with the capitalists attempting to restore profitability by holding down the living standards of workers (partly through devices like the social contract and schemes of worker participation), and the working-class movement striving to go beyond capitalist institutions in the direction of a fully socialist economy.

The Marxist accounts, whatever their merits as complete schemes of analysis, clearly dig deeper into the economic troubles of the country than most. The more immediately relevant problem is the character of the solutions proposed, or anticipated. Compared to the incisiveness of the analyses these are vague in the extreme. Holland's proposals for a programme of full, centrally controlled, nationalization seem to depend excessively on the rationality and public-spiritedness of governments and trade unions, for which there is little historical evidence. Moreover, in the face of his own evidence he nowhere shows how national governments can control the operations of the multinational companies, which evidently are in a position to adapt their strategies to suit the circumstances of any particular nation state. Glyn and Sutcliffe look forward to 'the control by the working class of its own fate in a democratic socialist system', but they don't anywhere spell out how this is going to be achieved, and certainly give no evidence that the working-class movement itself is moving in this direction in Britain. An all-out struggle for the diminishing fruits of capitalism is certainly in prospect – but this can as easily lead to bankruptcy or barbarism as to socialism. Over and above these difficulties, the Marxist analyses scarcely touch on the problems of large-scale organization, alienating technology, environmental destruction and scarce natural resources. Some attempts are currently being made to supply the missing pieces,[14] but it is no secret that traditional Marxist theory has few tools for handling these issues very convincingly.

The Marxist analysis does, however, form a bridge to the more specifically political analysis of the current crisis. I mean this not in the sense of anxieties about Parliament, welfare administration, local government and the like – although there is quite enough that could be said on those counts.[15] There is the more fundamental concern with the survival of the British state as such, threatened as it is at one level by the rise of 'peripheral nationalisms' (Welsh, Scottish and Irish), and at another by the forces of supranational economic and political organizations (the EEC, IMF, OPEC, the multinationals and so on). From the Marxist standpoint, the 'break-up of Britain' is seen partly as the consequence of the continuing internationalization of capital, and the consequent reduction in the importance of national sovereignty; partly the coming home to roost of the failure of the British state and British society to 'modernize' and 'rationalize' itself in accordance with the requirements of competitive capitalism.

The British political crisis is, in other words, once again both general and specific. Nationalist and separatist movements are offering powerful challenges to the integrity of many contemporary industrial states – France, Belgium, Spain, Canada – but the British political system seems especially vulnerable and impotent, despite its much longer tradition of political unity. The Conservative Party, for instance, has been virtually wiped out in Wales, Scotland and Ireland, to be replaced by nationalist parties; and the Labour Party has had to make repeated accommodations to nationalist demands in order to maintain its historic presence in those areas.

Northern Ireland has of course its own long troubled history behind the present conflicts; but the challenges from Welsh and Scottish nationalism are novel, in degree at least. The confusion they have caused in Westminster and Whitehall is none the less surprising, and reflects on the extreme brittleness of the current political consensus, and its very insecure base. In Tom Nairn's provocative account, following in the now familiar tradition of *New Left Review* historiography, the British state is doomed to dissolution.[16] The absence of a 'proper' or complete bougeois revolution in Britain at the period of its critical industrialization, the continued social and political ascendancy of the landed gentry and the corresponding lack of confidence of the bourgeois class, have left the antiquated political system defenceless and incapable of reforming itself, when once the advantages of being the pioneer industrial nation had been eroded away. The loss of Empire in the post-1945 period removed the economic shield that had protected, and disguised, the fundamental structural weakness of the old industrial base. Britain is now 'the sick man of Europe', like the Ottoman Empire of old; and, like that decrepit Empire, it is now destined to splinter into its component nationalities.[17] It has nothing now with which to hold or to tempt those, like the Scots, who see a rosier future in some other political grouping than the United Kingdom.

It is interesting, incidentally, to note how close in essence this kind of analysis is to the earlier 'managerialist' critiques of British society by writers such as Michael Shanks and Andrew Shonfield.[18] These, with their complaints of a 'stagnant society', and of feeble management in public and private enterprises, were also drawn to reflect on the archaic structures of the British polity and economy as compared with the up-to-date technology and powerful planning instruments of France, Germany and the Scandinavian countries. But, unlike Nairn, they seem to believe that economic rationalization is still on the agenda, given sufficient political will, and political skill.

The tangle of issues involved in the nationalist revival, the strange alliances made within it, are fairly reflected in the attitudes held towards it. Nairn's vision is frankly apocalyptic. The British political system will fragment, and out of the ashes of a disintegrated United Kingdom will rise the phoenix of the English working class, the bourgeois scales finally fallen from its eyes, and capable at last of realizing its common struggle and common destiny with the international working-class movement. Others, Marxist and non-Marxist sympathisers alike, are not so confident of either the inevitability or the desirability of a complete break-up of British political unity. But many of them are supporters of the nationalist and centrifugal tendencies on more traditional regionalist and decentralist grounds.

Everyone seems agreed that the peripheral nationalisms cannot be seen – as they themselves often wish to be seen – in their own terms, as a self-contained phenomenon. There is an intrinsic connection between the rise of these nationalist movements and the shifting balance of forces in the international system as a whole. It remains a very open question, however, how much they may be the signs of a regeneration of the British political system – on some pattern of federalism, say – or how much the signs of a continuing decay and decline, with no imminent prospect of recovery. The balance of gains and losses is a difficult one to calculate. For the decentralists, for instance, there is the obvious danger of being seduced by the appeal of a regionalism which is, so to speak, at the end of their noses, while being oblivious of the powerful centralizing forces gathering up over their heads at the level of European and American technocracy.

Indeed, in an incisive comment on Nairn, Eric Hobsbawm has argued that the current nationalist revival has to be seen less as an aspiration to independent statehood, than as one of the expressions of the fact of a growing dependence of most states, old and new, on the operations of an increasingly globalized capitalist economy. The internationalization of the economy, its dominance by a relatively small number of powerful multinational companies, has encouraged 'the Balkanization of the world of states'. Size is no longer, as it had been in the conditions of nineteenth-century capitalism, a relevant criterion for national independence:

the rise of the transnational corporation and international economic management have transformed both the international division of labour and its mechanism, and changed the criterion of a state's 'economic viability'. This is no longer believed to be an economy sufficiently large to provide an adequate 'national market' and sufficiently varied to produce most of the range of goods from foodstuffs to capital equipment, but a strategic position somewhere along the complex circuits of an integrated world economy, which can be exploited to secure an adequate national income. While size was essential to the old criterion, it appears largely irrelevant to the new . . . By these new standards, Singapore is as viable and much more prosperous than Indonesia, Abu Dhabi superior to Egypt, and any speck in the Pacific can look forward to independence and a good time for its president, if it happens to possess a location for a naval base for which more solvent states will compete, a lucky gift of nature such as manganese, or merely enough beaches and pretty girls to become a tourist paradise.[19]

In these changed conditions, the nationalist aspirations of small regions and groups can not only be encouraged, but are actually realistic – in the sense of aiming for formal political independence. But the price of that is a well-nigh crushing dependence in almost every other sense. The political imperative of the neo-capitalist economy, according to Hobsbawm, is 'divide and rule', as it was of the multi-ethnic empires of the past: 'The optimal strategy for a neo-colonial transnational economy is precisely one in which the number of official sovereign states is maximized and their average size and strength – i.e. their power effectively to impose the conditions under which foreign powers and foreign capital will have to operate – is minimized.'

Hobsbawm's line of argument I find to be generally convincing; and within this overall context of 'bastard capitalism' there seems little reason to pin one's hopes for the future of Britain on the Scottish Nationalist Party or Plaid Cymru (let alone the Irish Republican Army). If one does, and if they succeed, I find equally convincing Hobsbawm's widely shared expectation that 'by far the most likely effect of a secession of Scotland and Wales would be an enormous reinforcement of English nationalism, i.e. under present circumstances of a xenophobic, vicious and . . . a semi-fascist radical right'.[20] This, however, is not necessarily going to be the only consequence, or in the long run necessarily the most important. Such a regime, occupying a vacuum, may indeed prove to be only a transition to a more fundamental re-alignment and re-constitution of the political order, in which local groupings and local organizations emerge as the strongest units, as the only ones capable of attracting sufficient loyalty and commitment. The problem of the relation to international forces still applies, of course; but the balance may not turn out to be as asymmetrical and one-sided as Hobsbawm makes out. There may be a complementarity to the relationship which gives both sides more or less what they both want. The flea can be a source of great annoyance to the elephant, and it may serve the latter's interest to make genuine concessions, even where it isn't forced to. I return to this point later.

From politics to culture. Many commentators, impressed by the failure of repeated warnings, bribes and threats to arouse general enthusiasm for industrial renewal in Britain, have turned increasingly to a concern with the cultural values that they see as underlying the present economic crisis. They point to a specific cultural feature of British society that distinguishes it from most of its industrial competitors: a long-standing indifference to the values associated with industry and industrial growth, a preference for a more leisurely pattern of life at the cost of a greater commitment to work, a reluctance to offer sufficient status or rewards to the commercially adventurous and successful.[21] This is indeed a highly relevant part of the present problem, and no strategy is likely to succeed which does not come to terms with it.

This is a different matter, however, from simply belabouring the population for its uncaring attitude to industry, as if the values of a national culture can be changed overnight by tough ministerial talking on television, or addresses to schoolchildren by ageing industrialists with the light of old boardroom battles in their eyes. The educational system has become for many the chief culprit in perpetuating anti-industrial attitudes: as witness the veiled threats to commandeer the educational system contained in a much-discussed speech by the Prime Minister James Callaghan at Ruskin College, Oxford, in October 1976. But as Ralf Dahrendorf tartly retorted, 'British universities are not likely to be more industry-minded than British society'.[22] No more are British schools, as was acknowledged by Callaghan's own Secretary of State for Education, Shirley Williams.[23] The roots of these attitudes go far back into British history, and their persistence is a function of the social structure as a whole, its system of rewards and recognition, rather than of any particular set of institutions.

It is of course precisely at the level of values and cultural attitudes that the argument about future developments can go in a number of different ways. For those who believe that the way forward is to restore manufacturing strength and material growth, an alteration of these attitudes is crucial. For those who see future growth in different terms, these long-standing values may be exactly what provides the springboard for the desired development: as is suggested in the observations quoted at the beginning of this essay. Britain's future, on this view, may lie in a past even deeper than her relatively recent industrial era. A later section takes up this possibility.

There is, finally, the most general level of analysis, which subsumes the crisis of British society under the crisis of industrial society as such. The distinctiveness of this approach is marked. Even the Marxists, who see the

British predicament as a predicament of all capitalist societies, and to that extent deny its uniqueness, acknowledge the peculiar features of British history and social structure which have made the British position especially weak in relation to other industrial societies. In any case they look forward to a socialist future recognizably industrial in its main outlines. But the 'post-industrialists' – in Illich's, not Daniel Bell's sense – see the British crisis as symptomatic of the crisis of the industrial mode itself. The general lines of the argument we get in the writings of Illich himself, and Bookchin and Roszak in the United States, and from Schumacher, Robertson and some of the 'radical science/technology' theorists in Britain.[24] In this account the crisis is the inevitable product of the long-term tendency of industrialism towards larger scale, greater centralization, a finer specialization and division of labour, and the replacement of human labour and human skill by a resource-consuming machine technology. Britain is perhaps suffering more than most because she is an older and weaker industrial power. But the pangs may not necessarily be those of a continuing decline. They may be also the symptoms of the birth of a new order which in several important respects reverses the tendencies of classic industrialism, including the compulsive drive to economic growth. It is these post-industrialists who, not surprisingly, are most likely to see some signs of hope in the anti-industrial prejudices of British culture.

Are the options really as open as this last critique supposes? I think so, although there is inevitably a utopian element in some of the expressions of the more radical recommendations. This brief – and very selective – review of some current accounts of the British crisis has at least indicated my dissatisfaction with most of the proposed remedies. It is now time to look at some alternative possibilities.

II

Growth or no-growth?

On this subject, no passage seems more frequently quoted than the following from John Stuart Mill's *Principles of Political Economy:*

I cannot ... regard the stationary state of capital and wealth with the unaffected aversion so generally manifested towards it by political economists of the old school. I am inclined to believe that it would be, on the whole, a very considerable improvement on our present condition. I confess I am not charmed with the ideal of life held out by those who think that the normal state of human beings is that of struggling to get on; that the trampling, crushing, elbowing, and treading on each other's heels, which form the existing type of social life, are the most desirable lot of human kind, or anything but the disagreeable symptoms of one of the phases of industrial progress ... the best state for human nature is that in which, while no one is poor, no one desires to be richer, nor has any reason to fear being thrust back, by the efforts of others to push themselves forward ... the stationary state of capital and population implies no stationary state of human improvement.

The argument between proponents of expansive material growth, on the one hand, and human improvement or the quality of life as the sufficient end, on the other, is one of the oldest in Western thought, as many writers have pointed out.[25] It is to be found, for instance, in the distinction Aristotle makes in the *Politics* between *oiconomike* (household management) which 'attends more to men than to the acquisition of material things', and *chrematistike* (the pursuit of wealth), which must be the always strictly delimited means to the end ('human excellence') set by the former. It continues throughout the medieval period, in the concept of the 'just price', where Aquinas distinguishes between *commutatio*, 'fair exchange' in the satisfaction of needs as the basis of economic relations, and *negotiatio*, which is exchange not for needs but for profit. And it is to be found in the writings of the Physiocrats, and of Rousseau, in the eighteenth century, with their idea of the essentially limited needs of individuals, and the necessity therefore of limiting economic activity to the satisfaction of these needs.

No one will deny, however, that the argument has been powerfully revived in recent years, fuelled by anxieties about environmental destruction, and the possible exhaustion of the physical resources of the earth on which economic growth depends. Indeed with the renewed concern with the 'stationary state' has gone a new view of world history, and especially of the industrial epoch, which bids fair to become a new orthodoxy in certain circles. The period of world history up till the end of the eighteenth century is seen as one of a 'steady state' economy and society. The Industrial Revolution of the nineteenth and twentieth centuries introduces a period of acute destabilization, an 'exponential era' marked by rapid and unbalanced growth, especially but not exclusively economic. Now, in the last quarter of the twentieth century, a second turning point is discerned, bringing about a renewed switch to a steady state system.[26]

There is much that is attractive in this view, both in its conception of the past and its proposals for the future. But there are profound ambiguities in the whole conception of a 'no-growth' society. What is meant by no-growth? It seems fairly clear that what most of its proponents mean by it is a slow-down in the production of *material goods*, which they associate with an increasingly prodigal expenditure of men, machines and natural resources, as well as an increasingly intolerable level of environmental pollution and destruction. But of course we could switch production towards more *services* without in any way abandoning the goal of economic growth. Nor would this goal necessarily be affected by a radical change in the tastes and desires of the industrial populations. As Mancur Olson says, 'if the tastes of modern man were suddenly to change in such a way that he devoted most of the time and money he now devotes to cars and television, to cathedrals and art galleries, the change would not reduce economic output or growth: it could, like other changes in the composition of output, be perfectly consistent with an increase in the rate of economic growth.'[27] The link between welfare and economic activity, Olson goes on to assert, can be made far more inclusive than most people suppose:

Because of the arbitrariness involved in any restrictive definition of what is economic, I have, like other economists of the more single-minded sort, often defined utility or welfare from any source or of any kind as part of income or welfare. With this definition, there is an economic problem whenever people have wants which cannot be entirely satisfied with existing resources, and economic growth whenever existing wants are satisfied to a greater degree than they were in a previous period. Reality, in this view, is not divided into departments, like a university; the economic dimension has no logical outer limit.[28]

Accordingly, on this definition, there is no necessary link, say, between a pro-environment policy and a no-growth policy, and no necessary contradiction between environmentalism and growthmanship. All that would be involved, if one pursues the former, is a change of policies and regulations making it economically more attractive for firms to produce 'cleaner' or socially more useful goods, with cleaner processes of production (involving perhaps intensive re-cycling of waste materials), and economically punitive to do otherwise.[29]

It is obviously important for no-growth advocates to make precise, both to themselves and to others, exactly what they are opposing or proposing, if only to prevent people arguing past each other. Nevertheless, as Olson himself admits, it is usually not difficult to see what current proponents of no-growth are getting at, and to allow the strength of the case. What they are saying is that the *present* conception of economic growth, as reflected in the national statistics which are used to calculate Gross National Product, emphasizes the wrong priorities in the assessment of national wealth. It counts as wealth-creating, activities which are either actually harmful to human beings and their natural environment or are simply forms of 'defensive' and reparative expenditures caused by those activities. At the same time the statistics ignore activities – in the home, for instance, or in voluntary organizations – which are self-evidently valuable although currently don't involve market or state expenditure. Once we acknowledge the contribution of a whole realm of activities conventionally deemed 'unproductive', but which to some people may constitute the very basis of a creative and satisfying life, it certainly makes sense to oppose 'growth' as that is currently accounted and practised.

It may be true to say that, in principle, the composition of the GNP could be changed to suit the wishes of the no-growth advocates, in which case they would have no reason to oppose growth. But in practice the change of priorities involved may be so formidable, the vested political and economic interests so powerful, that the no-growth slogan may prove the most effective rallying cry in trying to bring about a change of direction. For there is, as Hugh Stretton has stressed, a real conflict of values and interests involved in the debate about growth.

Better social accounting which measured real net welfare might allow environmentalists to join in favouring growth as a general principle. But still not agree about in it detail – people with different interests and values would still want to count different things as 'real welfare' and weight them differently according to who was to enjoy them. It is a mistake ... to pin extravagant hopes to the development of better economic and social indexes. Indexes can't alter the fact that one citizen sees as goods what another sees as costs or wastes; what one wants to consume, another wants to leave in the ground. Indexes of net welfare have to be constructed by controversial judgements of good and bad . . . Better accounting can serve all sorts of good purposes, and reconcile some mistaken conflicts of opinion, but can't reconcile real conflicts of interest and value.[30]

It is this that makes so disingenuous the arguments of those who – like Wilfred Beckerman and the late Antony Crosland in Britain[31] – are fervent advocates of growth. They meet all the objections smoothly at the level of abstract economic theory. We *can* have our cake and eat it – in fact we must, if we are to have any cake at all. But they ignore the political facts which are equally relevant to the argument, and which in present circumstances almost inevitably tend to impose a particular direction on growth, for the benefit of particular interests.

Much of the discussion about growth has centred on the physical limits, as exemplified in the Club of Rome report, *The Limits to Growth*. In his powerfully argued book *The Social Limits to Growth*,[32] Fred Hirsch has added a fresh dimension. The basic argument turns on the difficulties encountered once a society gets beyond a certain level of material production, and enters on a competitive struggle for goods within the 'positional economy' – such goods as satisfying and creative jobs, quietness, privacy. The old law of imitation – 'what the few have today, the many want tomorrow' – continues to operate at the level of aspiration but, unlike the case with material goods, cannot work at the level of achievement. It breaks down in that sector of the economy where the satisfactions deriving from the good turn entirely on its restricted and reserved nature, thus making it self-defeating for all to pursue it. The positional economy, unlike the material economy, is a zero-sum economy. Hirsch's argument is not strictly speaking an argument against growth as such – indeed it presupposes a quite considerable level of material growth. Moreover to my mind it takes an excessively narrow and closed view of the character and potentialities of the positional economy. Hirsch's assumptions are evidently conservative ones – that the structure of work and organization will remain substantially as it is now, for instance, so that there will always be the same strictly limited number of creative and responsible jobs, or 'leadership roles'; or that we cannot use our imaginations to conceive of a better arrangement for the enjoyment of countryside, lakeland and sea-shore, such that we can mix both privacy and sociability, thus enriching the satisfaction of the good as well as increasing the number able to enjoy it.[33]

Nevertheless, Hirsch is surely right to point to the enormous problems encountered when the growth mentality becomes lodged in societies.[34] His own solutions are offered without any great conviction. Mostly they imply policies of 'levelling-down' as well as 'levelling-up', to lessen the fierceness of the struggle for positional goods. The pay given for intrinsically interesting jobs, for instance, should be lowered; the tie between the attainment of educational qualifications and the gaining of financially lucrative jobs should be loosened. Here he is close to those many others who have also offered bleak scenarios for the future of no-growth societies. Mostly they emphasize the acute distributional struggles which will ensue with the slowing-down or stopping of growth, leading either to a breakdown of the political order or, more likely, to the rise of strongly authoritarian political regimes. Charles Taylor grimly looks out on a prospect 'of a Byzantine society in which production and consumption are held in a static pattern by a myriad of controls, and in which the pattern of consumption is marked by the drab uniformity of the utility good. The economics of Byzantium combine with the taste of wartime Britain.'[35]

These melancholy predictions no doubt might lead us to incline to the view of those who briskly dismiss no-growth altogether, as 'a disguised ideology of privilege, or a form of romantic reaction'.[36] The haves are trying to stop the have-nots getting in on the act, as so often in the past. The Hudson Report, *The United Kingdom in 1980*, roundly puts the matter thus:

Britain is a country of 56 million people living on a crowded and poor island, in no sense self-sufficient in food or raw materials, and . . . decreasingly self-sufficient even in manufactured goods. There is no possibility of supporting Britain's population except through the mechanism of modern industrial society [i.e. growth]; the options of retreat into a rural stable-state or zero growth economy are sentimentalities.[37]

Sentiment can be a great thing, especially when there is a certain amount of necessity mixed in with the desire. Indeed, those who, like Hirsch, Heilbroner and Taylor, fear the consequences of the end to growth, pin their hopes to a remarkable extent on the development of strong collective feeling to take us through the difficult times ahead: a recurrence of 'the Dunkirk spirit', or a revival of religion.[38] Are they being too gloomy? Assuming that we have to look forward to something that is more like a steady state than a growth economy, need the transition be quite so much the vale of tears conjured up by these writers? Once more we need to see that the alternatives are being deployed on too restricted a plane. The accounting tends to leave out a good deal of the benefits that may be expected to come – and which in fact have already come – from the slowing down of material growth. Such things as a new concept of and attitude towards 'waste', a concern with the renovation, repair and recycling of materials, a renewed respect for the whole realm of nature. Put more strongly, there is in most of these accounts a failure to ask what kind of society ultimately we may want – and to see whether the check to our automatic, routine growth mentality may not be as full of opportunities as it is of threats and fears. In Britain's case particularly there are good grounds for thinking that the society is peculiarly well-placed to come to terms with the new situation.

III

Manufacturing or services?[39]

Whether or not Britain opts for renewed economic growth, or maintains economic output at something like the current level, it is clear that she will have to make a choice about what kind of economic activities to support and promote. Here is a typical statement from the Department of Industry, blessed by no less than four Secretaries of State: 'The success of manufacturing is vital to the country's future. The Government, through its industrial strategy, is committed to giving it priority over other objectives ... Society needs to recognise the contribution of manufacturing industry in creating wealth on which we depend to preserve and improve our social provisions and personal standards of living.'[40]

Nothing could be plainer than that, and nothing more likely to command heartfelt assent from all concerned with public affairs. Moreover, the Department of Industry's document is correct in noting that government policy has since the war consistently favoured manufacturing, and – though this is unspoken – been consistently hostile to service activities. As public policy the attitude seems to date back to Keynes,[41] with his incisive analysis of Britain's weak manufacturing sector in comparison with its world-wide financial operations. As a general view, however, the attitude clearly has deeper roots, and derives from the writings of Adam Smith, Say and others, on the nature of 'productive' and 'unproductive activities'. In this classification, manufacturing (and agriculture) are productive, services largely unproductive. This view has taken an almost religious hold on educated opinion. Politicians, trade unionists, their advisers, all have accepted the apparently common sense view that if something doesn't hurt when you drop it on your foot, it can't become an export. To champion services as against manufacturing, to suggest that the future might lie more in the development of the former than of the latter, is to invite the charge of crankiness, if not actual treason.

There has been a public consensus, unprecedented in its weight of advocacy and narrowness of content, on the need to 'get manufacturing industry moving again', to put more people back into 'productive', that is, manufacturing industry, whether or not this would be a good thing for manufacturing anyway, and at whatever cost to the rest of the economy and society. Services have been persistently penalized – most notoriously with the Selective Employment Tax of 1966–73, a product of Lord Kaldor's advisory role, and under the influence of his strongly pro-manufacturing economic writing.[42] Symbolically the official antipathy to services is shown by the fact that right up until 1970 the Queen's Award for Export could not be given to the exporter of a service. At a different level it was shown in the reaction of the backwoodsmen who returned their MBEs on the award of the same honours to the Beatles in 1965 for their contribution to Britain's overseas earnings.

For many people, the case against services was decisively put by the Oxford economists Robert Bacon and Walter Eltis, in their influential analysis of Britain's economic problems.[43] Carefully read, their book does not really back up the prescriptions popularly derived from it, but the authors' general emphasis – and the book's title – is such as easily to lead to misunderstanding. What seemed to follow from their account was that there had been an excessive movement of employees and investment funds from manufacturing to services. Manufacturing is seen as productive, 'wealth-creating', and is largely identified with the private, market sector. Services are seen as mostly non-productive and are largely identified with the non-market, public sector.[44] The fact that the state also manufactures and sells – for example, steel and ships – is acknowledged but not, apparently, regarded as very significant. Similarly the existence of a highly successful services branch – for example, retail and banking – in the private sector is recognized, but this too does not seem to carry much weight. Eltis and Bacon's analysis, popularized in an influential Sunday newspaper, led to a chorus of demands for cut-backs in services, and massive inducements to get more men and women back into manufacturing.

And yet the merest glance at some widely available figures tells a different story, for those with ears to hear. Consider this picture of manufacturing decline. For the first half of the nineteenth century, as was hardly to be wondered at in the world's first industrial nation, British manufacturing dominated the world. In 1870 British manufactured exports accounted for 40 per cent of all world trade in manufactures. By 1900 this was down to 30 per cent; by 1930, 20 per cent; by 1960 – following a period of temporary recovery largely owing to the smashed industrial economies of Japan and Continental Europe – it was 15 per cent; in 1976, less than 9 per cent.[45]

It could scarcely be clearer from these figures how long-term, basic and structural Britain's manufacturing decline must be; and so it has been widely acknowledged.[46] From about 1870 onwards, all the relevant economic indices – rates of growth, productivity, investment, technical innovation, and so on – take a downward turn. They have continued to plunge in this century, except for a few short periods. The reasons for this decline are complex and much discussed, but an obvious one was quite simply that other countries were now industrializing, and had many of the well-known advantages of latecomers. France, Belgium, Germany, Sweden, the United States, Japan, Russia, all grew at Britain's expense. They invaded not just her foreign but her home markets. Later came competition from Canada and Australia, later still the challenges from the intensely capitalist eastern enclaves: Taiwan, Hong Kong, Singapore, South Korea. Now countries like Brazil and India are also threatening some of Britain's traditional markets, and other competitors are already in sight. As *The Times* put it in 1971 – before the position could be seen to have actually worsened – 'Britain is now little more than standby capacity for world manufactured exports; the complete elimination of Britain's industrial capacity could now be made up by the expansion in the rest of the world inside a few months.'[47]

This being so, on what grounds do its advocates urge the strategy of economic recovery through manufacturing? No one surely can expect a reversal of so secular a decline within the foreseeable future. Certainly it would go against any historical parallel that springs to mind. Britain's manufacturng base has now become so precarious that every attempt to strengthen and broaden it has invited punishment. Every impulse to growth in the past two decades has been halted by the inescapable and finally unacceptable rise in imports, leading to a severe balance of payments crisis. To put it in the economist's terms, the income elasticities of demand for British imports are high, those for British exports are low. In other words, the British need other people's goods; other people seem neither to need nor to want British goods.[48] The British government's policy has for long been geared to the idea of growth through the export of manufactured goods. But as the Hudson Report puts it, 'there is a basic question of just what Britain will export. Manufactures have been a stagnant component of exports but a rapidly rising component of imports. It seems much more likely therefore that an increase in investment and output will create an increase in imports, not the desired exports.'[19] The change in the structure of imports reveals the pattern of increasing dependency. Britain imports half her food, and up to 1960 this accounted for a third of all imports. During the following twelve years this proportion dropped to 18 per cent of total imports. By contrast imports of manufactured goods and machinery rose sharply – by some 16 per cent – so that at the end of the same period they accounted for 55 per cent of total imports. The position with regard to fuels and raw materials has, it is well known, deteriorated even more sharply in recent years, especially following the OPEC decision to quadruple the price of crude oil in 1973. Britain imports two-thirds of her raw materials and half her fossil fuels (and North Sea oil and gas will be very short-lived). As a manufacturing nation she is, clearly, very dependent on overseas goods and resources. As these increase in price or scarcity her ability to compete with the rest of the world's industrial nations declines even further.[50]

But if British *manufacturing* glory seems over, the same thing cannot be said for British *services*. The contrast here with manufacturing could hardly be more striking. Britain is second only to the United States in the world trade in 'invisibles', i.e. services, with 12 per cent of the total trade. She has a permanent and rising surplus on current account. Whereas the import content of manufacturing exports is already 19 per cent and going up, that of service exports is less than 9 per cent. Productivity in service industries, though notoriously difficult to measure, seems to be higher than manufacturing in many branches (compare Marks and Spencer's to British Steel). In 1975 the insurance and banking services of the City of London earned twice as much in exports as the motor car industry. Tourism, one of the most successful and fastest growing industries, contributed in 1977 £3,000 million to the balance of payments, and had a surplus on account of £1,000 million. It earns for Britain more than the total sales abroad of electrical machinery and appliances. In fact services already account for more than 40 per cent of total overseas earnings, and on current trends bid fair to overtake manufacturing.[51]

One might have thought that these figures would be publicized and their implications seriously discussed. But they are not. A clear alternative to current official strategy presents itself – to promote and prosecute the service activities of the economy as vigorously as possible. And yet, as we have seen, strong suspicions and prejudices abound in this field. For instance, alarmed by the tourist invasion Sir Malby Crofton, leader of one of London's biggest boroughs, proposes the imposition of a tourist quota and special tourist taxes to discourage the trade. Moralists and economists, mindful of past manufacturing triumphs, denounce the wealth created by tourism as fleeting and insubstantial. There is an uneasy sense that Britain may turn into a nation of Benidorms, or of Arab bazaars selling cheap trinkets.

What is peculiarly misguided about these attitudes is that they think that they are reacting against some novel phenomenon, something more suited to foreigners and alien to the noble native manufacturing tradition. In fact tourism is simply one of the more recent[52] expressions of a field of economic activities – the tertiary or service sector – which of course long pre-dates the Industrial Revolution. But there is something more important about this, from the point of view of Britain's future. *Services are the thing that Britain has always been good at*, well before she launched the industrial revolution that turned her society – and the world – towards manufacturing. By the end of the eighteenth century Britain had already outdistanced her European competitors in the crucial services of banking, insurance and shipping. Over two centuries she had established the pattern and practice of overseas investment. London had superseded Amsterdam as the centre of the world's money market. Long before she was an industrial community, then, Britain was an organized commercial and financial community. On the basis of her service economy she had made herself by the end of the eighteenth century the richest country in the world.

Financial and mercantile services, together with overseas investment, constitute the historic core of the nation's foreign trade in 'invisibles', traditionally centred on the City of London. The trade has swollen by every new addition of marketable services, whether in the form of tourism, technical expertise, clothes design, symphony orchestras, pop groups, television programmes, health and educational services. Now there is a fact about Britain's trade in invisibles which ought to be widely known, and reflected on. For most of this century politicians and economists have worried us, and the economic system, over deficits in the balance of payments. They have concentrated almost exclusively, as most people tend to when they talk about the balance of payments, on deficits in the trade in 'visible' goods, now mostly manufactures. But as W.A.P. Manser established in his book *Britain in Balance*, a deficit in the visible trade has been the normal thing in Britain ever since regular trading records began at the end of the seventeenth century. Taking just the more recent period, there was a surplus on the visible trading account only in 9 out of the past 177 years. The deficit moreover was at its largest in the nineteenth century, at the height of Britain's manufacturing prosperity.[53] What has throughout made up the differences and – with the exception of a few years – bridged the gap between exports and imports of goods, has been the continuous and healthy surplus in invisibles. If Britain over the past couple of centuries has had a net surplus in its overall balance of payments, this has been entirely due to the earnings from the trade in invisibles. The service sector has bailed out the manufacturing sector.

But we may be able to go even further than this. Paradoxical as it may sound in the nation that created the world's first industrial society, there is actually something artificial, aberrant almost, in the rise to pre-eminence of British manufacturing industry in the nineteenth century. It went against the grain of the society's cultural values, as well as important parts of its social structure. 'Trade' in the form of the merchant banker or the West Indian planter was respectable. After an initial encounter with feudal values, the City became an accepted part of the Establishment. The sons and daughters of such 'tradesmen' married easily enough into the gentry and aristocracy, whose ample rural style of life continued to dominate the aspirations of all classes throughout the last century and well into this

But manufacturing: that was a different matter. Manufacturers were provincial. They were often Dissenters (which meant, for one thing, not being able to go to Oxford or Cambridge). They were looked down upon not just by the aristocracy and gentry but by the merchants and bankers of the City. Faced with such social pressure who can be surprised if their children hurried to escape from this despised social category – indeed were pressed to do so by their own parents. The historians monotonously record the movement out of manufacturing of the great industrial families, the Arkwrights, Boultons, Strutts, Wilkinsons, Wedgwoods, Courtaulds. 'From shirt-sleeves to hunting-jacket in three generations', is how David Landes sums up the process.[54] D.C. Coleman sees it as the result of the persistent pressure to cross the only important divide in English society, that between 'Players' and 'Gentlemen'.[55] The ideal of the English gentleman, originally thought up to tame the turbulent knights of the Tudor period, was refurbished in the nineteenth century – with the help of the public schools – to tame the rough energetic industrialists and technologists of the Industrial Revolution.

Some of this was true of other European countries as well. But nowhere – for reasons much discussed[56] – was the persistence of gentry culture and life-styles so deep and long-lasting as in Britain. The sheer energy and success of early industrialism carried it along for a time. But the weight of the stronger cultural tradition, always present alongside, eventually proved too much. The consequences were already apparent by the last quarter of the nineteenth century. British manufacturing then began its long downhill slide from its position of supremacy. From the 1870s we also begin to hear the litany of complaints, now so familiar, about Britain's backwardness in technical education, the lack of entrepreneurial ambition, the preference of the best brains for the professions and public service rather than for manufacturing industry.[57]

But there was a strong element of hypocrisy in the complaints. British society had *chosen* the values which it recognized and rewarded, and it was idle to expect ambitious individuals to ignore this fact. The structure of higher education which emerged at the end of the nineteenth century made this only too clear. It continued the divide between gentlemen and players, between commissioned and non-commissioned officers, between the two cultures of the cultivated amateur and the technical expert. For the governing class there were Oxford and Cambridge, to complete the work of the public schools. For the non-commissioned officers there were the new provincial universities with their strong utilitarian and technological bias. Matthew Arnold was driven to comment thus on the disturbing consequences:

So we have amongst us the spectacle of a middle class cut in two and in a way unexampled anywhere else, of a professional class brought up on the first plane, with fine and governing qualities, but without the idea of science; while that immense business class, which is becoming so important a power in all countries, on which the future so depends ... is in England brought up on the second plane, cut off from the aristocracy and the professions, and without governing qualities.[58]

Who, given the opportunity to choose, would deliberately opt to join the second rank? Commenting on the educational developments of this period, Michael Fores has aptly observed that '"pecking orders" of occupational groups in society determine which educational courses can be set up successfully, not the other way round. Exhortations to teach more "science" in schools and universities missed the point. It is more important to note that the middle – and late – Victorians preferred not to send their sons to learn the useful arts because these did not fit in well with the new type of society which they wanted to create.'[59]

By the end of the nineteenth century the British, it seems, had already had their fill of manufacturing. They gratefully reverted to the older, culturally more comfortable pattern of getting their wealth through services. As Britain's share of world manufacturing trade declined, her trade in invisibles increased its share of world market. 'It could well be said,' says Fores, 'that Britain changed from being the workshop of the world in about 1850 to being the service agency of the world about half a century later.'[60] Nothing much has changed in the course of the present century, either in the external environment or in the character of British society, to suggest that this direction could or should be reversed. At regular intervals the anguished national debates about Britain's poor manufacturing and technological performance have taken place, the last before the present round being the controversy over Sir Charles Snow's Rede Lecture, *The Two Cultures and the Scientific Revolution* (1959). These debates have nearly always simply recapitulated the nineteenth-century discussion of the same problem. And, for the same reasons now as before, attitudes towards manufacturing industry remain stubbornly negative.

A recent discussion paper from the Department of Industry, *Industry, Education and Management*,[61] underlines the point forcibly (and depressingly, from the Department's point of view). It states the problem with great clarity. It sees the need to improve the quality of British industrial management. It realizes that this will only happen if the society can improve the status and image of manufacturing industry, and of technology and science generally. Yet the document shows that the proportion of graduates going into manufacturing had dropped to an all-time low of 26 per cent by 1975. The fall is in actual as well as proportionate numbers, and represents a more or less steady decline from the 35–40 per cent of a decade ago. Even more worrying must be the drop in the proportion of science and technology graduates who go into manufacturing – from 42 per cent (technology) and 20 per cent (science) in 1961, to 26 per cent and 11 per cent respectively in 1975. Moreover the demand for science and technology places at universities continues to be static, while that for arts and social science subjects goes on rising. Add to this that the quality of students entering to read technological subjects is significantly lower than that for all other subjects, and the Department of Industry's disquiet is understandable. All this when both the quantity and quality of industrial management, backed by social esteem, continues to increase in most other industrial societies.

This section is not meant to be a tract against manufacturing. Manufacturing always has been and always will be a part of the nation's economy. The idea of a pure service economy is nonsense. But the important question is the balance of national endeavour, what we recognize and reward, what we see to be the strengths of the society in relation to what our industrial competitors can do. On that basis the prejudice against services, and the obstacles put in the way of their development, is extremely short-sighted. One suspects here a strong residual puritanism in economic matters: that 'there's only money where there's muck'. In the framework of a capitalist economy this is the sheerest hypocrisy. Why should anyone object if the Beatles make more money for Britain than British Leyland? There are good grounds moreover for thinking that the growth of services will benefit the society not just economically, but socially and culturally. In certain of the service areas, at least, the nature of the work, the scale of organization, the nature of the product and the social effects of the process of production, are all very much to be preferred than in the bulk of manufacturing industry.[62]

The country has in any case, because of the prevailing prejudices, so far only scratched the surface of its service potential. It has relied very much on the historic services of the City of London. Much imagination and enterprise must lie dormant or undeveloped for lack of encouragement. But there are some indications. The boom in English language schools suggests one additional line of development. So, too, does the success of the broadcasting organizations in selling their television programmes abroad, and of the Open University in selling its educational services. Tourism, for all its spectacular development, is still very much restricted to a few well-known English cities, and is clearly capable of much greater growth. Most far-reaching of all might be the opening up of the health and educational services. Passions are bound to be aroused by this. But properly handled there is no reason why these highly developed national resources should not pay handsomely without loss of quality or service to the native population. It is quite clear, from the demand for places in private health clinics and in British schools and universities, that these services are highly regarded and widely sought after by people overseas. Yet in the universities, for instance, at current fees of £650 a year for overseas undergraduates and £850 a year for postgraduates – something like a quarter of actual costs – no one could say that we were charging anything like the economic rate. A simple sliding scale could easily cope with the problems of students from the poorer countries. It seems foolish that with such obviously marketable services to hand, the government should cut back on these in the interests of a decaying manufacturing industry.

Britain launched the first industrial revolution on the world. For nearly a century she reaped the rewards of being a pioneer. Now she is suffering, inevitably and naturally, from industrial senility. To attempt to rejuvenate British society by propping up its creaking manufacturing industries is like trying to restore the looks of an ageing beauty with quantities of cream and rouge: pathetic and impossible. The world no longer seems to want or need British textiles, British steel, British ships, British cars, British electrical goods.

It does, however, want a whole host of British services and will pay well for them. To encourage these with as much political will as can be harnessed seems to promise not simply a sounder economic future but the possibility of a more lively, humane and satisfying society.

IV

The longer term – a household economy?

The strategy of going for services is conventional on most criteria. It is contained within the framework of a capitalist market economy. It assumes the goal of continuing economic growth, although accepting that such growth is likely to be slower for all industrial countries than has been the case in recent decades. It assumes that Britain remains heavily dependent on imports of food, fuel and manufactured goods, and therefore has to have something to sell in the overseas markets of the world. Although it provides a breathing-space, it may be short term.

On the other hand it may provide the bridge to a future that is radically different. It does at least break the psychological tie with the past, and is firm in its rejection of the nostalgic hope for a revival of old industrial glories. It may lead to a search for activities which, besides being commercially viable, call upon resources of enterprise, creativity and imagination that are rewarding in themselves. It may, in short, seriously raise the question of quality versus quantity, of a way of life satisfying by virtue of the values which it cultivates as against the goal of material growth for its own sake.

What, therefore, are the prospects for a move towards a society of welfare or well-being – something akin to Illich's 'convivial society'? A society in which considerations of continuing material growth are displaced by considerations of continuous personal growth? We are, doubtless, all for this in theory, but most people would regard such a goal as utopian in present circumstances. I want to suggest that it may be utopian in the sense that one cannot easily specify the mechanisms which will take us from here to there; but that it is properly utopian in confronting us with choices and values which we must decide upon in the pursuit of any long-term future goal. Moreover it goes to a considerable extent with, not against, many current developments.

Such a strategy would question, first, the current forms of social accounting, and the reality of the measurement of welfare contained within their terms. It inquires of the present order: by the criteria of genuine welfare, how efficient, productive and satisfying is it? It questions in particular current conceptions of 'wealth' and 'productive work'. We have already had reason to note the narrowness as well as the possible illusoriness of the concept of 'wealth creation' contained in the statistics of national income. James Robertson thus challenges the idea that it is only industry and commerce which create wealth:

We question the idea of 'wealth' as something created by manufacturers of cigarettes and sweets, but not by doctors and dentists; created by bankers and commercial lawyers, but not by housewives and social workers; created by agri-business, but not by people working their smallholdings, allotments, and gardens; created by advertising agencies but not by schools; created by the arms trade, but not by the peacepeople. Is it a law of nature that compels us to make more and more *things*, including many that are harmful or useless, before we can attend to the needs of *people*? ... The idea of wealth as something that has to be created by the economic' activities of industry and commerce, so that it can then be spent on something quite different called 'social' wellbeing, is part of the metaphysic of the industrial age.[63]

Once accept this broader, and patently saner, concept of wealth, and the goods, services and activities that go to make it undergo a change of character that may be very far-reaching. Tom Burke gives the following account of what it might mean to be truly accounted wealthy:

The new wealth might count as affluent the person who possessed the necessary equipment to make the best use of natural energy flows to heat a home or warm water – the use which accounts for the bulk of an individual's energy demand. The symbols of this kind of wealth would not be new cars, T.V.s, or whatever, although they would be just as tangible and just as visible. They would be solar panels, insulated walls, or a heat pump. The poor would be those who remained dependent on centralised energy distribution services, vulnerable to interruption by strike, malfunction, or sabotage, and even more vulnerable to rising tariffs set by inaccessible technocrats themselves the victims of market forces beyond their control. The new rich would boast not of how new their television set was but of how long it was expected to last and how easy it would be to repair. Wealth might take the form of ownership of, or at least access to, enough land to grow a proportion of one's food. This would reduce the need to earn an even larger income in order to pay for increasingly expensive food. Wealth might consist in having access to most goods and services within easy walking or cycling distance of home thus reducing the need to spend more time earning more money to pay for more expensive transport services. A high income would be less a sign of wealth than of poverty since it would indicate dependence on the provision by someone else of a job and a workplace in order to earn the income to rent services. Wealth would consist in having more control over the decisions that affected well being, and in having the time to exercise that control.[64]

The important point about re-conceptualizing wealth is that it changes the constraints normally supposed to exist on the amount of 'free' or 'leisure' time, and potentially expands this sphere greatly. More accurately, perhaps, it changes the very definition of 'work' and 'leisure' and suggests the possibility of a working life lived equally 'productively' in both spheres. At the moment most of us accept the utilitarian 'felicific calculus' of work being the necessary pain for the pleasure of leisure. Work is painful, and by virtue of that, necessary and productive; leisure is pleasure, and by virtue of that, contingent and passive. Commenting on this 'vision of inertia', C.B. Macpherson rightly says:

It is almost incredible, until you come to think of it, that a society whose keyword is *enterprise,* which certainly sounds active, is in fact based on the assumption that human beings are so inert, so averse to activity, that is, to expenditure of energy, that every expenditure of energy is considered to be painful, to be, in the economist's term, a disutility. This assumption, which is a travesty of the human condition, is built right into the justifying theory of the market society ... The market society is commonly justified on the grounds that it maximizes utilities, i.e., that it is the arrangement by which people can get the satisfaction they want with the least effort. The notion that activity itself is pleasurable, is a utility, has sunk almost without trace under this utilitarian vision of life.[65]

What are the practical possibilities of revising and reversing this utilitarian assessment? Can we move towards a society in which work done at home or in the community, normally thought of as spare-time activity, can become the central focus of an individual's life, the chief source of his identity? The interesting thing is the extent to which this has already been happening. Hugh Stretton has given us the most perceptive account of this development. 'The first industrial revolution,' he says, 'had moved production out of the family into the factory; the second industrial revolution moved a lot of it back again.' Mass-produced household goods, network water and gas and electricity, ubiquitous transport, all produced another great shift of productive resources. 'By 1970 the British housewife was using the horsepower the British factory worker had used in 1910. Households could *make* and *do* things: a steadily increasing number and variety of things. With materials and equipment supplied by the commercial economy, they were soon producing a good deal of the twentieth century standard of living for themselves.'[66]

In similar fashion, Jay Gershuny has shown that there is already under way a movement to what he calls 'the self-service economy'. Contrary to the views of some 'post-industrial' theorists such as Daniel Bell, people are consuming more, not less, goods, and less, not more, services supplied by the formal money economy. A process of substitution of goods for services has been going on steadily for some considerable time. Gershuny comments:

This change runs deeper than it sounds; it is more than just a simple modification of buying habits. Goods are not consumed in the way services are – goods consumption is much more akin to investment. What the evidence shows is a real transformation in investment patterns, from investment in the money economy to investment in the household, from investment in laundries and theatres and railways to investment in washing machines and televisions and motor cars. This pattern of change results from two ongoing economic trends. On the one hand rising costs – particularly labour costs – and on the other technical change enabling the substitution of labour by capital, reducing both the necessary time and the necessary skill levels. These together enable more and more final production by the final consumer himself – by 'direct labour'. This is the self-service economy.[67]

The implication of this shift from market to home, from the 'formal' to the 'informal' economy, is, as Stretton points out, that 'the flow of consumer goods has been overrated as the characteristic product of industrialization. The most profound achievement of modern industry – of the forty-hour week of organized alienated labour – has been to give people at home energy, equipment, materials and communications, and time and space and freedom, to produce for themselves: to make and do what they want, when and where and how they want, working together or apart as they feel inclined, and enriching their time and social experience in all sorts of ways freely chosen by themselves.' Already, as he further shows, in present-day industrial societies much more than a half of all working time is spent at home or near it. More than a third of all capital is invested there, more than a third of work is done there. Depending on what we choose to count as goods, some high proportion of all goods are produced there, and even more are enjoyed there. 'More than three-quarters of all subsistence, social life, leisure and recreation happen there. Above all, people are produced there, and endowed there with the values and capacities which will determine most of the quality of their social life and government away from home.'[68]

It would, clearly, be going too far to say that the desirable transformation is already more or less accomplished. Indeed aspects of the current development could lead to a society of a highly undesirable kind: privatized, passive, consumerist, characterized by an educated elite doing all the interesting work and running the society, and a majority employed in unrewarding tasks at work and undemanding consumption at home (something, in fact, like the scenario sketched in Michael Young's *The Rise of the Meritocracy*). The materials for the change exist. But they have to be given a definite shape and direction. The assumption underlying the design of current household tools and appliances, for instance, is that they should be time-saving and undemanding of skill and effort. Household work is regarded as a marginal activity, to be undertaken with the minimum effort and in the minimum time. 'Real' work takes place outside the home – in the money economy. The ideal home is a place of leisure and inactivity. It refreshes and recreates the worker for the serious and productive work elsewhere. The aim, then, should be to redefine the place and the function of the household. Here, only the briefest indications can be given of how we might achieve this.

First, make production in the formal, institutional, economy as efficient as possible. This may mean pushing capital intensity, specialization and mechanization as far and as fast as possible. The price may well be abandoning the hope of humanizing work in this sphere. It is a price we should not be afraid to pay. The extent to which work in a complex industrial economy can be humanized will always be limited. Alienation is its hallmark. The gain will be correspondingly great, however: cheapness of goods and, above all, increase in free time. Most of us will need to spend no more than two or three days at work in the formal economy. Some people, probably, with particular drives and aptitudes will want to spend most of their time on activities in the formal economy. The rest of us will be freed for activities in the household and the community.

Next, much of the technology of the household will need to be redesigned. The capital goods produced in the formal economy for use in the household must be of the kind that will enhance the skill and productivity of the individual user or small group (by household, of course, I mean anything from the nuclear family to a small village, urban or rural). A domestic cooker (or typewriter) is an ideal model: it aids, does not substitute for, time-intensive, skill-intensive, non-alienating, non-polluting, eminently productive activity.

Many of the tools that have accompanied the 'Black and Decker do-it-yourself revolution' have these characteristics. One can, for instance, now purchase domestic lathes for turning metal, wood, or clay, which can be installed in very small workshops. Similarly the miniaturization and simplification of print technology makes it perfectly feasible for small household units to print and publish newspapers, magazines and books. On this count, generally, many technological developments are going in the direction of scaled-down, household-size units.[69]   The goods made in the formal economy should be those that emphasize durability and reparability. They should be capable of being repaired and serviced by people with modest technical skills and relatively simple tools. They should as far as possible be components that can be assembled in small workshops.

Lastly there is the need to cut as far as possible reliance on imports of food, fuels and raw materials. This means going in for the familiar strategy of low-energy technologies, use of 'alternative' sources of energy (wind, water, sun), production of long-life durables and processes involving recycling, re-use, renovation and repair. For instance, the British electricity generating system is prodigiously wasteful, wasting three out of every four tons of coal consumed. The importance of this is seen in the fact that about one-third of all primary energy is consumed in the generation of electricity. Similarly one-quarter of all energy consumed in Britain is for domestic space heating in homes with very poor insulation standards. Consumption can be cut by about one-third at a cost to each house of about £200 spent on insulation.[70] Most far-reaching of all might be the savings possible in food imports (Britain imports half her food). Michael Allaby has shown how, by certain not very spectacular and often very desirable changes in the national diet, Britain could become well-nigh self-sufficient in food. The changes involve mainly cutting back by about half on the consumption of beef, veal, pig and poultry products (though leaving lamb and mutton consumption much as it is now), and making up the additional protein through increased grain consumption. There would also have to be less sugar consumed.[71]

We might, finally, note the relation of an overall strategy of this kind to two dominant anxieties of the present time: unemployment, and the power of the multinationals. As to the first, it must be clear how little 'unemployment' has to do with the lack of *work*. There are more than a million and a half unemployed in Britain at the time of writing. They are not, that is, 'in work', employed for wages in the formal economy. But are they all not working? How many unemployed husbands and wives now spend more time doing jobs around the home, renovating and extending domestic facilities ('building' and 'construction'), taking more time with their children ('education' and 'child-rearing'), growing more of their own food in gardens and allotments ('agriculture')? How many services and goods are being exchanged not involving cash transactions, or undeclared cash transactions – car repairs in return for examination tuition, tomatoes and lettuces in return for baby-sitting? How many of the young unemployed have used or developed skills to run small trades or businesses in the informal economy – small-scale construction and maintenance, gardening, window-cleaning, carpentry and furniture-making – for all of which there is unfilled demand both in large cities and in small country towns? How many of those who don't, who are demoralized and made apathetic by unemployment, are so because of the excessive valuation placed on employment in the formal economy?

There are many of those in employment who are already aware of a dissatisfaction, an uncertainty, about where the line between work and non-work should be drawn. Much of what they do at work strikes them as unproductive even if time-consuming. Much else that they do in their 'leisure time' seems worthwhile and rewarding. It is pointless to entice industry to create jobs that are often useless to the industry and degrading to the worker. There is no shortage of work to be done. It is mainly a matter of acknowledging this, of conferring legitimacy on particular activities. In an instructive Canadian example, the Canada Council 'creates' jobs by conferring legitimacy on tasks proposed by people in local communities. Worthwhile activities are not identified and organized from the top down, but from the bottom up – by people proposing and carrying out particular tasks. It is interesting that this process started through a conventional 'job creation' scheme, initiated by government agencies with traditional assumptions about work and employment. It was the local community workers and their 'clients' who redefined the tasks to suit the actual needs of the local community.[72] It hardly needs pointing out how much a move to a household-based economy would further obliterate orthodox distinctions between work done in the formal money economy and work done outside it. Once the latter sphere is acknowledged as legitimate and productive, the opportunities for creative work are boundless. A high level of official 'unemployment' could come to be a sign of a society that had changed its priorities from continuing material growth to personally satisfying work.

The multinational problem isn't so easily dealt with. There may be features of a move to a household economy that the multinationals view with alarm – specifically, the fact that there may be a declining demand for some of their goods and services. But in a number of ways there may be no great incompatibility, in the short term at least, between the interests of the multinationals and the growth of locality-based economies. Many commentators have in fact envisaged a future world division of labour in which the multinationals act basically as servicing agencies, supplying the products that cannot be produced locally, especially those requiring high-science, high-technology and high-energy inputs. Both the large and the small units may gain from this arrangement. This is the dual economy on the international plane.[73]

No doubt there is reason to suspect so neat a resolution. But assuming a conflict of interests in the long run, is there not more hope for small-scale communities from the rivalry between great powers, leaving the other elements as the *tertium gaudens?* Was it not the rivalry between Papacy and Empire which allowed the Italian city-states to revive and thrive after the fall of the Roman Empire? Was it not the rivalry between King and Parliament after 1688 which created the conditions for the intense social and economic developments in England in the subsequent century and a half? The spectre of omnipotent multinationals crushing the autonomy of small communities may be the stuff of demonology rather than of sociology. In the competition between nation states and international agencies, between national corporations and the multinationals, the small may still find the space to manoeuvre, and the means to retain their freedom.

'If you had to constitute new societies, you might on moral and social grounds, prefer corn fields to cotton factories; an agricultural to a manufacturing population. But our lot is cast; we cannot change it and we cannot recede.'[74] Thus spoke Sir Robert Peel in 1846 as, reluctantly but stoically, he forced upon the Conservative Party the repeal of the Corn Laws, and inaugurated the 'Golden Age' of manufacturing prosperity in Britain. He was right, of course, for the time and place. But might not a change of similar magnitude be upon us in Britain now? A century after Peel the certainties, the accomplished fact, of industrialism are breaking up. A definite new direction has not yet emerged. Our lot is not yet cast. Various options seem open to us, and we may, indeed must, on 'moral and social grounds' choose which to follow. The suggestion of this chapter is that there is much in Britain's tradition that, perhaps more than any other industrial society, prepares her for a social order going beyong the confines of classic industrialism. She has retained attitudes and values that may allow her to pioneer a post-industrial revolution. And if this involves recovering aspects of the past before industrialism, if it may include more people working once more in corn fields than in cotton factories, who can now say that this is either impossible or regrettable?

NOTES

Parts of this chapter were first given as papers at two conferences organized by the Acton Society Trust: the first at Cumberland Lodge, Windsor Great Park, in July 1977; the second at the Certosa di Pontignano, Siena, in September 1977. I should particularly like to acknowledge the help I received from the papers and comments of Jay Gershuny, Peter Harper and James Robertson. Thanks, too, to Ray Pahl for the continuing stimulus of conversation.

1 Peter Jay, 'Englanditis', in R. Emmett Tyrrell jnr (ed.), *The Future That Doesn't Work: Social Democracy's Failure in Britain* (New York, Doubleday, 1977), pp. 167–85.

2 J. K. Galbraith, interviewed in the *Sunday Times*, 21 January 1977. See also the similarly expressed sentiments of Arthur Koestler, interviewed in *The Times*, 21 February 1977.

3 Ralf Dahrendorf, 'A reply to the Britain-bashers', *Sunday Times*, 1 May 1977. For the report of the *New Society* survey, see T. Forester, 'Do the British sincerely want to be rich?', *New Society*, 28 April 1977.

4 R. Socolow, letter to *The Times*, 14 October 1976.

5 Jay, 'Englanditis', p. 169.

6 For a rare example, calling for a 'cessation of major Government-inspired change',

see the letter by Professor Ian Budge to *The Times*, 22 May 1977.

7 L. Silverman, 'Britain – the crisis of decline', in M.B. Hamilton and K.G. Robertson (eds), *Britain's Crisis in Sociological Perspective* (Reading, University of Reading, 1977), p. 8.

8 For one representative and considered statement, see the joint Trades Union Congress–Labour Party document, *The Next Three Years and into the Eighties* (London, Transport House/Congress House, 1977).

9 J.H. Goldthorpe, 'Social inequality and social integration in modern Britain', in D. Wedderburn (ed.), *Poverty, Inequality, and Class Structure* (Cambridge, Cambridge University Press, 1974), pp. 217–38.

10 Stuart Holland, *The Socialist Challenge* (London, Quartet Books, 1975).

11 A. Glyn and B. Sutcliffe, *British Capitalism, Workers, and the Profits Squeeze* (Harmondsworth, Penguin Books, 1972).

12 It has to be said that – as Holland shows in *The Socialist Challenge*, pp. 394ff – Glyn and Sutcliffe overestimate the decline in profitability by ignoring the practice of multinational firms of declaring low profits in high-tax countries, such as Britain, while often being highly profitable elsewhere. As Holland says, 'since multinational companies now account for more than half the output in British manufacturing industry, their capacity to understate real profits in the U.K. is considerable.' There is, further, the practice of 'transfer pricing', whereby the multinational companies charge themselves from foreign subsidiaries import prices higher than the real value of the imports (of raw materials, semi-manufactured goods, components, etc.). This means that within a given country they can show high costs and low or nil profits, thus paying little tax and often attracting generous subsidies from the government. See Holland, ibid., pp. 83–4.

13 Glyn and Sutcliffe, *British Capitalism*, p. 73.

14 See, for example, Hans Magnus Enzensberger, 'A critique of political ecology', *New Left Review*, no. 84 (Mar.–Apr. 1974), pp. 3–31.

15 One might mention here in passing an analysis that does focus more specifically and more narrowly on political institutions as such. This is the view associated with the more general thesis of the growing 'ungovernability' of Western industrial democracies. The thesis focuses particularly on the problem of 'organized overcomplexity' caused by governmental growth, such that governments become less efficient owing to policy conflicts in different departments, information overload, the need to accommodate powerful 'veto' groups, and so on; and on the problem of 'overloaded resources', caused by escalating demands for public services financed out of general taxation. Some have argued that Britain's low economic growth has made it an especial victim of these processes, given the greater ideological commitment to welfare in this country. There is a superficial appeal to the thesis, but generally it seems a very shallow, typically 'political science' kind of analysis, dealing mainly with the symptoms rather than the causes of the current predicament, and rather too much from the point of view of the governors than the governed. For a discussion, see Richard Rose, *Governing and 'Ungovernability': A Sceptical Inquiry* (Studies in Public Policy, no. 1, Glasgow, University of Strathclyde, 1977). A more systematic and penetrating discussion of the problems of government control and authority in the recent period can be found in James O'Connor, *The Fiscal Crisis of the State* (New York, St Martin's Press, 1973); Ian Gough, 'State

expenditure in advanced capitalism', *New Left Review*, no. 92 (July–Aug. 1975), pp. 53–92; and Harold L. Wilensky, *The Welfare State and Equality* (Berkeley, Ca. University of California Press, 1975).

16 See Tom Nairn, 'The twilight of the British state', *New Left Review*, no. 101–2 (Feb.–Apr. 1977), pp. 3–61; reprinted in Tom Nairn, *The Break-up of Britain* (London, New Left Books, 1977). For the original 'classic' statement of the New Left view of English history, see Perry Anderson, 'Origins of the present crisis', in P. Anderson and R. Blackburn (eds), *Towards Socialism* (London, Fontana, 1965), pp. 11–52.

17 Another favoured historical parallel in this genre of analysis is with the declining empire of seventeenth-century Venice. The parallel here is perhaps more apt, since Venice like England was a mercantile and maritime power. See Tom Nairn, 'The politics of the New Venice', *New Society*, 17 November 1977. Seventeenth-century Spain, another imperial power in decline, is also a favourite.

18 See M. Shanks, *The Stagnant Society* (Harmondsworth, Penguin Books, 1961); A. Shonfield, *British Economic Policy Since the War* (Harmondsworth, Penguin Books, 1959).

19 Eric Hobsbawm, 'Some reflections on "the break-up of Britain"', *New Left Review*, no. 105 (Sept.–Oct. 1977), pp. 6–7.

20 Ibid., p. 17. General predictions of authoritarian regimes of the Right or Left are of course two a penny. See, for the former, Peter Hall 'Scenarios of the unacceptable', and for the latter, Anthony Burgess, 'Tucland', both in *New Society*, 17 November 1977.

21 One of the best statements of the general cultural divide in British society remains Sir Charles Snow's Rede Lecture, *The Two Cultures and the Scientific Revolution* (Cambridge, Cambridge University Press, 1959). As Britain's economic condition continues to stagnate, such cultural analyses have become increasingly widespread. Among the more recent, see G.C. Allen, *The British Disease: A Short Essay on the Nature and Causes of the Nation's Lagging Wealth* (London, Institute of Economic Affairs, 1976); Correlli Barnett, 'The hundred year sickness', *Management of Human Resources*, 8 (1977), pp. 237–44; M. Burrage, 'Culture and British economic growth', *British Journal of Sociology*, 20 (1969), 117–33; M. Burrage, 'Nationalization and the professional ideal', *Sociology*, 7 (1973), 253–72; Noel Annan, 'The path to British decadence', *Sunday Times Weekly Review*, 22 May 1977; The Hudson Report, *The United Kingdom in 1980* (London, Associated Business Programmes, 1974), from which the following passage (p. 113) gives the characteristic flavour of the general cultural critique: 'We would argue that Britain's present economic difficulties and social difficulties derive ultimately from a kind of archaism of the society and national psychology: a habit of conciliation in social and personal relations for its own sake, a lack of aggression, a deference to what exists, a repeated and characteristic flight into pre-industrial, indeed pre-capitalist, fantasies, a suspicion of efficiency as somehow 'common', a dislike for labour itself – all of course accompanied by a deep inner rage at the frustrations and obfuscations which contemporary Britain demands of its citizens and an equally significant envy for the worldly goods that others, Americans, Belgians, Germans, French, have and which the stodgy pattern of a more traditionalist British society and economy cannot provide.'

22 Ralf Dahrendorf, *Times Higher Educational Supplement*, 19 November 1976.
23 'It was said that the present academic bias of the school system made pupils, especially the more able, prejudiced against work in productive trade and industry. While there was undoubtedly a need for much closer links between industry and schools, it was unreasonable to expect teachers alone to remove the antipathy of some young people towards certain jobs. If more young people were to be persuaded to make their careers in industry and commerce, the remedy lay with the companies and firms and only to a minor degree with the schools', *Education in Schools: A Consultative Document* ('Green Paper' presented by Shirley Williams, Secretary of State for Education and Science, London, HMSO, June 1977).
24 See I. Illich, *Tools for Conviviality* (London, Calder Boyars, 1973); M. Bookchin, *Post-scarcity Anarchism* (Berkeley, Ca, Ramparts Press, 1971); T. Roszak, *Where the Wasteland Ends* (London, Faber and Faber, 1973); E. F. Schumacher, *Small is Beautiful* (London, Blond and Briggs, 1973); James Robertson, *Power, Money, and Sex* (London, Marion Boyars, 1976); D. Dickson, *Alternative Technology and the Politics of Technical Change* (London, Fontana, 1974). Some thinkers of this school are prepared to go even further, and locate the current British crisis within a crisis of the whole of human history to date. Cf. Ronald Fletcher: 'Gradually, throughout history, man's knowledge had grown in extent, specialization, systematization, and accuracy. With knowledge has come power and control, and in the 20th century these tendencies have come to their global culmination. We are witnessing, living within, trying to work out, the most crucial point of arrival and departure in the entire destiny of man; the most crucial watershed of human history. In a very real sense we are the present-day inheritors of the historic fate of human nature – and all the problems which this presents. During the next 25 years – for good or ill – they will be worked out', 'The wider context', in Hamilton and Robertson (eds), *Britain's Crisis in Sociological Perspective*, p. 1.
25 I have drawn here on the historical discussion in J. Gershuny, *After Industrial Society* (London, Macmillan, 1978), ch. 1.
26 For such a sketch see Maurice Lamontagne, 'The loss of the steady state', in A. Rotstein (ed.), *Beyond Industrial Growth* (Toronto, Toronto University Press, 1976), pp. 1–21.
27 Mancur Olson, 'Introduction', to Mancur Olson and Hans Landsberg (eds), *The No-Growth Society* (London, The Woburn Press, 1975) p. 4.
28 Ibid., p. 4.
29 Cf. the following proposal by Roland McKean: 'The preferable course would be to attack directly conventional forms of pollution (making use of effluent charges and price mechanisms wherever they appear to be economical), and to tax the use of non-renewable resources. This direct and more finely tuned approach would, of course, reduce growth and final output, as conventionally measured, thereby generating some of the costs and benefits attributed to no-growth. Whether it reduced the growth of the GNP to 1 per cent, to zero, or to a negative 2 per cent would not be highly relevant as long as its impact on pollution and the exhaustion of resources was one in which gains exceeded sacrifices. The parts of the GNP that this policy would reduce are those that produce more social cost than gain, and the parts it would preserve are those that yield more social gain than cost', 'Growth vs. no growth: an evaluation', in Olson and Landsberg (eds), *The No-Growth Society*, p. 225.

30 Hugh Stretton, *Capitalism, Socialism, and the Environment* (Cambridge, Cambridge University Press, 1976), p. 314, n. 1.

31 See W. Beckerman, 'Why we need economic growth', *Lloyds Bank Review*, no. 102 (October 1971), pp. 1–15; 'What no-growth society?', *New Statesman*, 18 March 1977. For Crosland's view, see C.A.R. Crosland, *Socialism Now, and Other Essays* (London, Cape, 1974). It should perhaps be said here that, for all their gestures in an environmentalist direction, Beckerman and Crosland clearly stand for old-fashioned material growth, and have so been understood by both supporters and critics.

32 Fred Hirsch, *The Social Limits to Growth* (London, Routledge and Kegan Paul, 1977). This is a more radical statement than the earlier one by E.J. Mishan, *The Costs of Economic Growth* (Harmondsworth, Penguin Books, 1969), in that it cannot really be dealt with by proposed changes in the composition of Gross National Product, whereas Mishan makes clear proposals of that kind. For a lucid summary of the main physical and social objections to continued economic growth, see H.V. Hodson, *The Diseconomics of Growth* (London, Earth Island, 1972).

33 See the review of Hirsch by J. Gershuny, 'We cannot all stand on each others' shoulders . . .?', *Futures*, 10 (1978), no. 1.

34 In the bleak, Depression-like, conservationist no-growth scenario sketched by Stretton, he observes that things will be worse for the population of that society than for those in past societies living at comparable economic levels. For the new masses can remember that things were very different not so long ago: 'The generations since the environmental revolution are spoiled by the folk memory of that short glorious century when it was different: when it was for each generation better, warmer, growing more, knowing more, discovering and inventing, doing and making more, travelling far, living longer. When men have once tasted that wonderful apple of growth and lived through that springtime, nothing can be as good again', *Capitalism, Socialism, and the Environment*, p. 26.

35 Charles Taylor, 'The politics of the steady state', in Rotstein (ed), *Beyond Industrial Growth*, p. 60. For a similar prediction, see Jeremy Bugler, 'Towards the no-growth society', *New Statesman*, 11 March 1977; R. Heilbroner, *Business Civilization in Decline* (Harmondsworth, Penguin Books, 1977).

36 *The United Kingdom in 1980* (the Hudson Report), p. 58.

37 Ibid., p. 61.

38 Since historical analogies abound in the literature of the kind we're considering, we should here add the decline of Rome to Venice, Spain, Turkey. In Heilbroner's formulation: 'A crucial element in the transformation of the Roman system into the wholly different medieval period was the influence of the new religion of Christianity, which at first undermined the old order and later provided the spirit and shaped the institutional forms of the new order. So, too, in our future, I suspect that a major force for the transformation of business civilization will be a new religious orientation, directed against the canons and precepts of our times, and oriented towards a wholly different conception of the meaning of life and a mode of social organization congenial to the encouragement of that life.' He goes on to see the content of that religion as most likely to be a 'deification of the

state', a kind of 'religious politicism' already foreshadowed in Mao's China (*Business Civilization in Decline*, pp. 94–5).

39　In parts of this section I have drawn upon my article, 'A future in the past?', *New Society*, 24 November 1977.

40　Foreword by the Secretaries of State for Industry, Education, Scotland, and Wales, to the Department of Industry's Discussion Paper, *Industry, Education, and Management* (Department of Industry, London, July 1977).

41　See Marcello de Cecco, 'Keynes's analysis of the British disease', *The Spectator*, 19 June 1976.

42　See especially Nicholas Kaldor, *Causes of the Slow Rate of Economic Growth of the United Kingdom* (Cambridge, Cambridge University Press, 1966). A similar hostility to services is shared by many left-wing writers: see Glyn and Sutcliffe, *British Capitalism*, p. 121; and Holland, *The Socialist Challenge*, p. 394.

43　R. Bacon and W. Eltis, *Britain's Economic Problems: Too Few Producers* (London, Macmillan, 1976).

44　In their book, Bacon and Eltis settle on the terms 'marketable' and 'non-marketable' output sectors to indicate the distinction which they wish to make between 'productive' and 'non-productive' economic activities. Thirlwall comments: 'The distinction between marketable and non-marketable output is not to be confused with the distinction between privately produced and publicly produced output or with the distinction between goods and services. Having said that, however, substantial overlaps may exist. Marketable output tends to be privately produced and a large part of publicly produced output tends to be of the service variety not sold in the market place', A.P. Thirlwall, 'Britain's economic problem: too few producers or a fundamental balance of payments constraint?', *National Westminster Bank Review*, February 1978.

45　For these figures, see Phyllis Deane and W.A. Cole, *British Economic Growth 1688–1959*, 2nd edn (Cambridge, Cambridge University Press, 1967), pp. 30–3; Ajit Singh, 'UK industry and the world economy: a case of de-industrialisation?', *Cambridge Journal of Economics*, 1 (1977), 113–36. There is a parallel story to be told in the decline in manufacturing output. In 1850 British manufacturing output amounted to 40 per cent of the world's total; in 1870 it was still 32 per cent. By 1900 it was 20 per cent, by 1914, 14 per cent and – to cut the story short – by 1963 it had dropped to 4 per cent. See Glyn and Sutcliffe, *British Capitalism*, pp. 16–17.

46　See especially John Knapp, 'Pragmatism and the British malaise', *Lloyds Bank Review*, no. 90 (October 1968), pp. 1–21; Michael Fores, 'Britain's economic growth and the 1870 watershed', *Lloyds Bank Review*, no. 99 (January 1971), pp. 27–41; Barnett, 'The hundred year sickness'.

47　*The Times, The Prospect of Britain*, a collection of leading articles (Times Newspapers Ltd, London, 1971), p. 21.

48　See Singh, 'UK industry and the world economy'; and Thirlwall, 'Britain's economic problem. . .'. Singh comments (p. 132): 'The evidence suggests that the main reason for the UK's high income elasticity of demand for imports (as well as the unfavourable export elasticity) is to be found in the lower quality, design and general performance of its products relative to other countries . . . The faster growing, more dynamic economies are in a position to achieve greater technical progress and make product improvements in all the above-mentioned directions, and are therefore able to respond more effectively to changing patterns of demand as consumer incomes rise.'

49 *The United Kingdom in 1980*, p. 43. As they further comment: 'Much post war policy for growth has been firmly tied to "export-led" stimulation with a resulting emphasis on traditional manufacturing industries. For this reason, the motto "Export or Die" may contain the wrong conjunction: for it has guaranteed that Britain has maintained those manufacturing sectors often of greatest age or the most inefficient construction.'

50 Ibid., p. 53, table 13. For the later – and worse – position regarding imports, see V. Woodward, 'No cause for optimism over imports', *The Times*, 23 June 1976.

51 For these figures, and a general discussion of the contribution of services to the British economy, see *Britain's Invisible Earnings*, Report of the Committee on Invisible Exports (London, National Export Council, 1967); W.M. Clarke, *The City in the World Economy* (London, Institute of Economic Affairs, 1965); Russell Lewis, *The New Service Society* (London, Longman, 1973); Ian Bradley, 'Made in Britain', *Sunday Times Magazine,* 27 March 1977; S. Medlik, *Britain–Workshop or Service Centre to the World?* (Guildford, University of Surrey, 1977).

52 More recent only in its scale and organized nature, perhaps. I live in a city, Canterbury, which has lived off tourism ever since the martyrdom of Thomas à Becket in 1170, and which for long prospered mightily by it.

53 W.A.P. Manser, *Britain in Balance: The Myth of Failure* (London, Longman, 1971), esp. pp. 5–14.

54 D. Landes, *The Unbound Prometheus: Technological Change and Industrial Development in Western Europe from 1750 to the Present* (Cambridge, Cambridge University Press, 1969), p. 336. For the general discussion, emphasizing cultural and institutional factors, see pp. 326ff.

55 See D.C. Coleman, 'Gentlemen and Players', *Economic History Review*, 26 (1973), 92–116. The whole article is a splendid historical discussion of the culture of British economic life. The persistence of this set of cultural preferences in contemporary economic life is argued by J.P. Nettl: 'Consensus or elite domination: the case of business', *Political Studies,* 13 (1965), 22–44.

56 Especially in the New Left English historiography referred to in note 16, above.

57 For a good selection of the anxieties expressed by the Parliamentary commissions, educational committees and the like, see Barnett, 'The hundred years' sickness', and Allen, *The British Disease.*

58 Quoted Fores, 'Britain's economic growth', p. 37.

59 Ibid., p. 38. And cf. Coleman: 'How, historically, were the successful businessmen of Victorian or Edwardian England suddenly to learn to renounce the long traditions by which their predecessors had abandoned their counting houses and climbed into the gentry? And if, by some unlikely magic, they had turned themselves into single-minded, constantly profit-maximizing entrepreneurs, what sort of world might have resulted? If it is true that one of the costs of the Public Schools producing "first-class administrators" was some lag in industrial advance, how can we know that the price was not worth paying?' 'Gentlemen and Players', p. 115.

60 Fores, 'Britain's economic growth', p. 35.

61 See note 40, above.
62 For these characteristics of the service sector, see especially V. Fuchs, *The Service Economy* (New York, Columbia University Press, 1968). One must at the same time see that this is by no means true of all service activities, many of which are as routine and alienating – and worse paid – as in manufacturing. The direction given to the service economy is clearly of great importance in enhancing the social as opposed to the purely economic benefits.
63 James Robertson, letter to *The Times*, 16 February 1977. One is reminded here of Ruskin's distinction: 'Possession is in use only, which for each man is sternly limited; so that such things and so much of them as he can use, are indeed well for him, or Wealth; and more of them, and any other things, are ill for him, or Illth', *Munera Pulveris*.
64 Tom Burke, *The New Wealth* (London, Friends of the Earth, 1977).
65 C.B. Macpherson, *The Real World of Democracy* (Oxford, Clarendon Press, 1966).
66 Stretton, *Capitalism, Socialism, and the Environment*, p. 186. A number of other writers have picked out this trend and drawn similar inferences. See J. Goldthorpe, D. Lockwood, F. Bechhofer and J. Platt, *The Affluent Worker in the Class Structure* (Cambridge, Cambridge University Press, 1969); M. Young and P. Willmott, *The Symmetrical Family* (London, Routledge and Kegan Paul, 1973); James Robertson, 'Towards post-industrial liberation and reconstruction', *New Universities Quarterly*, 32 (1977/8), no. 1, 6–24; Hazel Henderson, 'The coming economic transition', *Technological Forecasting and Social Change*, 8 (1976), 337–51.
67 J. I. Gershuny, 'The self-service economy', *New Universities Quarterly*, 32 (1977/8), no. 1, 54–5.
68 Stretton, *Capitalism, Socialism, and the Environment*, pp. 183, 186–7.
69 See Peter Harper and Godfrey Boyle (eds), *Radical Technology* (London, Wildwood House, 1977), for detailed sketches of some possible combinations of household technology and workshop/garden-allotment units of production.
70 For a detailed specification of technologies relevant to Britain's condition, see J. D. Davis, 'Appropriate technology for a crowded world', *New Universities Quarterly*, 32 (1977/8), no. 1, 25–36.
71 Michael Allaby, *Inventing Tomorrow* (London, Sphere Books, 1977), ch. 8, 'Will we eat?'.
72 For an account of this episode, and an enlightening general discussion, see Gail Stewart and Cathy Starrs, *Re-Working the World: A Report on Changing Concepts of Work* (Ottawa, The Public Policy Concern, 1973).
73 See, for instance, E. G. Goodman, 'How the economies of scale can aid small enterprises', paper presented to the Acton Society Conference on 'Size and Technology' at the Certosa di Pontignano, Siena, September 1977.
74 Quoted Manser, *Britain in Balance*, p. 40.

BIBLIOGRAPHICAL NOTE

It is difficult to be certain how far the debate on the condition of Britain has been fundamentally affected by the principal development since this chapter was first written: I mean the coming to power of a Conservative government in 1979 and its continuance in office through two further elections. Certanly there has been a marked change of rhetoric. The 'Radical Right' is said to be triumphing everywhere in the West, forcing a change not just on traditional Conservatism but on the parties of the Centre and Left. The whole post-war consensus, based on the mixed economy and the welfare state, is said to be coming apart. This, it is further argued, is bound to affect the character of the discussion about Britain's future.

Time alone will tell. For the moment what must strike the dispassionate observer are not the differences but the basic continuities with the debates of the 1970s. (For a good summation, see Isaac Kramnick, ed., *Is Britain Dying? Perspectives on the Current Crisis*, Ithaca, NY, and London, Cornell University Press, 1979.) Britain's manufacturing decline continues to be the subject of intense concern. Four million, or more than a third of all jobs in manufacturing – 2 million of these since 1979 – have gone, a loss 'unparalleled anywhere in the world' (Thirlwall). Manufacturing employment, still 30 per cent of total employment in 1979, was less than 25 per cent by 1983 and continues to drop. Investment in manufacturing industry since the late 1970s has been negative: the rate at which plant has been scrapped has exceeded new investment, so that the real stock of capital equipment has fallen absolutely. The same is true of output: by 1986 Britain's manufacturing output was 10 per cent lower absolutely than it had been in 1974. Manufacturing output in Britain now accounts for only 21 per cent of GNP (compared with 28 per cent in 1972, and with 32 per cent for both Germany and Japan at the present time). This is not the result of a decline in demand for manufactured goods. Import penetration has accelerated sharply. Imports now amount to nearly 40 per cent of home demand (compared with 8 per cent in 1950), and in the past twelve years, while home output was falling, imports of manufactured goods have doubled. To the general consternation, in 1983 for the first time ever imports of manufactures exceeded exports: a deficit in the balance of trade in manufactures that has persisted since. Equally symbolic, or so it seemed to many, was the announcement in 1986 that Italy, traditionally one of Europe's weakest economies, had now overtaken Britain as the world's fifth largest economy. Italian pride at *il sorpasso* was a grim reminder to Britons of the devastating report on Britain's manufacturing decline produced by a select committee of the House of Lords the year before. Their lordships warned: 'It is neither exaggeration, nor irresponsible, to say that the present situation undoubtedly contains the grounds of a major political and economic crisis in the foreseeable future' (House of Lords, *Report of the Select Committee on Overseas Trade*, London, HMSO, 1985. For the figures in this paragraph, see also A.P. Thirlwall, 'Deindustrialisation in the United Kingdom', *Lloyds Bank Review*, no. 144 (1982), pp. 22–37; Stephen Bazen and A.P. Thirlwall, 'Deindustrialization in the United Kingdom', in B. Atkinson, ed., *Developments in Economics*, vol. 2, Liverpool, Causeway Press, 1986; D. Aldcroft, 'Britain's long-term economic decline, *The Economic Review*, 2 (1985), 8–10; Wynne Godley, 'A doomed economy?', *New Society*, 17 January 1986; Professor D.A. Bell in *The Times*, 14 January, 1987.)

Such a warning, based on a similar assessment of the situation in manufacturing, can be found in a score of books and reports published in the 1970s (not to mention the 1890s, as Correlli Barnett showed in *The Collapse of British Power*, 1972; paperback edn, Gloucester, Alan Sutton, 1984). Equally familiar is the current debate about the role of the service sector, which has continued its rapid post-war expansion. Services now account for 60 per cent of GNP and 65 per cent of total employment. Half of all service employees are in the 'tradable services', i.e. those capable of earning foreign income, and service earnings amounted to half the cost of Britain's total visible imports in 1985 (*The Times*, 2 February 1987; *Financial Times*, 27 February 1987; *Guardian*, 8 August 1987). The House of Lords Select Committee nevertheless, along with several other expert commentators such as Nicholas Kaldor, Wynne Godley and Wilfred Beckerman, poured scorn on the idea that the service sector could adequately compensate for the decline in manufacturing (see, for example, Beckerman in *The Times*, 23 March 1987). As against this, Mrs Thatcher's government – though not with a single voice nor with whole-hearted conviction – looked to the services as the basis of Britain's economic recovery. In a more familiarly euphoric vein there were those who fastened on the service sector as spearheading the move to a post-industrial society based on information technology (see, for example, Amin Rajan, *Services – The Second Industrial Revolution?*, London, Institute of Manpower Studies/Butterworth, 1987; William Rees-Mogg, on the 'new electronic class', *The Independent*, 5 May 1987; *Service Industries Review*, 1981 onwards).

It is hardly surprising, therefore, that much of the literature on the 'condition of England' that has appeared in the past ten years has a broadly familiar look. The 'British disease' continues to be diagnosed according to a well-established – or at least generally accepted – aetiology. The century-long decline in manufacturing, paralleled by a thriving and vigorous financial sector based on the City of London, has been documented and discussed in several trenchant analyses. A good end-of-the-seventies report is F. Blackaby (ed.), *De-Industrialisation* (London, Heinemann, 1979). A full survey, with the emphasis on the failure to modernize during the key period 1870–1914, is M.W. Kirby, *The Decline of British Economic Power Since 1870* (London, Allen and Unwin, 1981). Michael Fores, in a piece of radical revisionism, questions the very idea that there was an Industrial Revolution in the first place: 'The myth of British Industrial Revolution', *History*, 66 (1981), 181–98. (For a rebuttal, see A.E. Musson, *History*, 67 (1982), 252–8.) Others, while also pointing the finger at long-term structural weaknesses, are more inclined to date the real failure to the post-1945 period, and the low rate of investment in manufacturing over the past forty years: see, for example, S. Pollard, *The Wasting of the British Economy* (London, Croom Helm, 1982). Pollard also stresses the political failure of this period, the extent to which industry was sacrificed to the politically influential City interest and to a misguided attempt to maintain Britain as a world military power. This point is also well made in Andrew Gamble's *Britain in Decline*, 2nd edn (London, Macmillan, 1985); see also Malcolm Chalmers, *Paying for Defence: Military Spending and British Decline* (London, Allen and Unwin, 1985). From a related perspective, Porter has argued that Britain's industrial decline was implicit in the world-imperial role adopted by nineteenth-century British statesmen, as this undermined the liberal, free-market, international economy that was the linchpin of Britain's industrial dominance: Bernard Porter, *Britain, Europe, and the World 1850–1986: Delusions of Grandeur*, 2nd edn (London, Allen and Unwin, 1987). The penalty of being first, and the too easy British dominance this allowed, is also stressed in the wide-ranging account by Colin Leys, *Politics in Britain* (London, Verso, 1983).

The City–industry divide has for long been seen as a major cause of Britain's economic problems. For a discussion of this, see Marcello de Cecco, *Money and Empire* (Oxford, Basil Blackwell, 1974); Frank Longstreth, 'The City, industry and the state', in C. Crouch (ed.), *State and Economy in Contemporary Capitalism* (London, Croom Helm, 1979); *Report of the Committee to Review the Functioning of the Financial Institutions* (the Wilson Report) (London, HMSO, 1980); and, most useful of all, Geoffrey Ingham, *Capitalism Divided? The City and Industry in British Social Development* (London, Macmillan, 1984).

It has been standard, ever since the debates of the late nineteenth century, to see the root cause of Britain's economic weakness in aspects of the social structure and culture: especially the dominance of the landed gentry and the corresponding antipathy to manufacturing industry – an 'anti-industrial spirit' – that went with its style of life. Related to this was the neglect of scientific and technical education, as compared with Britain's chief rivals, Germany and the United States. A powerful and highly influential statement of this view is Martin Wiener, *English Culture and the Decline of the Industrial Spirit, 1850–1980* (Cambridge, Cambridge University Press, 1981). Echoing this, and with a venomous attack on the English Establishment and its pernicious influence, especially in the post-1945 period of reconstruction, is Corelli Barnett's latest philippic, *The Audit of War: The Illusion and Reality of Britain as a Great Nation* (London, Macmillan, 1986). Educational and attitudinal factors as the cause of the malaise are also stressed in the detailed and closely argued comparative study by S.J. Prais, *Productivity and Industrial Structure: A Statistical Study of Manufacturing Industry in Britain, Germany and the United States* (Cambridge, Cambridge University Press, 1982); see also Ian Jamieson, *Capitalism and Culture: A Comparative Analysis of British and American Manufacturing Organisations* (Aldershot, Gower, 1980). A major series of articles in *The Times*, 16–19 February 1987, documented Britain's weakness in scientific and technical research and development.

The aristocratic embrace, and the consequent hegemony of an anti-industrial gentry culture, was central to the 'New Left' analyses of Perry Anderson, Tom Nairn and others in the pages of the *New Left Review* in the 1960s and 1970s (see note 16, above). It has been powerfully restated, in a full review of the whole question, in Perry Anderson, 'The figures of descent', *New Left Review*, no. 161 (Jan.–Feb., 1987), pp. 20–77. A similar though more qualified view is taken by Daniel Bell, 'A report on England: the future that never was', *The Public Interest*, no. 51 (Spring, 1978), pp. 35–73. Some of the historical underpinnings of this view are roundly attacked by F.M.L. Thompson, 'English landed society in the Nineteenth Century', and J. Harris and P. Thane, 'British and European bankers, 1880–1914', both in P. Thane, G. Crossick and R. Floud (eds), *The Power of the Past: Essays for Eric Hobsbawm* (Cambridge, Cambridge University Press, 1984). Doubt on Britain's uniqueness in this respect is also cast by two works which emphasize the uniformity of European experience in the widespread persistence of the *'ancien régime'*: Arno J. Mayer, *The Persistence of the Old Regime: Europe to the Great War* (New York Pantheon Books, 1981); David Blackbourn and Geoff Eley, *The Peculiarities of German History: Bourgeois Society and Politics in Nineteenth-Century Germany* (Oxford, Oxford University Press, 1984). An attack on overarching 'culturalist' explanations, and a more careful attention to 'institutional rigidities' in industrial organization, industrial relations etc., is to be found in Bernard Elbaum and William Lazonick (eds), *The Decline of the British Economy* (Oxford, Clarendon Press, 1986); see also, on the historical pattern of trade unionism and its detrimental effect on industrial growth, A. Kilpatrick and T. Lawson, 'On the nature of industrial decline in the UK', *Cambridge Journal of Economics*, 4 (1980), pp. 85–102.

New Left thinkers were not alone in emphasizing Britain's 'missing', 'failed' or 'incomplete' bourgeois revolution as the basic cause of present discontents. As compared with her capitalist competitors, the absence – through an otherwise fortunate legacy of constitutional continuity and domestic peace – of an enforced 'modernization' of the old pre industrial political and economic structures of Britain was a theme of many of the popular diagnoses of Britain's ills presented in the press and on television. Several of these appeared as accompanying books: James Bellini, *Rule Britannia: A Progress Report for Domesday 1986* (London, Cape, 1981), an update on the earlier Hudson Report, *The United Kingdom in 1980*, with a grim forecast of a coming new feudalism and mass poverty; Rod Allen, Anwer Bati and Jean-Claude Bragard, *The Shattered Dream: Employment in the Eighties* (London, Arrow Books/LWT, 1981), a fearful appraisal of the impact of the new technology on Britain's antiquated industrial system; and, with a sharper focus, John Eatwell, *Whatever Happened to Britain? The Economics of Decline* (London, Duckworth/BBC, 1982), a popularization of the view of the 'Cambridge School' of neo-Keynsian economists. Ralf Dahrendorf's series, *On Britain* (London, BBC, 1982) was unusual in pointing up the strengths as well as the weaknesses of the British tradition. More idiosyncratic, but with a similar emphasis on the archaic structures of British society – especially in its southern reaches – is Norman Stone, 'The English Disease', *New Society*, 10 January 1986. Even more varied was the series on 'The British Disease' run by the *Times Higher Educational Supplement*, 8 May–26 June 1981. But there too – in the contributions by myself, Bill Wedderburn, Ralph Miliband, Roy Close and W.B. Reddaway – the common theme was the break-up of a social consensus formed in happier times and now no longer adequate to the challenge of a new age. This idea also formed the basis of a number of stimulating 'summer' essays written annually in the dead month of August by *THES*'s editor Peter Scott: see, for example, 'Britain in the 1980s', *Times Higher Education Supplement*, 1–22 August 1986. Finally, there are the provocative and racy essays written for *New Society* by R.W. Johnson, collected as *The Politics of Recession* (London, Macmillan, 1985).

Of all the sections of the foregoing chapter, the one perhaps most in need of revision is the last, the reflections on the move to a 'household economy'. The push to a 'self-service' economy has been charted anew by Jonathan Gershuny: see *Social Innovation and the Division of Labour* (Oxford, Oxford University Press, 1983); and 'The leisure principle', *New Society*, 13 February 1987. But Gershuny is even clearer now than before that the role of the household in the new economy will be a dependent and subordinate one. The technology – much of it of the 'information' kind – will be designed for the household, but the levers of power and control will remain outside, in national and international centres remote from the household and the local community. The drive, therefore, is less towards an autonomous household economy – as I tended to argue – and more towards a fragmented society in the context of a new international division of labour. My revised thoughts are briefly set out in 'The privatized society', *Universities Quarterly*, 40 (1986), 356–64; for similar impressions, see Lincoln Allison, 'The spirit of the Eighties', *New Society*, 25 April 1986. Against this more pessimistic prospect, some of the radical 'post-industrialists' continue to place their hopes on a decentralized system in which the 'informal' household economy will parallel and gradually displace the large-scale formal economy: see, for example, James Robertson, *Future Work: Jobs, Self-Employment and Leisure After the Industrial*

Age (Aldershot, Gower, 1985). A somewhat unlikely ally here is a former Conservative minister, David Howell, who also looks to the informal economy and the growth of 'ownwork' as the most hopeful solution to the present crisis of employment: see *Blind Victory: A Study in Income, Wealth and Power* (London, Hamish Hamilton, 1986).

To return finally to the present, and Thatcherism. Two-thirds of all homes in Britain are now privately owned; 18 per cent of the adult population own shares in publicly quoted companies (compared with 7 per cent in 1979); less than a third of the workforce is now unionized (compared with more than 40 per cent in 1979). Are these the intimations of 'a private future'? Is fragmentation and atomization the dominant trend? Or are there continuing structural tendencies inherited from the expanded welfare state of the post-war consensus which is shaping a future more in line with the developments of the 1960s and 1970s? All one can do here is to note the ideological warfare and conflicting interpretations of current trends. For the 'New Right', see Ruth Levitas (ed.), *The Ideology of the New Right* (Oxford, Polity Press, 1986); David Coates and John Hillard (ed.), *The Economic Decline of Modern Britain: The Debate Between Left and Right* (Brighton, Wheatsheaf Books, 1986). The Thatcher record, and the extent to which performance has matched ideology, are scrutinized in Stuart Hall and Martin Jacques (eds), *The Politics of Thatcherism* (London, Lawrence and Wishart, 1983); Colin Leys, 'Thatcherism and British manufacturing: a question of hegemony', *New Left Review*, no. 151 (May–June 1985), pp. 5–25; Joel Krieger, *Reagan, Thatcher, and the Politics of Decline* (Oxford, Polity Press, 1986); Dennis Kavanagh, *Thatcherism and British Politics: The End of Consensus?* (Oxford, Oxford University Press, 1987); Andrew Gamble, *The Free Economy and the Strong State: Thatcherism and the Future of British Conservatism* (London, Macmillan, 1987); K. Minogue and M. Biddiss (eds), *Thatcherism: Personality and Politics* (London, Macmillan, 1987). Perhaps it is symptomatic of the mood of the times that, unusually and somewhat idiosyncratically, the latest review of Britain's condition and prospects should conclude that there is no crisis and that Britain 'has responded politically and institutionally to pressure for change' (see Alan Sked, *Britain's Decline: Problems and Perspectives*, Oxford, Basil Blackwell, 1987). The complacency shown here, after a decade of further decline, is less pardonable than that found in the observations of certain foreign Anglophiles in the 1970s, for example Bernard Nossiter, *Britain: A Future That Works* (London, Andre Deutsch, 1978).

Index

governmental power, 64
Gramsci, Antonio, 118, 181
Greeks, Ancient
attitude to work, 229–30
Greenwood, Walter, 271
Gross National Product, 66
statistics used to calculate, 300
growth, economic, 298–302
and distributional conflicts, 112
industrialization and, 11–12
physical limits to, 301
growth, technical
self-sustaining, 82
Guevara, Che, 174
guilds, medieval, 228
Guttsman, W. L., 145

Harrison, Brian, 156
Hartz, Louis, 48
Harvey, David, 110, 119
Hawtrey, R. C., 268
Hegel, Georg Wilhelm Friedrich, 213, 232
Heilbroner, R., 302
Hellenic society, 101–2
Hilferding, Rudolph, 108
Hill, Christopher, 103
Hindley, Charles, 149
Hirsch, Fred, 118
on capitalism, 40–3, 51–4
on collectivism, 52–3
on limits to growth, 301
Hirschman, A. O., 38, 39, 40
Hobsbawm, Eric, 110–11, 143, 175, 187, 233, 261, 265–6
on nationalist movements in Britain, 296–7
Hobson, J. A., 267
Holland, Stuart, 293, 294
Hong Kong, 16
household economy, 312–16
in eighteenth-century England, 256–7
in nineteenth-century England, 261–3, 264, 265
household goods, 313–14
Hudson Report, 302, 305
humanists
Renaissance, 230
twentieth-century, 232
Hume, David, 37

Hungary
1956 rising, 177
risings after First World War, 178
Hunt, Henry, 137

identity
work and, 19, 226–7
IGOs (international governmental organizations), 85
Illich, Ivan, 65, 298, 310
imperialism, 45–7
income, guaranteed, 274–5
India, 26
individualism, 11, 19, 112
v. social responsibility, 41–2
industrial society
future of, extrapolated from the past, 59–64
individualism and, 11, 19, 41–2, 112
possible revolutionary groups in, 189–90
and pre-industrial society, 10–11
and science, 6, 11
specialization in, 11
industrial world
relationship with developing countries, 27–8, 86–93, 105–7
relationship with less-developed (PTM) countries, 88–90
industrialism
crisis of, 65, 67, 69–70, 102, 297–8
Industry, Education and Management (Department of Industry), 308
information technology, 30, 119
INGOs (international non-governmental organizations), 85
internationalism, 85–6
international system, *see* world system
Italy, 22, 119
unrest after First World War, 181–2

Jahoda, Marie, 239
Japan, 12, 25–6, 27, 28, 82
population, 14
urbanization, 16
Jaurès, Jean, 179
Jay, Peter, 290, 292
Jenkins, Clive, 235
job enrichment, 69
Jones, Stedman, 139

Index by Justyn Balinski